CONTESTING ZION

McGILL-QUEEN'S STUDIES IN THE HISTORY OF RELIGION

Volumes in this series have been supported by the Jackman Foundation of Toronto.

SERIES ONE G.A. RAWLYK, EDITOR

1 Small Differences
Irish Catholics and Irish Protestants, 1815–1922
An International Perspective
Donald Harman Akenson

2 Two Worlds
The Protestant Culture of Nineteenth-Century Ontario
William Westfall

3 An Evangelical Mind
Nathanael Burwash and the Methodist Tradition in Canada, 1839–1918
Marguerite Van Die

4 The Dévotes
Women and Church in Seventeenth-Century France
Elizabeth Rapley

5 The Evangelical Century
College and Creed in English Canada from the Great Revival to the Great Depression
Michael Gauvreau

6 The German Peasants' War and Anabaptist Community of Goods
James M. Stayer

7 A World Mission
Canadian Protestantism and the Quest for a New International Order, 1918–1939
Robert Wright

8 Serving the Present Age
Revivalism, Progressivism, and the Methodist Tradition in Canada
Phyllis D. Airhart

9 A Sensitive Independence
Canadian Methodist Women Missionaries in Canada and the Orient, 1881–1925
Rosemary R. Gagan

10 God's Peoples
Covenant and Land in South Africa, Israel, and Ulster
Donald Harman Akenson

11 Creed and Culture
The Place of English-Speaking Catholics in Canadian Society, 1750–1930
Edited by Terrence Murphy and Gerald Stortz

12 Piety and Nationalism
Lay Voluntary Associations and the Creation of an Irish-Catholic Community in Toronto, 1850–1895
Brian P. Clarke

13 Amazing Grace
Studies in Evangelicalism in Australia, Britain, Canada, and the United States
Edited by George Rawlyk and Mark A. Noll

14 Children of Peace
W. John McIntyre

15 A Solitary Pillar
Montreal's Anglican Church and the Quiet Revolution
Joan Marshall

16 Padres in No Man's Land
Canadian Chaplains and the Great War
Duff Crerar

17 Christian Ethics and Political Economy in North America
A Critical Analysis
P. Travis Kroeker

18 Pilgrims in Lotus Land
Conservative Protestantism in British Columbia, 1917–1981
Robert K. Burkinshaw

19 Through Sunshine and Shadow
The Woman's Christian Temperance Union, Evangelicalism, and Reform in Ontario, 1874–1930
Sharon Cook

20 Church, College, and Clergy
A History of Theological Education at Knox College, Toronto, 1844–1994
Brian J. Fraser

21 The Lord's Dominion
The History of Canadian Methodism
Neil Semple

22 A Full-Orbed Christianity
The Protestant Churches and Social Welfare in Canada, 1900–1940
Nancy Christie and Michael Gauvreau

23 Evangelism and Apostasy
The Evolution and Impact of Evangelicals in Modern Mexico
Kurt Bowen

24 The Chignecto Covenanters
A Regional History of Reformed Presbyterianism in New Brunswick and Nova Scotia, 1827–1905
Eldon Hay

25 Methodists and Women's Education in Ontario, 1836–1925
Johanne Selles

26 Puritanism and Historical Controversy
William Lamont

SERIES TWO IN MEMORY OF GEORGE RAWLYK
DONALD HARMAN AKENSON, EDITOR

1 Marguerite Bourgeoys and Montreal, 1640–1665
Patricia Simpson

2 Aspects of the Canadian Evangelical Experience
Edited by G.A. Rawlyk

3 Infinity, Faith, and Time
Christian Humanism and Renaissance Literature
John Spencer Hill

4 The Contribution of Presbyterianism to the Maritime Provinces of Canada
Edited by Charles H.H. Scobie and G.A. Rawlyk

5 Labour, Love, and Prayer
Female Piety in Ulster Religious Literature, 1850–1914
Andrea Ebel Brozyna

6 The Waning of the Green
Catholics, the Irish, and Identity in Toronto, 1887–1922
Mark G. McGowan

7 Religion and Nationality in Western Ukraine
The Greek Catholic Church and the Ruthenian National Movement in Galicia, 1867–1900
John-Paul Himka

8 Good Citizens
British Missionaries and Imperial States, 1870–1918
James G. Greenlee and Charles M. Johnston

9 The Theology of the Oral Torah
Revealing the Justice of God
Jacob Neusner

10 Gentle Eminence
A Life of Cardinal Flahiff
P. Wallace Platt

11 Culture, Religion, and Demographic Behaviour
Catholics and Lutherans in Alsace, 1750–1870
Kevin McQuillan

12 Between Damnation and Starvation
Priests and Merchants in Newfoundland Politics, 1745–1855
John P. Greene

13 Martin Luther, German Saviour
German Evangelical Theological Factions and the Interpretation of Luther, 1917–1933
James M. Stayer

14 Modernity and the Dilemma of North American Anglican Identities, 1880–1950
William H. Katerberg

15 The Methodist Church on the Prairies, 1896–1914
George Emery

16 Christian Attitudes towards the State of Israel
Paul Charles Merkley

17 A Social History of the Cloister
Daily Life in the Teaching Monasteries of the Old Regime
Elizabeth Rapley

18 Households of Faith
Family, Gender, and Community in Canada, 1760–1969
Edited by Nancy Christie

19 Blood Ground
Colonialism, Missions, and the Contest for Christianity in the Cape Colony and Britain, 1799–1853
Elizabeth Elbourne

20 A History of Canadian Catholics
Gallicanism, Romanism, and Canadianism
Terence J. Fay

21 The View from Rome
Archbishop Stagni's 1915 Reports on the Ontario Bilingual Schools Question
Edited and translated by John Zucchi

22 The Founding Moment
Church, Society, and the Construction of Trinity College
William Westfall

23 The Holocaust, Israel, and Canadian Protestant Churches
Haim Genizi

24 Governing Charities
Church and State in Toronto's Catholic Archdiocese, 1850–1950
Paula Maurutto

25 Anglicans and the Atlantic World
High Churchmen, Evangelicals, and the Quebec Connection
Richard W. Vaudry

26 Evangelicals and the Continental Divide
The Conservative Protestant Subculture in Canada and the United States
Sam Reimer

27 Christians in a Secular World
The Canadian Experience
Kurt Bowen

28 Anatomy of a Seance
A History of Spirit Communication in Central Canada
Stan McMullin

29 With Skilful Hand
The Story of King David
David T. Barnard

30 Faithful Intellect
Samuel S. Nelles and Victoria University
Neil Semple

31 W. Stanford Reid
An Evangelical Calvinist in the Academy
A. Donald MacLeod

32 A Long Eclipse
The Liberal Protestant Establishment and the Canadian University, 1920–1970
Catherine Gidney

33 Forkhill Protestants and Forkhill Catholics, 1787–1858
Kyla Madden

34 For Canada's Sake
Public Religion, Centennial Celebrations, and the Re-making of Canada in the 1960s
Gary R. Miedema

35 Revival in the City
The Impact of American Evangelists in Canada, 1884–1914
Eric R. Crouse

36 The Lord for the Body
Religion, Medicine, and Protestant Faith Healing in Canada, 1880–1930
James Opp

37 Six Hundred Years of Reform
Bishops and the French Church, 1190–1789
J. Michael Hayden and Malcolm R. Greenshields

38 The Missionary Oblate Sisters
Vision and Mission
Rosa Bruno-Jofré

39 Religion, Family, and Community in Victorian Canada
The Colbys of Carrollcroft
Marguerite Van Die

40 Michael Power
The Struggle to Build the Catholic Church on the Canadian Frontier
Mark G. McGowan

41 The Catholic Origins of Quebec's Quiet Revolution, 1931–1970
Michael Gauvreau

42 Marguerite Bourgeoys and the Congregation of Notre Dame, 1665–1700
Patricia Simpson

43 To Heal a Fractured World
The Ethics of Responsibility
Jonathan Sacks

44 Revivalists
Marketing the Gospel in English Canada, 1884–1957
Kevin Kee

45 The Churches and Social Order in Nineteenth- and Twentieth-Century Canada
Edited by Michael Gauvreau and Ollivier Hubert

46 Political Ecumenism
Catholics, Jews, and Protestants in De Gaulle's Free France, 1940–1945
Geoffrey Adams

47 From Quaker to Upper Canadian
Faith and Community among Yonge Street Friends, 1801–1850
Robynne Rogers Healey

48 The Congrégation de Notre-Dame, Superiors, and the Paradox of Power, 1693–1796
Colleen Gray

49 Canadian Pentecostalism
Transition and Transformation
Edited by Michael Wilkinson

50 A War with a Silver Lining
Canadian Protestant Churches and the South African War, 1899–1902
Gordon L. Heath

51 In the Aftermath of Catastrophe
Founding Judaism, 70 to 640
Jacob Neusner

52 Imagining Holiness
Classic Hasidic Tales in Modern Times
Justin Jaron Lewis

53 Shouting, Embracing, and Dancing with Ecstasy
The Growth of Methodism in Newfoundland, 1774–1874
Calvin Hollett

54 Into Deep Waters
Evangelical Spirituality and Maritime Calvinist Baptist Ministers, 1790–1855
Daniel C. Goodwin

55 Vanguard of the New Age
The Toronto Theosophical Society, 1891–1945
Gillian McCann

56 A Commerce of Taste
Church Architecture in Canada, 1867–1914
Barry Magrill

57 The Big Picture
The Antigonish Movement of Eastern Nova Scotia
Santo Dodaro and Leonard Pluta

58 My Heart's Best Wishes for You
A Biography of Archbishop John Walsh
John P. Comiskey

59 The Covenanters in Canada
Reformed Presbyterianism from 1820 to 2012
Eldon Hay

60 The Guardianship of Best Interests
Institutional Care for the Children of the Poor in Halifax, 1850–1960
Renée N. Lafferty

61 In Defence of the Faith
Joaquim Marques de Araújo, a Comissário in the Age of Inquisitional Decline
James E. Wadsworth

62 Contesting the Moral High Ground
Popular Moralists in Mid-Twentieth-Century Britain
Paul T. Phillips

63 The Catholicisms of Coutances
Varieties of Religion in Early Modern France, 1350–1789
J. Michael Hayden

64 After Evangelicalism
The Sixties and the United Church of Canada
Kevin N. Flatt

65 The Return of Ancestral Gods
Modern Ukrainian Paganism as an Alternative Vision for a Nation
Mariya Lesiv

66 Transatlantic Methodists
British Wesleyanism and the Formation of an Evangelical Culture in Nineteenth-Century Ontario and Quebec
Todd Webb

67 A Church with the Soul of a Nation
Making and Remaking the United Church of Canada
Phyllis D. Airhart

68 Fighting over God
A Legal and Political History of Religious Freedom in Canada
Janet Epp Buckingham

69 From India to Israel
Identity, Immigration, and the Struggle for Religious Equality
Joseph Hodes

70 Becoming Holy in Early Canada
Timothy Pearson

71 The Cistercian Arts
From the 12th to the 21st Century
Edited by Terryl N. Kinder and Roberto Cassanelli

72 The Canny Scot
Archbishop James Morrison of Antigonish
Peter Ludlow

73 Religion and Greater Ireland
Christianity and Irish Global Networks, 1750–1950
Edited by Colin Barr and Hilary M. Carey

74 The Invisible Irish
Finding Protestants in the Nineteenth-Century Migrations to America
Rankin Sherling

75 Beating against the Wind
Popular Opposition to Bishop Feild and Tractarianism in Newfoundland and Labrador, 1844–1876
Calvin Hollett

76 The Body or the Soul?
Religion and Culture in a Quebec Parish, 1736–1901
Frank A. Abbott

77 Saving Germany
North American Protestants and Christian Mission to West Germany, 1945–1974
James C. Enns

78 The Imperial Irish
Canada's Irish Catholics Fight the Great War, 1914–1918
Mark G. McGowan

79 Into Silence and Servitude
How American Girls Became Nuns, 1945–1965
Brian Titley

80 Boundless Dominion
Providence, Politics, and the Early Canadian Presbyterian Worldview
Denis McKim

81 Faithful Encounters
Authorities and American Missionaries in the Ottoman Empire
Emrah Şahin

82 Beyond the Noise of Solemn Assemblies
The Protestant Ethic and the Quest for Social Justice in Canada
Richard Allen

83 Not Quite Us
Anti-Catholic Thought in English Canada since 1900
Kevin P. Anderson

84 Scandal in the Parish
Priests and Parishioners Behaving Badly in Eighteenth-Century France
Karen E. Carter

85 Ordinary Saints
Women, Work, and Faith in Newfoundland
Bonnie Morgan

86 Patriot and Priest
Jean-Baptiste Volfius and the Constitutional Church in the Côte-d'Or
Annette Chapman-Adisho

87 A.B. Simpson and the Making of Modern Evangelicalism
Daryn Henry

88 The Uncomfortable Pew
Christianity and the New Left in Toronto
Bruce Douville

89 Berruyer's Bible
Public Opinion and the Politics of Enlightenment Catholicism in France
Daniel J. Watkins

90 Communities of the Soul
A Short History of Religion in Puerto Rico
José E. Igartua

91 Callings and Consequences
The Making of Catholic Vocational Culture in Early Modern France
Christopher J. Lane

92 Religion, Ethnonationalism, and Antisemitism in the Era of the Two World Wars
Edited by Kevin P. Spicer and Rebecca Carter-Chand

93 Water from Dragon's Well
The History of a Korean-Canadian Church Relationship
David Kim-Cragg

94 Protestant Liberty
Religion and the Making of Canadian Liberalism, 1828–78
James M. Forbes

95 To Make a Village Soviet
Jehovah's Witnesses and the Transformation of a Postwar Ukrainian Borderland
Emily B. Baran

96 Disciples of Antigonish
Catholics in Nova Scotia, 1880–1960
Peter Ludlow

97 A Black American Missionary in Canada
The Life and Letters of Lewis Champion Chambers
Edited by Hilary Bates Neary

98 A People's Reformation
Building the English Church in the Elizabethan Parish
Lucy Moffat Kaufman

99 Towards a Godless Dominion
Unbelief in Interwar Canada
Elliot Hanowski

100 Finding Molly Johnson
Irish Famine Orphans in Canada
Mark G. McGowan

101 Apparition Fever
Observing the Virgin Mary in Belgium
Tine Van Osselaer

102 Tradition and Tension
The Presbyterian Church in Canada, 1945–1985
Stuart Macdonald

103 Contesting Zion
The Vatican, American Catholics, and the Partition of Palestine
Adrian Ciani

CONTESTING ZION

The Vatican, American Catholics, and the Partition of Palestine

ADRIAN CIANI

McGill-Queen's University Press
Montreal & Kingston • London • Chicago

ISBN 978-0-2280-2461-3 (paper)
ISBN 978-0-2280-2518-4 (ePDF)
ISBN 978-0-2280-2519-1 (ePUB)

Legal deposit second quarter 2025
Bibliothèque et Archives nationales du Québec

Printed in Canada on acid-free paper that is 100% ancient-forest-free, containing 100% sustainable, recycled fibre, and processed chlorine-free.

This book has been published with the help of a grant from the Federation for the Humanities and Social Sciences, through the Awards to Scholarly Publications Program, using funds provided by the Social Sciences and Humanities Research Council of Canada.

Funded by the Government of Canada | Financé par le gouvernement du Canada | Canada | Canada Council for the Arts | Conseil des arts du Canada

We acknowledge the support of the Canada Council for the Arts.
Nous remercions le Conseil des arts du Canada de son soutien.

McGill-Queen's University Press in Montreal is on land which long served as a site of meeting and exchange amongst Indigenous Peoples, including the Haudenosaunee and Anishinabeg nations. In Kingston it is situated on the territory of the Haudenosaunee and Anishinaabek. We acknowledge and thank the diverse Indigenous Peoples whose footsteps have marked these territories on which peoples of the world now gather.

Library and Archives Canada Cataloguing in Publication

Title: Contesting Zion : the Vatican, American Catholics, and the partition of Palestine / Adrian Ciani.
Names: Ciani, Adrian, author.
Series: McGill-Queen's studies in the history of religion. Series two ; 103.
Description: Series statement: McGill-Queen's studies in the history of religion. Series two ; 103 | Includes bibliographical references and index.
Identifiers: Canadiana (print) 20250114623 | Canadiana (ebook) 20250114720 | ISBN 9780228024613 (paper) | ISBN 9780228025184 (ePDF) | ISBN 9780228025191 (ePUB)
Subjects: LCSH: Catholic Church—Foreign relations—Israel. | LCSH: Israel—Foreign relations—Catholic Church. | LCSH: Catholic Church and Zionism. | LCSH: Catholic Church—Foreign relations—United States. | LCSH: United States—Foreign relations—Catholic Church. | LCSH: Catholic Church—United States. | LCSH: Palestine question (To 1948) | LCSH: Palestine question (1948-)
Classification: LCC BX1628 .C53 2025 | DDC 327.456/340569409—dc23

This book was designed and typeset by studio oneonone in Minion 11/14.
Copyediting by Ryan Perks.

McGill-Queen's University Press
Suite 1720, 1010 Sherbrooke St West, Montreal, QC, H3A 2R7

Authorized safety representative in the EU: Mare Nostrum Group BV, Mauritskade 21D, 1091 GC Amsterdam, the Netherlands, gpsr@mare-nostrum.co.uk

To Courtney, to my mother, Johanne,
and to the memory of my father

Contents

Contents

Acknowledgments

Despite the single name on the cover of this book, the road to its completion was paved by the selfless and generous advice, encouragement, and support of fellow researchers, scholars, archivists, students, librarians, friends, and family members. I would like to express my heartfelt appreciation for their contributions over the many years since this project took root.

This study began as a doctoral dissertation for the Department of History at Western University. My doctoral supervisor, Robert Ventresca of King's University College at Western, has been a source of support and encouragement since the earliest days of this project. Through the various stages of research and writing, Robert was a model adviser, coaching me through challenging phases and providing valuable insights and perspective. At moments when I wavered, it was Robert's mentoring and confidence in the project that pulled me through. When it comes to supervisors, I know I was blessed. In the years since I completed the dissertation, Robert has continued to be a supportive confrere, providing opportunities for collaboration and facilitating my continued development as a writer and historian. For his patience, guidance, and friendship, I am so deeply grateful.

I would also like to thank a number of colleagues and mentors who have been so vital to my academic journey. The late Peter C. Kent of the University of New Brunswick introduced me to the field of Vatican diplomacy and guided me through my first research in the subject. It was Peter who set me along the path of "Vaticanology." Paolo Zanini of the University of Milan has provided advice, support, and true friendship throughout the writing of this work, as well as doses of good humor when I needed it most. Peter Meehan of St Jerome's University provided pivotal support and counsel as I built a career in teaching, all while encouraging me to carry the present study to completion.

Charles R. Gallagher of Boston College, who served as my external reader during my doctoral defense, has been an invaluable mentor and support in the years since. From offering advice on many aspects of my research, to expanding my scholarly network through invitations to symposia and conferences, to graciously hosting me at St Mary's Hall during my research stay in Boston, I am sincerely grateful.

I am also indebted to the archivists and librarians who guided me through the collections that were so vital to the completion of this book. In particular, I would like to thank Maria Mazzenga, curator of the American Catholic History Collections at the Catholic University of America, William LaFevre of the Walter P. Reuther Library at Wayne State University, Heidi Christein of the archives of the Archdiocese of Detroit, Annie Grunow of the archives of the Catholic Near East Welfare Association, Thomas Lester of the archives of the Archdiocese of Boston, Nicholas Scheetz of Georgetown University's Special Collections, and Kate Feighery of the archives of the Archdiocese of New York. I would also like to thank Monsignor Peter Vaccari, rector of St Joseph's Seminary in Dunwoodie, Yonkers, for graciously hosting me at the seminary during my research stay in New York. I am also deeply grateful to Roberto Benedetti for his assistance in Rome; in the midst of intermittent pandemic closures and travel restrictions, Roberto provided key material from the newly declassified Vatican archives that invaluably strengthened the final manuscript.

I am also sincerely thankful for the support of my publisher, McGill-Queen's University Press, which embraced this project from its earliest days. I would like to thank the anonymous reviewers for providing detailed, thoughtful, and timely reviews of the manuscript; the final study is undoubtedly much stronger for their perceptive and detailed commentary. I'd like to also thank managing editor Kathleen Fraser for her advice and guidance, as well as copy editor Ryan Perks, whose superb editorial eye has immeasurably enhanced the clarity and coherence of the work. I would like to express particular gratitude to my acquisitions editor, Kyla Madden. From the day that I submitted my manuscript proposal to the final stages of preparation for publication, Kyla provided sage advice, encouragement, and guidance, all with a spirit of collegiality and admirable patience. Her confidence and sincere interest in the project were so vital in carrying me to the end of the process.

Western University was a wonderful place to pursue my doctoral studies, and I am thankful for a number of mentors, colleagues, and friends who were so supportive during my time there: Timothy Compeau, Dorotea Gucciardo,

Richard Holt, Mark Humphries, Francine McKenzie, Eli Nathans, Ryan O'Connor, Jane Whalen, and Nicolas Virtue. I am also grateful for the financial support of Western's History Department, as well as to the Ontario Graduate Scholarship fund. I was hosted by the United States Holocaust Memorial Museum in Washington, DC, for an enriching two-week seminar in 2012, where Suzanne Brown-Fleming and Victoria Barnett offered their valuable insights and suggestions for my research. At Seneca Polytechnic I have been fortunate to work with teachers and friends who all have a hand in the pages that follow, including Jeffrey Bercuson, Glen Choi, Nanda Lwin, Amanda Nowensky, and Carmelo Tropiano. At St Augustine's Seminary in Toronto, I have had the chance to work with a supportive and collegial group of scholars and friends, including John Abad, Kevin Belgrave, Frederick Chung, Edwin Gonsalves, Donald Graham, Seamus Hogan, Josephine Lombardi, Colleen Mahy, Luis Melo, Patricia Murphy, Monsignor Robert Nusca, and Francesco Pica.

Over the last decade, the Sherk family has welcomed me with warm and open arms, and I am so grateful for their love and support. I'd like also to express my appreciation to Philip Savas and Neil Hrab, both for reading and commenting on large sections of this work, and for their genuine friendship and support over many years. I have been fortunate to have a network of true friends and colleagues who have been so essential to both my academic and my life journey: Evan Kazolis, Jim Apostolopoulos, Jason Chartrand, Enzo Verrilli, George Stavropoulos, Rosella Latini, and Frank Palcich. To the patrons of Seb's Café, thank you for your support, good humor, and friendship through the years. You have all sustained me more than you can know.

My paternal grandfather, Ercole Ciani, has also served as an inspiration for this work. Though he left us long before this project began, his life story – from world war to Kenyan POW camp to leading his family across an ocean to start a new life in a new world – offers a model of perseverance, hard work, and loyalty that has always inspired me. I hope that this book, in a small way, is a testament to his spirit.

Finally, I owe my greatest debt of gratitude to my wife, Courtney, whose love, patience, and spirit have guided me to the completion of this work. This book, with much love, is for her.

Abbreviations

AACI	Anglo-American Committee of Inquiry
ACPC	American Christian Palestine Committee
AHC	Arab Higher Committee
AJC	American Jewish Committee
AZEC	American Zionist Emergency Council
CAIP	Catholic Association for International Peace
CNEWA	Catholic Near East Welfare Association
CUA	Catholic University of America
DELASEM	Delegazione per l'Assistenza degli Emigranti Ebrei (Delegation for the Assistance of Jewish Emigrants)
IDF	Israel Defense Forces
IUCW	International Union of Catholic Women
NCCJ	National Conference of Christians and Jews
NCCM	National Council of Catholic Men
NCCW	National Council of Catholic Women
NCNS	National Catholic News Service
NCWC	National Catholic Welfare Conference (originally National Catholic Welfare Council)
PCC	Palestine Conciliation Commission
PCI	Partito Comunista Italiano (Italian Communist Party)
PMP	Pontifical Mission for Palestine
UN	United Nations
UNICEF	United Nations International Children's Emergency Fund
UNSCOP	United Nations Special Committee on Palestine
WZO	World Zionist Organization
ZOA	Zionist Organization of America

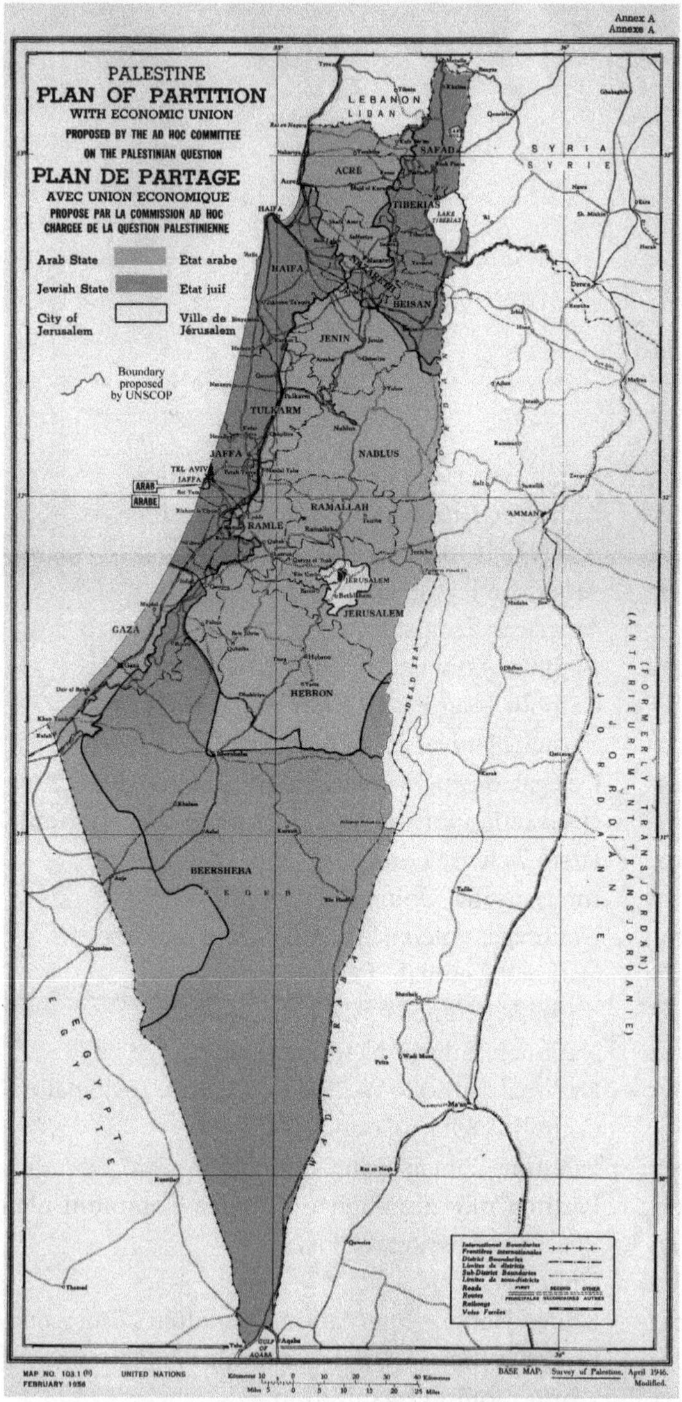

Map of UN plan for partition of Palestine, adopted 29 November 1947. Courtesy of Wikimedia Commons, https://commons.wikimedia.org/wiki/File:UN_Palestine_Partition_Versions_1947.jpg.

CONTESTING ZION

Introduction

On the morning of 30 December 1993, in the Vatican's Sala Regia, the magnificently frescoed antechamber to the Sistine Chapel, a "Fundamental Agreement" was signed by Monsignor Claudio Celli, the Vatican's assistant secretary of state, and Yossi Beilin, Israel's deputy minister of foreign affairs, paving the way toward full diplomatic relations between the two parties.[1] On its surface, this agreement between the Vatican and Israel was a conventional political accord, undertaken by two sovereign subjects of international law for the purpose of exchanging ambassadors. It was emblematic, however, of a significant and historic rapprochement. For decades after the creation of the State of Israel in 1948, its relations with the Vatican were strained by disputes over the status of the city of Jerusalem and the Holy Places, and the repatriation of Palestinian Christian refugees. The tensions that afflicted this relationship, particularly in the years immediately following the creation of the new state, had much deeper roots in the historical relationship between Roman Catholicism and Judaism. For nearly twenty centuries, the Roman Catholic Church had viewed Judaism as a fallacious and pariah faith, and the Jews a "witness people" destined to wander the earth for their complicity in the deicide – the death of the Christian savior, Jesus Christ. The historical "proof" of this theology, according to numerous early Christian theologians and church fathers, was evidenced by the first-century destruction of Judaea at the hand of the Romans: the overthrow of the Jewish king, the fall of Jerusalem, the destruction of the Temple, and the dispersal of the Jewish people. In this view, Christianity had definitively superseded Judaism in the eyes of God, and the Abrahamic Covenant, in which God had promised the land of Israel to Abraham and his followers, was null.

In the nineteenth and early twentieth centuries, papal aversion to the return of the Jews to Palestine (or "Zion" to Christians, a reference to both the earthly and the heavenly Jerusalem, as well as to the Holy Land more generally) continued to be shaped by this fundamental conviction. This theological view also shaped the Vatican's opposition to political Zionism, particularly as this movement consolidated and expanded in the later nineteenth century. The idea that the Jews might return to Palestine to establish sovereign control there, and that the most sacred holy sites of Christianity, directly related to the life and death of Christ, might fall under their jurisdiction, was unthinkable to the popes of the era. Theodor Herzl, the founder of modern Zionism, discovered this in 1904 when he was received by Pope Pius X in Rome. The pope, in no uncertain terms, made clear that the church, for reasons both historical and theological, could not endorse the Zionist program, despite Herzl's assurances of protections for Christian holy sites. As the Zionist movement gained prominence in the early decades of the twentieth century, and particularly after the Balfour Declaration of 1917, when the British government announced its support for a Jewish state in Palestine, Vatican opposition to the Zionist project intensified. Between 1917 and 1939, the Vatican attempted to thwart the momentum of the Zionist movement through its diplomatic channels and at the League of Nations. In the decisive decade after 1945, a period that witnessed the birth of the Israeli state, Vatican anti-Zionist politicking reached a zenith, first in attempts to block the very partition of Palestine at the United Nations, and next to secure Jerusalem and its environs, home to the most sacred sites of the Christian faith, as an international, extraterritorial *corpus separatum*, an enclave independent of either Israeli or Jordanian control.[2]

In recent decades, a small but commendable body of scholarship has emerged that examines the Vatican's response to the rise of political Zionism and to the creation of the State of Israel, as well as papal relations with the nascent state in its formative years.[3] While this study builds upon these works, it ranges beyond the existing historiography by examining this relationship through a distinctly transnational lens.[4] As defined and applied by scholars such as Akira Iriye, Ian Tyrell, and Petra Goedde, transnational history concerns the movement of people, ideas, technologies, and institutions across national boundaries.[5] This approach seeks to move beyond the limits of national and regional narratives, where borders and boundaries served to demarcate inquiry, to more adequately comprehend and integrate the influences of non-state actors and organizations. In the field of international relations history, this lens seeks to transcend the examination of relations between sovereign governments and their diplomats to consider the influence of a range of non-state actors who influence global affairs, including international cultural, religious, and social institutions and bodies, diaspora communities, nongovernmental organizations, and the international media.[6]

The Roman Catholic Church, as an international religious organization that maintains an extensive network of national hierarchies and oversees nearly three thousand territorial dioceses around the world, represents the quintessence of a transnational actor in global affairs. Though centered in Rome, the Roman curia (or Vatican government) stands at the head of a global network of nuncios (papal diplomats accredited to national governments), apostolic delegates (Vatican envoys to national Catholic churches), national episcopacies, religious orders, missionary and lay organizations, and the faithful.[7] The church must be understood, as James Chappel has recently noted, as a socially embedded and transnational "archipelago of institutions," and not simply as a closed nexus of popes, cardinals, bishops, and nuncios.[8] Despite this emerging transnational perspective, much of the traditional historiography on Vatican diplomacy, including work on the relationship between the Vatican and Israel, has centered on these conventional channels of diplomatic exchange.[9] While this focus has proven fruitful in examining the Vatican's formal relations with nation-states, particularly in the area of concordat (treaty) negotiations, where the church sought specific guarantees and rights for Roman Catholics in a given state or territory, it reveals only a part of the Vatican's power to shape the international order.

The influence of the papacy in international affairs, as such, must be understood not only as a function of the Holy See's juridical sovereignty, which allows it to engage in formal diplomatic relations with other states, but also as a consequence of the global presence of Catholic episcopies, institutions, and lay populations, which also augments the Vatican's influence.[10] As Timothy A. Byrnes has observed, it is this combination of the Holy See's sovereignty with the presence and agency of a global network of Catholic institutions and lay populations, led and administered by national bishop's conferences, that more fully reveals the papacy's power to shape international affairs.[11] In this sense, the Holy See can be seen as a "hybrid actor" in the international system, in which the Vatican's global network of formal diplomatic relationships is augmented by the power and influence of the transnational Catholic diaspora.[12] Recent scholarship has begun to examine the Vatican's diplomacy within this context. Lisa L. Ferrari has outlined the power of the Vatican as a transnational actor, positing that, as both a sovereign state and a nongovernmental organization, it exercises a significant degree of soft power (influence girded by neither a state economy nor military power) given its reputation as a moral arbiter, its network of lay and religious organizations, and the size and distribution of the global Catholic population.[13] Other recent studies by Mariano Barbato, David Ryall, and Verena Beittinger-Lee have similarly examined the Vatican's role in modern international history through this transnational lens, considering the agency of international Catholic institutions and lay constituencies alongside that of the Vatican itself.[14]

This study adopts the framework of the Vatican as a "hybrid actor" in international affairs in examining papal attempts to constrain the Zionist movement and to shape the Palestine question between the 1920s and the 1950s. It specifically argues that the Vatican's attempts to shape the fate of Palestine must be understood within this transnational context. It builds upon a recent historiography that examines Vatican initiatives to shape the twentieth-century international order along lines amenable to the church, and that reveals the agency of the transnational church in this endeavor. As Giuliana Chamedes's *A Twentieth-Century Crusade: The Vatican's Battle to Remake Christian Europe* (2019) reveals, the Vatican's project to place a Catholic stamp on the European and global order in the decades after the First World War necessitated the mobilization of a "Catholic International" comprised of religious and lay organizations, national groups of clergy and bishops, and an active Catholic media.[15] This study similarly emphasizes the agency of a "Catholic International," and places particular emphasis on the role of the American Catholic Church within this transnational network. I contend here that the transnational consensus that existed among Roman Catholics on the question of Zionism and on the fate of Palestine, combined with the growing political influence and fiscal power of the Catholic Church in the United States, particularly from the 1920s onward, gave American Catholic leaders and organizations a unique ability to transmit the Vatican's Palestine policy to both the United Nations (UN) and Washington, the most powerful capital in the world.

American Catholics, as such, became the primary advocates of papal policy on a number of postwar challenges, including the Palestine question.

A wide range of archival evidence reveals the leadership of the American bishops in attempting to shape the debate on Zionism and the future of Palestine along lines amenable to the papal curia. As formal diplomatic relations between the United States and the Vatican were not yet established, however, the apostolic delegate in Washington (the papal representative to the Catholic Church in the United States) could not relay papal positions on Palestine directly to the American government. These policies, instead, were disseminated to the American bishops through their national council, the National Catholic Welfare Conference in Washington, DC. The bishops, in turn, coordinated a pervasive campaign designed to steer American and UN policy on Palestine and Israel toward outcomes sanctioned by the Vatican and the international Roman Catholic Church. This campaign extended beyond the bishops themselves, and encompassed lay Catholic organizations, subcommittees of the National Catholic Welfare Conference, and papal associations under the jurisdiction of American Catholic leaders. The American Catholic press was also deployed in the battle for public opinion, as both the Vatican and the American bishops were cognizant of the potential clout of the "Catholic vote" in Washington's policy considerations. American Catholic activism, moreover, came at the head of an international Roman Catholic lobby on Palestine, underscoring the importance of considering the transnational dimension of the Vatican's relationship to Zionism and the nascent Israeli state.

In connecting the political advocacy of American Catholics to the papal curia in Rome, this study is primarily indebted to the work of Peter D'Agostino, whose *Rome in America: Transnational Catholic Ideology from the Risorgimento to Fascism* (2004) explored the transnational nature of Catholic ideology from the middle of the nineteenth century to the interwar decades.[16] D'Agostino posited that Catholics in the United States "forged an imagined community with myths, shared symbols and a calendar of prescribed rituals," with the Holy See in Rome comprising the spiritual and physical center of this community.[17] He revealed how American Catholics demonstrated solidarity with the popes through public rituals and political agitation that distinguished Catholics from their non-Catholic neighbors. D'Agostino traced this American Catholic activism from reactions to the Roman Question (the dispute on the temporal power of the popes after the dissolution of the Papal States in 1870) to the rise of Benito Mussolini's Fascist regime. Throughout the later nineteenth century, American Catholics rose to the defense of papal demands for territorial sovereignty in Italy, a position that placed them at odds with the American Protestant establishment, which generally regarded the emergence of a liberal, democratic, and secular Italy as a providential sign of an emerging global order shaped by Anglo-American progressivism. Similar patterns emerged with American Catholic sympathy and support for Mussolini and Fascist Italy, another stance that placed Catholics at odds with the non-Catholic majority. As D'Agostino outlined, American Catholics (particularly Italian Americans) followed the lead of papal Rome in participating in rituals legitimizing Mussolini's regime, as the Italian embassy in Washington forged strong relations with the bishops and Catholic laity. American Catholic sympathy for Fascist Italy was demonstrated, on a political plane, by demands that Washington repeal its embargo on Rome during the Italo-Ethiopian War of 1935–36. The absence of an anti-Fascist movement among American Catholics, moreover, underscored a solidarity with papal Rome (which had cautiously endorsed Mussolini's regime after 1929), and again generated frictions between Catholics and their non-Catholic fellow citizens.

American Catholic attitudes toward Zionism up to 1948, and the political activism of the church vis-à-vis the nascent Israeli state, dovetail neatly with the patterns revealed by D'Agostino. I contend, in fact, that the Vatican's diplomatic efforts to shape the Palestine question in the first decade of the Cold War must be understood in the context of this shared transnational opposition to Zionism. As chapter 2 of this study outlines, such a consensus did exist between Rome and American Catholics from the time of the Balfour Declaration onward. This was despite lingering frictions between Rome and the American bishops from earlier in the century, when papal fears of American episcopal autonomy led to a crackdown.[18] Transnational Catholic unanimity on Zionism, in fact, grew stronger in the interwar decades, as the Zionist lobby itself grew more powerful and strident. This enmity to Zionism also proved remarkably resilient. Even the Holocaust, which would create significant pockets of sympathy for Zionism in the United States, did not fundamentally alter Vatican or American Catholic opposition to the creation of a Jewish state in Palestine. While American Catholics expressed sympathy with the plight of European Jews, often in language bolder than that of Pope Pius XII, they stopped firmly short of endorsing the Zionist program. When a Catholic leader did express sympathy with Zionism, as the case of New Orleans Archbishop Joseph Rummel illustrates in chapter 3, the Vatican moved quickly to suppress it, evidence of the solidarity Rome would demand on the Palestine question.

After 1945, this transnational consensus melded into political action, with American Catholics at the forefront of efforts to shape developments on postwar Palestine. A number of factors had made the American bishops leading voices in the international church. Through the interwar decades and during the war, archbishops such as Detroit's Edward Mooney, New York's Francis Spellman, and Chicago's George Mundelein had cultivated close ties with President Franklin Roosevelt and the Democratic Party. Institutionally, the Catholic Church in the United States had expanded steadily after the First World War, bolstered by waves of Catholic immigration from Europe and high birth rates. This growth boosted the financial might of the American church. As John F. Pollard's study of Vatican finances reveals, New York, Boston, and Chicago, in that order, were the three wealthiest archdioceses in the world by 1939.[19] The Vatican, increasingly isolated in Europe and anxious to tap into the political, cultural, and fiscal power of the American church, grew progressively closer to the American bishops in the interwar years. This would lead to the creation of new associations such as the Catholic Near East Welfare Association and the Pontifical Mission for Palestine, which were placed entirely in the hands of the American bishops, and which would play an important role in the Vatican's postwar efforts to shape the Palestine question. The Vatican also placed American prelates in ever higher positions of authority in the papal secretariat, another sign of the interwar turn toward the American Catholic Church. President Roosevelt's creation of a "personal representative" to the Holy See in 1939, moreover, appeared to signal ever closer relations between the papacy and the United States.

As the postwar era dawned, it appeared that Washington, the Vatican, and the American Catholic bishops did comprise an informal, yet ideologically cohesive, strategic alliance that was primarily committed to the containment of Soviet communism. On the question of Palestine, however, a distinctive American Catholic lobby emerged that clearly diverged from Washington's policy on the territory. On this issue, the American bishops, and a number of leading American Catholic organizations, clearly took their ideological and political lead from papal Rome. The transnational consensus that D'Agostino revealed on the Roman Question and Mussolini's Italy had survived the war intact, manifesting itself most forcefully on the question of Palestine. And as in the previous cases identified by D'Agostino, American Catholic positions on Zionism placed them at odds with their non-Catholic fellow citizens, a majority of whom had come to support the creation of a Jewish state in the territory. The Vatican had high hopes that the American bishops, given their ties in Washington, increasing financial might, and growing public profile, as well as their role as linchpins in the postwar Vatican-American relationship, might be uniquely endowed to transmit the Vatican's postwar designs both in Washington and at the UN. The final chapters of this study trace the rise, and ultimate demise, of this American Catholic political lobby to shape the Palestine question along lines amenable to the Vatican.

This American Catholic crusade was ingrained, ultimately, in competing visions of a territory revered by Catholics and Jews alike. Since the birth of Christianity, the Holy Land had excited the visions of popes and Christian rulers who sought to establish a lasting sovereignty over a land sanctified by the sites associated with the life and death of Jesus. Though Christian theologians never developed a distinctive theology of land to underpin the church's stake in the territory, the negation of Jewish claims, which were rooted in the Abrahamic Covenant, became the basis of papal claims. This negation, embedded in a foundational antipathy to Judaism and centered on the notion of the deicide, would guide papal policy and wider Catholic activism on the sacred ground of Zion for nearly two thousand years.

CHAPTER 1

Terra Santa: The Church and the Land

The origins of Christianity in Palestine extend back to the life, and particularly the death and resurrection, of Jesus Christ. Through bouts of severe persecution by the Roman state between the first and third centuries, Christianity survived and spread throughout Palestine and other parts of the Roman world. The institutional establishment of the Christian church in Palestine began in the fourth century, when this oppression ceased, and the faith was given official sanction. Over the next fifteen centuries, this expansion continued with the construction of churches, basilicas, convents, monasteries, abbeys, and schools. Places related to the life and death of Jesus, moreover, had become important pilgrimage sites, drawing the faithful from all corners of the Christian world.

Against this backdrop, the rise of Zionism in the nineteenth century appeared to pose a direct threat to the Christian presence in Palestine. A product of the intensifying persecution of Jewish populations across the global diaspora, particularly in central and eastern Europe, Zionism sought to reestablish a Jewish home in Palestine both as a safe haven for the diaspora and as a fulfillment of the biblical covenant that hearkened a return of the Jews to the land promised to Abraham by God. The Vatican, for its part, opposed the movement from the outset, fearful that the church's ancient stake in the territory was threatened. Though the Catholic Church had never espoused its own distinct theology of land, as had existed in Judaism's Abrahamic Covenant, the notion of Jewish dominion over the Holy Land raised anxieties at the highest levels of the papal court. Attempts to constrain Zionist momentum, however, through both diplomatic channels and Catholic allies at the League of Nations would ultimately prove futile, necessitating the Vatican's eventual turn toward emerging branches of the international church.

A CATHOLIC THEOLOGY OF LAND?

The connection between Judaism and Zion – the land of Israel in the Hebrew Bible – is rooted in the Abrahamic Covenant, in which God promised Abraham and his descendants eternal guidance and protection in return for unyielding devotion and loyalty. In Genesis, the first book of the Hebrew Bible, the centrality of land in the covenant is unequivocal, as God says to Abraham, "I will give to you, and to your descendants after you, the land of your sojourning, all the land of Canaan, for an everlasting possession."[1] Judaism's subsequent connection to the land of Israel, as such, was recognized both by the authority of the Bible and by the significance of the covenant itself. During long periods of exile and dispersal, Judaism's attachment to the land remained constant, reflected in rituals such as facing Israel during prayers, praying for a return to the land, and commemorating the 70 CE destruction of the Temple at Jerusalem at the hand of the Romans with days of fasting and mourning. For adult Jewish males, pilgrimage to the Temple in Jerusalem, though not always possible, was commanded in the Torah during Passover, the Pentecost, and the Feast of Tabernacles. "Next year in Jerusalem" was the aspiration expressed at the end of every Passover meal, commemorating the Hebrew exile from Egypt and subsequent dispersal of the Jewish diaspora. The land of Israel, as it was interpreted and understood by rabbinical scholars, was no mere appendage to the concerns of biblical authors, but was a pivotal concept intrinsic to the notion of the covenant itself.[2] As historian Gershon Cohen has observed, "By the time Palestine ceased to be the central Jewish community, its centrality had been so impressed upon the Jewish mind that it could not be uprooted."[3] To deny the link between the Jewish people and Israel, then, was to deny the legitimacy of the Abrahamic Covenant and the Hebrew Bible itself.

Despite Christianity's obvious link to Palestine (or the Holy Land as it became known to Christians), which contained the sites related to the life and death of Jesus, a distinctive theological connection to the land, as exists in Judaism, is difficult to discern.[4] The earliest possible manifestation of such a "theology of land" would be found in the gospel sources, written between the late first and early second centuries. The writings of the apostles Mark, Matthew, Luke, and John, however, do not seem to espouse any coherent notion of a particular Christian homeland, and instead appear to implore the followers of Christ to turn outward toward the world, and to spread the faith beyond the bounds of Roman Judaea. In the Gospel of Matthew, Jesus says, "And everyone who has left houses or brothers or sisters or father or mother or children or lands, for my name's sake, will receive a hundredfold, and inherit eternal life," implying the universal, and not territorial, calling of Christianity.[5] The Gospel of Luke echoes this notion, when Jesus says to a follower, "Foxes have holes, and birds of the air have nests; but the Son of man has nowhere to lay His head."[6] The Gospel of John, believed to be the last of the gospel sources written, and comparatively distinctive from the Synoptic Gospels of Mark, Matthew, and Luke, similarly emphasizes the universality of Christianity. In a conversation between Jesus and a Samaritan woman, she said to him, "Our fathers worshipped in this mountain; and you say that in Jerusalem is the place where one ought to worship." Jesus answered her, "Believe me, woman, the hour comes when neither in this mountain nor at Jerusalem shall you worship the Father."[7] From this perspective, Christianity was to be an itinerant faith, not linked to a particular land or region, but rather universal and boundless.

The idea of Christianity as a universal faith, unbound to the land of the covenant, appeared again in the writings of Saint Paul. Following his conversion to Christianity, Paul tirelessly preached the new faith throughout the Roman world from the 30s to the 50s CE. His status as a full Roman citizen allowed him to travel freely through the empire, and his proficiency in several languages, including Greek, Latin, Hebrew, and Aramaic, made his ministry particularly influential. Paul's missionary efforts were indispensable to the early spread of Christianity through Asia Minor and Greece, and led to the establishment of permanent Christian communities at Ephesus, Smyrna, Athens, Corinth, and Antioch. His ministry eventually took him to Roman Spain and to the imperial capital of Rome itself, where he was martyred in the 60s CE. Though Paul had been raised a Pharisee Jew, and was reputed to have participated in the persecution of Christians before his conversion, the breadth of his ministry suggests the profound universalism of the new faith. Christianity was not to be limited by territory or nation, but instead was to be spread among

Jews, gentiles, and pagans alike. It was to be unbound by gender, ethnicity, geography, class, or indeed covenant, as traditional Judaism was.

The Epistles of Paul, comprising of a series of addresses to the Christian communities of the first-century Roman Empire, provide a clear exposition of the universalism of the new faith.[8] The Epistles make scant reference to land, as Paul explicitly proclaims Christianity as a faith that provided salvation through the person of Christ. The "Christocentrism" of Paul's Epistles appeared to announce a new covenant, in which salvation was achieved not through fulfillment of the Abrahamic Covenant, but through the worship of the Christian messiah. As such, the Epistles make little reference to Palestine, Jerusalem, the Temple, or the covenant. Paul's focus, rather, was Christ, and his vision was universal.[9] The new messiah, who represented a new covenant, would return to save all people of the faith of Christ, and not just the people of the original covenant. Paul's worldview, then, transcended the limitations of geography, law, or nation. For him, God could be found by all people in all places.[10]

By the second century, the view that the followers of Christ represented a new covenant, which had replaced (or superseded) the Abrahamic Covenant, had become ensconced among Christian theologians throughout the Roman Empire. The historical experience of Christians in these centuries illustrates this embrace of the new covenant represented by Christ, and the abandonment of any notion of an earthly, territorial homeland. The intensified persecutions of the Roman state, which feared the subversive potential of the expanding faith, only strengthened the idea that Christianity transcended fealty to any particular polity or territory. Exile and martyrdom, as such, became markers of prestige and supreme demonstrations of faith for early Christians. Geographical dispersal (and sometimes death) created new classes of exemplars and heroes, and became another sign that Christians had abandoned the Abrahamic Covenant, with its notion of a promised land, to seek salvation in a transcendental and universal new faith.

During the fourth century, a veritable revolution swept the Roman world, as Christianity moved from being a persecuted sect to the officially sanctioned religion of the empire. During the reign of the Emperor Constantine (306–337 CE), imperial support flowed freely to the church, as basilicas, monasteries, and churches were constructed across the empire, confiscated property was returned, and tax obligations were lifted. Though Constantine did not formally convert to the faith until his deathbed, and although Christianity did not become the official religion of the empire until later in the century, it was clear that the faith was ascendant, and that the era of persecution had ended. Despite the resulting expansion of the Christian church in Palestine, however, and the subsequent influx of pilgrims to the region, a distinctive theology of land did not emerge during the Constantinian era or after. Christian theologians continued to emphasize the universality of the faith, and implored Christians to seek God where they were. Gregory of Nyssa, the church father and bishop of Nyssa (Asia Minor) from the 370s to the 390s, strongly emphasized the universal nature of the Christian faith, and was an early proponent of the notion of universal salvation, where all baptized and pious Christians would achieve salvation. Christian attachments to the land, or obligations to pilgrimage, were not to be found in Gregory's theology, a view evident in his instructions to a friend: "You who fear the Lord, praise him in the places where you are. A change of place does not bring you any closer to God. But wherever you may find yourself, God will come to you. Therefore, my dear friend, give the brethren that advice, that they rather take a pilgrimage out of their body towards God, but not out of Cappadocia towards Palestine."[11]

Saint Jerome, the acclaimed fourth-century theologian, ascetic, historian, and church father, is widely known for his translation of most of the Bible into Latin, the *Vulgate*. Jerome's theological views on pilgrimage and land, however, were largely in accord with those of his contemporaries. Though living his final years in Jerusalem, he instructed his colleague Paulinus, the bishop of Nola, in southern Italy, not to feel implored to make a sojourn to the Holy Land. "The gates of heaven stand open in Britain quite as well as in Jerusalem. Do not think that anything is missing in your faith, because you have not seen Jerusalem. Do not consider us any better, because we are able to live in this place."[12] In his letter, Jerome appears to explicitly deny the very notion of a land-based covenant in Christianity. "It is not, I believe, for nothing that I, like Abraham, have left my home and people. But I do not presume to limit God's omnipotence or to restrict to a narrow strip of earth Him whom the heaven cannot contain. Each believer is judged not by his residence in this place or that, but according to the deserts of his faith."[13] Pilgrimage to Palestine did expand from the fourth century onward, as wealthier Christians sought to do penance, visit the sites associated with the life and death of Jesus, obtain important relics, and seek redemption for serious sins. The notion of an obligatory pilgrimage to the territory, however, did not emerge in the writings of the early theologians. Christianity, instead, was presented as a distinctly universal creed, where true pilgrimage was a deeper connection with the faith itself, and not a physical sojourn to the Holy Land.

This Christian universalism was contrasted with the Abrahamic Covenant by principal theologians of the early church. A key to interpreting later papal reticence to Zionism, in fact, emerges in the writings of Augustine of Hippo, the seminal fifth-century philosopher and church father. Like his predecessors, Augustine articulated the universality of Christianity and affirmed the transitory nature of earthly possessions and relationships. In a letter to the clergy and faithful of his diocese, he echoed the Gospel of John in declaring that "God is everywhere, and that He who made all things is not contained or confined to dwell in any one place."[14] Augustine's theology went further, however, in that it explicitly denied Jewish claims to Palestine as understood through the Abrahamic Covenant. As Carole Monica Burnett has noted, Augustine's emphasis on the transitory nature of earthly possessions and covenants contributed to his rejection of Jewish claims to the land of Palestine. His interpretation of the book of Joshua, in which God promised that the stones of Palestine would be "a memorial to the sons of Israel unto eternity," is indicative of his rejection of the Abrahamic Covenant. "How can it be unto eternity, since heaven and earth will pass away," he observed. "Can it be that these stones signify something eternal, since they themselves cannot be eternal?"[15] Augustine's exegesis of the books of Joshua and Genesis hinged on the notion that Christianity had essentially replaced, or superseded, Judaism in the eyes of God, a theological view that had become firmly ensconced by the fifth century. In this view, Christians were the new progeny of Abraham, and as such, any earthly or territorial covenant between God and the Jews was null.

For Augustine, the dispersal of the Jews from Palestine was prophetic and was divinely willed. "No one can fail to see that in every land where the Jews are scattered, they mourn for the loss of their kingdom," he triumphantly noted, "and are in terrified subjection to the immensely superior number of Christians."[16] Augustine's descriptions of the Passion of Christ dripped with anti-Judaic sentiment and allusions to deicide. "It was the Jews who held Him; the Jews who insulted Him; the Jews who bound Him; the Jews who crowned Him with thorns; who soiled Him with their spit; who whipped Him; who ridiculed Him."[17] Augustine also identified Jews with the fratricidal Cain, who was condemned to wander the earth for the murder of his brother Abel, as suffering examples to Christians who might be tempted to revolt against their faith. The Christian identification of the Jews with Cain repudiated, in essence, the very notion of a permanent Jewish home in Palestine, or anywhere. Augustine held out hope that the Jews would repent and find their salvation in

Christ, but until that time they would remain living witnesses to their crime. As Robert Andrew Everett has noted, it was a theological view that argued that the Jewish existence itself was one of exile: exile from the favor of God, exile from the Messiah, and exile from the land of Israel.[18] In this theological narrative, Jews were the heirs of a divine curse, the most tangible proof being their dispersal from the land of the Hebrew covenant.[19]

This theological rejection of the Abrahamic Covenant was closely connected to the growing anti-Judaism on the part of Christians during the fourth and fifth centuries.[20] As Christianity gained in power and influence throughout the Roman world, and as classical paganism declined precipitously, Judaism remained as both an existential and a theological challenge to the early church. This resulted in a steady expansion of anti-Judaic invective in the writings of the theologians and church fathers of the era, in which the "teaching of contempt" toward the Jews and Judaism, as historian and Holocaust survivor Jules Isaac notably described it, became a part of the very lifeblood of Christian thought.[21]

No theologian of the early church characterized this anti-Judaic turn as starkly as John Chrysostom, archbishop of Constantinople and the most influential Christian thinker of his age. His writings sought to drive a definitive wedge between Christianity and Judaism, evidence in part of the enduring link between the faiths well into the fourth century.[22] Rigidly doctrinaire and a talented orator, Chrysostom threw considerable energy into the denunciation of Judaism in an attempt to engender a Christian fear and mistrust of the rival faith. The synagogue was presented as the central theater of Jewish corruption and debauchery, "an assembly of criminals, a den of thieves, a cavern of devils, an abyss of perdition."[23] The Jewish character itself, in this view, was at the core of this debauchery, as Chrysostom describes the Jews as "lustful, rapacious, greedy, perfidious bandits."[24] The key notion in Chrysostom's anti-Judaic theology, however, was that of deicide, the murder of the Christian savior. Though the concept of deicide had appeared in the work of other Christian writers, it emerged with new force in the work of Chrysostom. He clearly charged that as a Jewish court had turned Jesus over to the Roman authorities, Jews were essentially responsible for the crucifixion of Christ. This heinous crime, to Chrysostom, was central to the rejection of the Jewish people in the eyes of God. It was a crime for which there was "no expiation possible, no indulgence, no pardon," and one that condemned the Jews to live "under the yolk of servitude without end."[25] In this view, the destruction of the Jewish Temple at Jerusalem in 70 CE, and the failure of the pagan Emperor Julian to rebuild it in the 360s, was divine proof that Christianity had indeed superseded Judaism in the eyes of God.

By the early fifth century, Christian theological views on Palestine had become widely accepted and firmly ensconced. As a universal and itinerant faith, in which salvation was achieved through the worship of Christ and not through the fulfillment of any territorial covenant, a distinctive theology of land did not emerge as it had in Judaism. Christian pilgrimage to Palestine expanded after the fourth century, and the institutional presence of the church there steadily grew, but a theological or covenantal claim to the territory did not emerge in the writings of the apostles, apologists, or theologians of the early church. Christians were not required to make a pilgrimage to the land of Jesus' life and death, as salvation could be achieved without it. Indeed, numerous Christian writers explicitly urged the faithful to seek salvation in a closer relationship with the faith and with Christ, and not in a physical journey to Palestine itself. Within the increasingly anti-Judaic writings of the church fathers, however, can be discerned a clear Christian rejection of Judaism's covenantal claim to the land of Israel. The theological view of the Jews as deicidal murderers, disavowed by God and destined to wander the earth for their crime against the Christian messiah, served as a Christian disavowal of the Abrahamic Covenant. The rejection of this covenant, rather than the emergence of a distinctive Christian theology of land to replace it, would remain at the core of the Christian view of the Holy Land for the next sixteen centuries.

PATRIA COMMUNIS: THE CRUSADES AND THE HOLY LAND

The Muslim conquest of the Levant – including Jerusalem and its environs – in the 630s, and completed within a decade of the Prophet Muhammad's death, created a new challenge in Christianity's connection to the Holy Land. For the first time in over three centuries, the church was forced to conduct its affairs under the auspices of a non-Christian power. From the seventh to the tenth centuries, Christian pilgrimage to Palestine continued, though the institutional expansion of the church was halted. Evidence suggests that a succession of Muslim caliphs tolerated this continued Christian presence, no doubt in part for the economic stimulus provided by waves of pilgrims visiting the various holy sites of the territory. Though the destruction of the Church of the Holy Sepulchre in 1009 on the orders of Caliph Al-Hakim bi-Amr Allah (the "Nero of Islam" to his critics) was a shock to the church, its rebuilding in the 1040s, and the resumption of regular pilgrimage to the region, signaled a return to normal relations between the caliphs and the Christian powers.[26]

It is tempting to seek the traces of a more coherent Christian (and specifically Catholic) theology of land in Pope Urban II's preaching of the First Crusade at the Council of Clermont in 1095. Called in response to an appeal from the Byzantine Emperor Alexios I, who requested papal aid to repel the advances of the Seljuk Turks into Anatolia, the reconquest of the city of Jerusalem, and indeed of the Holy Land itself, emerge as a central objective of the papacy both in remaining fragments of Urban's sermons and in contemporary commentaries on them. Urban's calls to crusade spoke vividly of the *liberatio* of the of the sacred city from the infidel Muslims as an objective that must unify and galvanize Christendom, and emphasized the notion that Palestine, and Jerusalem specifically, was the *patria communis* of all Christians, a legacy that could not be forfeited. This notion of the land as the rightful inheritance of Christians was expressed by a number of medieval chroniclers. As the fourteenth-century writer of Sir John Mandeville's *Travels* expressed, "Each good Christian man who is able, and has the means, should set himself to conquer our inheritance, this land."[27] In this view, crusading dovetailed neatly with the feudal obligation of a vassal to his lord, though in the spiritual context the Christian knight fought to restore the earthly estate of his heavenly lord and savior, Jesus Christ.

Stephen of Bourbon, the thirteenth-century preacher and church historian, expounded on the Catholic claim to the Holy Land explicitly, suggesting that as Christianity had superseded Judaism in the eyes of God, so had Catholic claims eclipsed the Abrahamic Covenant and its promise of land to the Jewish people. In this view, the territory was unequivocally the patrimony of the Christian church, which was now the true Israel. "We are descendants of the Holy Land both according to flesh and the spirit," he wrote. "According to the flesh, because our father Adam was created here and like the other patriarchs is buried in this country; according to the spirit because our father Christ and our mother the Holy Virgin were born, lived, died and were buried here. Moreover here our fathers the apostles were born and brought up, and here our mother the Church had its origin. Likewise the land is ours by right of succession as we are the true children of God."[28]

This notion of Palestine as the sacrosanct inheritance of universal Christendom, however, was bound up in the theology of salvation itself, where the earthly Jerusalem functioned as a ladder to its spiritual, heavenly counterpart. This connection between the earthly and the heavenly Jerusalem, between the reconquest of the Holy Land and Christian salvation, was expressed by no less a figure than Bernard of Clairvaux, the famed monastic reformer and impassioned preacher of the Second Crusade. In his *Letter to the English People*, he implored Christians to take up arms for the recapture of the territory as a means to salvation. "God has pity on his people and has prepared for them a means to salvation," he noted to potential crusaders. "He does not want your death but rather that you should turn to him and live. He puts himself in your debt, so that in return for your taking up arms in his cause, he can reward you with pardon for your sins and everlasting glory."[29] Pope Innocent III (r. 1198–1216), who called the Fourth Crusade (1202–04), similarly denoted the connection between crusading and salvation in a recital to be repeated after the daily mass. "O God, by thy admirable providence dispossessed of all things, we humbly beseech Thee to restore to Christian worship, the land which thy only begotten Son consecrated with His own blood; mercifully directing the vows of the faithful, who urge its liberation, upon the way of eternal salvation."[30]

Recent scholarship on the Crusades places this penitential character of crusading at the center of explanations as to why the endeavor was taken up by so many.[31] Though the reconquest of land was certainly an objective, the salvific act of crusading itself was perhaps the most powerful motivating force for a potential crusader. Pope Urban II himself appeared to have emphasized this notion in his crusade sermons, suggesting that a knight who fought as a soldier of Christ would sanctify his sins and restore his standing in the eyes of God. "Now become soldiers of Christ you who a little while ago were robbers," he implored at Clermont. "Now legally fight against barbarians, you who once fought against brothers and blood-relations ... Those who were the enemies of the Lord, now these will be his friends."[32] Crusading, in this view, was an act of salvation, a means for the sinner to atone for past transgressions and a way to sanctify one's role in the violent and often deadly power struggles of feudal society. This notion of the remission of sin (*remissio peccatorum*) permeated Urban's sermons, and even appeared in the decree of the Council of Clermont itself. "Whoever for devotion alone, not for gain or money, goes to Jerusalem to liberate the Church of God can substitute this journey for all penance." In launching the Third Crusade in 1187, Pope Gregory VIII wrote that, "to those who with contrite hearts and humbled spirits undertake the labour of this journey and die in penitence for their sins and with the right faith, we promise full indulgence of their faults and eternal life."[33]

This emerging view of the Crusades as an essentially penitential quest complicates the idea that these campaigns produced a distinctive Catholic theology of land. Though popes, bishops, theologians, and chroniclers spoke of the Christian "inheritance" of Palestine, the *patrimonium Christi*, crusade theology was consistently bound up in notions of pilgrimage, penance, salvation, and even martyrdom. For the medieval crusader, the quest provided the ideal means through which to expiate the sins accrued in the violent struggles of medieval life, to say nothing of the vainglorious appeal of the pursuit to the knightly class. The decline of crusading proposals after the thirteenth-century capture of the territory by the Mamluks provides further evidence that patrimonial views of the earthly Jerusalem were again giving way to a spiritual view of the heavenly city in Christian rhetoric and theology. The westward flow of numerous important relics from Palestine, including the skull of Saint Andrew (brother of Saint Peter), and the creation of important shrines dedicated to these repatriated relics, appeared over time to assuage Christian desires to maintain political dominion in Palestine itself.[34] The establishment of the Custody of the Holy Land in 1217, administered by the Franciscan order from Jerusalem to protect the sanctity of and access to the holy sites of Jerusalem and its environs, as well as to provide assistance to Christian pilgrims, further tempered demands for the military conquest of the territory. Assented to by the Mamluk conquerors, the Custody appeared to signal a new strategy to guarantee Christian protection of the holiest sites of Palestine in light of the ultimate failures of the later twelfth-century crusades. A bull issued by Pope Gregory IX in 1230, which urged bishops, abbots, legates, and patriarchs to support the work of the Custody by any means possible, similarly suggests that papal strategy on Palestine was gradually shifting away from the notion of outright political control of the territory, and toward a guarantee of Christian access to important shrines and pilgrimage sites.

By the end of the thirteenth century, as crusading to Palestine declined in both frequency and fervor, and as the Custody functioned to protect access to Christian sacred sites, the theological universalism of the apostles and theologians of the early church steadily reemerged. A connection with the heavenly Jerusalem, in essence, once again supplanted the notion of Christian political dominion in Palestine itself. The rise of both monasticism and mysticism in the late medieval church, which emphasized a detachment from earthly concerns for a deeper connection with God, similarly functioned to prioritize notions of the heavenly, mystical Jerusalem. Thomas à Kempis, the fifteenth-century author of the widely influential *Imitation of Christ*, exemplified the turn toward the universal, mystical spirituality of the age. "They who go on pilgrimage are but seldom the holier," he stated in the *Imitation*. "There are many people who run off to various places to see the relics of the saints. When men go to see such things, it is often out of curiosity and a wish for change of scenery. They come back little inclined to change their lives."[35] Walter Hilton, the fourteenth-century English Augustinian, emphasized a similar notion in his *Ladder of Perfection*, instructing Christians to seek salvation and grace through a deeper connection with faith itself, and not in any physical shrine or sanctuary. "If you really desire to attain this blessed vision of a true peace and to be a true pilgrim to Jerusalem," he advised, "I will set you on the right road as far as I can. The beginning of this high road is the reformation of faith, which is grounded in humility, faith and the laws of the church."[36] The views of Kempis and Hilton, emerging alongside calls for reform in the medieval church and a return to a simpler piety, echoed an earlier theology that emphasized spiritual over earthly concerns. If a theology of land could be discerned in Pope Urban II's call to crusade at Clermont in 1095, subsequent events, including military defeat, calls for reform within the church, and the reemergence of a mystical and penitential theology, served to once again preference a universal view of the faith, where God could be found by all believers in all places. Within this context, the pursuit of the heavenly Jerusalem once again took precedence over the conquest of the earthly city.

Though the reconquest of Palestine ceased to be an objective of the papacy and the Christian West from the fourteenth century onward, access to the Holy Places, and the protection of pilgrimage routes to the region, remained crucial. Following the Ottoman conquest of Palestine in 1517, Christian access to the territory was guaranteed by a series of treaties between the Ottomans and various European powers. The first of these, a Franco-Ottoman treaty in 1535, guaranteed the free passage of Christian pilgrims to the Holy Places, and protected them against forced conversion to Islam. In the seventeenth century, the Republic of Venice and the Netherlands completed treaties with the sultans, focused primarily on trade, but guaranteeing access to the Christian shrines of Ottoman Palestine. The tensions that did arise were often not between Muslims and Christians, but between Roman Catholic, Protestant, and Orthodox factions, all of whom claimed distinctive rights and access in the territory. As a result of increasing tensions between Christian sects, and on occasion between Christians, Jews, and Muslims, the Ottoman government decreed in 1757 a modus vivendi between the faiths, an agreement that sought to prevent future disputes over jurisdiction by preserving the status quo, as it existed in 1757, in perpetuity. The edict, which became known as the "Status Quo" agreement, applied to most of the sacred sites in Palestine, including Jerusalem's Wailing Wall, Tomb of the Virgin, and Sanctuary of the Ascension, and Bethlehem's Basilica of the Nativity and Field of the Shepherds.[37]

In the midst of such growing stability, and with the clear challenge posed by interdenominational struggles, the Holy See also sought to bolster its institutional presence in the territory. In 1837, Pope Gregory XVI (r. 1831–1846) extended the authority of the Melkite (Arabic Eastern Catholic) patriarch of Antioch to Alexandria and Jerusalem, reestablishing a Catholic ecclesiastical structure in Palestine absent for centuries.[38] In 1847, the Latin (Roman Catholic) patriarch was finally reestablished in the Holy Land, and the Uniate churches (Syrian Catholic, Maronite, Armenian, Chaldean Catholic), though small by comparison, were reorganized and strengthened in order to undertake new missions.[39] From the 1850s to the end of the century, the Roman Catholic Church opened dozens of new hostels for pilgrims, and even more schools, hospitals, clinics, and orphanages for the local Catholic population. These institutions were staffed by more than thirty male and female religious orders, sent by the Holy See to establish a firmer presence in the region. As the Ottoman grip on the region weakened in the latter decades of the century, over one hundred new churches and chapels were constructed or reconstituted in Palestine, evidence of a Roman Catholic resurgence in a land so long under the sultanate's yoke. The alarming decline of Ottoman power in the second half of the nineteenth century, however, combined with the emergence of Zionism, a product of both widening antisemitic persecutions and the age of nationalism, would soon pose a new and dangerous set of challenges to the Catholic presence in Palestine.[40]

NON POSSUMUS: THE CHURCH AND THE RISE OF ZIONISM

Zionism, the national movement that sought to restore a Jewish state and homeland in Palestine, emerged in the nineteenth century as a consequence of three interrelated phenomena: the civic emancipation of European Jewry in the decades after the French Revolution, the rise of modern nationalism, and the emergence of racial antisemitism, which regarded the Jews (now increasingly seen as a distinctive and revolutionary "race") as a threat to the social and cultural cohesion of Western states. While cultural Zionists sought a Jewish homeland in Palestine as a means to stem the diminishment of Jewish tradition and culture in a secularizing (and increasingly hostile) West, political Zionists sought nationhood as a means to alleviate the intensifying persecution and suffering of the diaspora. Zionism, as such, represented both an acceptance of the failure of Jewish emancipation and assimilation, and an acknowledgment that marginalization and persecution were the ultimate realities of Jewish life in the diaspora.[41]

From the 1850s onward, a small but steady flow of Jewish emigrants arrived in Palestine to establish agricultural settlements and religious communities. Primarily from the Russian Empire, where pogroms against Jewish communities were increasing in frequency and ferocity, but also from western Europe, North Africa, and the Near East, these emigres sought refuge from persecution in a return to the land of the covenant. Zionism as a political idea, which was inspired by the Enlightenment and the various European national movements of the nineteenth century, was provided its first acting manifesto by Moses Hess, a German Jew active in socialist circles and an associate of Karl Marx and Friedrich Engels. His 1862 work *Rome and Jerusalem* advocated for a return of the Jews to Palestine as the only feasible solution to the rising tide of antisemitic persecution in Europe and beyond. He connected the revival of Jewish life and culture to the creation of a distinct national home, and posited that the social and legal emancipation of European Jews would never be sufficient to solve the Jewish question, given the tide of antisemitic persecution that followed it. For Hess, this Jewish nationhood was tied inseparably with Palestine and the city of Jerusalem. "Without a soil," he observed, "a man sinks to the status of a parasite, feeding on others."[42]

In the ensuing decades, as antisemitic persecutions intensified and the trickle of emigres to Palestine became gradually larger, the logic of a national homeland in Palestine as a means to alleviate Jewish suffering became ever more compelling. By 1896, when the Hungarian-born, Vienna-based journalist and literary critic Theodor Herzl founded the World Zionist Organization (WZO), the movement for Jewish nationhood possessed a growing élan that would make it a powerful force in European and international politics. His experiences in Vienna, where he witnessed a rising tide of antisemitic persecution, had led to his disillusionment in the idea of Jewish emancipation and assimilation. The election of Karl Lueger's openly antisemitic Christian Socialist Party in the Vienna elections of 1895 only cemented Herzl's conviction that a Jewish national home was essential. And for Herzl, Palestine was the legitimate and rightful home of the Jewish diaspora. "Palestine is our ever-memorable historic home," he boldly proclaimed in his 1896 work *Der Judenstaat* (The Jewish state). "The Maccabees will rise again. We shall live at last as free men on our own soil and die peacefully in our own homes."[43]

From the start, the leading figures of modern Zionism understood the importance of harmonizing the goals of Jewish nationalism with the Holy See's position in Palestine, given the church's historical ties and institutional presence in the territory.[44] Herzl posited that careful, high-level diplomacy, rather than a grassroots national movement, was the key to realizing Zionist ambitions. To this end, Zionist leaders actively courted the support and sanction of the papacy. Herzl's first meeting with an official of the Vatican came in May 1896, when he secured an audience with Cardinal Antonio Agliardi, the papal nuncio in Vienna. Herzl had keenly anticipated Vatican anxieties regarding church property in Palestine, as well as access to the multitude of pilgrimage sites throughout the territory. As such, he sought to gain papal approval by assuring Agliardi that a future Jewish state would protect the extraterritoriality of the sacred sites of Palestine, keeping Jerusalem, Bethlehem, and Nazareth out of the proposed state.[45] Herzl stressed that these cities would be internationalized, and possibly placed under the authority of the Holy See, pledges that would be repeated by a succession of Zionist leaders down to 1948.[46] The nuncio appeared satisfied with these assurances of extraterritoriality, but expressed doubt as to what form the new state might take, and skepticism of how the European powers, in particular Russia (which acted as a patron and protector of Orthodox Christian claims in Palestine), may react to the creation of a new state in the Near East. Agliardi further expressed doubt that the creation of a Jewish state in Palestine would alleviate the antisemitism suffered by Jews throughout Europe. The brief audience, cut short by the arrival of the French ambassador, left little doubt that the Holy See was not prepared to endorse the Zionist project, despite Herzl's assurances. In his diary, he confided that he left the meeting with doubts about Agliardi's sincerity, fearing that the nuncio regarded the goals of political Zionism fundamentally untenable and at odds with papal designs for the territory. "I believe Rome will be against us," he recorded, "because she does not see in the Jewish State the solution of the Jewish Question, and perhaps even fears it."[47]

Herzl's growing skepticism of Vatican support was piqued again the following year. In August 1897, as over two hundred international delegates arrived for the first World Zionist Congress in Basel, Switzerland, the Roman Catholic Church issued its first unequivocal statement on Zionism.[48] The Rome-based Jesuit newspaper *La Civiltà Cattolica*, which closely mirrored the Vatican's line on international affairs and was tightly connected with the Vatican Secretariat, proclaimed its position on a Jewish homeland as Zionist delegates arrived in Basel. "One thousand, eight hundred and twenty-seven years have passed since the prediction of Jesus of Nazareth was fulfilled, namely that Jerusalem would be destroyed," the editorial declared. "As for a rebuilt Jerusalem, which might become the centre of a reconstituted state of Israel, we must add that this is contrary to the predictions of Christ himself who foretold that '*Jerusalem shall be trodden down of the Gentiles, until the time of the Gentiles be fulfilled*' (Luke 21:24), that is … until the end of the world."[49]

In no uncertain terms, the statement outlined the fundamental incompatibility between the church's theological view of the Jews as a dispersed people, and Zionist aims to reconstruct a Jewish state in Palestine. Papal reticence to Zionism flowed both from this theological view, and from the church's growing association of emancipated Judaism with liberalism, socialism, secular nationalism, and communism, the very ideological forces that had destabilized the church's prestige and power in the nineteenth century. While traditional depictions of the Jews as deicides, usurers, and traitors remained in the Catholic press, they were now increasingly depicted as a revolutionary race, whose emancipation and assimilation had only rendered them more dangerous.[50] The church, as such, now deemed the Jews as doubly complicit, as the unredeemed living witnesses of the deicide, on the one hand, unrepentant and obstinate, and on the other as accomplices in the modernist and revolutionary ideologies that had so diminished papal authority and autonomy. The papacy's own loss of territorial sovereignty during the process of Italian unification, whereby the Papal States were dissolved by a liberal, secular, and anticlerical nationalist movement, further cemented the impossibility of papal support for an autonomous Jewish state. Despite the lack of a specifically Catholic "theology of land," the church would not assent to a Jewish home in Palestine, as a succession of Zionist leaders would now discover.

In January 1904, Herzl was afforded the opportunity of audiences with both the Vatican secretary of state, Cardinal Rafael Merry del Val, and Pope Pius X (r. 1903–1914), evidence of his growing prestige as the recognized leader of the international Zionist movement. In his meeting with Merry del Val, Herzl made certain to emphasize the purely political aims of Zionism, and informed his host that a future Jewish state would not impede upon Catholic access to or sovereignty over the sacred sites and shrines of Palestine. "We are only asking for the profane earth," he assured the cardinal. "The Holy Places are to be extra-territorialized."[51] He further explained to Merry del Val that the WZO sought the spiritual sanction of the Vatican, and not solely the political support of the European powers, precisely because a future Jewish state sought to respect the Roman church's historical and institutional presence in the territory. The cardinal's response left little doubt that the Catholic position had only calcified since 1897. "As long as the Jews deny the divinity of Christ," he informed Herzl, "we certainly cannot make a declaration in their favour. Not that we have any ill will towards them … To us they are the indispensable witnesses to the phenomenon of God's term on earth. But they deny the divine nature of Christ. How can we, without abandoning our own highest principles, agree to their being given possession of the Holy Land again?"[52] Merry del Val's position invoked two long-standing Catholic views on the Jewish people: their fate as a "witness people," destined to wander the earth for their crime against the Christian savior, and the notion that Catholicism had superseded Judaism in the eyes of God, a fact that negated the Abrahamic Covenant – ideas that precluded the church from blessing or endorsing the Zionist project. "The history of Israel is our heritage," the cardinal reminded his guest, "it is our foundation … In order for us to come out for the Jewish people in the way you desire, they would first have to be converted."[53]

Three days after his meeting with Merry del Val, Herzl was received by Pope Pius X, a "good, coarse-grained village priest," he recorded in his diary, "to whom Christianity has remained a living thing, even in the Vatican." Herzl may have been encouraged by reports of the new pope's amicable relations with the Italian Jewish community, stretching back to his youth in Mantua and Treviso. Indeed, Pius X apprised his guest of this warm relationship. "I have always been on good terms with Jews … after all, there are bonds other than those of religion: courtesy and philanthropy. These we do not deny the Jews. Indeed, we also pray for them."[54] The pope's cordial relations with the Italian Jewish community, however, included friendships with a number of high-ranking anti-Zionist Jews. The day before Herzl's visit, Pius X had called on the Jewish Senator Giacomo Malvano, a general secretary at the Foreign Ministry and a staunch anti-Zionist, for a meeting that undoubtedly prepared the pontiff for his discussion with Herzl. Another longtime Jewish associate of the pope, the politician and future senator Leone Romanin Jacur, similarly shaped the pontiff's anti-Zionist views in a meeting just days before Herzl's arrival. Italian Jewry's general opposition to Zionism was conditioned by several factors, including a high level of assimilation into Italian society, an Italian nationalism that raised patriotism to the level of a religious duty, and a messianic view that tied the mission of Judaism to the international diaspora and not to any ascribed "homeland."[55] Within this context, and given the papacy's historic and theological apprehensions to the return of the Jews to Palestine, Pius X presented his case to Herzl in no uncertain terms.

In short order, the pope outlined the incongruity between Catholic and Zionist positions on Palestine. "We cannot give approval to this movement," he sternly informed Herzl. "We cannot prevent the Jews from going to Jerusalem, but we could never sanction it. The soil of Jerusalem, if it was not always sacred, has been sanctified by the life of Jesus Christ. As the head of the Church, I cannot tell you anything different. The Jews have not recognized our Lord, therefore we cannot recognize the Jewish people."[56] Though Herzl assured the pope that a future Jewish state would not impede on Catholic access to, or indeed potential control of, the holy sites, his host appeared little convinced. "*Gerusalemme*," he noted, "must not get into the hands of the Jews." Pius X continued that if the Jews were to go to Palestine "clinging to their faith," then the Vatican could not be in support, and if they went "without any faith," then the pope would be even less favorable to them. Pius X's opposition appeared to hinge both on the notion of the Jews as an unredeemed, deicidal people, and on the idea that emancipated, secular Judaism, with its connections to modernist and revolutionary ideologies, was also a threat to Catholic interests. He did not outline an alternative Catholic theology of land for his guest, but rather suggested that the Abrahamic Covenant had been nullified by the coming of Christ, which negated Jewish desires to return to Palestine. "The Jewish religion was the foundation of our own," he reminded Herzl, "but it was superseded by the teachings of Christ, and we cannot concede it any further validity." As had Merry del Val, the pope alluded to the notion that the Vatican could theoretically support Zionism only with the mass conversion of the Jews to Roman Catholicism. "If you come to Palestine and settle your people there," he infamously cautioned Herzl, "we shall have churches and priests ready to baptize you all."[57] At the close of the brief audience, Herzl recognized the impossibility of Vatican support for Zionism. "*Non possumus* [we cannot]" were the pope's closing words. Sitting in an antechamber after his meeting, Herzl gazed at a Raphael fresco of a seated Pope Leo III, crowning a kneeling and acquiescent Emperor Charlemagne. "That's the way Rome wants it," he recorded bitterly in his diary.[58]

Several months after Herzl's visit, Merry del Val elaborated on the Vatican's position in an interview with the Viennese Zionist journal *Die Welt*. While he repeated that the church could never "deliver up the country of our redeemer to people of a different faith," he explained that the Vatican would never oppose the emigration of Jews to Palestine to escape persecution, as the Holy See "never opposes an undertaking that alleviates human misery."[59] The Vatican, then, would not oppose migration of the Jews to Palestine on humanitarian grounds, but it could not endorse the establishment of a Jewish state in Palestine, which it regarded as untenable on both theological and political grounds. This notion was repeated to Heinrich York Steiner, an associate of Herzl, just weeks after the latter's Roman visit. Merry del Val assured Steiner that if the Jews wanted to establish agricultural colonies in Palestine, he would regard it as a humanitarian endeavor and not impede it.[60] At this stage the Vatican, however, did not anticipate the mass immigration that would lead to a Jewish majority in Palestine, nor the upheavals of the First World War, which would alter alignments of power and create new international allies of the Zionist movement.

Following Steiner's visit, nearly thirteen years would pass before the Vatican would receive another Zionist delegate. By the time Pope Benedict XV (r. 1914–1922) received Nahum Sokolow in 1917, however, the influence of the international Zionist movement had increased significantly. While the WZO had been plagued by infighting for several years after Herzl's death in 1904, it had grown to become a formidable and transnational movement by the eve of the First World War.[61] The growth of international Zionism was fueled by a rapid out-migration of Russian Jews escaping persecution and pogrom, a process accelerated by the chaos of the war. From 1880 to 1920, nearly two million Jews fled Russia, the majority heading for Germany, Britain, and the United States. As a consequence, Berlin, London, and Washington acted as international hubs of the movement through the war years. These states, in turn, remained keen to cultivate Zionist loyalties to further the war effort, an objective complicated by the fact that Germany would oppose Britain, and eventually the United States, on the battlefields of Europe. All mainstream Zionists, however, agreed on the general principle of a Jewish homeland in Palestine.

Sokolow's April 1917 visit to the Vatican came amid this flush of optimism within the international Zionist movement, and in the afterglow of the Sykes-Picot Agreement of 1916, which assigned the fate of Palestine to Britain and France after the inevitable fall of the Ottoman Empire. Sokolow's confidence was further buoyed by correspondence with Sir Mark Sykes, who had visited the Vatican a week earlier. Sykes, a Roman Catholic, soldier, Conservative parliamentarian, and principal adviser on Ottoman and Near Eastern affairs to the British cabinet, was also a recent convert to the Zionist cause, believing a Jewish state under British protection would best maintain London's interests in the region.[62] In private conversations with Monsignor Eugenio Pacelli (the future Pope Pius XII), Secretary of State Cardinal Pietro Gasparri, and Pope Benedict XV, Sykes came away with a strong impression that the Vatican was at last prepared to accept the aspirations of political Zionism.[63] Pacelli assured Sykes that the Vatican was not opposed to British protection of the Holy Places, and additionally that he did not oppose the Jewish settlement of Palestine, so long as these sites remained under foreign, and preferably Christian, jurisdiction. Sykes, on his part, assured Pacelli that the Zionists had no intention of annexing the Holy Places, repeating the assurances of Zionist leaders, including Sokolow, that the Vatican had "no reason to fear that any possession of the Christians in Palestine would be disturbed or harmed by the Jewish population of Palestine."[64] After brief meetings with Gasparri and Benedict XV, Sykes remained convinced of the Vatican's goodwill. On 14 April 1917, Sykes apprised Sokolow of his meetings in Rome. "I visited Msgr Pacelli, and was received in audience by His Holiness … I was careful to impress that the main object of Zionism was to evolve a self-supporting Jewish community … which should … be a proof to the non-Jewish people of the world for the capacity of Jews to produce a virtuous and simple population … I further pointed out that Zionist aims in no way clashed with Christian desiderata in general, and Catholic desiderata in particular, in regard to the Holy Places."[65]

Sokolow saw Pacelli on 29 April 1917, followed by meetings with Gasparri on 1 May and Benedict XV on 4 May. Despite his guarded optimism (bolstered by Sykes's letter), he was careful to present the Zionist program in a most moderate vein, wary of altering the Vatican's apparent change of view. Sokolow was aware of the papal desire to control an autonomous zone that encompassed a large swath of territory around the holy sites, a plan discussed at a conference at Chur, Switzerland, earlier in 1917, where prelates and leading German, French, Italian, and Swiss Catholics discussed a Vatican enclave in southern Palestine, and prepared to launch a diplomatic campaign to secure such a zone.[66] Armed with this knowledge, he was careful to downplay notions of an expansive Jewish state or of imminent Jewish political domination of Palestine. From the outset of his meeting with Pacelli, he noted that "in spite of the extraordinary courtesy shown … the interview was somewhat strenuous."[67] Despite presenting his aims in moderate terms, Pacelli remained skeptical, pressing his visitor for a more rigidly defined outline of Zionist territorial demands. On hearing Sokolow's general explanations of Zionist aims, Pacelli retorted sharply, "That is not enough. Borders must be determined, what the Holy Places are must be defined, for on this there are differences of view: some hold that they mean all the country, others – that they are only a few isolated sites. We must know in advance what you demand, in order to avoid conflicts and competition between us."[68]

While Sokolow intended to speak in generalities, and to present Zionism as a moderate and logical program, Pacelli continued to press for clarification on territorial specifics, lending credence to earlier reports that the Vatican indeed had designs on carving out an autonomous zone in southern Palestine. Sokolow had clearly underestimated the Vatican's territorial claims, which amounted to a virtual partition of the territory. Pacelli indicated that the reserved area, which would be off-limits to Zionist claims, was to extend well beyond the Holy Places themselves and would cover Jerusalem, Bethlehem, Nazareth, and their surroundings, as well as Tiberias and Jericho. Pacelli explained, cordially though firmly, that the legal and political status of the region would have to be established directly through negotiations between the Holy See and the powers, and the Zionists would be expected to abide by their decisions.[69] What Sokolow could not have known during his audience with Pacelli was that the Vatican was embarking on a new era of diplomacy centred on the concordat, a legal instrument, rooted in canon law, that sought to protect the civil and political rights of the church in the international sphere. Though concordats had existed for centuries, the codification of canon law, a project completed in 1917, revived the concordat as a tool to protect Catholic interests, carving out legal protections for the institutional church in the various jurisdictions that entered into such agreements with the Vatican. Concordat diplomacy, as Giuliana Chamedes has revealed, was envisioned as the Vatican's antidote to a liberal, secular (Wilsonian) global order, on the one hand, and a communist (often seen as Judeo-Bolshevik) order, on the other.[70] As the chief architect of this new diplomacy, Pacelli could offer no meaningful support to a national project that could subsequently curtail the rights of the church in Palestine.

Though Cardinal Gasparri also emphasized the Vatican's territorial claims, he expressed sympathy with the plight of Jews in Russia, reminding Sokolow that the church had condemned the persecution of both Catholics and Jews in czarist Russia, and that the Vatican would continue to condemn the religious persecution of Jews wherever it occurred. A number of topics were discussed during the short meeting, including the general situation of the Jews and their desire for Palestine, the question of the Holy Places and the church's stand regarding them, and the Vatican's attitude toward Zionism. Again, Sokolow sought to assuage Vatican fears of expansive Zionist ambitions in the territory. "We do not plan to create a state, but only an autonomous home," he explained to Gasparri. Though his host assured him that the Vatican was not opposed to Jewish migration to Palestine, particularly if it was prompted by religious persecution elsewhere, Gasparri's bold and juridical outlining of the Vatican's territorial demands left Sokolow skeptical that the church would ever assent to mere jurisdiction over the sacred sites themselves. "I felt a chill in my bones," Sokolow later recorded, as he listened to the cardinal's meticulously developed ideas on papal sovereignty in the territory. Though Gasparri's territorial demands differed little from those presented by Pacelli, he did end the meeting with Sokolow on a seemingly affirmative note. "Naturally," he exclaimed, "we are sympathetic to [Zionism]. You must do this and we will be extremely glad if you succeed in establishing the Kingdom of Israel."[71]

On 4 May 1917, Sokolow was received by Benedict XV in an audience lasting nearly an hour, much longer than the allotted twenty minutes. It was a sign of the pope's eagerness to receive his visitor, and an implicit nod to the growing significance of the Zionist movement, particularly given its growing base of support in Britain and the United States. To the pope, Sokolow characterized Zionist goals as the preservation of historical Judaism with its spiritual and moral traditions, rooted as it was in scripture. To this end, he stressed, it was not necessary to encourage large-scale Jewish immigration to Palestine, or to alter its existing demographic balance. The central issue, according to Sokolow, was to "inspire world Judaism by a new model of idealism."[72] Like Gasparri, the pope expressed sympathy with the plight of persecuted Jews and assured his guest that the Roman Catholic Church had no objection to the immigration of Jews to Palestine. On the return of persecuted Jews to the territory, in fact, the pope expressed his approval, affirming to his guest that "it is providential. God has willed it."[73] The pope concluded his meeting by repeating to Sokolow, several times, "Si, si, io credo che saremo buoni vicini" (Yes, yes, I believe we will make good neighbors), suggesting that he, like Gasparri, approved of a Jewish "kingdom" in Palestine, so long as Roman Catholic sovereignty over religious sites and centres remained intact.[74] Sokolow was sufficiently encouraged that he submitted a report to Chaim Weizmann, chemist and leading British Zionist, suggesting that the Holy See's demands were finally dovetailing with Zionist ambitions for Palestine. Just two weeks later Weizmann, relying on the report, felt confident enough to tell a London Zionist conference that "we have assurances from the highest Catholic circles that they will view with favour the establishment of a Jewish National Home in Palestine, and from their religious point of view see no objections to it and no reason why we should not be good neighbours."[75]

The Vatican's brief and apparently conciliatory position on Zionism did not, in fact, signal a change in the church's long-standing views, and must be read within the context of the frenetic diplomacy of the closing months of the First World War. As the Ottoman Empire rapidly imploded, and as Germany's allies suffered a string of defeats, it became apparent that the Western powers, and Britain in particular, would play a decisive role in postwar Palestine. The Vatican, for its part, was not opposed to British suzerainty in Palestine as it would signal the conquest of the territory by a Christian power. It presented an opportunity, moreover, to carve out an autonomous zone, under papal dominion, around the holy sites and their environs. The notion of a sovereign, papal-controlled zone in southern Palestine was further buoyed by the fall of the czarist government in the spring of 1917, an event that appeared to suspend Russia's traditional role as protector of Orthodox Christian interests in the territory. For the Vatican, this represented the opportune moment to establish its own sphere of authority. Weizmann himself later reflected on the extent of the Vatican's territorial ambitions. "Practically all of Palestine could be regarded as a Holy Place," he noted. "There was Galilee, the Jordan Valley, Jerusalem, Bethlehem, and Nazareth. On such principles, very little of Palestine was left."[76] Given these ambitions of an autonomous region under papal jurisdiction, Benedict XV's promise to be "good neighbors" with the Zionists must be read in a geographical, and not spiritual, sense. The Vatican would only consent to a return of the Jews to Palestine if the Holy Land itself, which encompassed much of central and southern Palestine, was to remain firmly within the ambit of the Roman Catholic Church.[77]

Sokolow's visit, in fact, marked the end of the Vatican's presumptive sanction of political Zionism for decades to come. The events of the next several months served to harden Vatican opinion on the subject and hearkened the return of the unambiguously anti-Zionist line of the prewar era. In November

1917, British Foreign Secretary Lord Arthur James Balfour issued the Balfour Declaration, drafted with the assistance of Weizmann, Sokolow, and the British Zionist Lord Walter Rothschild.[78] Promising British support for a Jewish homeland in Palestine, it contained assurances of protection to non-Jewish communities in Palestine, though it ominously neglected to discuss the rights of Palestinian Arabs, who constituted nearly 90 percent of the population.[79] The declaration, followed by General Edmund Allenby's triumphant entrance into Jerusalem in December, after British troops had captured the city from the control of the Ottomans, aroused latent anxieties in the highest levels of the Vatican Secretariat. It seemed that the Vatican's designs on an autonomous enclave in southern Palestine were being supplanted by Britain's imperial ambitions for the territory, which appeared to cede the Zionists a much larger stake than had previously been assumed.

Benedict XV still considered Great Britain the ideal power to administer Palestine after the fall of the Ottoman Empire, and outwardly, the Vatican signaled relief that Jerusalem had been wrested from the Ottomans by a Christian state. The Vatican's semiofficial organ, *L'Osservatore Romano*, went so far as to call the capture of Jerusalem a "victory for the Christian civilization," a sentiment echoed by the Catholic press the world over.[80] What concerned curial officials, however, was that the Balfour Declaration appeared to disregard papal claims to sovereignty over the Holy Places, making no mention of sites considered sacrosanct by the Holy See. In fact, the declaration appeared to sanction the eventual Zionist domination of the whole territory, including the Holy Places and the indigenous Arab and Christian populations. The day after Allenby's entrance into Jerusalem, Gasparri, speaking to Charles Loiseau, the French attaché in Rome, confided that since the Ottomans had left, the status of the Holy Places would reemerge as a source of conflict between the Christian powers, and that "Zionism, of which Mr Balfour had just made a gift to Palestine, would not fail to engender other conflicts."[81] In concluding, he added that it was "difficult to take a piece of our hearts away from the Turks in order to give it to the Zionists."[82]

The next five years would mark a period of intensifying Vatican opposition to Zionist plans for Palestine, as it appeared that a Jewish state in the territory was rapidly moving from idea to reality. Added to this were fears of a "Bolshevist" Zionism using the territory as a beach head to further communist expansion, a concern that caused genuine disquiet in both Vatican and wider circles in the aftermath of the Russian Revolution. As Nina Valbousquet has observed, networks close to the papacy had long conflated the spread of Bolshevism and Zionism, a fact that led to a series of articles in *L'Osservatore Romano* and the influential Jesuit paper *La Civiltà Cattolica* warning of the destructive and revolutionary potential of "Judeo-Bolshevism."[83] In the same period, the priest, seminary professor, and curial official Umberto Benigni, who had served in the Secretariat of State under Pope Leo XIII (r. 1878–1903), coordinated the distribution of the forged and antisemitic *Protocols of the Elders of Zion* through Catholic networks both in Italy and beyond.[84] Though no pope had ever endorsed the *Protocols*, the latitude and autonomy of figures such as Benigni spoke volumes on the Vatican's implicit linking of Bolshevism and Zionism.

Benedict XV's pronouncements and allocutions increasingly reflected this growing apprehension. His March 1919 allocution to the College of Cardinals amounted to a forceful restatement of Vatican policy and was clearly intended to trumpet the Vatican's demands to the delegates of the Paris Peace Conference, who had been deliberating since January. The pope explained that there was "one matter on which We are most specifically anxious and that is the fate of the Holy Places, on account of the special dignity and importance for which they are so venerated by every Christian ... Our anxiety is most keen as to the decisions which the Peace Congress at Paris is soon to take concerning them. For surely it would be a terrible grief for Us and for all the Christian faithful if infidels were placed in a privileged and prominent position; much more if those most holy sanctuaries of the Christian religion were given to the charge of non-Christians."[85] If the papacy had ever harbored any notions of an accommodation between Zionist and Catholic interests in Palestine, they had clearly evaporated in the postwar period.

By early 1919, however, it appeared increasingly evident that the Vatican would play a marginal role both in the immediate future of Palestine and in the negotiation of peace. Despite the frenetic lobbying of papal diplomats on the eve of the Paris Peace Conference, the Vatican would not be afforded a seat at the conference table, an outcome that piqued fears of a postwar order dominated by liberal, democratic, and secular powers who would move to limit the authority and autonomy of the church. *La Civiltà Cattolica*, echoing the words of Cardinal Gasparri, denounced Woodrow Wilson squarely, stating that the American president would bear the ultimate responsibility for the "odious offense" of excluding the Vatican from participating.[86] The creation of the League of Nations, which began its deliberations in January 1920, was met with similar scorn by the Vatican, which saw the new organization as merely the permanent instrument of Wilsonian internationalism. In April, the Vatican's petition to secure sovereignty over the Holy Places of Palestine was also rejected at the San Remo Conference (which made official the British Mandate in Palestine), an outcome that clearly signaled the Vatican's feeble diplomatic clout. The appointment of Sir Herbert Samuel, the Anglo-Jewish parliamentarian and Zionist advocate, as Britain's high commissioner to Palestine only heightened Vatican anxieties. As a result, the pope's subsequent statements on the issue reflected deep unease on the rapidity of developments in Palestine, and the potential for Rome to lose control and influence in a territory inexorably bound to the tradition and history of the church.[87]

In 1920 leading Zionists were still convinced that the Vatican, wielding influence with Catholic-majority states at the League of Nations, represented a roadblock to the implementation of Britain's Mandate for Palestine and the eventual implementation of the Balfour Declaration. France and Italy, in particular, remained resistant to ceding to Britain too much control in the Near East, particularly as Ottoman power was imploding rapidly. Informal cooperation with the Vatican on the question of Palestine, in this context, served larger French and Italian interests while checking British expansion in the region. France, as the traditional guardian of Catholic interests in the Near East, sought with the Vatican a special status for the Holy Places, a plan opposed by Britain as it would lead to a dual administration in Palestine.[88] In February 1920, Weizmann apprised the British foreign secretary, Lord Curzon, of the particular challenge Italy posed, "foremost among the powers which display a considerable and somewhat dangerous propaganda." On the question of Palestine, he informed Curzon, "the Vatican and the secular Italian government seem to be identical," adding that the Banca di Roma, a Vatican bank, was also attempting to exploit the delicate situation in the territory.[89] Also dangerous, warned Weizmann, was the politicking of the Catholic religious orders in Palestine, led by the Franciscans, who had acted as the spiritual wardens of the Catholic sacred sites in the territory since the thirteenth century. Bishop Luigi Barlassina, who had been appointed the Latin patriarch of Jerusalem in 1920, was identified by Weizmann as a particularly vitriolic and fanatical anti-Zionist propagandist, a character sketch not without merit. In September 1920, upon returning to Jerusalem from Rome, where he had informed the pope of Zionist intrigues, Barlassina published a pastoral letter urging the internationalization of Palestine, lest Catholics become "servants of Zionism." "The speeches which the Latin Patriarch has been making in Rome," Weizmann informed the Palestine Zionist Executive in 1922, "are almost unbelievable in their unscrupulous malignity."[90] Barlassina, for his part, called for a "new crusade" to defend Catholic interests in Palestine, and he disseminated his views through a journal, *La Palestine*, that was published by the Patriarchate. "Palestine is under an oppressive domination a thousand times more dangerous than Turkish rule," he declared in a 1922. "Only corruption and immortality reign in the sacred land … The whole Zionist movement, directed by a few fanatics, is waging war against both Catholic and Arab elements."[91]

Just prior to the presentation of the draft Mandate for Palestine to the League of Nations Council in April 1922, Weizmann made a final attempt to shape Catholic opinion in a visit to the Vatican. Though, notably, he was unable to secure an audience with the pope, he was granted a meeting with Gasparri.[92] Little was gained from the discussion. Though he was "very genial and friendly," Gasparri pressed Weizmann on the increasing Jewish immigration to Palestine, inferring that Jews were quickly supplanting Arab and Christian populations in the territory and gaining a privileged position vis-à-vis these groups. The cardinal also expressed dismay at several articles of the draft Mandate for Palestine, including "all of the Zionist provisions," evidence that the Vatican was preparing to challenge the document at the League of Nations. Weizmann later reflected on the distinctive parallels between views in the Vatican and those of the Arab delegations in Palestine, suggesting to Nahum Sokolow weeks later that there was "no doubt in my mind that to a great extent the Arab agitation is due to the encouragement of the Vatican."[93] He further opined that France and Italy would have been amenable if it were not for the "implacable hostility of the Vatican, which has been moving heaven and earth to get the ratification of the Mandate postponed and to bring about a reversion of the whole policy."[94] If nothing else, the audience with Gasparri confirmed to Weizmann and the Zionist Executive that the Vatican could not be counted among the allies of Zionism as the draft Mandate moved to debate at the league. Several weeks later, an exasperated Weizmann informed Albert Einstein that the Vatican could simply be added to a list of foes the Zionist movement faced at this crucial juncture. "Rich servile Jews, dark fanatic Jewish obscurantists, in combination with the Vatican, with Arab assassins, English imperialist anti-Semitic reactionaries – in short, all the dogs are howling."[95]

On 6 April 1922, just four days after Weizmann's visit, Gasparri forwarded a memorandum to the British Foreign Office voicing Vatican fears of Zionist hegemony in Palestine. The document stated that while the Vatican did not oppose the extension of equal civil and legal rights to the Jewish population in the territory, it could not consent to the Jews being given "a privileged and preponderant position over other nationalities and confessions."[96] The memo further expressed fears that the Mandate did not adequately protect the rights of the Catholic populations of the territory. On 15 May 1922, Gasparri formally submitted a Vatican memorandum to the league critiquing several of the Mandate's articles. It argued that articles 2 and 4 (those that ensured the creation of a Jewish national home in Palestine) contradicted the League of Nations Covenant itself, in that the Mandate appeared to be designed less to serve the interests of the indigenous population and instead to facilitate Jewish immigration into Palestine.[97] In time, argued the memo, this would lead to "an absolute preponderance of the Jewish element in the economic, administrative, and political field" to the detriment of Arab and Christian populations.[98] Gasparri further critiqued the Balfour Declaration as incompatible with the spirit of the Treaty of Versailles itself, which stated that Mandates were supposed to be a "tutelage" that one power assumed over "peoples not able to support themselves under the strenuous conditions of the modern world."[99] The Vatican, as such, did not consider the Zionists in Palestine to constitute such a fragile population. Gasparri reminded both the British government and the league that the Mandate, which purported to support "the well being and development of the peoples of Palestine," was in fact becoming "an instrument for the subordination of the indigenous population for the advantage of other nationalities."[100]

Through the summer of 1922, Gasparri also tried to stir up opposition to the Mandate from Catholic-majority states at the league, including France, Italy, Spain, Poland, and Brazil. Though each of these powers had their own objectives for backing the Vatican, if only to thwart British influence in a Jewish-dominated Palestine, a variety of factors prevented the emergence of a unified Catholic response to the Mandate. Though France, the historic protector of Catholic interests in Palestine, had renewed diplomatic relations with the Vatican after the First World War (which were earlier severed during the Dreyfus Affair), anticlericalism continued to shape the politics of the Briand and Poincaré governments, complicating support for papal initiatives. In Italy, ongoing tensions between the Holy See and the state over the Roman Question (which concerned the territorial sovereignty of the Vatican), combined with pockets of senatorial support for Zionism, similarly impeded support of Gasparri's protest. Spain, for its part, was wary of French influence in Palestine should the Mandate be defeated, given France's historic role in the territory.

Poland, having regained independence only four years earlier, wielded little singular clout at Geneva, despite its willingness to toe the Vatican line. Brazil, in the midst of a political crisis that would topple its First Republic, was similarly unable to influence the outcome, despite its close ties to the papacy. In the end, then, no such unified front materialized. As a first attempt by Rome to rouse a "Catholic international" in opposition to Zionist aspirations, it was a failure. In July 1922 the League of Nations approved the Mandate of Palestine, and by September 1923 it officially came into effect. The rebuff spoke volumes on the limits of post-Versailles Vatican diplomacy, despite the reputed support of traditional Catholic allies at Geneva.

Papal failure to achieve results through conventional diplomacy, with the strategic cooperation of traditional and powerful allies, was particularly stinging to the Vatican, given that the fate of the Holy Land was a singular issue on which it felt it had a sound and persuasive case. It could certainly be argued that the Roman Catholic Church had an ancestral and legitimate stake in the territory, yet this amounted to little in the end. The Vatican's loss of confidence in its ability to influence international affairs through the league was made evident in the first encyclical issued by Pope Pius XI (r. 1922–1939), who had assumed the papal throne in February 1922. *Ubi arcano Dei consilio* critiqued the persistence of materialism, militarism, and class warfare in the postwar world, and it urged Catholics to use their faith as the true instrument of peace and social progress. "No merely human institution of today," he wrote, "can be as successful in devising a set of international laws which will be in harmony with world conditions as the Middle Ages were in the possession of that true League of Nations, Christianity."[101] Despite the Vatican's disdain for the secular, liberal, and democratic order envisioned by Wilson and embodied in the League of Nations, however, it was clear that the struggle to influence its traditional allies through conventional channels had been checked. Defeat on the Palestine question, in the end, would soon open the door to Vatican cooperation with less traditional partners within the "Catholic international."

CHAPTER 2

Toeing the Roman Line: American Catholics and the Palestine Question

From its sixteenth-century origins as a mission field, the Roman Catholic Church in the United States grew exponentially between 1800 and 1950, an expansion fueled by steady immigration and a high birth rate.[1] In the course of one hundred and fifty years, the American Catholic population had increased from 150,000 to over 30 million, representing one-fifth of the national populace and becoming the largest single denominational group in the country, Christian or otherwise. This growth led to the expansion of the institutional presence of the church, as the construction of Catholic hospitals, universities, schools, and seminaries ensconced the faith into the fabric of American life. Despite this growth, the relationship between the Vatican and the American church did not develop without strains. Papal fears of the social and political independence of the American bishops manifested in the well-documented "Americanist" crisis of the later nineteenth and early twentieth centuries, when a series of popes sought to curtail the autonomy of the American episcopate. While the American bishops struggled to create an identity for the faithful that was both authentically Catholic and American as a means to more deeply assimilate the faithful into the nation's social and political life, popes fretted over their embrace of ideals such as democracy, liberalism, and pluralism.

Though papal anxieties about the American church would last through the First World War, the Vatican's growing diplomatic isolation in postwar Europe would lead to a progressively closer alliance with the American bishops, who in turn were developing ever closer ties to Washington. American Catholic money was indeed a factor in the growing relationship between Rome and the American church, and would become a source of funding that would underpin the Vatican's own postwar projects. The collective voice of the American bishops, expressed through the Washington-based National Catholic Welfare Conference (NCWC; the organization had changed its name from the National Catholic Welfare Council in 1922), would also emerge in the interwar decades as an influential pulpit for papal visions of a postwar order. On a number of international questions, including the anticlericalism of the Mexican regime of Plutarco Calles, the persecution of Catholics in the Soviet sphere, and support for Franco's Nationalists in the Spanish Civil War, American Catholics emerged as powerful advocates of Vatican policy. Key to this was the transnational consensus that existed between papal Rome and its American faithful. This consensus between the Vatican and the American bishops would be particularly evident on the rise of Zionism, as the Vatican's hardening reticence to the notion of a Jewish state in Palestine was mirrored by Catholics in the United States. It was a reality that would, in short order, make the American church the leading advocate of papal policy on the future of Palestine.

A COLLECTIVE VOICE FOR AMERICAN CATHOLICS: THE BIRTH OF THE NCWC

The Vatican's apprehensions about the independence of the American bishops lingered into the First World War, and were aroused again when, upon the United States' entry into the war, the American bishops met collectively to establish a temporary council to coordinate Catholic support for the war effort. The group's first spokesman, John J. Burke (who edited the influential weekly *The Catholic World*), received the approval of Cardinal James Gibbons (of "Americanist" notoriety) to convene a meeting of the hierarchy in December 1917 at Washington's Catholic University of America. It was the first collective meeting of American Catholic churchmen in over three decades, and it resulted in the creation of National Catholic War Council, an emergency body that was dissolved at the end of the war.[2] Gibbons had pledged Catholic support for the war in an open letter to President Woodrow Wilson in April 1917 in which he powerfully outlined the collective duty of the American church. In creating the council, Gibbons reiterated the imperative of Catholic support. "The Catholic Church cannot remain an isolated factor in the nation," he asserted to the faithful. "The Catholic Church possesses the spiritual and moral resources which are at the command of the nation in every great crisis. Parochial, diocesan and provincial limits must be forgotten in the face of the greater tasks which burden our collective resources today. Today, as never before, the Catholic Church in the United States has an opportunity for doing a nation-wide work. No one, honestly, doubts Catholic loyalty to the principles of the American nation."[3]

It was a statement that unequivocally aligned Catholicism with American patriotism, and American Catholics did respond resoundingly to the war effort, enlisting in numbers that exceeded their proportion of the population.[4] In pledging steadfast support for the war, and in backing that up with a collective and coordinated effort, the American bishops also earned considerable legitimacy in larger American society, and a degree of political capital in their dealings with Washington. Indeed, the function of the council to express the collective will of the American episcopacy ushered in a new era in the relationship between the bishops and Washington in which the unified demands of American Catholics would become more difficult for policymakers and politicians to ignore.

After 1918, Burke and Gibbons led a campaign to establish a permanent bishops' council, a reflection of the rising profile of the church in American public life, particularly given the ardent support of Catholics for the war effort. Burke envisioned the new body as having a specifically political mandate – a collective voice that could advocate on behalf of American Catholics. It was a vision that grew directly out of the experience of the wartime council. In September 1919, at a gathering of representatives from 87 of the nation's 100 dioceses at the Catholic University of America, the National Catholic Welfare Conference was created as a permanent replacement of the wartime council. Archbishop Edward Hanna of San Francisco was elected as its first chairman, and it was decided that the organization would be centered around five departments – those focused on education, legislation, social action, lay organizations, and a press bureau – each headed by a bishop, coordinating the activities and advocacy of the church on a national level. Hanna described the specifically political role of the nascent body as "deal[ing] directly with the United States government and its numerous departments on matters that affect Catholic interests."[5] Bishop Peter J. Muldoon of Rockford, Illinois, who served as the first chairman of the NCWC's administrative committee, also saw the utility of the new body to galvanize Catholic opinion in the United States, creating a more unified and forceful lobby. "We do not hesitate to say that some representative body could accomplish untold good by directing editors, teachers, and even the clergy, on general matters pertaining to the welfare of the Church," he wrote in 1919, as the bishops met to form the NCWC. "There is an incessant demand for instructions on 'how to act' on many bills that are now before the legislatures of the country."[6]

While many American bishops were enthusiastic about the possibilities of speaking with a unified national voice, the idea caused apprehensions in Rome, where fears of the Americanist crisis still lingered. Gibbons's involvement in the NCWC, given his role during that crisis, only added to the air of mistrust. In January 1922, as Pope Benedict XV lay gravely ill with pneumonia, powerful members of the Roman curia moved to suppress the NCWC, fearing that a collective voice for the American bishops could only lead to a revived and potentially more dangerous form of Americanism.[7] Benedict's death on 22 January 1922, however, and the election of Milan's cardinal archbishop, Ambrogio Achille Ratti, as Pope Pius XI, appeared to signal a sea change in relations between the Vatican and the American bishops. Ratti's recent mission as nuncio to Poland had apprised the new pope of the growing threat of Bolshevism in eastern Europe, and of the general futility of Vatican diplomacy with Moscow. In the first year of his pontificate, the new pope would also witness the accession of Benito Mussolini's National Fascist Party, a development that placed the Vatican within the jurisdiction of an authoritarian regime with anticlerical leanings. Evidence suggests that these new realities shaped the pope's views on the utility of American Catholic power. On 6 February 1922, the very day of his installation, Pius XI was presented with a petition, representing a wide swath of American bishops, to preserve the NCWC. The new pope was also visited personally by Bishop Joseph Schrembs of Cleveland, who eloquently advocated for the body's survival. Cardinal Gasparri, who had arranged for Schrembs's meeting with Pius XI, clearly foresaw the utility of the American hierarchy speaking with a unified voice, and imparted to the new pontiff its potential advantages. In what could only be considered a nod to the growing power of the American church, the pope overturned the dissolution of the new body, stipulating only that episcopal councils take place less often than every year, that attendance at NCWC meetings remain voluntary, and that its decisions not be binding to all bishops of the American church. The decision was a watershed moment in the relationship between the Holy See and the American hierarchy, and one that would usher in a new era of American Catholic political advocacy.

Following its brush with disbandment, the NCWC quickly established itself as the leading voice, and political lobby, of the American Catholic Church. Opportunity to test the potency of this lobby soon presented itself. The repressive anticlericalism practiced by the Mexican regime of Plutarco Calles, who had won the presidency in 1924, provided the NCWC its earliest opportunity to advocate for a specifically Catholic policy response on an international issue.[8] A Freemason, Calles initiated anticlerical legislation in June 1926 that included the outlawing of religious orders, the exiling of numerous bishops and clergy on trumped-up charges, a suspension of the civil liberties of the clergy, and denial of the vote to the entire hierarchy. Within weeks, the situation descended into a protracted struggle between Calles's anticlerical allies and the supporters of the church and the conservative, traditional order (the so-called *Cristeros*).

The response of American Catholics to the Mexican crisis was indicative of the growing confidence and unity of the church, undoubtedly aided by the existence of a national body that could express a collective will. Catholic pressure comprised of public statements issued by the bishops, cloistered diplomacy conducted by high-ranking members of the hierarchy, and a broad-based press campaign aimed at bringing public pressure to bear on issues dear to American Catholics. In September 1926, the American bishops issued an open letter of sympathy to their Mexican coreligionists, assuring them that Catholics in the United States – both clergy and laymen – remained committed to their struggle for religious freedom and an end to persecutions, promising to stand with their Mexican brethren "to the end."[9] This was followed by the bishops' *Pastoral Letter on Mexico*, which was issued following the hierarchy's annual meeting in December.[10] This statement drew clear parallels between the bishops' concerns as both Catholics and American citizens, juxtaposing the freedoms enjoyed by American Catholics with the denial of religious liberties in Calles's Mexico. The statement was carefully worded so as not to appear to advocate for direct American intervention in the Mexican crisis, particularly military intervention, but it was clearly intended to galvanize Catholic pressure in expecting a firmer policy response from Washington.[11]

A wider campaign of public awareness was initiated by the NCWC between 1926 and 1929, spearheaded by Baltimore's archbishop, Michael J. Curley, who had succeeded Gibbons upon the latter's death in 1921. Curley engaged in the type of direct political activism that his predecessor would have advised against. On the issue of Mexico, Curley was active on the lecture circuit, delivering public speeches that sought a wider civic awareness and engagement on Mexican religious persecutions, and demands that Washington adopt a firmer hand on Calles. Through the NCWC, he also encouraged grassroots activism on the issue, and sought to mobilize organizations such as the Knights of Columbus, the National Council of Catholic Men, and the National Council of Catholic Women to spread awareness of the plight of their Mexican coreligionists.[12] In August 1926, the NCWC called upon the local chapters of these organizations to petition state and national leaders, including President Calvin Coolidge, the secretary of state, and numerous congressmen, to pressure Mexico to cease its persecution of the Roman Catholic Church.[13] To expand the base of Catholic activism even further, the NCWC's administrative committee sought to form a national committee of laypersons dedicated to stimulating a moral public opinion that would prompt Washington to more definitive action, an initiative resulting in the creation of the National Committee for the Protection of Religious Rights in Mexico, chaired by the prominent Catholic judge Morgan J. O'Brien.[14] In addition, the NCWC's press department supplied diocesan newspapers with a steady stream of dispatches from Mexico, where the organization had stationed a number of correspondents, resulting in pervasive coverage of Mexican atrocities in the widely circulated American Catholic press.[15] By the later 1920s, nearly five million copies of diocesan newspapers and magazines were distributed monthly. This campaign of awareness mounted by American Catholics was in full swing months before Pope Pius XI issued his own formal denunciation of the Mexican situation, which he outlined in the November 1926 encyclical *Iniquis afflictisque*. The NCWC's response also entailed direct political advocacy. This included a letter from the organization (which carried the weight of the entire American episcopate) directly to Coolidge in April 1926. The letter, which requested the president's attention to the growing atrocities committed by the Calles government, was published widely in the diocesan press in May.

The most profound aspect of the NCWC's advocacy on the Mexican crisis, however, was the role it played as an intermediary between the American government, the Vatican, and the Calles regime. The organization's central figure in this matter was John J. Burke, whose efforts had been instrumental in the organization's founding.[16] Between 1927 and 1929, Burke functioned as an unofficial envoy of the Vatican to Calles, a role approved of and encouraged by Secretary of State Frank Kellogg, as well as by Dwight Whitney Morrow, who had been named the American ambassador to Mexico in 1927. Morrow considered Burke to be a churchman of exceptional diplomatic skill and tact, and one who might be able to persuade Calles to cease his persecutions of the church and allow for the return of the apostolic delegate, George Caruana. Significantly, this sentiment was shared by the apostolic delegate to the United States, Pietro Fumasoni-Biondi, and the Vatican itself, which preferred an American churchman to conduct the delicate negotiations over its own official delegate to the American church. Before a series of meeting with Calles in 1928, Burke met with Fumasoni-Biondi to be briefed on the Vatican's demands, which included the return of the exiled Caruana, as well as bishops and priests who had been spuriously ousted by regional officials. In his meetings with Calles, Burke presented the Vatican's demands first and foremost, underscoring his role as the pope's de facto envoy. His efforts were instrumental in achieving a modus vivendi with the Calles regime in 1929, which resulted in the lifting of a number of restrictions on the Mexican church and defused a situation that had bedevilled Mexican-American and Mexican-Vatican relations.[17]

The lobbying efforts of the NCWC during the Mexican crisis signaled the emergence of the American Catholic Church as an organized and unified political force. Washington's reliance on Burke to conduct negotiations with Calles was emblematic of a growing relationship between the NCWC, the American bishops, and leading Catholic figures, on one side, and the American government, on the other. The fact that Burke was able to forge a satisfactory agreement in difficult circumstances only deepened esteem for the NCWC. It was a relationship that would grow much stronger in the 1930s, when Franklin Roosevelt would develop an even closer relationship with American Catholic leaders, and when American Catholics would again press their demands on a number of international questions, including the fate of Palestine.

The NCWC's efforts on the Mexican crisis also drew the American church closer to the Vatican. The entrustment of Burke to the negotiations with Calles, while it might have been desired by Washington, was consented to by Rome, a decision that spoke volumes on the Vatican's growing trust in the NCWC and the American bishops on political and diplomatic questions. In a 1927 letter to the four American cardinals, Pius XI praised the "splendid zeal" of American

Catholic activism on Mexico and lauded the various elements of the American church for "vigorously defending and furthering the cause of the Holy Roman Church."[18] He reserved particular praise for the NCWC, and its News Service, for bringing public attention to the Mexican situation. It was a far cry from the Vatican's grave suspicions of the NCWC just five years previous, and it signaled a closer working relationship between Rome and the American bishops that would strengthen further in the next decade.

"AMERICAN GOLD": MONEY AND THE RISE OF AMERICAN CATHOLIC POWER

There were other signs in the 1920s of growing ties between the Vatican and the American church. As with Mexico, it involved the diplomacy of a prominent American Catholic and academic, Edmund Walsh, SJ, who in 1919 had founded Georgetown University's School of Foreign Service (five years before the United States Foreign Service came into being). Since the Bolshevik Revolution of 1917, the Vatican was cautiously optimistic that a modus vivendi could be established with Moscow. The popes had denounced atheistic communism since the mid-nineteenth century, but the events of 1917 raised fresh fears of religious persecution in Russia and an expansion of Bolshevism beyond its borders. The Vatican had hoped that religious freedoms could be secured in exchange for official recognition from the pope, an important legitimizing and symbolic link for the fledgling Soviet Union. Part of the Vatican's outreach strategy was a pledge of assistance to famine-stricken regions of Russia, with a call to Catholics worldwide to raise funds for the endeavor. Of the nearly $2 million raised, a majority was donated by American Catholic organizations and dioceses. The relief mission had a practical purpose as well – it allowed the Vatican to dispatch a legion of religious to the Soviet Union, providing Rome an important source of intelligence from inside the country. Notably, the Vatican chose an American prelate, Walsh, to coordinate the Papal Relief Mission from Moscow.[19] Walsh, who would find later fame as a chief American consultant at the Nuremberg Trials, was uniquely suited to the role. Between 1922 and 1924, he was in regular contact with Rome, apprising the Vatican on the condition of the Catholic Church under Soviet rule. Though he was recalled from Moscow in 1924, allegedly because of his brusque (the Russians said "American") diplomatic manner, he did manage to open up a dialogue between the Vatican and the Soviets.[20] Despite his recall, the mission bolstered an increasingly closer working relationship between the Vatican and the American church. Upon his return from Russia, Walsh was sent by Pius XI to Washington with a letter for President Warren Harding on the urgent need for Russian relief. While in the capital, Walsh was also able to secure additional Catholic aid for Russia, a development that impressed upon the pope the financial might, as well as the fervent spirituality, of American Catholics.

The fiscal clout of American Catholics in financing Vatican initiatives by the middle of the 1920s can hardly be overstated and was another key factor in the growing influence of the American church at the Vatican. The pope's ambitious building program in Rome in the later 1920s, which included new seminaries, colleges, and the restoration of the Catacombs of St Sebastian, was largely funded by the American faithful.[21] Through the decade, the Archdiocese of Chicago sent over $100,000 a year to the Holy See, a figure matched or exceeded by other wealthy dioceses such as New York and Boston. By this time, New York, Boston, and Chicago, in that order, were the three richest archdioceses in the world.[22] As early as 1923, the increasing influence of American churchmen, and American dollars, in the Vatican became evident to observers in Rome. Odo Russell, the British minister to the Holy See, commented in his annual report for that year that "American gold" had a role in the elevation of two American archbishops, Chicago's George Mundelein and New York's Patrick Hayes, to the College of Cardinals. "The Catholics of New York and Chicago," he continued, "are by far the greatest contributors towards Vatican funds. It is, indeed, difficult to see how the present administration could be preserved without their support."[23] Russell also commented on the increasing numbers of American Catholic religious in Rome, evidenced by plans to build a new American college on the Janiculum Hill financed by a $600,000 gift from the American bishops. "The increasing strength of the Catholic Church in America means increasing influence at the Vatican," he noted, "and it is not so much of an exaggeration to say that the United States is now looked up to as if it were the leading Catholic nation."[24]

By 1925, then, it was clear that a sea change had occurred in the Vatican's view of the place of the American church in the international Catholic firmament. This was further evident in the role of the American church in the Vatican's global missionary efforts, an endeavor that was expanding in the postwar era. Russell's report for 1925 indicated that American support of Catholic foreign missions had become considerable, "not in personnel, but in terms of money," a fact that had influenced the Holy See to increasingly remove missionary enterprises from French Catholic control, "it being understood that American Catholics prefer to have the funds they contributed under direct Vatican control."[25]

In short order, the American bishops would have a missionary organization in their own hands. In 1926, after consulting with the apostolic delegate in Washington, Pius XI created the Catholic Near East Welfare Association (CNEWA) as a permanent umbrella organization for Vatican aid in Russia and the Near East, an organization placed entirely under the control of the American bishops. The fundraising capacity of American Catholics was again a key factor in this decision. The example of the Vatican's Russian relief efforts between 1921 and 1923 had clearly demonstrated the fiscal might of the American faithful, when nearly $2 million had been raised in the United States.[26] The CNEWA's charter stipulated that funds raised (through mass stipends, special collections, and donations) would be forwarded directly to the Vatican's Sacred Congregation for the Oriental Churches, and were to be dispensed at the behest of the pope himself. The association's "annual" for 1927 suggested that Catholics who joined the CNEWA pledge "a yearly minimum of one dollar," and expressed "the Holy Father's hope that every American Catholic who can possibly do so will join this association."[27] Given a Catholic population of nearly twenty million in the United States, the fundraising potential of the new association was considerable. The creation of the CNEWA had, in effect, allowed the Vatican to tap into the vast wealth of the American church while retaining firm control of the disbursement of funds.

The new association was intended to provide Catholic assistance to eastern and central Europe, the Balkans, and Palestine, the very regions where the Vatican feared a declining influence. In March 1926, the Vatican named Edmund Walsh the CNEWA's first president.[28] In September, Walsh described "the wish of the Holy Father to form a permanent society somewhat like the International Red Cross or the American Near East Relief. It will be a centralized Catholic distributing agency which can materially assist the Holy See to meet the daily demands made on the Holy Father for assistance in humanitarian works, education, and in social welfare work all over the world, as well as in distinctly religious and missionary activities."[29] Its charitable efforts occasionally extended beyond the Near East, such as a $100,000 donation made by the Vatican, through the CNEWA, to victims of the Great Mississippi Flood of 1927, a donation that raised the domestic profile, and fundraising repute, of the association.[30] Its board comprised the leading archbishops in the United States, and included Cardinals William Henry O'Connell of Boston, Dennis Dougherty of Philadelphia, and Patrick Hayes of New York.[31] In entrusting the new association to the American bishops, the Vatican expressed "complete confidence in the [American] bishops, and the Holy See leaves to them full liberty in the practical working out of this project." On the organization of the CNEWA's departments and functions, Cardinal Luigi Sincero, head of the Pontifical Mission for Russia, expressed that "the Holy See relies, as always, on the judgement of the American bishops."[32]

The placing of the CNEWA in the hands of the American episcopate was another sign of the Vatican's growing trust in, and reliance upon, the American Catholic Church, an alliance girded by the financial might of the American faithful. The CNEWA, as the primary Roman Catholic aid organization for Russia and the Near East, was tasked with collecting funds from every American diocese, with proceeds placed "at the direct disposal of the Holy Father himself."[33] Its objectives for 1927 included the commencement of a Russian seminary at Rome, as well as aid for Russia, Greece, Syria, and Palestine. A target amount of US$1 million was set by the Vatican, a figure that was surpassed by June.[34] The success of the CNEWA attracted attention beyond Catholic circles. Secretary of Commerce Herbert Hoover, who would become president in 1929, lauded the work of American Catholics in this sphere, connecting the alleviation of famine and disease to the combating of Bolshevism and other antidemocratic forces.[35]

The generosity of American Catholics, as well as the stalwart leadership of the American episcopate and clergy, was certainly recognized by the pope himself. In June 1927, Pius XI praised the American church, which had "once more demonstrated its traditional loyalty to this Holy See, manifested in their spirit of generosity."[36] In the same year, he credited them further with underwriting the Vatican's program for the "safeguarding of international peace through international understanding," praising the "great, permanently organized body of American Catholics forming a solid phalanx" behind him, "unfailing in their loyalty and devotion."[37] In October 1928, he again extolled the leadership of the American bishops in their development of the CNEWA. "We are indebted to you, Venerable Brothers," he exclaimed, "in who the sacred hierarchy of the United States finds its personification, and without whom nothing ever could or can now be accomplished."[38] He further praised the American church for "the substantial financial help given Us in support of two works of religion which are the object of intense daily, and ... harrowing concern of Our Apostolic ministry."[39] The first of these were funds for the Propaganda Fide, the Vatican office tasked with carrying the faith to non-Catholic states and regions. The second "work" were funds for the Roman Catholic Church in Palestine, where the Vatican clearly sought to bolster its institutional presence in the midst of rising Arab-Jewish tensions. The pope, in an implicit allusion to rising Zionist influence in Palestine, urged the bishops to keep in mind "that East which once was a most flourishing garden of the Catholic Church and which later, separated, or rather torn, from the Church, fell into so wretched a plight ... that East which now as never before fills Us with hopes ... of seeing her return to the One Fold, but which for this very reason is more than ever beset and tempted by propaganda (only too well equipped with worldly resources of every kind) hostile to Christ and His Church."[40] As early as 1928, then, it was clear that American Catholic money was supporting the Roman Catholic institutional presence in Palestine, a territory now firmly a priority of the Vatican Secretariat. Though the Vatican would ultimately fail in its efforts to establish relations with Moscow, the CNEWA would remain central to Rome's outreach in the Near East, and as such would play a vital role in postwar Palestine.

Increasing diplomatic isolation in Europe was another factor drawing the Vatican closer to both the American Catholic Church and Washington in the interwar decades, despite signs of optimism in the 1920s. In 1921, the Vatican had managed to reestablish diplomatic relations with France, the "eldest daughter of the Church," which had been severed for two decades by disputes over laicization and anticlericalism. Through the decade, the Vatican also set about securing its legal position with a number of European governments through the concordat, the church-state agreements that protected the social and civic privileges of the church, as well as securing tax-exempt status for its considerable land and property holdings.[41] The Lateran Treaty of February 1929, which offered Italian recognition of the sovereignty of the pope in Vatican City in return for papal recognition of the Kingdom of Italy (and Mussolini's Fascist regime), was the most significant concordat completed by the Vatican in the postwar period. The agreement saw an indemnity paid to the Holy See to settle accounts outstanding since Italian unification in 1860; it also provided guarantees on the position of the church in Italian society.[42] The agreement appeared to settle, once and for all, the tensions between the popes and the Italian state (the so-called Roman Question) that had bedevilled this relationship for six decades. By the end of the 1920s, then, it appeared that the Holy See had buttressed its position with a number of important European states, and had established its standing as a sovereign, neutral, and autonomous entity in continental and international affairs.

The stability of the later 1920s, however, would prove to be short-lived, not only for the Holy See but for the wider continent. The economic crash of 1929 strained preexisting political fault lines and renewed the Vatican's diplomatic anxieties. Despite completing a concordat with the Nazi government in 1933, relations between Rome and the new regime quickly deteriorated. Though Gasparri had severe doubts about Nazi sincerity at the signing of the agreement, fears of Bolshevism and a paucity of options led to its completion. True to form, the Hitler government disregarded most elements of the accord, and the Catholic Church in Germany was offered little protection against Nazi arrogance and ruthlessness. Papal relations with Fascist Italy held up little better, as disputes over the autonomy of Catholic Action, as well as the embedded anticlericalism of Fascist ideology, functioned to strain the relationship. The creation of the Rome-Berlin Axis in 1936, which drew Italy firmly into the German orbit, created distance between Pius XI and Mussolini; this would only widen as the Italian dictator moved closer to Hitler throughout the decade.[43] Mussolini's adoption of antisemitic racial laws in July 1938 further strained relations between Pius XI and the Fascist state. Just as it appeared that the papacy had reintegrated itself into the postwar states system, economic deterioration and political crises, combined with the rising hostility of authoritarian regimes in Italy and Germany, once again placed the Vatican in a precarious position.

THE AMERICAN BISHOPS BETWEEN ROME AND WASHINGTON

In the midst of such political volatility, and faced with diplomatic isolation, the Vatican began to cultivate ever closer connections both to the American bishops and the American government. Though the industrialized world had been shaken by the financial crash of 1929, American political structures remained remarkably resilient and stable, attributes admired and sought by the papacy. Alfred E. Smith's 1928 run for the presidency, while ultimately ending in failure, illustrated the extent to which Roman Catholics could penetrate American political life, even if pockets of anti-Catholic sentiment remained.

And the effective diplomacy of the NCWC on the Mexican crisis, as well as the administrative and fundraising acumen of the CNEWA and other American Catholic associations, had revealed the potential, both political and financial, of the American faithful. As European political instability deepened, and as it became increasingly clear that the United States had supplanted Britain as the world's most stable and powerful democracy, Vatican attentions increasingly turned toward Washington and the American church.

In the 1930s, a number of American Catholic leaders rose to prominence, a development that only bolstered their prestige in Rome. The principal figure among the American bishops was Francis Spellman of New York, a close associate of Eugenio Pacelli (who would become Pope Pius XII in 1939), and friend of presidents from Franklin Roosevelt to Lyndon Johnson.[44] Spellman, who had studied for the priesthood in Rome, had served in 1925 as the first American attaché to the Vatican Secretariat of State, where he became familiar with leading figures of the secretariat, including Pope Pius XI, Gasparri, and Domenico Tardini, who would later advise Pius XII on political matters and serve as secretary of state to Pope John XXIII. In 1927, Spellman's long and close friendship to Pacelli began during a visit to Germany, where the future pope was serving as apostolic nuncio. This relationship, which would strengthen over the 1930s and endure throughout Pacelli's pontificate, would guarantee Spellman, and by extension the American church, an important voice at the Vatican both during and after the war. In 1939, the pope would move Spellman from Boston (where he served as auxiliary bishop) to New York, where he was named archbishop of the nation's preeminent archdiocese. In the consistory of 1946, Pius XII would make Spellman a cardinal, cementing his position as the foremost leader in American Catholicism.

Other important national figures included Chicago's Archbishop George Mundelein, a close associate and key political ally of Roosevelt, credited with delivering the Illinois Catholic vote to the Democrats in the 1933 and 1936 federal elections. Mundelein's early and unequivocal support of the New Deal firmed up Catholic support for Roosevelt in the heavily Catholic Midwest, and his public praise of the Roosevelt administration's action on Mexico further cemented Catholic approval. Between 1932 and the cardinal's death in 1939, Roosevelt could count on the political support of Mundelein, who, by his very association with the president, had become the most visible figure in American Catholicism. The pair would meet fourteen times in this period, and they shared an active and frequent correspondence. That no other religious figure, Protestant or Jewish, would share such a relationship with Roosevelt was emblematic of the rapidly growing prestige of American Catholicism in the 1930s.[45]

Archbishop Samuel Stritch, who succeeded Mundelein in 1939, and who was also named a cardinal by Pius XII in 1946, maintained a similarly close relationship with Roosevelt throughout the 1930s, as did Boston's Cardinal William O'Connell. O'Connell was succeeded in 1944 by Richard J. Cushing, who would advocate for the Vatican on the Palestine question after 1945, and who later achieved national renown as the churchman to deliver the invocation at John F. Kennedy's 1960 inauguration.[46] Other key figures included Detroit's Edward Francis Mooney, a former chairman of the NCWC, and Archbishops John F. O'Hara of Philadelphia, Michael Curley of Baltimore, Patrick O'Boyle of Washington, and Timothy McNicholas of Cincinnati, all of whom cultivated important political ties in the postwar years. Howard Carroll, who served as the general secretary of the NCWC from 1944 to 1957, and Monsignor Thomas McMahon, who served as the acting head of the CNEWA from 1943 to 1955, would similarly emerge as influential figures in the postwar American Catholic firmament, particularly on the question of Palestine. By the end of the 1930s, the Vatican's expanding relationship with the American church was clear to observers in Rome. The British minister at the Vatican, Francis D'Arcy Osborne, reflected in his review of 1939 that "the steady increase of the Catholic populations of the New World, compared with the relative stability of that of the old, has during the last quarter of a century made the Vatican less dependent than formerly on Europe, and more anxious to adopt a democratic attitude in conformity with the spirit of America, to which the papacy may one day have to look for its main support, financial as well as spiritual."[47]

The Vatican, for its part, was anxious to take the initiative in strengthening bonds with the American bishops. The foresighted Pius XI, perhaps preparing his secretary of state, Eugenio Pacelli, for the papal throne, sent him to the United States in 1936 to acquaint him personally with the leading figures of American Catholicism.[48] It was Spellman who coordinated Pacelli's 1936 visit, the first ever of a future pope to the United States. The visit, along with strengthening the bond between Rome and American Catholic leaders, also highlighted the preeminence of Spellman in the American church, despite the misgivings of some more senior figures in the hierarchy.[49] If the tour signaled Spellman's rising status, it also initiated a Vatican effort to develop closer ties to the American government. Though the visit was classified as unofficial by the Holy See, it was clearly intended to draw the nominal allies closer together. Pacelli's agenda was threefold: to consult with Catholic leaders and the American government on official Vatican-American diplomatic relations; to seek American cooperation in the Vatican's various anticommunist endeavors; and to muzzle Father Charles Coughlin, the populist, antisemitic, anti-Roosevelt "radio priest" who had become a dangerous nuisance to both Washington and Rome.[50]

Pacelli's tour, which was covered extensively by the mainstream secular press, included meetings both with Catholic leaders and government officials. Through Joseph P. Kennedy, a prominent Catholic and a major contributor to Roosevelt's campaign chest, Spellman arranged a meeting between Pacelli and Roosevelt at Hyde Park on 5 November 1936 at which diplomatic relations, the suppression of Coughlin, and closer Vatican-American cooperation were discussed.[51] Spellman was the linchpin in the strengthening ties between Rome and the American church. In the early 1930s he had worked with Pacelli in the Vatican Secretariat of State, where the two became close friends and Spellman Pacelli's protégé.[52] After becoming auxiliary bishop of Boston in 1932, Spellman continued to cultivate his Roman contacts. Throughout the 1930s Spellman, in addition to his close relationship with Rome, also developed strong ties with Roosevelt. Along with Cardinal George Mundelein of Chicago, Spellman actively supported the New Deal, wielding spiritual authority and political sway in a Democratic Party stronghold.[53] Spellman also cultivated a closer political relationship with Kennedy, a fellow Bostonian, which opened additional avenues for the ambitious prelate.[54] From 1933 to 1936, Spellman discussed the virtues of formal Vatican-American diplomatic ties with both Kennedy and James Roosevelt, the president's son, a message he would later take to the president himself during Pacelli's visit.

As Spellman's star steadily rose, and as he increasingly acted as the primary envoy between the Vatican and the American government, American Catholic activism continued to grow and mature. The Spanish Civil War (1936–39) served to again highlight the increasing stridency of American Catholic activism on international questions. Upon the outbreak of hostilities in Spain, the Roosevelt administration sought, above all else, to avoid entanglement in what was regarded as a European civil war, a policy that fit neatly into the isolationism of the New Deal. Over time, however, a steadfast isolationism became more difficult to maintain, particularly given the clear evidence of Nazi and Fascist assistance to Francisco Franco's Nationalist forces, and in the face of growing atrocities on both sides. Though few Americans advocated direct intervention in the Spanish conflict, a wide range of civil and religious lobbies, which included many mainstream Protestant and Jewish groups, advocated for lifting, or at least revising, the American embargo on arms shipments to the Spanish Republic, a barrier that they claimed only aided Franco's Nationalists. A number of prominent Protestant and Jewish figures spoke out on the urgent need for embargo revision, including theologian Reinhold Neibuhr, Albert Einstein (then at Princeton University), and a cross section of literary, entertainment, and academic figures.[55] The various proponents of this view appeared to secure a victory in January 1938 when over sixty congressmen issued a statement expressing solidarity with the Spanish Cortes (legislature) as a stirring example to the world in its fight to protect democracy, a development that appeared to portend the lifting of Washington's embargo.[56]

This opposition to the Spanish embargo was counterbalanced by a majority of American Catholic leaders. Though few American Catholics advocated intervention, most were horrified at the atrocities perpetrated against Spanish religious by republican Loyalists and regarded Franco as a defender of religious freedom (even if many Catholics were uncertain of his political legitimacy). Michael J. Ready, general secretary of the NCWC, responded directly to the congressional statement of support for the Spanish Loyalists with an open letter, carried widely in the Catholic press, and sent directly to the State Department, in which he expressed "shock and amazement" that democratically elected American congressmen could so cavalierly support such an undemocratic, repressive, and anticlerical regime.[57] Ready's letter followed the statement of the American bishops, issued following their annual meeting in November 1937, expressing support and sympathy for their Spanish coreligionists, a declaration bolstered by a wave of reportage in the Catholic press highlighting the rape of nuns, the shooting of bishops, and the burning of churches.[58] In addition, a number of Catholic organizations, at the suggestion of the NCWC, passed resolutions condemning the anticlericalism of the Barcelona government, forwarding them to key figures in Washington, including Roosevelt and Cordell Hull, the secretary of state.[59] In December 1938, the National Council of Catholic Men created the "Keep the Spanish Embargo Committee," which constituted another flank in American Catholic efforts to shapes Washington's policy on Spain. The intensity of American Catholic political pressure on maintaining the Spanish embargo did not go unnoticed in Washington. In a May 1938 conversation with Roosevelt, Harold Ickes, the secretary of the interior, noted that the president feared that the lifting of the embargo "might have meant the loss of every single Catholic vote next fall," a predicament that made the Democrats justifiably wary.[60] Though Ickes later quipped in his diary that Catholic political pressure was "the mangiest, scabbiest cat ever," the administration was clearly cognizant of the need to strategically appease it.[61]

Although Catholic pressure did not, in the end, sway the administration's decision on the Spanish embargo, the episode endowed the American Catholic Church with a deeper confidence in its ability to express a collective voice.[62] The fight to maintain the embargo emboldened the NCWC's political lobby, and created the impression in non-Catholic circles (and particularly among mainstream Protestant and Jewish groups) that Catholics held a special sway in Washington. In fifteen short years, the American Catholic Church, organized through the NCWC, had emerged as a cogent and unified voice in American public and political affairs, and a powerful advocate of Vatican interests within the American body politic. Its dioceses and associations had become crucial fundraising sources for the Vatican's coffers, bolstered by the demographic and economic growth of the American faithful. Its bishops, once regarded by Rome as stubbornly autonomous and potentially radical, had coalesced into a powerful and unified collective, organized through a national council to express the mutual concerns of Rome and the American faithful.

CONFRONTING "THIS ROSEATE IDEA": AMERICAN CATHOLICS AND ZIONISM

Throughout the interwar period, Vatican attitudes on political Zionism remained unfavorable, becoming more hardened in the 1930s as increased Jewish immigration to Palestine lent a renewed urgency to the question of Jewish statehood. Despite the periodical strains that had existed between the Vatican and the American bishops, American Catholic attitudes toward Zionism mirrored Rome's quite closely, evidence of an analogous transnational outlook that appeared to supersede earlier tensions. An examination of the American Catholic press over this period illuminates these parallels. Reflecting Vatican sentiment, American Catholic journals regarded the 1917 British capture of Jerusalem by General Edmund Allenby as a positive development, delivering the city from the clutches of Ottoman Muslim rule and into the hands of a Christian power. Cincinnati's *Catholic Telegraph*, the oldest diocesan newspaper in the nation, feted the "deliverance of Jerusalem from the rule of the Turks," calling for a Sunday mass "of rejoicing over the British capture of the Holy City."[63] Mistrust of Zionism, however, remained a prominent theme, and was evinced almost immediately. Chicago's Catholic diocesan paper, *The New World*, expressed optimism in December 1917 that "whatever fate awaits the Holy Land, of this we have surety – never again will it depart from Christian control," but in the same article it expressed fears that a Zionist-dominated Palestine would unleash repression against its Catholic population. Similar sentiments were echoed the following April by *The American Catholic Quarterly Review*, which published a lengthy article attacking Zionist claims to Palestine on both theological and historical grounds.[64] The journal warned that Zionists had "erroneously based their political expectations upon some passages of the Holy Scripture," and further warned that the "Jewish nationalism" advocated by Zionists was a virulent colonizing force that would attempt to sweep aside all "opposing kingdoms."[65] Zionism, in this view, was a theologically bankrupt and historically unsubstantiated idea that had the potential to unleash revolution and war in Palestine and beyond. Despite this, *The Catholic Telegraph* warned in April 1918 of the "preparedness of Israelites to take charge of their inheritance," and that "the movement for the establishment of a Jewish State is making progress among statesmen and journalists with irresistible force."[66] A host of other diocesan papers, including *The Boston Pilot*, *The Michigan Catholic*, and *The Tidings* (out of Los Angeles), expressed similar concerns.[67]

Through the early 1920s, the American Catholic press gave extensive coverage to the Vatican's various protests of the Balfour Declaration and its general apprehensions of the Zionist project. The notion of internationalizing Jerusalem and the Holy Places, whereby these sites would be kept out of the jurisdiction of any sovereign state (particularly a Jewish state), was also given wide coverage. A policy endorsed by Monsignor Luigi Barlassina, the Latin patriarch of Jerusalem, internationalization was intended to assuage fears "that the Zionists might use their 'National Home' to infiltrate ... into the administrative and political affairs of the Holy Places."[68] Following a September 1920 meeting between Barlassina and the British high commissioner to Palestine, Sir Herbert Samuel ("a Jew," as Catholic journals never failed to mention), *The Catholic Telegraph* quoted the Latin patriarch that "it would be better for Palestine to be internationalized than become the servant of Zionism."[69] *The Catholic Columbian*, the newspaper of the diocese of Columbus, Ohio, placed the roots of modern Zionism in revolutionary Bolshevism, a force that threatened to usurp the Holy Places under the guise of a spiritual and humanitarian cause. "The Zionists are primarily and principally nationalists," it affirmed. "For the most part they are contaminated by Bolshevism. They were projected into Western Europe by the Russian Revolution. Fomenting unrest wherever they appear, these zealots of Zionism are spreading social diseases in all quarters. It is they who are trying to get the upper hand in the Holy Land."[70]

Pope Benedict XV's June 1921 allocution to the College of Cardinals, in which he protested "the position of preponderance and privilege" given the Jews in Palestine, and in which he speculated that an objective of Zionism was "to take away the sacred character of the Holy Places," was also given wide exposure in the diocesan press. Similar attention was given to Gasparri's April 1922 protest to the League of Nations, in which the Vatican critiqued the Zionist project as wrongheaded and ultimately untenable. For the remainder of the 1920s, American Catholic journals echoed papal critiques of Zionism, citing its threat to the status of the Holy Places, its true nature as an ideological (and not religious) project, and, as the decade progressed, the connection of Zionism to Bolshevism, an ideology that had long been condemned at the Vatican.

These initial anxieties, however, were tempered by several developments. The implementation of Winston Churchill's "White Paper" of 1922, which amounted to a significant watering down of promises made in the Balfour Declaration, was applauded in the American Catholic press.[71] A joint resolution of Congress in September 1922 affirming that the United States favored the establishment of a Jewish homeland in Palestine similarly did not appear to raise American Catholic ire, particularly as it clearly outlined the civil and religious rights of Christian populations in the territory.[72] Vatican protests, both privately and to the League of Nations, appeared to have been effective in diluting the Balfour Declaration, as expectations of imminent Jewish statehood began to diminish. The next several years, in fact, marked a more benign period in Catholic-Jewish relations in the United States. The resurgence of nativism in this period, particularly during Al Smith's run for the presidency in 1928, caused Catholic and Jews to find common cause in the face of Protestant bigotry. Since nativists often lumped Catholics and Jews together as unpatriotic and potentially subversive, the Catholic press struck back by emphasizing that bigotry itself was unpatriotic and "un-American." In doing so, Catholic writers often defended Jews alongside Catholics, placing overt critiques of Zionism temporarily aside.[73]

Also mollifying Catholic opinion in the 1920s was the steady expansion of the church and its institutions in Palestine, combined with the decline of political tensions there after 1922. Under the protection of the British Mandate, and in an atmosphere of political stability, the Roman Catholic Church underwent a rapid expansion in Palestine. The Jesuits opened a Jerusalem branch of the Pontifical Biblical Institute, and a number of churches, monasteries, schools, and hospitals were erected in Haifa, Jaffa, Nazareth, and Jerusalem.[74] Institutions destroyed during the First World War were rebuilt, and twelve new Roman Catholic parishes were constructed to minister to Palestine's growing Catholic population. In February 1924 Boston's cardinal archbishop, William O'Connell, toured Palestine and committed American Catholic support to the continued institutional expansion of the church in the Holy Land.[75] The journey, which took O'Connell to pilgrimage sites in Nazareth, Jericho, and Bethlehem, and culminated with a mass at the Holy Sepulchre in Jerusalem, highlighted the rapid expansion of the Catholic institutional presence in the territory. Underpinning this expansion was American Catholic money, which flowed to institutions in Palestine from the CNEWA via the Vatican's Oriental Congregation. The NCWC's John Burke, who traveled to Palestine in April 1929 with Pietro Fumasoni-Biondi, the apostolic delegate to Washington, praised the American Franciscans in particular for their prolific institution-building activities in the Holy Land, and intimated that this Catholic presence in the territory was essential to the Vatican's continued stake there. Fumasoni-Biondi specifically cited the importance of American Catholics to this effort, whose "financial and political support help in securing and extending the right of Catholics to care for the Holy Places."[76]

America, the Jesuit journal founded in 1909 and edited by the firebrand Richard Tierney, SJ, exemplified this trend toward a muted response to Zionism. Under Tierney, who a later *America* editor described as a "man of strong personal views, detesting sham and doubletalk, and shirking from no controversy," the influential journal took bold positions on a number of national and international affairs, including Mexican anticlericalism (for which Tierney received a letter of thanks from Benedict XV), Irish nationalism, and Palestine. Through the mid-1920s, however, it reflected Rome's general satisfaction with the situation in Palestine. *America* reported approvingly on the British Cardinal Francis Bourne's 1924 visit to Palestine (several months after O'Connell's visit), where he observed that the Arab population had "learned to be patient," and that he did not notice "the same unwise insistence on an untenable domination on the part of the Zionists" as he had in 1919.[77] The temporary cessation of tensions in Palestine turned the attention of the majority of Catholic journals elsewhere in these years. The apparent check of

Zionist ambitions after 1922, combined with Catholic institutional expansion in Palestine, tempered American Catholic editorial opinion on the subject for nearly the remainder of the decade.

Events in Palestine in the later 1920s, however, led to a resurfacing of Catholic anxieties on the Zionist project. Riots erupted in the territory in 1929 that were the result of long-mounting tensions. Despite British-Vatican cooperation in the region, which had facilitated the expansion of Roman Catholic institutions in Palestine, Arab-Jewish relations had continued to degrade. By 1928, leading Zionist groups had overcome hobbling political and ideological divisions, and the movement began to regain its former momentum.[78] American Zionism, led by the Zionist Organization of America (ZOA), was now the leading fundraising source of the global movement, a development that also piqued American Catholic concern that Jewish-American money was fueling a Zionist triumph in Palestine.

Palestinian Arab leaders, also recognizing the resurgent threat of Jewish statehood, pressed British authorities on negotiations for a separate Arab state in Palestine, pointing to other successful Arab national movements in the region.[79] In a bitter atmosphere of growing mistrust, Muslim-Jewish tensions erupted over rights at Jerusalem's Western Wall. Though Muslims maintained control of the wall (known as the Al-Buraq Wall to Muslims), Jews were allowed to pray on the pavement beyond it, so long as they did not erect benches, chairs, or other accommodations in the area. Days before the 1928 Jewish Day of Atonement (28 September), Jews erected a screen at the wall to divide male and female faithful. Muslim reaction led to an order to dismantle the screen, which British officials deemed an "infringement of the status quo ante."[80] British officers began to dismantle the screen during Atonement Day services, to which Jews reacted angrily, and which Muslim leaders mistook as British pro-Arab sympathy. The incident sparked both Jewish and Arab demonstrations and placed the incompatibility of Jewish and Muslim claims in sharp context.

The demonstrations piqued latent Arab nationalist fervor. Over the next several months, in an effort to underscore Muslim jurisdiction over the wall and its surrounding area, an extension was built over its northern portion, and a large muezzin was stationed on a nearby roof to call the faithful to prayer five times daily. In the summer of 1929, a passage was created from the Haram Al-Sharif to the pavement, effectively making the area a Muslim thoroughfare.[81] Jewish leaders claimed that these alterations constituted a more severe infringement of the "status quo ante" than had the prayer screen, to which

Arab leaders responded with a host of accusations, including a purported Jewish assault on the Mosque of Omar itself. Tensions surged in August, when Arabs attacked Jewish districts in Hebron, Safad, and several other places. In Hebron alone, over sixty Jews were murdered, prompting a Zionist writer to observe that, "were it not for the miracle that the Arabs attacked in broad daylight instead of night, giving the Jewish self-defence an opportunity to organize, the Jewish *Yishuv* would have been wiped off the map of the Near East."[82] British officials, overwhelmed by the impulsiveness and ferocity of the attacks, called in troops from Egypt for assistance. Though order was restored, the incident severely poisoned the well of Arab-Jewish relations in Palestine, and served to gird the Zionist movement for future challenges.

While the Vatican did not issue a direct statement condemning the violence, its position could be gleaned from the reactions of *L'Osservatore Romano*, the Holy See's de facto mouthpiece, which in effect represented papal views. It deplored the violence unleashed by Arab mobs but noted that the Vatican had warned the British of rising tensions and had recommended "certain changes in policy" in order to avert a bloody conflict.[83] According to the Vatican, unrest in Palestine was clearly linked to economic injustice stemming from unchecked Jewish immigration. Barlassina, who had earlier described Zionism as "a vampire which sucks on Arab blood," posited that both Christians and Muslims opposed continued Jewish immigration to the Holy Land, citing it as a root cause of the recent unrest. Barlassina, who along with the apostolic delegate to Cairo, Valerio Valeri, advised Vatican policy on Palestine and staunchly defended both Christian and Arab rights, had presented the Vatican's objections to the Balfour Declaration to the British government in 1921, and gave anti-Zionist speeches on scores of occasions.[84] The Latin patriarch was, perhaps, the most vocal Catholic anti-Zionist in Palestine, and he maintained an adversarial relationship with both the Zionists and British officials, undoubtedly shaping Vatican responses as a result. Valeri, the Vatican's chief authority in the region following the February 1929 expansion of the Cairo apostolic delegation to include Palestine, Transjordan, and Cyprus, urged Catholic communities to remain aloof from Arab-Jewish conflicts, fearing the repercussions of either Zionist or Muslim hegemony in the territory.[85] Valeri's main effort, along with steering Catholics away from the violent conflict, was aimed at improving Vatican relations with the British government on Palestine, which had been strained by Barlassina's overt anti-Zionism. Though Valeri warned the Vatican of the threat that Arab nationalism also posed in the region, his private reports to Rome concurred with Barlassina's view that

Zionism represented a distinct threat to the Catholic presence in Palestine.[86]

The initial responses of the mainstream American Catholic press to the riots of 1929 were not entirely unsympathetic to Jewish losses, a reflection, in part, of generally amicable Catholic-Jewish relations in the 1920s. Journals such as *America*, *The Commonweal*, and *The Pilot* that had, throughout the decade, defended Catholics alongside Jews in the face of Protestant bigotry, were generally prompt in condemning Arab violence. *The Commonweal*, the New York–based lay Catholic journal noted for its liberal editorial positions, carried a full report on the massacre at Hebron, chiding Muslim leaders for inciting violence, and included a message of condolence from New York's Cardinal Hayes to American Jewish organizations.[87] The journal further expressed an implicit sympathy with Zionist aims, urging that Jewish access be granted to worship at the Western Wall, given that – as it put it – Jewish rights were "anterior to the Moslem's in history; and speaking as Christians, we hold that his right is spiritually superior as well."[88]

Sympathy for Jewish losses, however, did not translate into support for a "Jewish home" in Palestine. A majority of the American Catholic press was condemnatory not only of Arab violence, but also of political Zionism, which a number of Catholic correspondents regarded as a cause of the 1929 uprisings. The NCWC's correspondent in Palestine and an associate of Barlassina, Alessandro Mombelli, filed a series of reports on the Arab-Jewish riots of 1929 that were widely reprinted in the American diocesan press.[89] He traced the root of recent unrest to the Balfour Declaration, in his opinion a flawed agreement that gave oxygen to an ultimately untenable political goal: Jewish statehood in Palestine. Arab violence was carefully explained as an inevitable reaction to Jewish political and economic hegemony in the territory, a situation exacerbated by increasing Jewish immigration. In stressing the political, and not religious, origins of the riots, Mombelli attempted to diffuse the idea that the uprisings could be ascribed to "Moslem fanaticism," a notion widely expressed in the mainstream secular press. Zionism was described as a purely political program, divorced of any theological legitimacy and "foisted upon pious Jews" only to strengthen its chances of success.[90] He further suggested that the agitations at the Western Wall had been sparked by Zionist groups, who had demonstrated there a day before the violence had erupted. His critiques of Zionism were surpassed only by his reports on the embattled position of the Catholic Church in Palestine, which he filed throughout the 1930s.[91]

As was frequently alluded in the Catholic press, Mombelli highlighted the "Bolshevistic" nature of Jewish communes in Palestine, associating Zionism with revolutionary communism, an ideology long since condemned by the Vatican. Zionist settlements were described as "communistic communities" where private property and capital did not exist, and in which "work," and not Judaism itself, was "the only religion."[92] In 1931, Mombelli warned of Moscow's use of propaganda to exploit Arab-Jewish tensions and disagreements within the Zionist movement itself, where moderates such as Chaim Weizmann and militant fundamentalists such as Ze'ev Jabotinsky vied for control.[93] The Soviet aim, as such, was to spark "a revolutionary fight, continuous and untiring … to strengthen communist influence among Jewish workers."[94] His reports also highlighted the lack of support from most Jews for Zionism, painting the movement as the ill-conceived brainchild of a small group of quixotic agitators. Mombelli deemed the violence of 1929 a necessary check on Zionist ambitions, and ominously suggested that the idea only piqued the potential for a violent Arab revolution in Palestine. "Zionism has had a very severe trial – its colonies devastated, its buildings robbed, its initiatives paralyzed … If the Arabs in future should rise and be supported by their co-religionists of Transjordania, Syria, Iraq and the Arabian Peninsula, what might be the result?"[95]

Mombelli's reportage, which was carried by a number of high-circulation diocesan weeklies, did not escape the attention of American Jews. The tensions that had previously played out between Zionist leaders and the Vatican now appeared to pit Catholics against Jews in the United States. Jewish leaders expressed concern with Catholic coverage of events, which, contrary to the mainstream secular press, appeared to fault Zionism exclusively for political tensions in Palestine. Morris Lazaron, an influential Baltimore rabbi who would play a significant role in Jewish-Protestant dialogue in the 1930s through the National Conference of Christians and Jews, expressed reservations at the implicit biases in Catholic coverage. Though not a supporter of the American Zionist movement, Lazaron took exception to what he regarded as an antisemitic propensity in Mombelli's reportage, a position he expressed in letters to John J. Burke, executive secretary of the National Catholic News Service.[96] In a response to Lazaron, Burke conceded that his correspondent did advocate an anti-Zionist position, but that he did not "show an anti-Jewish spirit," and that he did highlight Arab atrocities. "He does show bias," Burke admitted, "against the extreme form of Zionism, and he does play up the Arab side and the Arab defence. Yet at the same time, he shows the Arabs in a bad light in two respects – in the violence they commit and in their non-conciliatory spirit."[97] Burke expressed a view that was to define the position of mainstream American Catholicism for the remainder of the 1930s: a denunciation of antisemitism and Jewish persecution, combined with a forthright opposition to the tenets of political Zionism, which was consistently characterized as aggressive, radical, and violent. In closing, Burke dismissed the rabbi's concerns, implying the distinction between antisemitism and anti-Zionism in Mombelli's reports. "The impression I have reading his weekly correspondence is that he is not at all anti-Jewish, but that he is certainly in favour of a lessening of the Zionist status … Only when the material is grossly wrong do we interfere, and in this case we hardly think it merits intervention."[98]

This enduring disdain for Zionism, coupled with a claimed affinity for Jews and an abhorrence of religious persecution in general, closely mirrored the Vatican's position, and was amplified by the riots of 1929. The Balfour Declaration, which had received little analysis or comment in the Catholic press in 1917, was now regarded as the chief source of political and social instability in Palestine. The Jesuit review *The Month* critiqued the Balfour agreement in a series of articles, regarding it as having been "drafted by Jewish ambition and imposed by Jewish finance."[99] "What right had Lord Balfour or anybody else," the journal observed in 1930, "to further the mass immigration of Jews or any other nationality, into territory belonging to the Arabs?"[100] *The Commonweal* observed that the Balfour Declaration, and particularly the interpretation placed upon it, created "not a step toward the establishment in Palestine of a national home for the Jewish people, but a determination to convert that country into a Zionist theocracy," suggesting a Jewish dominance that would supplant the Arab population, "ensuring prerogatives and protection to a progressive, industrialized minority."[101] In this view, the riots promulgated by Muslims were tied to legitimate grievances stemming from Jewish political and economic dominion in Palestine, and were not eruptions of purely religious violence. *America*, which adopted an editorial line increasingly sympathetic to Arab concerns, emphasized the subjugation of Arabs by Jews in Palestine, the latter having "every advantage – capital, science and organization."[102] Despite this position of advantage, Zionists were portrayed as a ravenous group bent on further dominance. As Chicago's diocesan *The New World* reported, Zionists demanded "a Jewish police force, a Jewish defence force, and a Jewish administration."[103] In discounting charges of "Moslem fanaticism" in the riots of 1929, editor Patrick Scanlan of *The Brooklyn Tablet* reminded readers that "there was once a religious warfare in the Holy Land.

The papers said nothing about it. It was when Christ was crucified" – a clear allusion to Jewish complicity in the crucifixion and an example of the thinly veiled antisemitism that characterized the paper through to the early 1950s.[104]

The British commission charged with investigating the 1929 riots reached a conclusion agreeable to the Catholic position. Appointed by Lord Passfield (Sidney Webb) and headed by Sir Walter Shaw, the commission arrived in Palestine in late October 1929 to observe and report on the political and social condition of the British Mandate. The Shaw Commission's subsequent White Paper essentially amounted to a check on the national ambitions of both Palestinian Arabs and Zionist Jews. As both movements appeared to be gaining momentum and international support, with American Zionism rising in power and influence, and regional support for Arab Palestinians coalescing, British surveyors feared losing control of the territory to either group. Jewish immigration, which had caused the Jewish population of Palestine to double in ten years (from 84,000 in 1920 to 175,000 in 1930), was cited as a central cause of Arab discontent, and the limiting of Jewish immigration to Palestine was suggested.[105] Maintenance of the status quo became central to the Shaw Commission's report. The Labour government of Ramsay MacDonald adopted Shaw's suggestion that the Balfour Declaration had really imposed on Britain two separate but equal obligations to both Jews and Arabs.[106]

The Vatican was generally approving of the British resolution, which appeared to hobble Zionist national ambitions. Echoing British policy, the Vatican also feared Arab-Muslim control of the territory, which was regarded as a similarly dangerous threat to Roman Catholic interests in the Holy Land. Both Britain and the Vatican also feared Soviet influence, which the Shaw report, by maintaining some semblance of order, appeared to have staved off. For the time being, the synchronous goals of the Vatican and Britain – namely, to prevent the hegemonic dominance of either Arab or Jewish nationalism in Palestine, and to ward off communist infiltration – appeared to be secure. The Vatican's public stance on Palestine again subsided, as the prescriptions of the Shaw report appeared to have created a temporary calm. The Vatican Secretariat continued to air its concerns to Britain through diplomatic channels, but its public positions became focused on countering Bolshevism and promoting religious freedom in Mexico, Spain, and Russia.

While expressing some satisfaction with the cessation of hostilities, American Catholic journals, particularly the diocesan papers, which received dispatches from the NCWC News Service, were less quiescent in their evaluations.

Mombelli, who remained in Palestine as the NCWC's correspondent, placed the blame for the 1929 riots squarely on the Zionists, and considered the roots of discord in the Holy Land to be ideological and political, and not racial or religious, a tack that allowed Roman Catholic observers to critique Zionism while avoiding the smear of antisemitism. The unrest of 1929, he maintained, was the inevitable end result of Zionist belligerence. "This roseate idea that a solid and admirable new homeland for the scattered Jewish people, with the current faith of Moses as its centre, has been rearing itself here and has become far too widespread," he wrote in October 1929. "Regrettable as these recent events have been, it was time that something came about to bring the truth of the matter to the fore."[107] In early 1930, Mombelli quoted Robert Gordon-Canning, the noted British fascist, antisemite, and supporter of Arab nationalism who visited the territory in 1929, and concurred that "the fundamental unrest in Palestine and the hatred of the Jew by the Arab is political, and neither racial nor religious."[108] In stressing that the movement was essentially based on a cynical realpolitik, Mombelli emphasized its incompatibility with mainstream Judaism, and indeed its links to Bolshevism and communism, assuring readers that Zionists had "every intention of making Palestine a battlefield."[109]

Another journal that underscored the dangers of Zionism in Palestine was *The Crusader's Almanac*, published by the Washington-based Franciscan Commissariat for the Holy Land, a pontifical agency tasked with maintaining the Holy Places and raising funds for missionary, educational, and aid work in Palestine and the Near East.[110] In an editorial style both vivid and emotive, the journal apprised American Catholics of the faith's ancient and legitimate stake in the territory through examinations of Christian archaeological work, the history of the Crusades, and the enduring presence of Catholic institutions in the territory through twenty centuries. References to the rising tide of violence between Arabs and Jews, and in particular to the dangers of a Jewish Palestine dominated by Zionists to the exclusion of Christians, appeared frequently in its pages in the 1930s.[111] As a response, the journal implored American Catholics to support the commissariat's initiatives in the Holy Land by becoming "Promoter[s] of the Crusade," a status that gave members "spiritual benefits granted to them by the Holy See" and a "blessed Crusade-Scapular medal," reminiscent of the crucifix badges worn by medieval crusaders.[112] In its view the antidote to Catholicism's delicate stake in Palestine, due to Arab-Jewish tensions and the distinct challenge of Zionism, could only be reversed by an entrenchment of the church's position in the territory. "Don't envy the crusaders," the journal sharply reminded its readers, "be one!"[113]

The portrayal of Zionism as a dangerous, ill-founded, and belligerent movement, cynical in its methods, based in power politics, and divorced from mainstream Judaism in spirit and action, formed the essence of American Catholic characterizations of it for the remainder of the 1930s.[114] Steady Jewish immigration to Palestine, and the periodic flare-ups of Arab-Jewish tensions over the decade, only entrenched the anti-Zionist caveats of the Catholic press.[115] Through the latter half of the decade, as Arab nationalists intensified their resistance to increased Jewish immigration into Palestine, numerous American Catholic journals outlined the incompatibility of Zionist demands with the principle of national self-determination as established by the Versailles Treaty.[116] In response to growing congressional support for a Jewish Palestine, the journal of the Passionist order, *The Sign*, noted the illogic of Zionist demands. "Since the seventh century Palestine has been an Arab country and the Jews are as surely aliens and invaders as the English in Ireland or the Japanese would be, were they to take over our Pacific Coast."[117] Another editorial in the same journal epitomized the persistent duality of Catholic thought, between an affinity for Jews and Judaism and a disdain for the Zionist project. "One cannot but feel sympathy for the Jews. Crushed under the iron heel of the Nazis in Germany, harassed in Poland and elsewhere, unable to find a refuge because of immigration quotas, they are often in a sad plight indeed. But it is a rather strange kind of justice that because of this would deliver over to them a land so long in the possession of another people."[118]

As the war approached, and as tensions between Jews and Arabs in Palestine became more acute, *America* examined the competing claims of Jews and Arabs in Palestine, favoring neither for absolute political jurisdiction over the territory.[119] James E. Coleran, a Jesuit theologian and biblical scholar, presented both camps as fanatical and utopian, and sympathized with Britain in the precarious role it occupied as the Mandatory power. While denying Arab claims to complete control of Palestine, Coleran highlighted the fact that the Arab position was based on a fifteen-hundred-year occupation of the territory, and opined that if the Jews were to have any kind of national home in Palestine, it should have to be in consultation with, and with the consent of, Palestinian Arabs.[120] Given the rate at which Jews were successful in supplanting Arabs in Palestine, both in numbers and in economic and political control, he doubted that any such cooperation could exist in a new state.

While he agreed that both Jews and Arabs could rightfully appeal to the Wilsonian principle of national self-determination, he questioned whether Palestine could be considered the legitimate homeland of the global Jewish diaspora. In reflecting on Zionist ambitions, he observed that

> Even after the Romans finally destroyed their nation they never ceased to look upon Palestine as their land, and for the past centuries since that destruction countless Jews have longed to return, and many have actually filtered back to live and die in the "Land of Israel." Some seem to think that these facts constitute a sort of title to the land. However, if the fact that a people desire to regain their land, and a few do return to it, constitutes a just title to the land, what havoc might be wrought of the boundaries of more than one nation today, not excluding the United States![121]

Coleran did not deny the need for a Jewish national home, particularly in the context of escalating Nazi brutality, but he did suggest, as did the Vatican Secretariat, that a Jewish state be established somewhere other than Palestine. "Some part of this large earth," he opined, "should be given to them as their own. Some colony should be given to them where they would be their own masters, and never again to fear that the people among them, where they live, would someday rise against them and send them bleeding and impoverished to seek the calculating charity of strange lands."[122] He questioned, however, whether Palestine possessed the "absorptive capacity" for such an endeavor. "All must admit," he observed, "that Palestine cannot hope to provide for all of these. The more prosperous nations are all hesitating about throwing wide their doors to these unfortunates. Why insist that a poor Palestine do it?"[123] Coleran's notions on Palestine's "absorptive capacity" stood close to the Vatican's own position on the future of the *Terra Santa* and were emblematic of the unanimity of Roman and American Catholic views on the future of Palestine.

In a later article, published on the very eve of war, Coleran mused critically on the increasing "force and vehemence of international Jewry," observing that "the union of sentiment, the similarity of method, the use of propaganda, the moral pressure of Jews in every nation, particularly in the British Commonwealth and the United States, all manifest that Jewry is an international power, that it is aggressive and may be ruthless, and that it is determined to champion its interests against any and all who would question its aims."[124] The article was a reflection of the concern, in segments of the American Catholic hierarchy, of the growing stridency, profile, and effectiveness of American Zionist lobby, particularly the ZOA.[125] Coleran warned of the possible outcomes of unchecked Zionist zeal in the United States, and suggested that Washington act to brake American Zionist demands in the interests of peace and security. "The problem of Palestine may provoke a new orientation of ideas in regard to the place of the Jewish race in world affairs. In the United States, likewise, there is in process a new Jewish consciousness, characterized by militancy and acumen. This, also, requires a new American evaluation and orientation."[126]

The Brooklyn Tablet weighed in similarly on the "Palestine question." In a number of articles published in 1938 and 1939, the paper presented a decidedly pro-Arab perspective on the struggle for Palestine. It characterized Arab nationalism as primarily defensive in character, in contrast to the hegemonic ambitions of Zionism, and as supported by the majority of the Palestinian population, in contrast to the minority position of the Zionists.[127] As did *America*, *The Brooklyn Tablet* opined that "little Palestine" had reached its "absorptive capacity," and that further Jewish immigration to the territory would only serve to deepen political tensions there. The Arab struggle was likened to "the American struggle against British imperialism and the fight of George Washington and his men against that same imperial power. They, too, wished to secure themselves life, liberty and happiness."[128] *The Brooklyn Tablet*'s articles emphasized the fact that Palestinian Christians also opposed Zionist designs for the territory, echoing Vatican concerns that Christian rights were being trampled by Zionist aggression. On this theme, the paper quoted Dr George Ibrahim Kheirallah, the noted Egyptian American surgeon, academic, and secretary general of the Arab National League, who observed that "One hundred thousand Christian Arabs stand shoulder to shoulder with their Muslim brothers – patriarchs, bishops, priests, and ministers, all standing as one nation threatened by this ruthless treatment. Our forefathers once before generously fertilized the sacred soil of Palestine with their blood. May we be spared the necessity of doing it again."[129] Such allusions to a new crusade for the Holy Land would reappear in the Catholic press through the duration of the war.

Intensifying Nazi persecution of Jews in Germany, however, would give a new urgency to the question of a Jewish homeland in Palestine as the decade wound to a close. Nazi brutality also steeled the Zionist lobby in the United States, which, by the eve of war, was strenuously advocating its positions in

Washington. As American Catholic and Vatican positions on Zionism continued to coalesce, and as American Catholics more confidently advocated their views on a number of international questions, so, too, had the American proponents of Zionism (which included a number of Protestant leaders) become more strident. The Second World War, and its immediate aftermath, would serve to place these opposite camps in sharp relief.

CHAPTER 3

Into the Abyss: The Church and the Holocaust

The Second World War, and particularly the genocide perpetrated in its midst, lent an urgency and indisputable legitimacy to Zionist demands for a Jewish state in Palestine. The need for such a safe haven was laid bare by the horrors of the death camps, and international support for Zionism reached new heights by 1945. In the United States, political support for Zionism expanded during the war, evidenced by the January 1944 hearings in the House of Representatives, which revealed broad congressional support for Jewish statehood. By war's end, this support would extend to the Oval Office itself, as President Harry Truman emerged as the movement's most prominent international ally. Caught between its enduring disapproval of Zionism and its warming relations with the United States, the Vatican opted for public circumspection on the issue through the war, preferring to air its views through diplomatic channels. American Catholics, on their part, enthusiastically embraced the war effort, a fact that only strengthened relations between the bishops and Washington. On the question of Jewish suffering during the war, American Catholics were unequivocal, expressing sympathy and offering support more fervently than any other branch of the international church, and indeed more clearly than the Vatican itself. On the question of Zionism, however, American

Catholics remained firmly in accord with Rome, a stance that would soon place them at odds with a majority of their fellow citizens and with the federal government itself.

THE WARTIME "STRATEGIC EMBRACE"

As the clouds of war gathered over Europe, ties between the Vatican, Washington, and the American bishops continued to coalesce.[1] The appointment of New York industrialist Myron C. Taylor as Roosevelt's "personal representative" to the Vatican in December 1939 highlighted the president's desire to establish a direct link to the pope, despite the stiff objection of Protestant and Jewish groups. Roosevelt's ties with American Catholic leaders were also strong on the eve of war, and he could soon count on the support of the bishops to transform a staunch Catholic isolationism into support for the war effort. Spellman's connection to Roosevelt, combined with his long-standing and close relationship with Pacelli (who had been elected as Pope Pius XII in March 1939), similarly created a clearer diplomatic channel between the Holy See and the White House.

The war years witnessed a steady consolidation of this informal tripartite alliance, which the conflict itself made increasingly vital. These relationships, of course, had been building since the early 1930s. The Vatican had long been cognizant of the rising influence of the United States in international affairs, acknowledged by Pacelli's American "tour" of 1936, and was anxious to build on its collegial and constructive ties to both American Catholics and their government. By the late 1930s, Roosevelt had spent nearly a decade cultivating relations with American Catholic leaders, as his close ties to Mundelein, Stritch, Mooney, and Spellman attested. A New Deal coalition between Catholics and the Democratic Party had been a key factor in delivering Roosevelt electoral victories in 1932 and 1936, and the president remained committed to maintaining amicable relations with the church, particularly as the European situation worsened.[2] Roosevelt's appointment of Taylor as his personal representative to the Vatican was a tacit sign of the significance the president placed on a diplomatic channel directly to the pope. The idea of a representative had the additional support of Cordell Hull, the secretary of state, and Sumner Welles, his undersecretary, and was negotiated through Amleto Cicognani, the apostolic delegate in Washington, and Spellman.[3] During a private

White House dinner with Spellman in October 1939, Roosevelt affirmed that he saw an envoy to the pope as a "mission for the contribution to peace," and that Vatican-American cooperation on the issue of refugees displaced by war would be similarly crucial.[4] Spellman's central role in the negotiations, in fact, signaled his increasingly important function as a conduit between the Vatican and the president, enhanced by his accession to archbishop of New York in May 1939. Hull and Welles considered the Vatican an important wartime "listening post," a repository of diplomatic intelligence that could only enhance American strategy. The Vatican, for its part, recognized the urgency of maintaining a clear line of communication with Washington, particularly as Europe slid closer to war. The American church, an institution and a constituency loyal to both nation and faith, was now poised to become the crucial intermediary in the wartime Washington-Vatican axis.

Throughout the war, Spellman himself would play a unique role in this axis. Upon the outbreak of hostilities, he led American Catholic support for intervention, both in his vociferous advocacy for American entry into the war, and in his capacity as the head of the American Catholic military chaplaincy. As archbishop of New York, Spellman was also named apostolic vicar of the United States Armed Forces, a position that took him to Rome several times during the war.[5] Spellman's close connection to Pacelli led to his entrustment with confidential assignments of high importance. One of Spellman's key wartime duties, for example, was to administer Vatican funds that had been shipped out of Europe and deposited into American banks for security, evidence of the trust and esteem the pope held for his point man in the American church.[6] Throughout the conflict, Spellman would prove his value to the Vatican as an effective financial manager, diplomat, and administrator, and was the only American churchman, contends historian Gerald Fogarty, whom the pope regarded as a personal and trusted friend.[7]

The American Catholic bishops, on their part, did largely abandon their isolationism of the 1930s to wholly endorse the American war effort. Though isolationism had defined mainstream American Catholic positions on the war debate in the later 1930s, and while pockets of Italian American and German American Catholics remained reticent to support a war against their homelands, the bishops adopted the position that the struggle against European fascism was indeed a fight for the survival of Christian civilization. In December 1941, two weeks after the Pearl Harbor attack, Mooney, acting as the chairman of the administrative board of the NCWC, issued a statement assuring Roosevelt that the United States could count on the unconditional support of the American Catholic Church.[8] In equating Catholicism with unreserved patriotism, it informed the president that "the historic position of the Catholic Church in the United States gives us a tradition of devoted attachment to the ideals and institutions of government we are now called upon to defend." Mooney assured Roosevelt that the bishops, "spiritual leaders of more than twenty million Americans," were "keenly conscious of [their] responsibilities in the hour of the nation's testing."[9] In concluding, the bishops' statement reiterated resolute Catholic support, assuring Roosevelt of the American church's "whole-hearted support in the difficult days that lie ahead" to hasten "a victory that will be a blessing not for our nation alone but for the whole world." Spellman's 1942 book *The Road to Victory*, in essence a manifesto for intervention, highlighted similar themes. As the archbishop reminded his readers, "In the storm that has struck America, the ship of state will be held firm by two anchors – religion and patriotism."[10]

In short order, support for the war effort was widely trumpeted in the Catholic press, which characterized the struggle as a stark confrontation between Christian civilization and barbarism.[11] In January 1942 the Vatican, through Cicognani, virtually demanded that the American episcopate present a unified public stand of support for American intervention, despite the lingering of isolationist sentiments among some bishops.[12] The bishops' statement, which was released to the press, was also reported on widely in mainstream papers, including *The New York Times*, which reprinted the letter in its entirety on Christmas Day.[13] In his response to the NCWC, Roosevelt thanked the bishops for their pledge of support, and assured them that an Allied victory would be a victory for Christian civilization. "We shall win this war and in victory we seek not vengeance," he intoned, "but the establishment of an international order in which the spirit of Christ shall rule the hearts of men and of nations."[14] As the United States entered the war, Roosevelt could certainly count on broad Catholic enlistment, which would surpass even the high levels of the First World War.

Events of the war itself drew the parties even closer. Soon after the American entry into the conflict, the NCWC again assured Roosevelt of the unswerving loyalty of American Catholics to the war effort. In a memorandum to the president, Mooney, speaking on behalf of the NCWC, presaged a fruitful postwar cooperation between the Vatican and the United States, "when anti-Christian philosophies which have taken the sword will perish by the sword," and he outlined the unanimity of papal pronouncements and American objectives.[15] The nation was united in the war effort, he continued, and "among the architects of this unity are the foremost Catholic leaders in our country."[16] The American bishops' annual statement for 1942, "Victory and Peace," affirmed the sentiments of Mooney's earlier statement.[17] Roosevelt, on his part, sought to assure the Vatican that he shared papal visions of a postwar order. In September 1942, he prepared a lengthy and confidential memorandum for Pope Pius XII, to be delivered personally by Taylor, in which he praised the moral leadership of the Roman Catholic Church, particularly in denouncing Nazi racialism, and pledged to fight the Axis to the bitter end.[18] He further praised the support of the American bishops, who had engaged "the lives, the treasure and the sacred honour of American Catholics in the defence of their freedom against aggression." He further emphasized the enduring unity of purpose between Washington and papal Rome. "We want nothing better," he concluded, "than a continuation of those parallel efforts made by the Pope and the President before the war became general."[19]

The war also highlighted the growing role of American prelates as intermediaries between Washington and the Vatican, despite the existence of an American envoy to the pope. The Allied bombings of Rome in 1942 and 1943 vividly underscored the diplomacy of the American bishops, particularly Spellman, Mooney, and Stritch, on behalf of the Vatican. Intensified strategic bombing of the Italian capital from spring through autumn 1943, designed to loosen the Nazi grip on the Eternal City, strained relations between the Vatican and Washington. Publicly, the bishops said little about the bombings, eager to maintain a unified front in supporting the war effort, and reticent to incur the hostility of non-Catholic groups. Privately, however, the bishops strenuously conveyed to Roosevelt the pope's desire to spare Rome further bombings.[20] In September, the NCWC issued a letter to Roosevelt, in the name of the entire American episcopate, reminding the president of his responsibility to protect Rome from further damage.[21]

Spellman, for his part, had visited Rome in February 1943, where he met with top Vatican officials, including Luigi Maglione (the cardinal secretary of state), Domenico Tardini (the substitute secretary of state for extraordinary affairs), and Pius XII. Over five audiences with the pope, the bombing of Rome was discussed extensively, and Spellman was tasked with apprising Roosevelt of the pope's anguish at the "bombardment of the capital of the Catholic world."[22] Spellman's meetings with Pius XII affirmed the Vatican's growing reliance on both the American bishops and the American government, which was regarded as the keystone among the Allied powers.[23] Through the spring and summer, Spellman implored Roosevelt to negotiate a cessation. During a meeting with the president in September 1943, Spellman presented a statement, also signed by Mooney and Stritch, recommending that Rome be declared an "Open City," and immediately be spared Allied bombs.[24] The trio didn't hesitate to draw parallels between their demands and American domestic politics, alluding to the political power "of more than twenty million American Catholics, [who hoped] that their government will not have to share further responsibility for even more disastrous developments that threaten the Holy See under the conditions." The statement further warned against ignoring the international political influence of the Roman Catholic Church, and that "military measures which offend the religious sense of so many citizens in so many nations may have consequences fatally prejudicial to the interests we all have at heart."[25] In response, Roosevelt pledged to his guests the creation of a free zone of twenty miles around the city, and assured them that the Allied cause was in full unison with the Holy See's.

On 11 November 1943, just weeks after the meeting with Roosevelt, the American bishops convened in Washington for their annual meeting. While the annual statement issued for 1943, "The Essentials of a Good Peace," expounded on the necessary conditions of a Christian postwar order, the meeting was also significant for the adoption of a resolution where the bishops pledged their "filial devotion to the Holy See."[26] In it, they vowed to raise public awareness through the Catholic press, and to keep Washington apprised of any threats to Vatican City or other church interests. Though the bombings of Rome were not mentioned explicitly, they were clearly implied. The resolution was a call to action for the American bishops, echoing the pope's July request, on visiting a shelled Roman neighborhood, that the American church "demonstrate its dissatisfaction in such great grief." Though the bishops never publicly criticized the Allied bombings of Rome, the American Catholic press expressed evident dissatisfaction, clearly revealing the position of the episcopate.

The war, then, drew the pope, the president, and the American bishops closer together, but it also raised hopes that the bishops might more effectively press the Vatican's demands on Washington. The bishops, on their part, had responded to the nation's call to duty, and their protests on the bombing of Rome represented their first attempt since the American entry into the war to shape Washington's policy on an issue germane to the Vatican. It was a lobby that would soon be mobilized again on a number of postwar questions, including the fate of Palestine.

THE POPE AND THE SHOAH

The Second World War and the Holocaust proved to be cataclysms that shaped subsequent European and international affairs in profound and irrevocable ways. The conflict, besides proving to be the crucible of a new and dangerous postwar ideological divide, produced a genocide that made the logic of a Jewish homeland and safe haven difficult to deny. As the Mandatory power, Britain had constrained Zionist ambitions for much of the 1930s, and the British White Paper of 1939 appeared to have placed renewed obstacles in the path of such a goal.[27] The horrors of the Holocaust, however, and the growing sense of the depth of the Jewish refugee crisis created a sense of dire urgency on the issue from 1943 onward. The tragedy of European Jewry underscored the political, historical, and moral legitimacy of Zionist claims. Much scholarly attention has been focused on the question of the Vatican's efforts, or lack thereof, to assist European Jews during the darkest days of their modern history.[28] Significant, however, is the fact that a growing awareness of the tragedy affecting European Jewry did not alter the Vatican's fundamental opposition to Zionism, a position it had presented in its 1922 "aide-mémoire" to the League of Nations, and which remained unchanged throughout the war.

The Vatican's response to the Holocaust was shaped by Pius XII's diplomatic training and experience, which privileged circumspection and caution in the maintenance of the Holy See's official neutrality.[29] The preservation of neutrality, though leading to criticism both during and after the war, was not without precedent in Vatican diplomatic practice, and had shaped papal policy in the First World War as well.[30] This produced a statecraft in which the Vatican avoided specific condemnations, instead alluding to spiritual principles and moral teachings. As papal diplomats were keen to point out to critics, this approach was applied regardless of the religious or racial identities of the persecuted, even in cases where the victims were Catholic. During the Nazi and Soviet occupations of Poland, which produced widespread abuses against Catholics and their institutions, Pius XII steadfastly maintained this diplomacy of discretion, preferring to use back channels in an attempt to protect Catholic populations. This was despite the growing critiques of Catholic leaders in Poland who implored the pope to publicly condemn these abuses and who grew embittered at the Vatican's perceived lack of will. The bishop of Włocławek, Karel Radonski, wrote to Maglione in September 1942 outlining the abuses suffered by Catholic Poles, and lamenting that "the people, deprived of everything, die from hunger, and the pope remains silent as if he did not care for his sheep."[31] Radonski's sentiments were shared by a wide swath of Polish prelates, including Cardinal August Hlond, who implored Maglione for an "explicit word" from the pope on the plight of Catholics in Poland. Such a bold statement would never come, as Pius XII cleaved to a policy of prudence and official neutrality throughout the war, despite the critiques that emerged from various quarters.[32] For the pope, papal circumspection was designed to avoid greater reprisals against the church and its mission. As Pius XII explained to Bishop von Preysing of Berlin in 1943, his aim was to avoid a greater evil – *ad majora mala vitanda* – a phrase that neatly encapsulated his diplomatic training and his approach to the horrors of the Second World War.[33]

Pius XII's response to the Holocaust was also influenced by a theological anti-Judaism that had shaped papal relations with the Jews for centuries prior to his accession.[34] As Nina Valbousquet has revealed, even more ominous antisemitic notions according to which the Jews were regarded as a separate and retrograde "race" had permeated the church in Italy, extending to members of the curia itself.[35] To these "clerico-fascists," Jews in Italy represented an alien population that had been separated from Christians since Roman times, leading to justifications of the Mussolini regime's racial laws as a preservation of Christianity itself. There is no evidence to suggest that Pius XII adhered to such views, as his numerous critiques of Fascist and Nazi racialism, statism, and antisemitism, beginning in the early 1930s during his tenure as Pius XI's secretary of state, attests. The pope, however, did accede to the customary view that Jewish questions were not the primary concern of the church, regarding these as political, and not spiritual or religious, matters. Though Pius XII might criticize antisemitic "excesses," grounded in the Vatican's "universal mission" to show charity to all humanity, issues pertaining to Jewish persecution remained outside the purview of the Roman pontiff.[36] In this view, the church would lament the persecution and genocide of the Jews on humanitarian grounds, and seek to assist where it could, but its mission remained the preservation of the institutional church and the safeguarding of Catholic populations.[37] It was an approach that resulted in Pius XII's infamous "silence" on the persecution and eventual genocide of European Jews.

Though this public circumspection has been widely critiqued as an abdication of papal duty, the Vatican did consider the Holocaust a tragedy for humankind, and several papal initiatives to assist Italian and European Jews have been documented. Despite the ambiguity of the Vatican's wartime pronouncements, official denunciations of Nazi racialism and antisemitism were made public even before the outbreak of the conflict. In Italy, the Vatican had protested Fascist antisemitic laws since their inception in 1938, a reflection of Pius XI's deep enmity for racialist ideologies. The pope's 1937 encyclical *Mit brennender Sorge* (With deep anxiety), composed with the assistance of Pacelli, was written in German, addressed to the German bishops, and took direct aim at the Nazi cult of "race and blood" and the division of humanity on the basis of ethnicity and biology. In 1939, when Italy's decrees excluded Jews from a number of professions, including medicine, law, teaching, and journalism, Cardinal Maglione, the Vatican secretary of state, openly criticized the "so-called racial laws," and stressed in a note to the Mussolini government that the laws created a "good deal of suffering, desolation and ruin."[38] The Vatican maintained official protests against Italian racial laws for the duration of the war.[39] Papal nuncios in Nazi-occupied territories such as France, Slovakia, Hungary, Croatia, and Greece similarly protested to local officials against antisemitic decrees, and with some success, particularly in Catholic states.[40]

Efforts to assist European Jews extended beyond official protests. Between 1939 and 1945, more than three thousand Jewish converts to Catholicism ("non-Aryan Catholics") obtained passports, ship tickets, and travel money from the St Raphael Society, a German organization committed to assisting German Catholic emigrants. During the war, the society received encouragement and some financial support from the Vatican's coffers. The Vatican also sought to facilitate the emigration of Italian Jews (primarily converts to Roman Catholicism) to safer wartime havens. One of the more noted of these initiatives was the provision of Brazilian immigration visas to Italian Jews to provide safe passage from Rome to Rio de Janeiro, a plan that saw more than a thousand visas issued.[41] The Vatican similarly provided significant financial support to DELASEM (Delegazione per l'Assistenza degli Emigranti Ebrei, or Delegation for the Assistance of Jewish Emigrants), a Jewish resistance organization that operated in Italy throughout the war, providing false identity papers and finding shelter in religious houses, and which facilitated the emigration of nearly nine thousand Jews from Italy, primarily to neutral states such as Spain, Portugal, and Ireland.[42] Nearly $2 million, much of which was raised through American Catholic sources, was channeled to DELASEM through the American and British delegations at the Vatican. Father Marie Benoît, one the leading figures of DELASEM who was known as *le Père de Juifs* (father of the Jews) for his efforts to rescue French Jews, was known to Pius XII and was received by the pope in a rare private audience in July 1943. During the meeting, the pope praised Benoît's efforts, assuring Vatican support for DELASEM's efforts and agreeing to pressure the Spanish government to take in Jews facing persecution and death in Nazi-occupied Europe. As confidence in papal efforts to assist persecuted minorities increased, funds flowed to the Vatican from various international sources, primarily the United States. In January 1941, the Chicago-based United Jewish Appeal for Refugees forwarded $125,000 as a contribution to Vatican rescue efforts. Throughout the war, the Vatican distributed American federal funds through its various aid organizations in Rome and throughout Italy, for the benefit of Jews and non-Jews alike.[43]

During the Nazi occupation of Rome in 1943 and 1944, nearly ten thousand Jews were sheltered in Catholic institutions, churches, religious houses, and private homes, including within the walls of the Vatican itself, all with the knowledge of the pope and consistent with his opposition to Nazi and Fascist racialist policies.[44] In October 1943, on the eve of the infamous Nazi roundup and detention of twelve hundred Roman Jews, Pius XII approved the lifting of the so-called barriers of canonical cloister, which allowed men and women to shelter together in monasteries and convents in the city. Though the Vatican allowed various Catholic institutions and religious houses to exercise their own discretion in assisting Jews, evidence suggests that Pius XII encouraged these efforts and provided material aid where possible. The Vatican Relief Commission, at a cost of nearly $1 million, supplied food, clothing, and medicine to untold thousands of refugees, prisoners, and partisans during the winter of 1943–44, including at least six thousand Jews in Rome alone.

These various initiatives, though beneficial to Jews fleeing Nazi terror, fit neatly into the Vatican's long-standing position on Zionism. The Vatican recognized the legitimate plight of persecuted Jewry, and it sought to offer material and logistical aid where it could, but it consistently suggested emigration to destinations other than Palestine, in accordance with the view that the *Terra Santa* was sacred to Roman Catholics and could not be jeopardized by the fulfillment of the Zionist program. Papal opposition to the Zionist program continued to be rooted in the theological view of the Jews as an unrepentant people, unwilling to accept Jesus as the Messiah, and unwilling to accept salvation through conversion. As John Connelly has revealed, this was a view held not only by the Vatican curia, but also by progressive theologians such as Johannes Oesterreicher, Karl Thieme, and Waldemar Gurian, figures who would be central to the postwar revolution in Catholic-Jewish relations realized at the Second Vatican Council.[45] Particularly after Kristallnacht, these prelates forged a theological framework that implored Catholics to see persecuted Jews as their brethren, and to regard antisemitism as contrary to the very nature of Christianity. Oesterreicher consistently impugned Nazi conceptions of biological race, while Thieme urged Catholics to forge a new solidarity with the Jews, their "blood brothers" in Christ, a concept that vividly underscored the common bonds linking the faiths, and which undercut Nazi views on blood and race. This evolving theology on the Jews, however, continued to be rooted in the eschatological desire to see the Jews return to the Christian fold as preparation for the final judgment. It was even suggested in some of Oesterreicher's writings that Jewish suffering was a precursor to this conversion and salvation. "Antisemitism," he wrote in 1940, "sated as it was in the meanness and malice of the human being, remains a judgement of God."[46]

Given the endurance of this eschatological view of the Jews and Judaism, even among progressive voices in the church, papal support for a project calling for the return of the Jews to the land of the Abrahamic Covenant would remain an impossibility. As such, a distinct bifurcation remained in the Vatican's response to the persecution of Europe's Jews, characterized on the one hand by assistance to Jews where feasible, and by opposition to the goals of political Zionism on the other. Simply put, the tragedy of the Holocaust and the refugee crisis that it created would not translate into Vatican support for the creation of a Jewish state in Palestine. Assistance to European Jews was regarded as a Christian duty, an obligation to lend assistance to one's fellow man. Monsignor Domenico Tardini, the Vatican's undersecretary of state, expressed as much in the spring of 1943 when he observed that "the Jewish question is a question of humanity. The persecutions to which the Jews in Germany and the occupied or conquered countries are subjected are an offence against justice, charity, humanity … Therefore, the Catholic Church has full reason to intervene, whether in the name of divine law or natural law."[47] Despite this, the Vatican would not support the immigration of Jews to Palestine, regardless of the dangers they faced. As Tardini informed the papal delegate to Istanbul, Angelo Roncalli, in March of 1943, the Vatican could not facilitate the escape of twenty thousand Slovakian Jews to Palestine, despite their impending deportation to the death camps in Poland. The Holy See, advised Tardini, should "continue to follow the same line of conduct, endeavouring, that is, as in the past, to prevent the creation of the feared Jewish supremacy in Palestine."[48] Support for a Jewish homeland, despite the catalyst that the Holocaust had created toward that very end, was unfailingly opposed by the Vatican of Pius XII, based on the ancestral Roman Catholic tenet that the *Terra Santa* was sacred to the faith, and must never fall under the political jurisdiction of the theocracy proposed by Zionism.

This was despite the Vatican's awareness of the genocide unfolding in Nazi-occupied Europe. As early as the fall of 1942, the Vatican had received intelligence reports that Nazi detention camps were the sites of mass executions, but a May 1943 internal memo confirms the Vatican's clear cognizance of the scale of the Holocaust. The memo outlined the fate of Poland's three million Jews, there being "no doubt that most have been liquidated … There are special death camps in Lublin [Treblinka] and Brest-Litovsk. It is said that by the hundreds they are shut up in chambers where they are gassed to death. Transported in tightly sealed cattle trucks with lime on their floors."[49] As Allied diplomats became more fully apprised of the tragedy of the Holocaust in the first months of 1943, however, Cardinal Luigi Maglione, Pope Pius XII's secretary of state, reiterated the Vatican's opposition to Zionism in stark terms. In a March letter to William Godfrey, apostolic delegate to London, he expressed disappointment that Britain, which had recently facilitated the immigration of Jews from all corners of Europe to Palestine, had "altered its course," and appeared to be contravening the limits on immigration outlined in the 1939 White Paper.[50] It was clear that Maglione equated Jewish immigration to Palestine with the creation of a Jewish state there. "The Holy See has never approved the project of making Palestine a home for the Jews," he continued. "Palestine has always been more sacred to the Catholic than the Jews."[51] Maglione's notes from April revealed similar sentiments. He reflected on the "particular historical rights" held by Catholics on the Holy Places, which extended "with deep piety and devotion to Palestine itself, made sacred by the presence and memory of the divine redeemer," alluding that the whole territory was sacred to the church.[52] As such, he concluded that "Catholics would be injured in their religious sentiment and rightly fear for their rights if Palestine would belong exclusively to the Hebrews," echoing sentiments that could be traced back to the writings of Origen, Tertullian, and Augustine.

In the same month that reports of Nazi genocide reached the Vatican, Maglione wrote to the apostolic delegate to Washington and reiterated that the Vatican's 1922 aide-mémoire to the League of Nations would continue to define the Vatican's position on Palestine.[53] The Holy See, he expressed, could not accept the creation of a Jewish state in a territory that held such deep historical, theological, and spiritual significance for the world's Roman Catholics. It was a territory, he reminded Cicognani, that constituted the very cradle of Christianity. Though he admitted that, "at a time, the Jews did have a home in Palestine," he questioned "how this historical criterion could be adopted to restore a people to a territory they occupied more than nineteen centuries ago."[54] He suggested that another home could be found for the Jews outside of Palestine. Pushing forward the Zionist program, he warned, would be dangerous. "It would create serious new international problems, and would lead to a justifiable lament from the Holy See, which has always provided charity and assistance to non-aryans." Maglione's statements reflected the duality of Roman Catholic attitudes toward the Jewish plight, which joined a professed Christian duty to assist fellow men in need with a resolute rejection of the solution proposed by Zionism. It was a dichotomy almost perfectly mirrored by the institutional response of the American Catholic Church.

"WE ARE ALL SPIRITUAL SEMITES": AMERICAN CATHOLICS AND JEWISH PERSECUTION

For all the critiques of papal "silence" on the persecution of Europe's Jews, the same could not be said for the public response of American Catholics. From the time of Kristallnacht forward, bold expressions of solidarity with Europe's Jews, and denunciations of Nazi brutality, were largely forthcoming from the various organs of the American Catholic Church. At the same time, leading figures in the American church were working to effectively constrain the progressively antisemitic "radio priest," Father Charles Coughlin, whose popularity on the airwaves had contributed to strained Catholic-Jewish relations in the later 1930s. Maria Mazzenga has argued that a crassly antisemitic broadcast of Coughlin's, delivered in the immediate wake of Kristallnacht, galvanized his opponents in the American church to present a more definitive stance of support for European Jews.[55] The brutality of Kristallnacht, which aroused sympathies across the American political and religious spectrum, combined with Coughlin's crass response to it, did appear to spur American Catholics to speak out more openly against Nazi crimes.

In the aftermath of Kristallnacht, the Knights of Columbus published an open letter to Roosevelt expressing the organization's "deepest sympathy for the distressed Jews of Europe" and urging the American government to use its diplomatic channels and political clout to help secure the refuge of Jews to Palestine and other safe havens.[56] Father John A. Ryan, one of the foremost progressive American Catholic thinkers of the prewar era, provided firm and public rebuttals to Coughlin's thinly concealed antisemitism.[57] In a July 1938 address to the annual convention of Minnesota's B'nai B'rith, Ryan denounced Nazi persecution of the Jews as "contrary to the moral law of nature," and deemed Nazi racial theories as "utterly without scientific basis."[58] He continued that "Hitler's theory and practice with regard to the Jews contradicts, as he well knows, the very doctrines of Christianity." Ryan assured his audience that "authorized teachers and expounders of Catholic doctrine do not indulge in anti-Semitism," and he reiterated the "outspoken espousal of the Jewish cause" by Catholic editors and writers in the United States.[59] Later in 1938, he wrote that Nazism, which was "excessively nationalistic, adheres to ... [theories] of racial superiority and racial purity which are without foundation in fact, and which have been used as a pretext for an enormous amount of injustice and uncharity towards the Jewish race."[60] In 1939, Ryan told the audience of a Jewish civic forum in New York that antisemitism was "contrary to Christianity and violates the basic principles of American democracy. Followers of Christ cannot believe He would hate the race from which He sprang or any other people."[61]

Ryan did not stand alone in expressing such sentiments, as American Catholic solidarity with, and sympathy for, European Jewry was expressed emphatically and passionately both in Catholic newspapers and over the airwaves. A thirty-minute radio address, broadcast from the Catholic University of America (CUA), and carried by NBC to a nationwide audience, was emblematic of this spirit of kinship. Organized by Maurice Sheehy, professor of religion at CUA, and airing in November 1938, just two weeks after Kristallnacht, the address featured a number of prominent American Catholic leaders, including Sheehy, Bishops John Mitty of San Francisco, John Gannon of Erie, Peter Ireton of Richmond, and former Democratic presidential candidate Alfred E. Smith.[62] Sheehy's opening remarks were indicative of the tone of the broadcast. "The world is witnessing a great tragedy in Europe today," he warned listeners, "and after sober, calm reflection, various groups and leaders of the Catholic Church have sought permission to raise their voices, not in mad hysteria, but in firm indignation against the atrocities visited upon the Jews in Germany. The Catholic loves his Jewish brother because, as Pope Pius XI had pointed out, we are all spiritual Semites."[63] The address amounted to a resolute condemnation of Nazi racialism, and implicitly served to counter the recent antisemitic vitriol espoused by Coughlin. In effect, it proposed an alternative to Coughlin's defensive Catholicism, beckoning American Catholics to champion religious freedom and democratic ideals, and to pray for their persecuted Jewish "brothers."[64] It was this enlightened strain of American Catholicism that informed Catholic responses to Jewish persecution throughout the war.

Declarations of solidarity with persecuted Jews featured prominently in a wide range of Catholic journals from 1938 forward, reflective of broad American Catholic sympathy for the Jewish plight. The widely circulated *Commonweal*, edited by Edward S. Skillin, was at the forefront of Catholic sympathy and solidarity with European Jewry.[65] On the question of Jewish persecution, it was unequivocal. The journal criticized Charles Lindbergh's antisemitic Iowa speech of 1941, in which the former aviator and ardent isolationist identified Jews as the "principal agitators for war," citing "their large ownership in our motion pictures, our press, our radio and our government."[66] An editorial in *The Commonweal* strongly rebuked Lindbergh's theory, questioning his faulty logic in linking Jews to either media control or to pro-war agitation. In critiquing Lindbergh's crude and barely concealed antisemitism, it further argued that the fate that had befallen European Jews was a scourge that could only spread if not opposed by all faith groups, including Roman Catholics. "Anti-Semitism is an element and a symptom," it concluded, "of the calamity from which all groups and classes of America should want to save as much of the world as possible."[67]

Through 1942 and 1943, as Nazi plans for Jewish genocide moved from theory to reality, the American Catholic press continued to denounce antisemitism in the strongest terms. In those years, *The Commonweal* ran a series of articles by the exiled French Catholic philosopher Jacques Maritain that attempted to discredit Nazi racialist theories, and their resultant policies, on philosophical, moral, and scientific grounds.[68] Recent scholarship has demonstrated the degree to which Catholic philosophers such as Maritain pioneered modern conceptions of human rights, rooted in a universal concept of human dignity and the right to liberty, and particularly religious liberty.[69] For Maritain, this liberty was understood within the framework of natural law, and was subject to the moral precepts of a divine order. Maritain's conception of human rights encompassed all people of faith (as well as secular humanists working toward social progress), and he urged Catholics to be a part of "the progressive movement of humanity" toward justice, civic amity, and equality.[70] In these articles, Maritain eloquently imparted to his readers the notion that antisemitism had historically been, and remained, repugnant to any genuine interpretation of Christian history, and was the result of human weakness and distorted biblical and theological interpretations. German racial laws, he asserted, represented a complete and total abandonment of any genuine Christian morality, and stood in opposition to God's natural law, a point that Pius XI had recently emphasized in the 1937 encyclical *Mit brennender Sorge*. As to whether or not Catholics should embrace the American entry into the war to fight totalitarian persecution, Maritain was unequivocal. "The only conclusion possible," he observed in 1943, in the face of "an unutterable horror of the mind and heart," and of "the human degradation of which racist crimes are the expression," was "a resolution to fight this degradation to the death."[71]

The Catholic weekly *America*, published by the Jesuits since 1909, and considered moderate and judicious in its editorial line, presented similar denunciations of Nazi crimes and offered messages of Catholic solidarity with the persecuted Jews of Europe. Like *The Commonweal*, it was edited in this period by another leading Catholic progressive, John LaFarge, SJ, who would gain later acclaim as a champion of racial equality, establishing the National Catholic Conference for Interracial Justice in 1960. *America*'s relatively wide circulation and weekly magazine format, combined with its reputation for attracting noted non-Catholic contributors, made it an influential journal in both Catholic and wider circles.[72] Particularly from the summer of 1942 forward, as news of Nazi atrocities became more widely circulated in the mainstream American press, *America* drew consistent attention to Jewish persecution. A September 1942 article by the Jewish American field reporter Maurice Feldman detailed the depravity of Nazi oppression of German and central European Jews, outlining the dire situations in Hungary, Slovakia, Romania, and Croatia. Feldman warned of the unfolding "Final Solution" in observing that "there is no doubt that the Nazis have plans not only for the destruction of the Jews in Europe, but throughout the whole world."[73]

By the spring of 1943, *America* denounced Nazi pogroms in the most explicit manner. In June, it reprinted from *The Commonweal* parts of Maritain's passionate and erudite refutation of Nazi racist laws, assuring that his ideas received wide exposure in the Catholic press.[74] In solidarity with Maritain's positions, *America* warned its readers that any equivocation in Catholic attitudes to the Jewish plight amounted to a grave error. "It is not a question of this or that human being," the editorial intoned, "it is a question of all human beings and methods of destruction which exceed the nightmares of the most diabolical imagination."[75] It opined that Jewish sufferings could not be dismissed as mere "atrocity stories" – they amounted, rather, to a program for racial genocide carried out to "an inexorable and well-defined plan." Through 1943 and 1944, *America*'s editorials reminded readers that the tragedy unfolding for Jews, which stemmed from wrongheaded antisemitic vitriol, could befall Catholics as well. The atrocities, it stated, were "but a step" from Catholics if they condoned the spread of this "moral poison in the world, rooted in hatred of God and Christ Himself, which spreads like a forest fire and soon cares little what victim its violence destroys."[76] Similar sentiments were voiced by Louisiana's Father Elliot Ross, who told the New Orleans *Catholic Action of the South* that there were "Catholics who do not realize that if anti-Semitism comes [to the United States], anti-Catholicism will not be far behind. If anti-Semitism ever becomes formidable among us, every probability points to the prejudice breaking bounds and including Catholics as well as Jews."[77]

Though *America* and *The Commonweal* represented the leading edge in the denunciation of Nazi racialism and solidarity with European Jewry, similar expressions could be found across the American Catholic press. The large-circulation weekly *The Catholic World*, published by the Paulist fathers, offered a severe and lengthy critique of antisemitism in an October 1939 essay, calling it "unjust, brutal, and opposed to the teachings of Christ."[78] Large-circulation papers such as *The Michigan Catholic*, *The Catholic Mind*, *The Boston Pilot*, and *The Catholic Worker* offered similar sentiments.[79] Virtually no paper stood "silent" on the issue. Even *The Brooklyn Tablet*, which had offered a platform to Charles Coughlin throughout the 1930s, echoed these wider denunciations of Nazi racialism.[80]

Expressions of Catholic-Jewish solidarity were not limited to the American Catholic press. Catholic leaders such as Fathers John Ryan and Maurice Sheehy, and Archbishops John Mitty and John Mark Gannon, building on their efforts following CUA's Kristallnacht broadcast, continued to decry Nazi brutality throughout the war.[81] In an address to a civic forum in June 1944, Detroit's Archbishop Edward Mooney hailed the heroism of the victims of the Warsaw Ghetto Uprising, and denounced Nazi brutality in clear terms. Mooney further expressed revulsion at the plight of Jews through the centuries, and outlined the need for Catholics to "give full play to our instinctive revulsion and horror against this latest instance of mass cruelty in the story of the Warsaw Ghetto, to prepare ourselves for the impending task of putting together the shattered pieces of a war-torn world."[82] In pointing up the anti-Christian as well as antisemitic elements of Nazism, he concluded, "May we not hope that in the fires of a common tribulation new bonds of human solidarity and mutual goodwill are being forged between Catholics and Jews?" In the same speech, Mooney stressed the incompatibility of antisemitism and Christian faith, and indeed the historic brotherhood of Judaism and Christianity. "Catholic teaching exalts the historic and religious role of the Jewish people, and glories in the heritage from Judaism which is an essential element in Christianity," he reminded his audience. He then paraphrased Pope Pius

XI, who in a decree of 1928 had stated that "anti-Semitism is not compatible with the sublime reality of the faith. It is a movement in which Catholics cannot participate. We are all spiritually Semites."[83] In concluding, Mooney echoed other American Catholic leaders in emphasizing the fundamental unity of Catholics and Jews in the struggle against oppression and persecution. "The security of Jew and Christian," he warned, "and the promise of their living together as men and brothers lies in our common devotion to the moral order as a reflection of the mind and will of God our Maker."[84]

Fulton Sheen, the future auxiliary archbishop of New York and "television priest," and a leading Catholic voice both before and after the war, also tackled the issue of Nazi antisemitism on his weekly radio program *The Catholic Hour*, which had attracted an audience topping one million by the early 1940s.[85] In a broadcast delivered on 10 January 1943, Sheen reflected on Pius XII's Christmas allocution of 1942, in which the pontiff had bemoaned the totalitarian and militaristic ideologies destroying Europe both physically and spiritually.[86] While the pope's message lamented "the hundreds of thousands of persons who, without any fault on their part, sometimes only because of their nationality or race, have been consigned to death or a slow decline," Sheen's address denounced the Nazi persecution of Jews with unambiguous clarity. He impugned Nazi racialism as a policy based wholly on the warped ideology of a despotic madman, with no grounding in scientific fact, and critiqued the persecution of European Jews in the most explicit terms. To Sheen, Nazism, like communism, denied the basic equality of all humans, a pillar of Nazism that had led to Jewish persecution. "The disdain of the human person," he observed, "is the first dogma of all totalitarian systems. It explains why the individual Jew has no value or rights under Nazism: Because he is not a member of the revolutionary race. The persecution of Jews arises, therefore, not because, as Hitler first claimed, they were too wealthy, but simply because they were not Nordic."[87] Like Maritain, Sheen linked Nazi disdain for Judaism and Christianity. Speaking at a November 1942 meeting of the National Conference of Christians and Jews (NCCJ), he announced that the world had entered into a new historical phase "in which there will be no persecution of Jews without persecution of Christians."[88] In light of this view, he implored American Catholics to abandon lingering isolationist sympathies and support the war effort. "What we were once intolerant to as a wicked idea," he urged, "we must now be intolerant to as a deed." Sheen and other American Catholics were doing what many of the pope's critics were demanding – namely, to issue explicit denunciations of Nazi crimes rather than the vague allusions and abstractions of the encyclicals. Sheen's sentiments, in fact, were reflective of the dual nature of the American church. His words reflected, of course, the pronouncements of Rome, as expressed through the encyclicals, but they also spoke to the American reality of confronting the Nazi threat directly, and to the need to rally American Catholics to the war effort. It was the melding of two loyalties, both Roman Catholic and American.

As a national body, the American Catholic bishops similarly expressed revulsion at the fate of European Jewry. At a 1940 meeting of the NCCJ, Bishop Robert Lucey of Amarillo, Texas, declared that "We, as Christians, as citizens, as human beings, must cry out against the horror of this Nazi [debauchery] against Jews." In warning his listeners against the false comfort of isolationism, and in rallying his audience to the defense of "Western civilization," he intoned that "what is happening to the people of Europe is our business."[89] The American bishops' annual statement for 1941, issued through the Washington-based NCWC and titled "The Crisis of Christianity," addressed the evils of "totalitarian systems," singled out Nazism and communism as ideological forces threatening both Christianity and Western civilization more broadly, and implicitly urged American Catholics to support the larger effort to defeat these "systems." The statement also referred specifically to the suffering of Europe's Jews, stating that "Our sympathy goes out again to the peoples of those countries who have been crushed under the heel of the invader, and indeed, to all upon whom war has imposed so heavy a burden of suffering and sacrifice. We cannot too strongly condemn the inhuman treatment to which the Jewish people have been subjected in many countries."[90] The bishops' annual statement for 1942, entitled "Victory and Peace," addressed a range of similar themes. It endorsed the war effort emphatically, signaling a definitive end of the hierarchy's lingering debate on isolationism. It urged an Allied victory under American stewardship as the only outcome that could guarantee an enduring peace and in which Christian principles would guide and inform the international order. The statement, signed by a national cross section of leading bishops, including Spellman of New York, Mooney of Detroit, Stritch of Chicago, and John Mitty of San Francisco, also deplored Nazi brutality, and addressed the question of European Jews in clear terms. "We feel a deep sense of revulsion against the cruel indignities heaped upon the Jews in conquered countries and upon defenceless peoples not of our faith … We raise our voice in protest against despotic tyrants who have lost all sense of humanity by condemning thousands of innocent victims in concentration camps, and by permitting unnumbered persons to die of starvation."[91]

THE AMERICAN CHURCH AND "ZEALOUS ZIONISM"

This deep and widespread condemnation of the persecution of European Jewry, reflected in the Catholic press, over the radio waves, and through public statements from the American bishops, however, did not translate into American Catholic support for Zionism. American Catholic positions on the issue remained unchanged through the war and adhered closely to Rome's longstanding position. If American Catholic expressions of sympathy for the Jewish plight were expressed in terms bolder than those emanating from Rome, there was no substantive deviation on the question of a return of the Jews to Palestine. Simply put, the Zionist aim of a Jewish home in Palestine was an aspiration that Roman Catholic leaders, both at the Vatican and in the United States, continued to oppose on historical and theological grounds, despite the unfolding tragedy of the Holocaust.

In line with its diplomatic caution, the Vatican was reticent to trumpet this policy too loudly during the war itself. An analysis of the wartime *L'Osservatore Romano*, the Vatican's semiofficial journal, reveals little on the question of a national home for European Jews, despite the fact that the Holocaust severely underscored the growing importance of that very question. Given the highly fluid and rapidly evolving progression of the war, particularly from 1942 onward, Vatican policymakers preferred to keep discreet any public stance on the future of Palestine. Privately, however, Pius XII and his secretary of state, Cardinal Luigi Maglione, continued to express severe reservations about the creation of a Jewish state in Palestine, fearing a loss of control over Christian sites in the Holy Land, and concerned with the possibility of a Jewish bridgehead for communist influence and infiltration in the Near East.[92] These sentiments were shared by a number of the Vatican's most powerful cardinals and diplomats, including Angelo Roncalli, the future Pope John XXIII, who as nuncio to Istanbul was noted for his efforts to save Jewish lives, but who was unreceptive to the solutions posed by political Zionism.[93] In a September 1943 letter to Maglione, Roncalli expressed discomfort about the degree to which Vatican aid to Jews would later be considered an endorsement of their "messianic dream," adding that the "reconstruction of the Kingdom of Judah and the Israelites would not create a utopia."[94]

As in the case of American Catholic expressions of sympathy for persecuted Jews, however, warnings of the dangers of Zionism were clearer and more unequivocal in the American Catholic press than anything that emanated from the wartime Vatican. In 1942, a series of articles in *The Catholic Mind* squarely critiqued Zionist aims as quixotic and dangerous, and questioned the legitimacy of a "national home" for a diaspora seen as historically nomadic and dispersed. More ominously, the articles presented the Jews as a revolutionary and distinct race, echoing the clerico-fascism of the previous decades. "Everywhere the Jew is a Jew," the paper noted. "He is international. He is not fixed; he is *déraciné*; he is ready to take up his tent pegs at any moment and settle somewhere else."[95] Palestine was not a solution to the problem, the paper further suggested, as the territory lacked the "absorptive capacity" to accommodate the Jewish diaspora, echoing a position espoused by Vatican diplomats. In September, the same publication warned of the growth and influence of the Zionist lobby in the United States, a product of the "alert propaganda spirit of the Jews that causes them to be actively at work during the present World War, outlining the program and making the contacts that enable them to be confident of a place at the peace table when Hitler is defeated."[96] As such, it warned of infinitely expanding Zionist demands. "That is why they are no longer satisfied with the 'homeland' promised in the Balfour Declaration; they positively demand a Jewish Commonwealth that includes Transjordania."[97]

The Jesuit journal *America* continued its assault on Zionism long after the existence of Nazi death camps had become more widely known. In an October 1944 editorial, it advised that, despite the disproportionate suffering of European Jewry during the war, the United States should be wary of supporting "zealous Zionists."[98] The unchecked inflow of Jewish refugees, it warned, was a solution "fraught with dangers that should be recognized now." It cautioned Washington leaders that had warmed to Zionism of the dangers of intervening in a dispute between Jews and Arabs, and cited the example of Britain, whose "fingers had been burnt by competing commitments." In concluding, it suggested that while a home would need to be found for Europe's displaced Jews, securing that home in Palestine would raise more problems than it would solve.[99]

American Catholic critiques of Zionism juxtaposed sharply with growing support for a Jewish Palestine in the United States. Indeed, the unfolding tragedy of the Holocaust had created a groundswell of sympathy among American lawmakers, and had bolstered the hopes of American Zionist organizations, as Zionist leaders began to regard the emergency faced by Europe's Jews as their last best chance to push for the creation of a Jewish state in Palestine. The American entry into the war, furthermore, had created a shift in the focal point of Zionist lobbying from London to Washington, making the United States the clear epicenter of the international Zionist movement. Zionists had been bitterly disappointed by the British White Paper of 1939, and British reluctance to support a proposed Jewish army marked a sea change in relations between Britain and leading Zionist groups. The American Palestine Committee, which had been created in 1932 to foment high-level support for a Jewish state among non-Jewish leaders and politicians, claimed fifteen thousand members by 1941, among them nearly two-thirds of the United States Senate and numerous members of the House of Representatives.[100] Though Britain remained the Mandatory power, Zionist leaders were cognizant that the American government would likely dictate the terms of an allied victory, and were buoyed by the growing support of a large Jewish American community. The gathering of the leading Zionist organizations at New York's Biltmore Hotel in May 1942, attended by Chaim Weizmann and David Ben-Gurion, signaled a definitive shift that would affirm the United States as the new center of the international Zionist campaign. A keynote speaker at the conference was Dorothy Thompson, the renowned journalist and radio broadcaster whose impassioned advocacy for a Jewish Palestine drew significant Christian support to the Zionist cause.[101] The platform of the Biltmore Conference not only advocated for unlimited Jewish emigration to Palestine, but also forcefully endorsed the creation of a sovereign Jewish state, claiming that the lands of Palestine were "unoccupied" and "uncultivated" and that Jewish settlers "made the waste places to bear fruit and the desert to bloom."[102] In sum, Biltmore delegates saw a Jewish Palestine as not only a solution to the immediate problem of Nazi persecutions, but also as a permanent solution to Jewish dislocation since the time of the Roman Empire.[103]

This rising tide of sympathy for Zionism in the United States did not escape the attention of the Vatican. In May 1943, Cardinal Maglione instructed Cicognani to keep the Holy See apprised of any developments in the Zionist lobby and to outline any shifts in public opinion toward or against the idea of a Jewish state in Palestine.[104] To this end, the apostolic delegate filed several reports to Rome on the emergence of new and robust Zionist associations in 1943 and 1944, including the Hebrew Committee of National Liberation, which included among its leadership the Revisionist Zionist Eri Jabotinsky and Peter Bergson, a prominent Zionist who had escaped Nazi-occupied Poland in 1939, and who tirelessly lobbied the American government for assistance to persecuted Jewry.[105] Other groups identified by Cicognani, with the assistance of the NCWC, included the American Friends of a Jewish

Palestine and the American League for a Free Palestine, both of which raised funds for the immigration of Jews to Palestine and for Zionist paramilitary organizations such as the Irgun and the Haganah.[106]

Maglione also urged Cicognani to remind the American bishops of the dangers of political Zionism, and to disseminate these concerns, where possible, through the American diocesan press. In June 1943, Maglione forwarded the Vatican's 1922 aide-mémoire on Palestine to Michael Ready, the general secretary of the NCWC.[107] The memo, which delineated the Vatican's opposition to a Jewish Palestine on theological, historical, and political grounds, was evidence that the Holocaust had barely altered the Vatican's formal position of Zionism, and was intended to act as a template for American Catholic responses to the Palestine question. Early in 1944, Maglione again implored the apostolic delegate to "appeal to the sentiments of the Government and public opinion of America" in shaping the debate on Zionism, and to remind Washington policymakers what they "might achieve from their involvement in such a just cause as supporting the Christian communities in the Middle East."[108] In May, Cicognani forwarded to Ready another memo on the Vatican's position, stating that, "since the question is one of much discussion at the present time, it may be well for the point of view of the Holy See to be brought to the attention of the Most Reverend Bishops."[109]

THE OUTLIER: ARCHBISHOP JOSEPH RUMMEL OF NEW ORLEANS

In the same month, Cicognani forwarded a copy of the memo directly to Joseph Rummel, the German-born archbishop of New Orleans who had been appointed by the Vatican as the chairman of the Catholic Committee for Refugees in 1941.[110] Rummel's case reveals the extent to which the Vatican expected the American bishops to speak with one voice on the question of Palestine and on Zionism generally. The apostolic delegate rebuked Rummel for publicly critiquing the limits placed on Jewish immigration to Palestine in the British White Paper in an open letter to Rabbi Emil Leipziger. Rummel's sentiments were reported in the local diocesan press. "If the Jews needed protection in 1917 and the solace of a homeland in 1922," wrote the archbishop in February 1944, "they stand in greater need of help after all the sufferings endured in Europe, and Winston Churchill now has the opportunity to unmake what, in 1939, he criticized so vehemently in parliament as the violation of a pledge."[111] In the face of the unfolding tragedy in Europe, Rummel critiqued a policy that made "further Jewish immigration subject to the acquiescence of the Arabs in Palestine," and which protected "the numerical and political preponderance of the Arab population" in perpetuity.[112] "In a word, to promulgate and implement the White Paper," Rummel concluded, "does seem to be contradictory to the Balfour Declaration of 1917 and the letter and spirit of the mandate of 1922."[113] Rummel's statements, though brief, were directly at odds with the Vatican's policy on the future of Palestine, and Rome wasted little time in issuing its response.

Cicognani expressed to Rummel that he could "understand the humanitarian motives which induced [you] to make the statement referred to," but that it would "be useful for [your] future guidance to know the attitude of the Holy See, and to consider certain Catholic and Christian aspects of the problem which are commonly neglected in the public agitation being carried on in the United States for a Jewish Home Land."[114] The apostolic delegate added that he hoped Rummel, in his influential capacity as archbishop, would "be in a position to utilize this statement of policy on many occasions."[115] The "statement of policy" forwarded to Rummel, which was identical to that sent to the NCWC, amounted to a summary of the Holy See's long-standing "Palestine policy," positions barely changed since the end of the First World War. The statement outlined the Holy See's recent efforts to spare European Jewry the worst of the Nazi wrath but stated that Jewish suffering did not revise the Vatican's long-standing opposition to a Jewish homeland in Palestine, as expressed by Pope Benedict XV at a 1919 consistory of Cardinals, and reiterated by Pope Pius XI in his 1922 aide-mémoire to the League of Nations. On the Holy Places, the memo emphasized the importance of Catholic control, stating that generations of popes had "made every effort to keep them from falling into the hands of infidels, and because their possession had now become secure, all precautions must be taken to see that it be protected and strengthened."[116] On Palestine itself, it stated that "Catholics the world over are piously devoted to this country, hallowed as it was by the earthly presence of the Redeemer, and esteemed as it is the cradle of Christianity. If the greater part of Palestine is given to the Jewish people, this would be a severe blow to the religious attachment of Catholics to this land. To have the Jewish people in the majority would be to interfere with the peaceful exercise of these rights in the Holy Land already vested in Catholics." It further suggested that Jewish occupation of Palestine two millennia previous did not legitimize a modern claim to the territory, and it echoed a familiar Vatican refrain that while Jews would certainly require a postwar home, Palestine was not ideal. "If a 'Hebrew Home' is desired," it concluded, "it would not be too difficult to find a more fitting territory than Palestine. With an increase in the Jewish population there, grave, new international problems might arise. Catholics the world over might be aroused. The Holy See might then be hindered in its care of the Holy Places, and it might be kept from giving charitable assistance in the measure which it would wish."[117] On 9 June 1944, Ready forwarded copies of the memo to the entire American episcopate.[118] Rummel made no public utterances on the question of Jewish refugees and Palestine after February 1944, despite his central role as chairman of the Catholic Committee for Refugees.

In the wake of Rummel's censure, some bishops took the initiative to make certain that diocesan priests were fully cognizant of the Vatican's policy. On 24 July 1944, Thomas McLaughlin, bishop of Paterson, New Jersey, forwarded his priests a memo outlining the church's historic, and unaltered, position on the "Jewish Homeland Idea."[119] He instructed clergy to discourage parishioners from "participating in the current agitation on the British White Paper to the end that Britain may relax her immigration laws to Palestine," stating that as the issue "was economic and political rather than strictly religious … the Church and its organs and representatives should not as such take sides or make commitments on this matter." The letter was far from a neutral statement, however, clearly delineating the Vatican's historic position on the Holy Land. In addition to reiterating the points in the NCWC's "Rummel memo," McLaughlin warned his clergy that a Jewish majority in Palestine would imperil Catholic jurisdiction in the territory, and that "a noteworthy increase in the permanent Jewish population" would almost certainly produce "grave new international problems." Such "problems," the memo suggested, would severely hinder the church's ability to protect the sanctity of and access to the Holy Places.[120] In paraphrasing Cardinal Gasparri's 1922 aide-mémoire, which remained the backbone of Vatican policy on Palestine, it continued that "there is no principle in history or justice to establish the necessity of the return of a people to a country which they left nineteen centuries ago. There are other places on this earth where a 'Hebrew Home' could be set up without causing international repercussions and difficulties." In concluding, McLaughlin warned his priests to remain cognizant of the papal line, while avoiding entanglements that a defined public stance might produce. "In a word, we are to defend Catholic interests and not lend ourselves to propaganda for a cause [lifting British immigration quotas] which has no bearing upon our life here, but contains the seeds of difficulties for the authorities of the Church in maintaining recognized rights."[121]

The Vatican was aware of the grave repercussions likely to stem from losing the battle for public opinion to the Zionists in these years, and was keen to maintain the support of the American Catholic press on the issue, prompting an August 1943 request from Cardinal Maglione that Catholic journals more clearly delineate Rome's concerns on the Zionist program.[122] American Catholic journals that did comment on the Palestine question from the summer of 1943 forward obliged the Vatican's directive. They cast an increasingly critical shadow over the Zionist idea, and continuously drew a line between the denunciation of antisemitism and support for a Jewish homeland in Palestine. The tragedy of the Holocaust, and the daunting refugee crisis that it spawned, did not alter mainstream American Catholic positions on political Zionism, which continued to be regarded as a dangerous experiment, and one that, in combination with an emergent Arab national movement, threatened the very security of Roman Catholics in the Holy Land.

In a series of editorials in the fall and winter of 1945, *America* further elaborated on its opposition to Zionist demands. It decried the increasingly desperate tactics employed by Zionists by the end of the war, and scolded the movement for its "violent disagreement" with British foreign policy, referring specifically to the 1945 progress report of the Anglo-American Committee of Inquiry (AACI), the body assembled to study the social, political, and economic conditions of Mandatory Palestine and the feasibility of Jewish immigration to the territory.[123] While recommending the admission of 100,000 European Jews to Palestine, the AACI also proposed that the Mandatory government regulate all future immigration to the territory (stating that Palestine alone could not solve the Jewish refugee problem), and that neither a Jewish nor an Arab state would be created there. Its final report, released in 1946, appeared to heed the Vatican's concerns, stating that "Palestine is a Holy Land, sacred to Christian, to Jew, and to Moslem alike; and because it is a Holy Land, Palestine is not, and can never become, a land which any race or religion can justly claim as its very own."[124] Seizing on the AACI's rejection of Zionist aims, *America* advocated an international settlement for the territory, and opined that, in resorting to violence, it "appeared that the Zionist nationalists no longer fight the battle primarily to seek a refuge for persecuted brethren, but rather to further nationalist ambitions." While the journal didn't fault Jews for seeking a place of refuge following the war, it argued that the Jewish dilemma was a humanitarian question, not a political one, highlighting that "unity among [Jews] is based on religion rather than nationality." On that score, it advised against "a nationalistic treatment of a humanitarian problem."[125] It advised that the Palestine question be turned over to an international body, such as the nascent UN, a position the journal claimed it shared with a majority of Jews who, it asserted, found the claims of Zionists "embarrassing and politically dangerous." In concluding, it suggested a number of alternatives to the Zionist program, including the reinstatement of Jews as free citizens of their homelands and increased immigration quotas by Britain and the United States.[126]

A number of other Catholic journals also advised referring the Palestine question to an international body such as the UN, warning that leaving the Jews and the Arabs to their own devices would only lead to conflict and bloodshed. In a series of articles in *The Boston Pilot* and *The Michigan Catholic*, Monsignor Michael Assemani, the representative of the Latin patriarch of Jerusalem to Washington, raised these and other issues.[127] Assemani opined that while Jews and Arabs had legitimate historical and sentimental claims to the Holy Land, so, too, did Christians, and he implored that their rights not be undermined by the larger Jewish-Arab struggle. The Holy Land was sacred to Christians, he asserted, because "Jesus was born in Bethlehem, walked the dirt roads to Nazareth, through Samaria and to Jerusalem. It is the land which witnessed His miracles, the country in whose language He preached. It was on Mt Calvary that He was crucified. Palestine is the cradle of Christianity."[128] In concluding, Assemani hinted that Catholics would be prepared to take a firm stand in defending the neutrality of Christian holy sites in Palestine. "From the 12th century onward," he intoned, "Christians have fought and died to regain control of the holy sites in Palestine. And while the crusades of the armed Knights who went out to fight the non-believers now belong to history, the Christian world is no less keenly interested in the preservation of its holy places in Palestine."[129] His appeal to Christian historical and spiritual ties to the Holy Land would be repeatedly echoed by the Vatican in the early postwar years, and was intended to elicit an emotional response in American Catholic attitudes toward the struggle for Palestine. By reemphasizing Christianity's own ancestral stake in the territory, the diocesan press helped to shape Catholic opinion for later Vatican claims for the internationalization of the Holy Places, a focal point of postwar Catholic efforts.

An April 1945 press release by Anthony Bruya, an American Franciscan who served as the Palestine correspondent for the NCWC News Service, emphasized the notion that no suitable solution for the territory could be found that did not address Christian concerns in the Holy Land. In addressing the theme of Palestine's "absorptive capacity," and implicitly questioning Jewish primacy in the territory, he observed that "talk about providing a home for the persecuted millions of Europe is all very good and edifying, but is 10,000 square mile Palestine able to remedy, or even to alleviate, the plight of those unhappy peoples – by no means limited to those of the Jewish race, but knowing neither racial nor religious lines?"[130] Bruya further criticized a proposed Anglo-American partition plan for Palestine, inspired by a solution presented by the influential British journal *The Economist*, that would have ceded the Zionists a large portion of Palestine, including important Christian centers, save only Jenin and Nablus.[131] Though the plan was never made official, let alone implemented, Bruya's dispatches were widely reprinted in the American diocesan press under headlines such as "Christian Rights Overlooked" and "Christianity Ignored in Battles over Arab, Jewish Control of the Holy Land."[132] In concluding, Bruya reemphasized the notion that no solution was acceptable that did not preserve Christian control of the holy sites in Palestine. "Any attempted solution of the 'Palestine Question,'" he declared, "which does not provide a definitive and practical safeguard for the Christian position here, and hence for the peculiarly Catholic rights which are as old as Christianity itself, will be no solution at all. Such a makeshift will merely postpone the day when a real solution will have to be faced by all concerned."[133]

As the war drew to a close, and as the Palestine question was about to enter a decisive new phase, American Catholic opposition to Zionism had become firmly entrenched, despite the fuller airing of the tragedy of the Holocaust. It was a position, moreover, that drew direct inspiration from the Vatican itself. The political lobby of the American bishops on Mexico, Spain, Ethiopia, and, most recently, the Allied bombing of Rome was now set to press its case on the question of Palestine. American Catholic anti-Zionism was about to be applied as concrete political pressure. It would be countered, however, by an increasingly powerful American Zionist lobby that similarly sought to shape Washington's policy on the fate of the territory.

CHAPTER 4

"Impatient Zionism" and the Transnational Catholic Crusade for the Holy Land

The end of the Second World War would mark the beginning of the most crucial phase in the Zionist quest to establish a Jewish state in Palestine. In short order the horrors of the Holocaust, and the refugee crisis it had spawned, became more widely known, creating significant pockets of sympathy for Zionism even among groups previously agnostic or even hostile to the idea. This would come to include not only a majority of American Jewry, but also the new president, Harry S. Truman, and a large group of senators and congressmen. As the tide of sympathy for Zionism rose in the United States, British Mandatory control of Palestine rapidly weakened as postwar developments in the territory and the wider region became ever more difficult to manage. As a result, the international Zionist lobby shifted its gaze firmly to Washington as it became evident that the American government, the preeminent political, economic, and military power in the West, would be instrumental in securing its ends.

The Vatican and the American bishops, on their part, continued to cultivate their informal yet effective alliance with Washington. On a number of postwar questions, including displaced Catholic refugees in Europe, the containment of communism (particularly in Italy), assistance to persecuted Catholics in the Soviet sphere, and American aid to Germany and Poland, Washington and the American bishops did successfully collaborate. By the summer of 1947, the strategic coalition between Washington and the Vatican had become widely known, and the Vatican diverged from its traditional neutrality for a clearer alignment with the United States and its Western allies. For this reason, the American bishops were initially hesitant to express their opposition to Zionism too glaringly, lest it hamper progress in other areas of cooperation. Developments in Palestine in 1946 and 1947, however, pushed the Zionist dream of a Jewish state much closer to reality, which in turn spurred a more focused and determined institutional response from the American Catholic Church. The Catholic lobby on Palestine would finally emerge. American Catholic activism, inspired by the Vatican's own visions for the territory, now reached beyond the anti-Zionist rhetoric of the Catholic press to concrete political and diplomatic action.

COLD WAR CONSENSUS: THE VATICAN, AMERICAN CATHOLICS, AND TRUMAN

The postwar relationship between Washington, the American bishops, and the Vatican was built upon shared interests and values. The Vatican clearly recognized the preeminent power of the postwar United States and was eager to deepen its ties to the strongest international foe of communism. The Vatican similarly recognized the growing power of the American Catholic Church, not least for its financial might, and moved to place a number of American churchmen closer to the center of power in the Roman curia. Washington, meanwhile, regarded the Roman Catholic Church as a key ideological ally in the emerging global struggle against communism. Truman's maintenance of the Taylor mission after Roosevelt's death, despite stiff and persistent opposition to the appointment, was evidence of his commitment to preserving a Vatican connection.

After 1945, the Catholic Church in the United States entered a period of unprecedented vitality, confidence, and institutional expansion. Ardent Catholic participation in, and support of, the war effort, girded by the explicit endorsement of the American bishops, dampened much of the anti-Catholic bigotry of the prewar era, when critics had charged that Catholic isolationism served as a cover for deeper fascist and totalitarian sympathies. The war, to be sure, contributed significantly to the mainstreaming of American Catholics in the postwar era, further blurring the line between patriotism and Catholicism that had persisted (in the anti-Catholic mind) for nearly two centuries.[1] The Catholic population stood at twenty-five million in 1945, and would rise to nearly forty-five million (roughly 20 percent of the population) in the next two decades, bolstered by high birth rates and waves of Catholic immigrants from southern and eastern Europe.[2] The Catholic clergy grew by nearly 50 percent in the decade following the war, and numbers of enrolled seminarians nearly doubled. The economic prosperity of postwar America was mirrored by the institutional expansion of the American church. Over a hundred new hospitals, three thousand new Catholic elementary and high schools, and ninety-four new Catholic colleges were built in the postwar decade, evidence of the institutional vigor of the postwar church. Enrolment in Catholic educational institutions concurrently rose. The 1944 GI Bill, which provided college or vocational training for returning servicemen, was a particular boon to Catholic colleges, which saw their enrolment increase by 300 percent (from 92,426 in the prewar era to 384,526 in 1950), a development that further contributed to the mainstreaming of American Catholics after the war.[3] It was a vitality that did not escape the attention of the Vatican, which had long since recognized the unique role of American Catholic leaders to speak both as Catholics and as loyal Americans. The steady integration of Catholics into mainstream political and social life, partially facilitated by their unflinching support of the war effort, coupled with the preeminence of the United States in the postwar global order, only served to enhance Rome's view of the expanding potential of the American church.

Keen to tap into this, the Vatican acted to facilitate the organizational expansion of American Catholicism. Six new archdioceses were created for the United States between 1941 and 1952.[4] To minister to its growing flock, particularly in the postwar decade, a legion of new bishops and archbishops were appointed by Rome, bolstering the American episcopate by 1950 to 60 percent above its prewar numbers. In private conversations, Pius XII expressed the need to give prominent American prelates a more visible presence in the administration of the universal church, both in the College of Cardinals and in the Roman curia, to reflect the growing clout of American Catholics. He expressed as much to Harold H. Tittmann, secretary to Myron Taylor, who recorded in July 1945 that the pope "was emphatic that the Holy See must 'look to the United States' and that many non-Italians should be brought to the Holy See in important positions."[5] The pope's words were backed with action, as he quickly moved to integrate American prelates into positions of greater power. In July 1945 he named Cincinnati's Father Valentine Schaaf, a former dean of canon law at CUA, as the first American minister general of the Franciscan order, passing over more senior European candidates. It was an appointment that allowed the pope "to express his appreciation of the generous donations extended for relief purposes to the Holy See by American Catholics and the Catholic hierarchy in the United States," as well as to make a "gesture of appreciation and good-will to the Government and the people of the United States."[6] Perhaps not coincidentally, the Franciscans also controlled the office of Custodian of the Holy Land, a centuries-old institution that administered the order's extensive property in Palestine, which included Jerusalem's Church of the Holy Sepulchre, Bethlehem's Basilica of the Nativity, and Nazareth's Basilica of the Nativity.[7]

In his first postwar consistory, held in February 1946, Pius XII elected four new American cardinals. Joining Archbishop Dennis Dougherty of Philadelphia were Archbishops Francis Spellman of New York, John Glennon of St Louis, Edward Mooney of Detroit, and Samuel Stritch of Chicago. The fivefold increase in American cardinals in a single consistory further underscored Rome's postwar turn toward the United States. The pope also named a number of American bishops to key postings in the Vatican's diplomatic service. Bishop Joseph Hurley of St Augustine, Florida, was named regent of the nunciature in Yugoslavia, Bishop Gerald O'Hara of Savannah, Georgia, was named regent of the nunciature in Romania, and Bishop Aloysius Muench of Fargo, North Dakota, would soon be named apostolic delegate to Germany.[8] The rapid promotion of American Catholics prompted Lord Halifax, British ambassador in Washington, to observe that it was "an indication that the Vatican recognized America's pre-eminent position as a world power," and that "the greater voice she will now have in Church affairs is regarded as only proper."[9] It did not escape Halifax that "creeping Bolshevism" drove the Vatican's renewed interest in the American church, noting that "the lengthening shadow of the Soviet Union is leading to an increase in the influence of its most inveterate antagonist."[10]

The urgency with which the Vatican sought to place American prelates at the very height of curial power was also revealed in September 1945, when Spellman was tabbed by Pius XII to succeed Luigi Maglione as secretary of state. Spellman's suitability was emphasized on several fronts; to acknowledge a greater role for Americans in the curia, to facilitate the continuation of the Myron Taylor mission (in light of the war's end, and of Roosevelt's death), to tie the Vatican more closely to the strongest international foe of communism, and to ensure the cooperation of the United States in assisting with the resettlement of Catholic refugees displaced by the war. It also would have achieved the pope's objective of naming a longtime friend and confidant, one with close ties to Wall Street, to the vacant position.[11] Spellman asked for time to ponder the offer, which he ultimately declined, arguing that he would be of more use to Pius XII as archbishop of New York than as secretary of state.[12] Though Spellman had been offered the second most powerful position in the Vatican, a job Pacelli himself had held before becoming pope, he feared the potential constraints of working from within the curia. On several foreign questions, the pope had already consulted more extensively with Spellman than with Maglione, and there was no guarantee he would not turn to someone else in the future. Upon reflection, Spellman concluded that, as archbishop of New York, he could enjoy greater freedom from Vatican constraints, and act instead as a political linchpin between Rome and Washington. His decision to remain in the United States, given Rome's increasing desire to draw talented Americans into the curia, spoke volumes on the growing prestige and influence of the postwar American church in the international Roman Catholic firmament.

In the summer of 1945, Myron Taylor urged the incoming US secretary of state, James F. Byrnes, to establish formal diplomatic relations with the Vatican, citing it as a strategic advantage in Washington's relations with South American and European states, emphasizing that in the cause of peace, order, and stability, the United States and the Holy See "shared a fundamental similarity of purpose in the postwar era."[13] Though President Truman opted not to exchange ambassadors with the Vatican in 1945, wishing to avoid further piquing the ire of Protestant opponents of the Taylor mission in the infancy of his presidency, he did choose to extend Taylor's mission as personal representative to the pope indefinitely. This was despite Roosevelt's assurance in 1940 that the mission was "both special and temporary," highlighting the importance Truman placed on maintaining an informational channel with the Holy See.[14] The very public exchange of letters between pope and president in the summer of 1947, where each affirmed commitment to creating a world order based on peace, democracy, and freedom, underpinned by Christian morality, also seemed to buttress the Vatican-American relationship.[15] Truman, furthermore, pressed Harold Tittmann for a resident archbishop for Washington, giving him a high-ranking member of the hierarchy "right at hand, [whom] he could talk to whenever he wanted."[16] The Vatican erected the Archdiocese of Washington in November 1947, installing Patrick O'Boyle as its first archbishop.

This informal alliance of the American government, the Holy See, and the American church was bound by a mutuality of concerns in the postwar global order. Chief among these was the containment of Soviet communism. The American bishops' annual statement for 1945, "Between War and Peace," anticipated George F. Kennan's Long Telegram of 1947, and even Winston Churchill's Iron Curtain speech of 1946, on the need for Soviet containment.[17] In it, the bishops emphasized the need for peace, democracy, justice, and religious freedom as the underpinnings of a stable world order, and they expressed extreme reservations at the "soft hand" with which the United States and Britain treated the Soviet Union. Presaging Domenico Tardini's 1946 warning to Taylor never to "trust lions disguised as lambs," the bishops urged a firmer hand in dealing with Stalin.[18] A frank admission of the "clash of ideologies" that existed between East and West, the statement continued, and an insistence on a universal adherence to justice and democracy, were crucial to shaping a stable world order.[19]

By the early winter of 1947, the American Catholic press was roundly lauding Washington's renewed foreign policy objectives, as outlined in a speech by the president to Congress on 12 March 1947.[20] The Truman Doctrine, in vowing military and financial support to Greece and Turkey, signaled a shift in American policy from detente to containment of Soviet expansion. The policy was extolled both at the Vatican and by leaders in the American church, who had advocated a tougher line on Moscow for some time. Edmund J. Walsh, SJ, dean of the School of Foreign Service at Georgetown University and recent consultant to the American government at the Nuremberg Trials, praised Truman's resolute policy in a speech to twelve hundred foreign service and diplomatic staff at Washington's Statler Hotel. In comparing the Monroe Doctrine with the "equally historic Truman Doctrine," Walsh exclaimed that "the non-colonization of the world by communist aggression is now declared to be a cardinal principle of American foreign policy. The speed with which the American principle of free democracy rushed in to occupy the political vacuum created by the withdrawal of British power from the Middle East is an index of awakened responsibility in high places. It was a question of immediate response to an impelling emergency or else progressive surrender to the calculated advance of world communism."[21]

Walsh's sentiment was echoed by the Vatican itself, which offered its unqualified endorsement of the Truman Doctrine in a series of articles in the *L'Osservatore Romano* and *Il Quotidiano* (the paper of the church's powerful lay organization, Catholic Action) in the summer of 1947. Though the Vatican had valiantly sought to maintain an official neutrality through 1946 and 1947, its open support for Soviet containment amounted to a de facto alignment with Washington. The public exchange of letters between Truman and Pius XII in August 1947, circulated in the secular and religious press to maximum effect, appeared to seal the Washington-Vatican axis. The exchange coincided with Myron Taylor's return to Rome, following Truman's decision, despite a rising tide of domestic opposition, to send his personal representative back to the Vatican indefinitely. That Moscow considered the exchange of letters nothing short of a working alliance between the Vatican and the United States was suggested to Taylor's office by Don Manuel Sotomayor Luna, the Ecuadorian ambassador to the Holy See. "The communists consider the exchange of letters between the President and the Pope," he noted, "as tantamount to an alliance and as a source of moral strength to the United States. Accordingly, if it can defeat and weaken the Holy See, they will also be weakening the United States." The ambassador recalled a recent meeting with the pope at which he informed Pius XII that in Moscow he was now referred to as "that American."[22] Sotomayor's inference was confirmed during a September 1948 meeting between the Vatican's pro-secretary of state, Giovanni Battista Montini (the future Pope Paul VI), and James Dunn, the American ambassador to Italy. Montini informed his guest that he saw little hope of Vatican relations with any Soviet-controlled government, and that Moscow was "using the Orthodox Church as a political instrument to undermine the Vatican, whose favourable attitude toward the Marshall Plan … was particularly resented by Stalin."[23] In closing, Montini pledged the Vatican's unwavering support for the Marshall Plan, repeating three times to Dunn that it "must succeed for the good of mankind."[24]

Open cooperation between Washington, the Vatican, and the American church would reach an apex during the 1948 Italian elections, which pitted a left-wing bloc of Communists and Socialists, led by the Italian Communist Party (Partito Comunista Italiano, or PCI), against a center-right bloc led by Alcide De Gasperi's Christian Democrats. The Vatican, through the organs of Catholic Action, organized a capillary-like network of diocesan and parish organizations intended to steer Italian Catholics away from the PCI and into the voting booth on Election Day.[25] The American government, through the Central Intelligence Agency, channeled money, supplies, and expertise to the Holy See and the Christian Democrats. On a public level, the Truman administration, until the eve of the election, subtly reminded Italians that American aid, including Marshall Plan dollars, would not necessarily continue flowing to a "red" Italy. The American Catholic Church, at the suggestion of Luigi Gedda, head of Catholic Action, initiated a letter-writing campaign that saw Italian Americans writing relatives in Italy to warn them of the consequences of a PCI victory. Coordinated by the NCWC, through the office of Cicognani, the apostolic delegate, the campaign focused on dioceses and archdioceses with the highest concentrations of Italian American faithful.[26] Chicago's 200,000-member Holy Name Society, at the behest of Cardinal Samuel Stritch, mobilized to encourage the letter-writing campaign, and special devotional services were planned to "pray for the defeat of godless philosophies."[27] By mid-March 1948, the United States Post Office reported that mail to Italy had already doubled.[28] American and Vatican efforts appeared to have succeeded, as De Gasperi's coalition achieved a comfortable victory in the April election. The Vatican did not hesitate to thank the American church for its services rendered. Through Cicognani, it relayed to the NCWC the "deep gratitude" of the secretary of state "for the very active and efficient part taken by the NCWC in this campaign and its promotion."[29] If Pius XII looked to Washington to shape a postwar order based the principles of democracy, peace, justice, and religious freedom, the United States could equally regard the Vatican and American Catholics as committed and reliable ideological partners in such a task.

ZIONISM AS THE "NEW *LEBENSRAUM*"

Though a clutch of mutual concerns did draw Washington and the Vatican closer together in the years after 1945, Roman Catholic attitudes toward Zionism and the fate of Palestine grew increasingly at odds with positions beginning to prevail in the Senate and State Department, where support for a Jewish state was steadily growing. Favorable opinion on Zionism was also growing among the American public. By the summer of 1945, newsreel footage of Auschwitz, Buchenwald, and other Nazi concentration camps had vividly brought the horrors of the Holocaust to bear on the American conscience, creating a groundswell of support for Zionism that had been building through the war years. It was a development that was about to put American Catholic opposition to Zionism in much sharper relief.

The Vatican was certainly cognizant of the humanitarian calamity that the Holocaust had created for European Jews, which contributed to a widening refugee crisis at war's end. This emerging reality did not, however, alter the Vatican's long-standing policy of opposing a Jewish Palestine, as was outlined in the 1922 aide-mémoire issued by Cardinal Gasparri to the League of Nations.[30] A series of private meetings with Pius XII in 1945 confirmed this. In a papal audience in April of that year, Moshe Sharett, then the head of the pre-state Jewish Agency government and a future prime minister of Israel, assured the pope that there was "no clash between [Zionist] aspirations in Palestine and the high interests of Christianity and the Catholic Church."[31] The pope acknowledged his guest's claims, but continued to express concerns on the feasibility of the Zionist program. "There are Arabs in Palestine … They are the majority," Pius XII expressed in response. Though Sharett tried to emphasize the specific importance of Palestine to the Jewish diaspora, "the only place we have in the whole world," he remained unconvinced that the Roman Church would be supportive moving forward.[32] Forty years after Theodor Herzl's rebuff from Pius X, Sharett experienced his own disappointment at the papal court. By his own later admission, his attempt to elicit some kind of Vatican sympathy for the program of postwar Zionism, based on a rational explanation of the political and humanitarian reality, and in the immediate wake of the Holocaust, "went nowhere."[33]

In September, Pius XII received Rabbi Philip S. Bernstein, a member of the Zionist Emergency Committee, who would be assigned in 1946 by President Truman as an official adviser to the United States Army in Europe on the resettlement of nearly 200,000 European Jews. During the audience, held at Castel Gandolfo, Bernstein thanked the pope for his assistance to European Jewry during the war, and for his continuing assistance to Jewish refugees in postwar Italy.[34] The rabbi was impressed by the pope's genuine anguish at the fate of European Jews, which he repeatedly described as "dreadful." On the question of Jewish resettlement, however, Pius XII continued to disregard the option of a Jewish Palestine, informing his guest that Jewish immigration to the United States or to South America would be a suitable solution to the postwar refugee crisis. Bernstein then apprised the pope of the resistance to Jewish immigration in the United States and elsewhere, coupled with a desire among many displaced European Jews to settle in Palestine. "Yes, I recognize that as their desire," Pius XII admitted to Bernstein, but he suggested that "the United States was best equipped to absorb them."[35] Bernstein left the meeting with only vague assurances. He noted, plaintively, that the pope ended the audience with "another handshake, not firm but with enough pressure to suggest a positive clasp."

That the American Catholic hierarchy was to maintain a line on Palestine parallel to that of the Vatican was made clear in December 1945 when prominent archbishops in the American church, including Spellman, Stritch, Mooney, and Glennon, were again forwarded copies of the Vatican's 1922 aide-mémoire, as well as copies of Cardinal Gasparri's 1922 note to the British minister to the Holy See, both of which outlined Rome's opposition to a Jewish state in Palestine on political, theological, and historical grounds.[36] The statements, now thirty years old, and composed long before the rise of the Nazis and the eventual tragedy of the Holocaust, were still to be regarded as the definitive positions of the Roman Catholic Church on the question of Palestine. That the statements were reissued at the end of 1945, after having been distributed to the entire American episcopate through the NCWC in June 1944, was evidence that the cessation of hostilities in Europe, and a clearer appraisal of the tragedy of European Jewry, had not altered the Vatican's fundamental position.[37]

This continued resistance to the Zionist program was not, however, a policy widely aired by the Vatican in the immediate aftermath of the war. This was chiefly because Rome's rapidly warming alliance with Washington centered squarely on the Vatican's postwar priorities: the containment of Soviet expansion, the distribution of American aid to rebuild Italy and Germany, American assistance with Europe's Catholic refugees, and cooperation in halting the expansion of communist political movements in western Europe. As American public support for Zionism continued to grow (with a slim majority of Americans coming to support the idea by 1947), and as the American government increasingly pledged its support, the Vatican opted for circumspection on the question of Palestine.[38] President Truman's growing personal commitment to the Zionist idea made an overtly disproving stance more difficult still.[39] In the interests of maintaining sound relations with Washington, and particularly not to jeopardize the Taylor mission, the Vatican remained initially silent on the question of Zionism, though resistance to the establishment of a Jewish state in Palestine remained the formal policy of the church both in Rome and in the United States.

Given the convergence of interests between the American church and Washington in the postwar years, leading figures in the American hierarchy were similarly reticent to trumpet an opposition to Zionism too loudly. As increasingly important intermediaries between Rome and Washington, the American bishops shared the Vatican's apprehensions on clashing too openly with Washington's emerging postwar foreign policy precisely at the moment when relations with the Truman administration appeared progressively fruitful. As such, the bishops preferred to remain circumspect, withholding public statements as they pursued other areas of cooperation.

The American Catholic press, however, expressed opinion more freely than the hierarchy could. While the bishops exercised strategic restraint on the issue of creating a Jewish state in Palestine, anti-Zionist musings continued to be expressed liberally through the diocesan and wider American Catholic press, in line with Cardinal Maglione's call in August 1943 that the Catholic press trumpet the Vatican's line on the matter. By 1945, such opinion in Catholic journals became increasingly important in shaping public opinion on the Palestine question, particularly as sympathy for a Jewish home in Palestine grew in the wake of the war. Anthony Bruya, an American Franciscan and the Jerusalem correspondent for the NCWC News Service, produced a series of such articles, eventually carried by *The Brooklyn Tablet*, *The Boston Pilot*, *The New World* (Chicago), *The Catholic Mind*, and other large-circulation journals.[40] Bruya, closely echoing the Vatican, questioned the "absorptive capacity" of Palestine to accommodate Europe's displaced Jews. He criticized Jews who looked to the territory as a "new lebensraum for commercial enterprise and expansion," crassly linking Zionism to the Nazi drive for empire, and questioned whether Palestine should be "developed into a business undertaking, when there is room elsewhere on this planet without invading the sacred precincts of this Temple which is the Holy Land."[41] As the pope had expressed privately, Bruya touted alternatives for Jews seeking refuge and settlement, suggesting North and South America as ideal points of emigration. He also juxtaposed the safeguarding of Christian sacred sites in Palestine with Zionist dreams of a Jewish state, arguing that the latter was wholly incompatible with the former, a position more firmly expressed in the Catholic press after 1945. "For thousands of years Palestine has been the Holy Land," Bruya observed. "In defence of its sacred character and its Holy Places the flower of European manhood once purpled with Crusader blood many a Palestine battlefield. It would be unthinkable that now, from the unspeakable wreckage of this war … should come a new desecration of the home land of Jesus Christ."[42] The article reflected the increasingly dire, Crusade-inspired rhetoric that had appeared in prewar American Catholic reportage on Palestine. In concluding, Bruya posited that an international trusteeship for the territory, under the auspices of the recently formed UN, was the only solution that could reliably protect Roman Catholic interests in the Holy Land, a suggestion that the Vatican and American Catholic leaders had only revealed in private conversations.[43]

As Bruya's condemnations of Zionist designs for Palestine grew progressively more acerbic in the spring of 1946, however, the NCWC News Service became reticent to proclaim such a conspicuously anti-Zionist editorial line in its numerous papers. This was particularly so after the release of the AAIC's report on Palestine in January 1946, which recommended that a UN commission be established to administer the territory, instead of the partition of the territory sought by Zionists. The report also placed limits on Jewish immigration to Palestine and pledged that access to the Holy Places would be protected by "international guarantees." As it appeared that Catholic designs for the territory were being fulfilled by the recommendations of the report (in that it discouraged the imminent creation of either a Jewish or an Arab state in Palestine), the NCWC adopted a progressively vague line on Palestine, preferring not to inflame public opinion, particularly as sympathy for Zionism continued to rise. Much like the Vatican's de facto organ, *L'Osservatore Romano*, American diocesan papers adopted an increasingly ambivalent line on Zionism through the spring and summer of 1946, confident that a settlement on the territory amenable to the Vatican and the American church – namely, UN administration of the territory – was unfolding.

This editorial restraint exhibited by the NCWC, however, was not as evident in other organs of the American Catholic press. While the various diocesan papers published by the NCWC were under the imprimatur of local bishops, other Catholic journals operated with more autonomy. The national Jesuit weekly *America*, for example, continued to openly criticize Zionist demands, characterizing them as belligerent and wholly incompatible with Christian and Muslim rights in the territory. Publishing outside the auspices of the NCWC, *America* largely abandoned its wartime editorial line, which alternated between a show of Catholic solidarity with persecuted Jews and a stern skepticism of Zionism, to focus more singularly on the latter. The journal admitted that a home had to be found for Europe's displaced Jews, but it clearly expressed its reservations with a Jewish Palestine as that solution. As early as December 1945, *America* accused Zionist organizations of exploiting the suffering of Jews as an expedient to the erecting of a sovereign Jewish state.[44] The journal suggested that unity among Jews was based on religion rather than nationality, and that Zionism sought to create a question of national sovereignty out of what was properly a humanitarian crisis. The journal seconded Hans Morgenthau's November 1945 assertion that Palestine be placed "under the auspices of the UN," and it claimed to stand with Jews "embarrassed at aggressive Zionism."[45]

Through the first half of 1946, *America* criticized the increasingly violent tactics adopted by Jewish nationalists in Palestine as it touted the AAIC report as the most pragmatic solution to what was becoming an intractable political situation. "A fairer compromise," the journal described it, "in view of the complications that thirty years have added to the original 1917 arrangement, could scarcely have been forthcoming."[46] It charged that Zionist belligerence, which was spilling into violence, hampered the "Jewish cause" more severely than even Arab intransigence, and urged that British diplomacy, which favored an international mandate for the territory, be given a chance to succeed. *America* repeatedly criticized the "narrow nationalism" of the Zionists, charging that it "[appeared] that the Zionist nationalists no longer fight the battle to secure a refuge for persecuted brethren, but rather to further national ambitions."[47] In a later editorial, the journal accused Zionist leaders of exploiting the refugee crisis to fuel the "religio-nationalist mystique" of Zionism, all to push forward "an obscure claim for a Jewish 'nationality' and a small strip of land where it may be expressed." *America* also invoked the trope of Judeo-Bolshevism, suggesting in a number of editorials that the success of the Zionist program in Palestine would only give a stronger toehold to the Soviets in the region, a notion that now appeared with regularity in the Catholic press.[48]

These severe critiques of the Zionist program were echoed in the winter of 1946 by the Paulist *Catholic World*, which cautioned against ignoring the Christian and Arab stake in the territory. In January, the journal ran a lengthy article by the anti-Zionist Lebanese American scholar Jabir Shibli. In warning Americans against seeing Palestine "through Zionist spectacles," Shibli proposed the termination of the British Mandate and the creation of a single Palestinian state, observing that the territory had reached its absorptive capacity, and had been continually occupied by Arabs for two thousand years. The Holocaust, in this view, did not make the idea of a Jewish Palestine more compelling, as "political Zionism," an aggressive and cynical movement, sought merely to supplant the native population for the benefit of Jewish commercial and industrial interests. "The aim of political Zionism," Shibli observed, "is to get as many Jews as possible into Palestine to attain a Jewish majority in the population and convert Palestine into a Jewish state in which the Arabs would be dominated or uprooted and transferred to other lands."[49] Though Palestine was the "spiritual home" of devout Jews, he concluded, "it does not follow that it should be the haven or refuge for the Jews of the world." The next month, the journal sounded a grimmer warning on the dangers of privileging Zionist claims to the territory. "Americans do not hear the Moslem muezzins who mount to the top of the minarets inside the walls and chant their calls to prayer. It has sounded on the air of Palestine for thirteen centuries. If Zionism imposes a political state on their Holy Land, a cataclysm of blood will again begin to drench the earth."[50]

The appearance of Arab perspectives in the Catholic press came at a time when the Arab League and the Arab Higher Committee (AHC) were expanding a series of information bureaus (known as "Arab Offices"), in Washington, DC, New York, Boston, Chicago, and San Francisco.[51] The purpose of these offices was to disseminate an Arab viewpoint to the American public, and to counter similar Zionist efforts to shape discourse on the Palestine question. The offices were staffed by figures such as the Palestinian journalist and future Palestine Liberation Organization Chairman Ahmed Shukairy, the Lebanese diplomat and scholar Charles Malik, the Palestinian nationalist Musa Alami, and the British intelligence officer Cecil Hourani, brother of the noted Lebanese British historian Albert Hourani. That the offices featured a number of Christian Arabs, such as Malik and Hourani, was evidence that they were intended to tap into Catholic disdain for Zionism in building a common front against the creation of a Jewish state. Despite this shared contempt for Zionism, however, the Vatican's enduring mistrust of Arab nationalism prevented deeper cooperation between Arab and Catholic interests in the United States.

Events in Palestine itself would only harden Catholic opinion, as tensions there continued to intensify through 1946. In the immediate aftermath of the war, Zionists were confident that Britain would deliver on the promises of the Balfour Declaration and acquiesce to their demands for a Jewish state. The victory of Clement Attlee's Labour Party in the July 1945 British election only heightened Zionist hopes, given Labour's explicit support of Jewish statehood at its party conference in the autumn of 1944. This optimism quickly soured, however, when it became evident that Attlee's foreign minister, Ernest Bevin, had no intentions of facilitating Zionist ambitions. Bevin extended Britain's cautious course on Palestine, imposing renewed immigration quotas and promising only to launch another inquiry into the situation. This inquiry, which culminated in the AAIC's 1946 report, reinforced the limits on Jewish immigration as outlined in the 1939 White Paper, and established the principle that neither Jew nor Arab should dominate Palestine, nor should it be ceded to either Jewish or Arab national interests. As such, it represented a severe check on the momentum that mainstream Zionist organizations appeared to have gained during the war and contributed to decaying relations between Jewish Palestinians and British occupying forces in the territory.

Maintaining stability in the territory from early 1946 forward proved an increasingly difficult task for Britain, which stationed nearly eighty thousand soldiers there to preserve order. Zionist paramilitary organizations such as the Irgun, which was formed by disaffected members of the mainstream Haganah, sought a more aggressive form of action than its predecessor, whose leadership generally favored a defensive approach. Increasingly frustrated with Britain's stonewalling of Zionist ambitions and piqued by the limits imposed by the AAIC, the Irgun waged an intermittent campaign of sabotage and bombings through the spring and summer. This resistance had been initiated by the sinking of two British police boats in Haifa in October 1944 and continued with attacks on other symbols of British control in the territory, including railroads, police stations, and military bases. By the summer of 1946, imperial officials became increasingly desperate to stifle the rising tide of resistance activity, closely monitoring groups such as the Irgun and its offshoots. On 29 June 1946, the Jewish Sabbath, British authorities launched Operation Agatha, arresting nearly twenty-seven hundred suspects in Jerusalem, Tel Aviv, and Haifa, a sweep that included Moshe Sharett. In an attempt to find a link between the recognized Jewish Agency government and violent terrorist groups, the raids effectively drove an irrevocable wedge between imperial officials and mainstream Zionism. Though the Jewish Agency officially criticized the terror campaign of certain clandestine groups, it became clear that Britain's postwar Palestine policy was an affront and a threat to recognized and sanctioned Zionist organizations as well. Irgun attacks increased in frequency and severity in the summer and autumn. On 22 July 1946, purportedly in response to Operation Agatha, a massive bomb ripped through Jerusalem's King David Hotel, which served as Britain's administrative and military headquarters in Palestine. The attack, which killed ninety-one, was followed by the Irgun's bombing of the British embassy in Rome in October, signaling a widening campaign of terror designed to loosen Britain's grip on Palestine.

The increasing use of terror tactics provoked renewed critiques of Zionism in the Catholic press, as the moderation shown in some journals gave way to a progressively unanimous condemnation. The bombing of the King David Hotel drew a predictable response from *America*, which again linked Zionism to a crude "crypto-nationalism" that was little interested in seeking a genuine solution to the Jewish refugee crisis.[52] The violence of 1946, the journal suggested, "encourages the suspicion that certain elements of the Zionists are no more responsible or politically mature, despite superior material culture, than some Arab extremists who would resort to the same means if they got the chance and hope of success. Zionism is now in the difficult position of having to prove the possibility of peaceful government in Palestine."[53] The stability of the whole region, let alone the security of Roman Catholics, the journal later opined, was put at risk by "impatient Zionism" and its quixotic drive to carve out a national state.[54] *America*'s position closely reflected that of the Vatican, which viewed both Jewish and Arab nationalism with deep suspicion, consistently preferring an international mandate over the territory than the victory of either of these national movements.[55]

The liberal Catholic journal *The Commonweal*, which had previously offered only a convoluted and cautious opinion on Zionism in the period immediately following the war (in line with the Vatican's own circumspection), sharpened its critique from this point forward. It linked the bombing of the King David Hotel, not to the underground groups that had planned and undertaken it, but "to Zionism itself," which, it claimed, "must bear responsibility for an act that threatens all it ever aimed to create."[56] Like *America*, *The Commonweal* characterized the aims of Zionists as distinct and separate from those of a majority of world Jewry who, in the opinion of these Catholic journals, only sought to live in peace and security in the various states that would accept them as immigrants. "Zionists," it observed, "never in contemporary times a majority of the Jews, sought to use intimidation and violence to achieve an end not widely supported by their global co-religionists." It further opined that it "could not conceal [its] anger and distress now that a long and mistaken campaign has brought one more bitter nationalism into a world that has too many of them."[57] Denunciations on similar grounds could be found in a variety of American Catholic journals and papers, including *The Boston Pilot*, *The Sign*, *The Catholic Mind*, *The Catholic Worker*, *The Brooklyn Tablet*, and others, evidence that the circumscribed and cautious anti-Zionism of the immediate postwar period was giving way to a more uniform chorus denouncing the idea of Jewish statehood in Palestine.[58]

CORPORA SEPARATUM: THE UN PARTITION PLAN FOR PALESTINE

Events in Palestine after the bombing of the King David Hotel made it evident that Britain's Mandatory control over the territory was becoming dangerously fragile. The Irgun and other underground Zionist groups were becoming progressively emboldened in their successes against British targets and stepped up their campaign in the fall and winter of 1946 and the spring of 1947. Their tactics included bombing and mortar attacks on British police stations and supply depots, the planting of land mines on key transportation routes, and the sabotaging of key railway lines. Irgun gangs retaliated against arrests and imprisonments by capturing and beating British officers, prompting officials to move British families in Palestine into military bases for protection. Adding a sinister odium to the struggle was the capture and hanging execution of two British sergeants in July 1947 in retaliation for the execution of three Irgun prisoners. The discovery of the bodies in a eucalyptus grove near Netanya, booby-trapped to cause further injury, inflamed British opinion and led to a wave of antisemitic riots in Birmingham, Liverpool, and Manchester.

As international sympathy for Zionism continued to gain traction, particularly in the United States, and as the struggle against underground Zionist groups continued to intensify, necessitating an occupying force of now nearly 100,000 personnel, the British Foreign Office began to seriously question its commitment to the Mandate. Even before the violent events of the summer of 1947, the Foreign Office had decided to turn the question on the future of the territory over to the UN. In February, Britain requested that the UN study a solution, stipulating only that any proposed solution would have to be acceptable to both Arabs and Jews in the territory.[59] By May, the General Assembly had established the United Nations Special Committee on Palestine (UNSCOP), a body created to investigate the conflict in the territory, and to propose a viable solution.[60] Throughout 1947, UNSCOP delegates examined a variety of political solutions for Palestine, including a Jewish state with guaranteed rights for Arab minorities, an Arab state with guaranteed rights for Jewish minorities, UN trusteeship for the territory, and two partitioned states.[61] By early September, the committee had prepared a report calling for the termination of the British Mandate, and proposing two visions for the future of the territory. The first proposal, the majority report, favored partitioned states, one Jewish, one Arab, with economic union and UN trusteeship for the Old City of Jerusalem. The second proposal, the minority report, recommended one federated state with Jerusalem as its capital. Zionist groups largely favored the partition plan, while Arab nationalists dismissed both plans, charging that UNSCOP had taken little heed of Arab concerns. Significantly, both solutions proposed by UNSCOP vowed to protect the holy sites, "in recognition of the proper interests on millions of Christians, Jews and Moslems abroad," and that the preexisting rights of religious communities in Palestine "be neither impaired nor denied."[62] Following the release of the report, an Ad Hoc Committee on the Palestine Question was formed on 24 September to assess the two proposals and recommend a course of action. The partition plan suggested in the majority report prevailed, and on 29 November 1947, the UN adopted Resolution 181 to create both a Jewish and an Arab state in the territory. The Old City of Jerusalem and the center of Bethlehem were to be protected as an "international zone," or *corpus separatum*, under the auspices of the UN, reflective of the unique and historic character of the city's Holy Places and the sacredness of these sites to Christians, Jews, and Muslims alike.

News of the UN resolution on Palestine elicited little official reaction from either the Vatican or leading figures in the American church. The Holy See remained opposed to the establishment of a Jewish state in Palestine, but it continued, on an official level, to cloister this policy, cognizant of the broad international support for the partition plan, and desirous to maintain its growing strategic and ideological alliance with the United States (which had firmly supported the partition plan). This Vatican "silence" on Resolution 181, however, did not go unnoticed in the Arab world. Archbishop Arthur Hughes, the apostolic delegate to Egypt (the first Muslim state to exchange ambassadors with the Vatican), wrote to Tardini in December 1947, informing him that Arab leaders were questioning the Vatican's apparent vacillation on the Palestine question. Hughes wrote of the Arab impression of the Vatican's "severe indifference" and surprise that the church was not more concerned with the fate of the Holy Places, particularly those outside of Jerusalem.[63] More concerning, to Hughes, was the sense among Arab leaders that the Vatican preferred Jewish to Arab sovereignty. Following a meeting with Egypt's King Farouk, Hughes relayed his host's "deep regret and disappointment at what he calls the continuation of the mentality of the crusades on the part of the Holy See, in that it would continue to prefer Jews to Arabs." Azzam Pasha, the Arab League's first secretary-general, relayed to Hughes the Arab world's desire for a firmer public stance from the Vatican against the partition plan, and a clearer papal defense of the Arab Christian minority in Palestine. In closing, Hughes advised Tardini to be wary of alienating the Arab states at this crucial juncture. "The Arabs fear," he wrote, "that the Holy See has placed too much faith in the promises of the Jews and their American friends."[64]

Vatican circumspection, of course, did not infer support of Zionism or the partition plan. Though the Vatican remained opposed in principle to a Jewish Palestine, it was equally wary of an Arab state in the territory, a prospect that it had long since regarded, like Zionism, as a threat to Roman Catholic interests in the territory. The Vatican's mistrust of Arab nationalism was shared by Myron Taylor, who expressed his apprehensions in a memo to Cordell Hull during the closing months of the Second World War. "I have repeatedly expressed the opinion," Taylor wrote, "that no encouragement should be given to a ... pan-Arab confederation." He discouraged the creation of a "racial and religious bloc" that would hamper American authority in the region. "It seems to me," Taylor concluded, "that the whole plan to encourage a consolidation of the Arab world is full of dangers of many kinds."[65]

Taylor, whose views were clearly aligned with those of the Vatican, was similarly wary of imposing change too quickly, linking American security to the maintenance of the status quo in Palestine. As late as the summer of 1947, Taylor advised rejecting the Zionist plan, urging Truman to support the creation of an alternative "home" for Europe's Jews, and suggesting that Palestine itself was nearing its "absorptive capacity." "America should continue to support a democratic Palestine," he wrote to Truman on 30 July 1947, "but only for a reasonable number of convinced Zionists – a number that conforms to the limited resources of Palestine as they now exist and as they are gradually developed hereafter."[66] Leading figures in the American Catholic hierarchy similarly reflected the Vatican's apprehensions of either Jewish or Arab sovereignty in the territory, preferring UN trusteeship for Palestine. New York's Monsignor Thomas McMahon, secretary of the CNEWA from 1943 to 1955, expressed American Catholic support for UN trusteeship of Palestine as early as June 1945, when he weighed in on the options for the territory: "Palestine is international, an international UN government is another idea proposed; the idea is good, in fact far better than the others, because it does safeguard the sacred character of Christ's homeland."[67]

The partition plan of 1947 did appear to create for the Vatican a double bind: a situation in which two non-Christian states would be created, each of which would presumably pose challenges to Roman Catholic influence in the region. Given the broad-based support for partition, particularly that of the United States, an outright denunciation of the plan to divide Palestine between the Arabs and the Jews, either from Rome or from leaders of the American church, was fraught with risks. The Vatican remained keen to maintain sound relations with Washington and was reluctant to create a breach by openly rejecting the partition plan. This was particularly so considering that in the lead-up to Italy's 1948 elections, the PCI continued to expand its political influence on the peninsula, a threat the Vatican would need continued American assistance to counter.

In lieu of UN trusteeship for Palestine, which Maglione considered optimal, the Vatican seized upon promises made in Resolution 181 to maintain Jerusalem and its environs (including Bethlehem and Nazareth) as a UN-administered international zone, a *corpus separatum* protecting the Holy Places by placing neither Jews nor Arabs in control of the Old City or the wider zone.[68] In this way, the holiest sites of Christendom would remain outside of the political jurisdiction of a non-Christian sovereign power, preserving for the Roman Catholic Church a base for continued influence in the region. The *corpus separatum*, in many ways, reflected the plan that Pacelli (now Pope Pius XII) had presented to Nahum Sokolow during the latter's visit to the Vatican in 1917. This plan had included zones of exclusion that encompassed large swaths of southern Palestine that would function to protect the sacred sites and Roman Catholic jurisdiction and power in the region. The *corpus separatum* proposed in 1947 appeared to echo Pacelli's plan (though in circumscribed form) and provided a starting point for negotiating a Catholic zone of influence around the Holy Places.

By late 1947, then, American Catholic leaders, in accord with the views of the Vatican Secretariat, had accepted the partition of Palestine as a virtual inevitability, and focused their efforts on guaranteeing the maintenance of Jerusalem and its environs as a UN-administered international sphere. Spellman, the foremost figure in American Catholicism, expressed as much to an American diplomat in the winter of 1947, stating that though the Catholic Church "strongly [opposed] any form of partition, primarily on the ground that the whole of the land [was] sacred to Christ," he conceded that "a carefully conceived, detailed regime of guarantees and safeguards for the Holy Places and for the Christian minorities, both under the supervision of appropriate organs of the United Nations," would be the least that the church would expect in properly resolving the issue.[69]

That the Vatican and the American bishops conceded defeat on the partition plan spoke volumes on the limits of conventional papal diplomacy in the early Cold War. The close cooperation of the American bishops and Washington on a number of areas of mutual concern, foremost on the containment of Soviet expansion, combined with growing American support of the partition plan, effectively nullified the Vatican's long-standing opposition to a Jewish homeland in Palestine. Within a matter of weeks, Gasparri's 1922 aide-mémoire, which had been trotted out frequently to outline the Vatican's long-standing policy, had largely been rendered a dead letter. The prospect of a *corpus separatum* for Jerusalem and the Holy Places, however, appeared as a chance to salvage a victory from the jaws of defeat, an opportunity for the Vatican to save face on the Palestine question, and to preserve the very heart of the *Terra Santa* from either Jewish or Arab sovereign control. Supporting the plan, moreover, would allow for a continuation of fruitful relations between the Vatican, the American bishops, and Washington, a tripartite relationship that appeared to be gaining strength. Vatican figures, no doubt, also saw in the plan the potential for wider papal authority in Jerusalem, another factor contributing to Catholic acquiescence on the partition plan. Though anti-Zionist sentiment continued to be expressed in both Vatican and American Catholic quarters, particularly in the context of delays to the internationalization of Jerusalem, the establishment of a functioning *corpus separatum* became the focal point of Catholic lobbying from the summer of 1947 forward. Truman, meanwhile, sensing the Catholic stand-down on the partition plan, specifically vowed "support for the internationalization of Jerusalem and the protection of the Holy Places in Palestine" in the Democratic platform for 1948, evidence of the president's careful politicking on the Palestine question.[70] American Catholics, both in Washington and at the UN, would now strenuously advocate for just such an outcome.

CATHOLIC WOMEN AT THE UN: THE NCWC OFFICE FOR UN AFFAIRS

The National Catholic Welfare Conference, established in 1919 as a permanent replacement for the National Catholic War Council, had, by 1945, served as the organizational nerve center of the Catholic Church in the United States for nearly three decades.[71] Essentially a council of the American bishops, its various bodies and departments had lobbied the American government on a variety of domestic and international questions pertinent to Roman Catholic interests, which had included Washington's interwar relations with Spain and Mexico.[72] As the first bureaucracy of a major religious denomination to be headquartered in the national capital, the NCWC was specifically mandated to "organize, unify and coordinate Catholic activities for the general welfare of the Church, near the seat of federal power."[73] By 1945 the organization, emboldened by an increasingly constructive relationship with the American government and by the steady growth of the church in the United States, continued in its attempts to shape domestic and international questions along lines amenable to the Roman Catholic Church.

An American Catholic presence at the UN was deemed vital, both by the Vatican and by the American bishops, in attempts to impart an authentically Catholic worldview to the nascent global body. Though the Vatican was wary of an international forum that afforded the Soviet Union a significant voice, it remained optimistic that the UN would be central to the construction of a peaceable world order. During the Second World War, Pius XII had issued a series of addresses that envisioned a postwar system based on genuine international cooperation, coordinated by just such an organization. Echoing the Atlantic Charter of 1941, this papal framework emphasized global disarmament, the security and sovereignty of all peaceable nations, religious freedom, the protection of human rights for all, including persecuted minorities and refugees, and economic justice.[74] Pius XII underscored the need for a new body, free of the entanglements that had plagued the international order after 1919, that was committed to a genuine and collegial quest for justice and peace. Above all, it was to be an order that rested on the idea of a divine and universal morality, a vision based in natural law and its belief in the inherent virtue and dignity of the human race as endowed by God. In such an order, religious freedom was essential, and states that sought to persecute religion or infringe on the rights of religious minorities were to be justly chastised. In the early postwar years, it was evident that Pius XII was pleased with the UN, and he urged Catholics to support its work. "Nobody," he declared in 1947, "who has taken to his breast, as a sacred obligation, the fight for a worthy peace should renounce the use of this possibility … to stir up the conscience of the world from a place so high and clear."[75]

That the UN was based in the northeastern United States, first at Lake Success, New York, and later in New York City itself, also made the NCWC a natural liaison for Roman Catholic advocacy at the new world body. The NCWC first appointed consultants to the 1945 United Nations Conference on International Organization at San Francisco, where delegates lobbied to modify the Dumbarton Oaks and Yalta proposals along lines suggested in Pope Pius XII's *Five*

Point Peace Program of 1939 and in the American bishops' annual statements during the war.[76] The latter statements pledged fealty to the ideals of the Atlantic Charter, and emphasized the need for a global body that defended international law (including a world court with real authority and based in moral law), human rights, global economic cooperation, and international sovereignty and security. This vision of a universal order was also shaped by influential American Catholic thinkers such as Monsignor John A. Ryan (who had urged American Catholics to show solidarity with persecuted Jews during the war) and John Courtney Murray, SJ, a theologian and leading authority on church-state relations and religious liberty. Though American Catholic delegates to the Conference on International Organization experienced frustration in placing a distinctively Catholic stamp on the UN Charter, the NCWC was sufficiently encouraged to appoint a permanent observer at the UN. The nominee would be someone who could track developments at the various agencies, prepare summaries of debates for use by the bishops and by the Catholic press, and who, when opportunity presented, could advance Catholic perspectives and positions among members of the world body. The NCWC's Father Edward Conway, SJ, who was charged with creating the organization's UN office, also envisaged the post as creating a bridge between the American Catholic Church and the American diplomats at the UN, producing an envoy who could serve in the dual capacity of "rapporteur to the NCWC and as liaison between the NCWC and the American delegation."[77]

On 11 September 1946, the NCWC's Office for UN Affairs was formally established, using available space in Spellman's New York archdiocesan headquarters. The establishment of the office was not a surprise, given the growing consensus among the bishops of the advantage of having a liaison team at the UN.[78] The choice to lead the new office, however, was unorthodox. In August, at the behest of Chicago's Cardinal Samuel Stritch, Catherine Schaefer, an officer in the powerful lay National Council of Catholic Women (NCCW), was tabbed to head the new endeavor. Schaefer, who held a master's degree in economics and international relations from CUA, had also served as the Secretary for the influential Catholic Association for International Peace (CAIP). Her selection, given the availability of more senior candidates, and given the paucity of women in the upper echelons of the NCWC and the Roman Catholic Church generally, was significant. It was particularly so as Conway, who had been central to conceiving the mandate of such an office, had also coveted the position. The noted intellectual and Catholic convert Dr Ross Hoffman, chairman of the Department of History at Fordham University, who had served as a NCWC observer at the Security Council sessions, also expressed an interest.[79] Schaefer's selection, then, spoke volumes on the faith that senior figures placed in her ability to succeed in such a role. In expressing her understanding of the new position to which she had been appointed, Schaefer's vision and ambition were evident. She suggested that her role not be too rigidly defined, "since the field was somewhat a *terre inconnue*," and that if she was truly to assist the NCWC in formulating and shaping international policy, she should have the authority to "establish relationships with persons and organizations concerned, both within and without the United Nations."[80]

In addition to her roles with the NCCW and the CAIP, Schaefer had also been employed in the NCWC's social action department, which had been established in 1920 to promote the social thought of the Roman Catholic Church in the United States, and which used Catholic doctrine and papal teachings as guides in framing solutions to modern social questions. The department examined questions both domestic and international, with a particular eye on the threat that communism posed to the interests of the international church. Schaefer's role included the writing of speeches and the production of books and pamphlets, which impressed upon Stritch her potential in an even larger capacity. The noted British Catholic economist and policy adviser Barbara Ward, in encountering Schaefer at the social action department in early 1945, described her as "a delightful girl … rather overworked but full of life and guts," traits that would serve her well for the arduous task ahead.[81] As the nascent "UN Office" expanded in importance in the years after 1946, and as it became central to American Catholic attempts to shape the Palestine question, the bishops would be well pleased with their nominee.[82]

Once in New York her purview, as she had envisioned, extended well beyond the stated mandate of the office. Though she had been authorized to observe and report on developments at the UN for the purposes of keeping the American bishops updated and informed, it was clear that her vision for the office was broad. She clearly conceived of an activist organization that sought contact both with other Catholic organizations at the UN, as well as international NGOs and delegations. Six months after she had established the office, she revealed this ambitious mandate in an annual report to NCWC general secretary Howard Carroll. "As Catholics at the UN get to know each other better," she apprised Carroll, "and as Catholic organizations are admitted to consultative relationships, the utility of the NCWC's Office for UN Affairs should increase, in the informational, liaison and other assistance it may be able to render, and in its efforts to integrate Catholic principles into the formal action and atmosphere of the UN and of international life."[83]

As such, in addition to observing and reporting on the numerous sessions and committees, Schaefer actively sought to build bridges between the major American and international Catholic organizations accredited to the UN. In this respect, her objective appeared to have been the establishment of an "international Catholic circle" along the lines of which had existed among the Catholic powers at the League of Nations.[84] She also envisioned the NCWC's office as the coordinating body for those delegations. Within months of its establishment, Schaefer had established links with a number of international Catholic observer groups at the UN, including the International Federation of Christian Trade Unions, the International Union of Catholic Women's Leagues, Caritas International, and Pax Romana. By the end of 1946, the NCWC office was already established as the convening agent for American Catholic observer groups at the UN, which included the powerful NCCW and the CAIP.[85]

Schaefer's office monitored a number of issues relevant to Catholic interests, including the development of the UN's Universal Declaration of Human Rights, the status of and assistance to European refugees (particularly Catholics), religious freedom in eastern Europe, the development of UNICEF (the United Nations International Children's Emergency Fund), and the debates at the UN Commission on the Status of Women. No issue, however, commanded the time and attention of the office as did the Palestine question and, specifically from the spring of 1947 forward, the status of Jerusalem and its environs as an internationally administered *corpus separatum*. In addition to producing a monthly bulletin on UN affairs entitled *Foreign Affairs*, which summarized aspects of the various debates winding through the UN, the office also produced numerous reports specifically examining the debates on Jerusalem. Between 1947 and 1950, Schaefer would produced nearly forty lengthy and detailed papers on a score of aspects on the Palestine issue, providing a key source of information on the debate for both the American hierarchy and the Catholic press.[86] On a number of occasions over the same period, the Holy See also requested Schaefer's memos and monthly bulletins, evidence of the importance the Vatican placed on the NCWC's UN Office as a source of information.[87] By this time, Schaefer was assisted by Alba Zizzamia, who had been appointed as the office's associate director in June 1949. Another remarkable Catholic laywoman, Zizzamia had earned a doctorate at the University of Rome and had served as a professor of Italian language and literature at St

Joseph's College in New York and Trinity College in Washington, DC. She would represent the World Union of Catholic Women to both UNICEF and the UN Economic and Social Council, in addition to serving as director of the Archdiocese of New York's Office of Justice and Peace. An author, lecturer, and translator of works in Italian, French, and English, Zizzamia would remain at the NCWC's UN Office for decades, working alongside Schaefer in the tireless effort to maintain an American Catholic presence at the UN. It would not be until 1964, in fact, that the Vatican appointed its own permanent observer to the UN, underscoring the importance of the NCWC office as a clearinghouse of information for the international church.[88]

From the formulation of the partition plan in the summer of 1947 to the creation of the State of Israel in May 1948 (when Britain formally relinquished its mandate and withdrew its troops from the territory), Schaefer's office kept the NCWC apprised of the myriad debates on the Palestine question. This included a series of reports in the spring of 1947 revealing the stands of various states on the partition plan itself, from Egyptian, Iraqi, and Lebanese calls for an Arab-dominated state, to a disparate collection of countries (including the United States and Britain, but also Czechoslovakia, Guatemala, and Uruguay) who favored the creation of both an Arab and a Jewish state (as was eventually adopted in the partition plan).[89] Schaefer consistently tracked the question of the protection of the Holy Places, an issue central to both the Vatican and American Catholic interests. She expressed concern in the early stages of the UNSCOP meetings that Christian rights in the Holy Land were not a priority to delegates, citing the refusal of the committee to grant a hearing to the New York–based CNEWA, which sought to speak "in the interests of universal Christendom in the Holy Places."[90]

During the April 1947 meetings that led to the creation of UNSCOP, Schaefer, while reporting that the Christian stake in Palestine "did not receive much formal discussion," was encouraged by a draft resolution passed by El Salvador recommending that careful consideration be given to "the interests of the Christian world in the Holy Land and of the Christian population of Palestine."[91] The following day, the Brazilian delegation, along with a number of smaller South American states, endorsed the "religious interests" clause, evidence that the question of the Holy Places and the plight of Arab Christian refugees was gaining traction. The inclusion of the clause was eventually passed by a vote of 27 in favor, 9 opposed, and 16 abstaining, with the Soviet Union, which had been steadfastly opposed to its inclusion, representing the most notable of opposing states. In late April, Schaefer raised the issue of the Christian stake in Palestine directly to Warren Austin, the American ambassador to the UN, who assured her that concern for Christian rights in the territory would receive the full consideration of UNSCOP delegates.[92]

It was at this point, in the spring of 1947, that Schaefer's office began to more actively press the Catholic case at the UN. In consultation with Schaefer, who provided copious notes from her discussions with the various delegations, the NCWC formulated a detailed position paper on Roman Catholic demands for the future of Palestine. In May, Schaefer forwarded copies of the NCWC's "Resolution on the Holy Places" to both Austin and Chester Williams, public liaison of the American delegation to the UN, which stated that "all our sanctuaries will be respected and continuously and unconditionally accessible, and that the Christian minority will actually enjoy not merely that vague, frequently distorted and facetiously neutralized right of freedom of religion, but also freedom of religious assemblage, freedom of religious organization in conducting schools, orphanages, hospitals, and other institutions of welfare and mercy and freedom from civil, social and economic discrimination."[93] The statement was clearly centered on the notion of prescribed rights for Catholics in the territory, both for displaced Catholic refugees and for the institutional church itself. Presented six months before the adoption of the partition plan, it appeared to anticipate the increasing inevitability of a Jewish and an Arab state in Palestine, and consequently sought to carve out a Catholic sphere of legal and social jurisdiction in the territory.

In the same month, Schaefer presented a lengthier NCWC position paper on the future of the territory to UNSCOP. Penned by James Griffiths, who had been appointed by Spellman as chancellor of the Military Ordinariate in 1943, the statement represented as comprehensive an American Catholic position on the future of Palestine as had yet appeared.[94] It argued, chiefly, that the Palestinian problem was "not merely bipartite, but tripartite," and that Christian rights had for too long been ignored in the struggle between Jews and Arabs for control of the territory.[95] It emphasized that for the world's 700 million Christians, the territory was sacred, representing "the cradle of their religion." The document outlined the historical legitimacy of Christian claims to the territory and rejected suggestions that they be relocated to neighboring Christian states, such as Lebanon. "The Christians of Palestine are not new arrivals," it declared. "They have been there for nearly twenty centuries. They are rooted in the subsoil of their Holy Land. They have suffered every type of totalitarian persecution and countless thousands have shed their blood precisely because they would not disavow the principles of the Master whose land was their land. The Christian minority has been reluctantly tolerated, civically ostracized and economically pauperized because they have clung to the teachings of Christ in the very footsteps of Christ."[96] It was a bold statement that underscored both the historical and theological stake of Christianity in the territory and cautioned delegates not to frame the issue as a dispute between only Jews and Muslims. The document continued to endorse the British White Paper of 1939, which advocated an international trusteeship for the territory, while permitting the complete internationalization of Jerusalem and its environs as the minimally acceptable solution to the Roman Catholic Church. Finally, the statement raised the Bolshevik specter, tying Roman Catholic concerns for the future of Palestine to wider Cold War objectives. In insinuating that Moscow had already "infiltrated" the territory through the state-controlled Russian Orthodox Church, it argued that the protection of Christian (and specifically Roman Catholic) rights was imperative to checking the spread of communism in the region, a notion clearly intended to catch the attention of the American delegation.[97] The statement was disseminated by Schaefer during the UNSCOP special committee meetings, and it received wide coverage in the Catholic press, apprising American Catholics of the church's detailed position on the Holy Land.[98]

The activism of American Zionist observer groups at the UN was not unknown to Schaefer, and this activity provided additional impetus to her lobbying efforts. The importance Schaefer placed upon disseminating and publicizing the American Catholic viewpoint was lauded by Karol Krczmery, a Catholic and member of the Czechoslovakian delegation, who assured her that the influence of observer organizations such as the NCWC and the CAIP was significant, and that Jewish observer organizations at the UN, including the Jewish Agency for Palestine (which included powerful American Zionist leaders such as Nahum Goldmann and Rabbi Abba Hillel Silver), the American Jewish Committee (AJC), and the World Jewish Congress, were "operating like mad" with UNSCOP delegates.[99] Along with advocating Catholic positions, Schaefer's office also tracked the positions of the various international Jewish and Zionist observer groups at the UN, which, in general, favored the partition plan and accepted the internationalization of Jerusalem as a necessary concession in gaining a sovereign Jewish state. This also included, however, a number of non-Zionist Jewish groups, which often worked at cross-purposes with mainstream Zionist organizations, and emphasized the need for a strengthened international Jewish consciousness and greater protections under international law, but which did not advocate for a political and juridical state in Palestine. In May, Schaefer forwarded the policy of one such UN-accredited group, the Agudas Israel World Organization, back to the NCWC for the use of the bishops and the press office.[100] In May and June, the diocesan press disseminated the program of Augudas Israel in a range of papers, underscoring the idea that Jews were not unanimously in support of the Zionist program.

By the fall of 1947, Schaefer had developed a significant list of contacts within the various delegation and committees to the UN. Among American delegates, this included Warren Austin, Chester Williams, and later Secretary of State George Marshall, who confided to Schaefer in October that Zionist groups were disappointed that the United States was not doing enough in "getting the votes out" for the partition plan, an implicit suggestion that Catholic pressure was having an effect at the world body.[101] Schaefer also maintained contacts with members of delegations sympathetic to Roman Catholic concerns on Palestine, which often included Catholic-majority and Arab states. These delegates, which comprised numerous chiefs of missions, included Mahmoud Pasha of Egypt, Asaf Ali (India's first ambassador to the United States), Dr Fadhel Jamali (Iraqi foreign minister and future prime minister), and Dr Ramon Muniz of Brazil. Schaefer's closest contact at the UN between 1947 and the early 1950s, however, was the head of the Lebanese delegation, Dr Charles Habib Malik (whom Schaefer described as an "intensely sincere Christian"), who consistently pressed positions amenable to Roman Catholic interests in Palestine, and who regularly apprised Schaefer of committee-level progress, and setbacks, on the Palestine question.[102] Malik, an active contributor to the aforementioned Arab League information bureau in New York, would become a key ally of the NCWC and Schaefer's office as the UN debate on fate of Jerusalem wore on in the later 1940s. His own reputation undoubtedly lent additional credence to Roman Catholic claims at the UN. A Greek Orthodox Arab, Malik had been raised in a cosmopolitan Beirut, where he was exposed to Islamic, Christian, Arab, and Western influences. A graduate of Harvard and a student of philosophers Alfred North Whitehead and Martin Heidegger (on whom Malik wrote his doctoral dissertation), he served as the Lebanese ambassador to the United States and the UN from 1945 to 1948. His fluency in Arabic, French, German, and English only enhanced his repute among delegates. As a rapporteur for the Commission on Human Rights, he was instrumental in the drafting and adoption of the Universal Declaration of Human Rights in 1948.[103] In the same year, he was named president of the UN's Economic and Social Council, underscoring the influence and clout that he wielded at the world body.

Schaefer had less success in collaborating with the Protestant churches. Though both American Catholic and Protestant groups were present at the UN in observer roles, evidence suggests little coherence and cooperation between them, particularly on the question of Palestine. This was despite the fact that both Catholic and Protestant groups shared similar concerns for the future of Palestine, particularly in regard to the protection of the Holy Places.[104] Though some evangelical churches, particularly in the United States, had begun to see connections between a Jewish state and their own eschatology, most mainline Protestant churches favored neither Arab nor Jewish control over Palestine, but rather an international trusteeship for the territory administered by the UN, much in line with the Vatican's own policy.[105] This sentiment was expressed by the Reverend William Clark-Kerr, moderator of the Jerusalem Presbytery of the Church of Scotland, in July 1947. As one of the first Christian leaders to testify before UNSCOP on the issue of religious freedoms in Palestine, he declared that, "to the Western Christian mind, this whole country is holy," suggesting that plans to protect only Christian heritage sights and their immediate surroundings were futile and ill-advised.[106] Clark-Kerr's notion was seconded by a majority of Protestant leaders on both sides of the Atlantic, including Cyril Forster Garbett, Anglican archbishop of York, who declared in a radio address early in 1948 that "no one who has personal knowledge of Jerusalem believes that it is practical to divide it in this way," and warned that any such attempt "would lead to endless trouble and bloodshed."[107]

In the same address, Garbett urged American Christians to "do all they [could] for the protection of their fellow Christians in Palestine from persecution, and of the Holy Places from desecration." He asked them, in addition, "to use their great influence to save Palestine from lapsing into anarchy."[108] Despite his sentiment, Catholic-Protestant joint action on the question of Palestine was not forthcoming. Schaefer alluded to this early in 1948 when she revealed that relations with Protestant observer groups at the UN "were friendly and cooperative when possible," but that in some cases, "it had been impossible to enlist active cooperation."[109] This reticence to collaborate, to be sure, emanated from both sides. The Vatican had already waged a campaign against the influence of the Protestant churches in Italy before the Second World War, a struggle still fresh in the minds of curial officials.[110] Added to this were concerns about spheres of authority between Christian denominations once the *corpus separatum* was implemented, with some Protestant churches undoubtedly fearing the Vatican's dominance of an internationalized city. As such, collaboration at the UN was nominal.

Eliciting a joint Catholic-Protestant declaration on the Palestine issue was one such area of contention. In April 1947 Samuel McCrea Cavert, general secretary of the Churches of Christ in America, approached his counterpart in the NCWC, Howard Carroll, on the possibility of releasing a "parallel Catholic-Protestant statement on Palestine," emphasizing to Carroll that "it was not only Jews and Arabs that had a vital interest in Palestine."[111] At an NCWC board meeting later in the same month, the question of a joint statement was raised, and it was determined that no such parallel stand would be issued. It was also determined that any Catholic statement would be vetted by the apostolic delegate, Amleto Cicognani, "so that the Holy See ... would have the opportunity, if time permitted, to offer suggestions on the topic."[112] At the same meeting, the Holy See's 1922 aide-mémoire on Palestine was again circulated to attending bishops, emphasizing the degree to which Vatican reticence to the partition of Palestine continued to guide American Catholic advocacy on the issue. No Catholic response on the question of a parallel statement was issued until early May, when the Churches of Christ forwarded the NCWC a draft of their own statement, at which time Carroll informed the Protestant body that his organization had not yet formulated their own definitive statement.[113] Schaefer, as noted, presented the NCWC's position to UNSCOP just weeks later, evidence that the American bishops had, in fact, been preparing a policy statement for the UN. While Catholic and Protestant groups shared a cluster of concerns on the future of the Holy Land, the NCWC preferred to steer an independent course, advocating in parallel lines with Protestant organizations on certain issues, but rarely in close cooperation or conjunction.

Further complicating Catholic-Protestant cooperation on the Palestine question was the demand by certain Protestant groups for the recall of Myron Taylor from Rome on the grounds that his appointment violated the American constitutional separation of church and state. From the fall of 1946 forward, groups such as the Northern Baptist Convention agitated loudly for Taylor's removal, publicly urging Truman, a Baptist himself, to terminate the office of his personal representative to the Holy See. This was despite a general support for the Taylor mission in the secular press, including an editorial in *The New York Herald Tribune* by former Undersecretary of State Sumner Welles emphasizing the strategic advantages of Taylor's posting. The Taylor mission was also endorsed by several prominent Protestant leaders, who similarly noted the benefits of a Vatican link.[114] These included Harold Staasen, a Baptist and former governor of Minnesota, who expressed in May 1947 that, "in this postwar situation of world emergency and of conflicting ideological views, if President Truman wishes to have a representative at the Vatican … it is not the kind of situation either constructive or helpful for [Baptists] to protest."[115] He was seconded by Dr Everett Clinchy, founder and first president of the interfaith NCCJ, who stated that there was "nothing in the [Taylor] mission which need alarm any sincere Protestant."[116] Despite this, the chorus of anti-Taylor rhetoric among a number of mainstream Protestant groups continued to grow. Spellman, for his part, did little to assuage Catholic-Protestant tensions over the Taylor mission, attributing opposition to the mission to "the anti-Catholicism of un-hooded Klansmen sowing seeds of dissension and disunion."[117] The situation was strained further in August 1947 when a public exchange of letters between President Truman and Pope Pius XII, which emphasized the common stand of the United States and the Vatican in the post-war world order, also served to strengthen the president's commitment to Taylor's mission, further piquing Protestant groups committed to his recall.[118]

The representations of Schaefer's UN Office, then, were to remain distinctly Roman Catholic in character, advocating for positions that emanated specifically from the American bishops and, ultimately, the Vatican. Joint statements with other Christian denominations were to be avoided, a reflection of the Vatican's desire to claim its own independent stake in the future of Palestine. Schaefer's efforts over the spring and summer of 1947 did not go unrewarded. That the internationalization of Jerusalem and the creation of a wider *corpus separatum* was ensconced in the November partition plan could be credited, in part, to the persistent pressure of both Catholic and Arab states and observer organizations to the UN, exemplified by the NCWC's UN Office, which raised the issue clearly and consistently over these crucial months.

THE CARDINAL'S ENVOY: MONSIGNOR THOMAS MCMAHON AND THE CNEWA

The NCWC's UN Office was supported on the Palestine question by the New York–based and Vatican-funded Catholic Near East Welfare Association. Founded in 1926 by Pope Pius XI, and headed from its inception by American churchmen, the CNEWA's original mandate was to ensure the protection of the Roman Catholic Church in the Soviet Union in the aftermath of the Bolshevik Revolution of 1917. The provision of aid to famine-stricken Soviet citizens was intended to create a beachhead for future evangelization, as well as to create a functioning diplomatic relationship with the Soviet government.

By 1930, the Vatican had essentially abandoned any pretence of normalized relations with Moscow, particularly in light of Stalin's widescale program of state atheism, which saw the repression of Roman Catholic clergy and the confiscation and destruction of church property.

The CNEWA, however, was never formally suspended, and in 1931 it was placed under the permanent control of the American hierarchy. The archbishop of New York, resolved Pope Pius XI, would serve in perpetuity as the association's president. Through the 1930s, the CNEWA assumed a revived mandate to deal specifically with the Christian populations of Palestine and the wider Levant. Francis Spellman, who as archbishop of New York also assumed the presidency of the CNEWA, took a keen interest in the advocacy of the association, particularly as it pertained to Palestine. In June 1943 he named thirty-three-year-old Monsignor Thomas McMahon, a priest in the New York Archdiocese, as the association's assistant national secretary, a position he would hold until 1955. Upon his appointment, McMahon had been professor of church history at St Joseph's Seminary in Yonkers, having recently completed a doctoral degree at Fordham University.[119] Though he had served, in 1935, as a secretary at the Sacred Congregation for the Oriental Churches in Rome (the Vatican congregation that controlled the CNEWA), his selection was unexpected, given his age and the gravity of such a posting. His fervor, however, was not unknown in Vatican circles. Cardinal Eugène Tisserant, his superior in Rome, later described him as being "literally on fire for the cause of Christ," an effervescence that would, at times, hamper his diplomatic efforts. His appointment as master of ceremonies to Spellman, also in June 1943, further indicated the close working relationship between the young prelate and the most powerful figure in American Catholicism.[120] The appointment would move McMahon from the obscurity of the seminary to the head of an association that wielded significant diplomatic and financial clout, and with a mandate to defend Roman Catholic interests in Palestine. In short order, McMahon would become the leading advocate, both for the American hierarchy and for the international church, on the question of Palestine. Under his leadership, the CNEWA would play a crucial role in the Vatican's attempts to steer American and UN policy toward lines amenable to the church. In the immediate postwar period, this of course meant an international trusteeship for Palestine, which both the Vatican and American Catholic leaders considered optimal. McMahon had proposed trusteeship as early as 1945, when in the Catholic journal *The Sign* he advocated for the internationalization of the whole territory, citing the example of Trieste (which would be internationalized in February 1947). "No partition of the Holy Land can satisfy us," he explained, "because some part of it would thereby be without Christ."[121]

McMahon's rise coincided with a period in which the Vatican's position on Palestine appeared to be evolving. By the late winter of 1947 the Vatican and American Catholic leaders, for a number of aforementioned factors (including a growing international consensus on the partition plan and the surging support for Zionism in the United States), had come to regard the partition of Palestine as a fait accompli, and had turned their attention to ensuring the internationalization of Jerusalem as a means of preserving a base for Roman Catholic influence in the region and protecting the rights of Palestinian Catholics, the "living stones" of the territory. Spellman apprised the State Department of the Vatican's revised objectives during a meeting with the American ambassador to Iraq, George Wadsworth, at which he expressed continued dismay with the partition plan but signaled that the Vatican would acquiesce if the sanctity of Jerusalem and the Holy Places and protection of the Roman Catholic minority in Palestine could be guaranteed. The archbishop placed particular emphasis on the plight of the Arab Catholic minority, and suggested a "carefully conceived, detailed regime of guarantees for the Holy Places *and* for the Christian minorities ... the latter to be such as might serve as a model, accepted by the Arab and all other Eastern states, for the treatment of their religious minorities."[122] In essence, the guarantees sought by Spellman for the extraterritoriality of the sacred sites (which were not limited to Jerusalem) was a return to the "spheres of influence" plan Eugenio Pacelli had presented to Nahum Sokolow in 1917. Guarantees for the Catholic minority in the territory, while not a new concern, would emerge with more urgency from this point forward. The genuine internationalization of Jerusalem and its environs, as well as UN safeguards for the "living stones" of the faith in the territory guaranteeing their security, rights, and autonomy, would now constitute the twin pillars of Vatican policy on Palestine.

The CNEWA, like the NCWC's UN Office, attempted to disseminate this Roman Catholic vision for the future of Palestine directly to the UN, commencing with UNSCOP in the spring and summer of 1947. As an observer group at the UN, however, the CNEWA, like its sister organization, was not permitted to present petitions or testimonials directly to UNSCOP, a circumstance both Spellman and McMahon regarded as a threat to Catholic interests. In late February McMahon, at the behest of Spellman, was granted a meeting with Senator Warren Austin, head of the American delegation to the UN, and

Ambassador Wadsworth.[123] During the hour-long visit, McMahon detailed the Vatican's territorial demands, citing the internationalization of Jerusalem and its environs as a minimum starting point. McMahon, as he had in his 1945 *Sign* article, used the example of Trieste as a model of functional internationalization, and suggested a similar scheme be employed at the UN for Jerusalem. This suggestion, he reported optimistically to Spellman, "awakened a responsive chord in the Senator."[124] Austin suggested that an autonomous zone for southern Palestine, much in line with Vatican policy, would be acceptable to Britain as well, which "would submit to any plan that guarded the imperial lifeline and spared British blood," and further indicated that partition, with an internationalized zone, would also be acceptable to the Arabs, who "would not easily submit to an international trusteeship under UN control."[125]

Spellman, meanwhile, took full advantage of a meeting with the UN's Political and Security Committee in early May to emphasize the need for observer groups such as the CNEWA to be heard in committees and subcommittees, particularly on issues as crucial as the future of Palestine. During this meeting, Spellman presented the CNEWA's formal petition, penned by McMahon, which emphasized the necessity for a Christian, and specifically Roman Catholic, voice at the UNSCOP hearings. The statement refuted suggestions that the CNEWA did not directly represent the Christians of Palestine (a charge made by certain UNSCOP delegates who refuted the need to consider petitions and testimonies from faith organizations), emphasizing both the universality of the CNEWA's voice, as well as the international nature of the Palestine question itself. "It is our considered opinion that the CNEWA," it stated, "an international body, qualifies as an organizational representative of a considerable portion of the population of Palestine, since it officially represents the Roman Catholic population of Palestine."[126]

McMahon's petition also drew attention to the 1946 report of the AAIC, which maintained that no solution to the Palestine problem could be found without addressing its "religious phase." The Catholic stake in the territory, McMahon insisted, had to be addressed. In emphasizing the international nature of the problem, and the legitimacy of the CNEWA's right to present its views, the statement continued that

> The character of Palestine sets it in a unique class, totally different from all other nations. The interests of universal Christendom in the Holy Land transcend the political and national interests of the minority Christian population of Palestine. Although there may be included in

> the personnel of the Arab Higher Committee one or two spokesmen for the Christian minority, nevertheless the Committee itself, by reason of its tradition, its leadership, its overwhelming Moslem majority and by the fact of its purpose to present the case for a predominantly Arab Moslem population of one million, cannot reasonably be charged with the task or expected to represent adequately the interests of universal Christendom in the Holy Land.[127]

The statement clearly indicated the Vatican's skepticism of the AHC's capacity and inclination to advocate for the Arab Catholic minority. It further suggested that not only would the CNEWA advocate for the rights of Catholics in Palestine, but that it would represent "the interests of universal Christendom there," clearly inferring that Spellman's organization represented the desires of the Vatican and the international church on the question of Palestine. Despite stiff opposition to the consideration of religious factors in debating the future of Palestine, including that of Soviet delegate Andrei Gromyko, who considered religious concerns "superfluous detail," the "religious clause" was accepted by UNSCOP after a heated two-hour debate on 22 May 1947.[128]

Having won the right to submit its views to UNSCOP, the CNEWA presented a report to the committee on 5 June 1947.[129] It stressed that the Roman Catholic Church did not favor or endorse any particular political arrangement for Palestine so long as the sanctity and the international status of Jerusalem and the Holy Places were preserved and protections guaranteed for the territory's Catholic population. This Vatican impartiality signaled a concession from its early postwar desire for an international trusteeship for the whole of Palestine, in that it now assented to the creation of Jewish and Arab states. As McMahon reminded UNSCOP, this impartiality did not mean indifference, and any solution "would be unjust if it does not take formal cognizance of the Christian stake in Palestine, or in the fact that in this Holy Land of millions of Christians throughout the world, there still dwell thousands of indigenous Christians, with a centuries old right to be protected in any regime set up around them." The statement echoed Pius XII's August 1946 address to a delegation of the AHC in Rome, where the pope informed his guests that while his church did not favor either Jewish or Arab control of Palestine, and "had always observed this attitude of perfect impartiality, even in the most diverse circumstances," no solution that did not protect Christian populations could be acceptable.[130] While the pope's 1946 stance continued to endorse trusteeship, the CNEWA's 1947 representation to the UN revealed the church's moderated demands, accepting the partition plan if the creation of a *corpus separatum* and juridical protections for Roman Catholics in Palestine and the wider region could be guaranteed. As it was the CNEWA that officially represented Catholic institutions and populations in the Middle East, the 1947 statement can be read as a change in the policy of the Vatican itself. Though Gasparri's aide-mémoire of 1922 was still circulated among Catholic officials as a reminder of the Vatican's reticence toward partition, it had definitely been superseded by the circumscribed demands presented by McMahon. This was evidence, no doubt, of papal pragmatism on the question of Palestine, and was a policy designed to salvage core, nonnegotiable rights in the territory while maintaining amicable relations with Washington.

The statement underscored Roman Catholicism's ancient stake in the territory, highlighting twenty centuries of unbroken presence in Palestine. "The concern of Christians for the Holy Places is no recent development in world affairs," McMahon reminded the committee. "The Church of Jerusalem is the first Church of Christianity," and Christians had their "roots deep in the subsoil" of Palestine. The legal presence of the Catholic Church in Palestine, it continued, referring to the establishment of the Franciscan Custody in 1217, had been "uncontrovertibly and juridically established since the thirteenth century."[131] It further asserted that, "although persecuted and, indeed, decimated, [Roman Catholics] have never left or given up."[132] It specifically refuted the claims of the ESCO Foundation for Palestine, which maintained in a 1946 publication that Christianity "was not an indigenous force in Palestine, although it [was] based on the life and teachings of Jesus. As an organized religion it is the creation of Rome and always represented in the East the introduction of a foreign civilization."[133] McMahon termed this "spiritual jingoism and an intolerant indictment of Roman Catholics throughout the entire world." In evoking the Crusader imagery that the Catholic press had so prominently employed in its anti-Zionist editorials, McMahon spoke to the long-standing Roman Catholic struggle for the territory. "If only for these centuries of heroism, sacrifice and blood-letting," he apprised UNSCOP delegates, "Christendom can hardly be expected to stand by silently and be ignored, as your estimable Committee seeks an answer to the riddle of Palestine."[134]

The statement, however, did not dwell on historical precedent, but rather outlined the contemporary Roman Catholic stake in the territory, including the extensive charitable and educational activities administered by the Latin Patriarchate of Jerusalem (the official representation of the Holy See in Palestine). This network included over two hundred churches and religious houses, one hundred and thirty schools (which educated male and female students in almost equal numbers), and thirty charitable institutions, all of which, the statement continued, contributed to the stability and prosperity of both Roman Catholics and the wider community. McMahon, therefore, sought tangible guarantees for Roman Catholics and their institutions, which included "a freedom of religious organization and development, unimpaired by confiscatory taxation or disabling legislation, in building and conducting churches, schools, orphanages, hospitals and similar institutions of welfare and mercy." In essence, McMahon demanded protection for the institutional livelihood of the church in Palestine, regardless of the form of the regime decided upon by UNSCOP. His objective reflected that emanating from the Vatican Secretariat itself, where safeguarding Roman Catholic interests through legal guarantees and the internationalization of Jerusalem had supplanted the grander desire of establishing a UN trusteeship for the entire territory.

That it was the CNEWA that spoke at the UN for Vatican interests in Palestine, and not the Latin Patriarchate in Jerusalem (represented, at that time, by Monsignor Luigi Barlassina), was made clear in the conclusion of McMahon's statement. "This Association," he noted, "under the presidency of His Eminence, Francis Cardinal Spellman of New York, is the sole official mission and relief agency of the Sacred Oriental Congregation in Rome. This Congregation, of which Pope Pius XII is direct superior … has jurisdiction over all the above-mentioned activities of the Catholic Church in Palestine. Thus, our Association has an international scope and is expected to supply not only financial aid but also intellectual support, wherever the interests in the Holy Land are at stake."[135] The statement culminated with a veiled warning that an infringement of the freedoms of Palestinian Roman Catholics, whose claims were as ancient as any of their compatriots, would be considered a "crime" against not only the indigenous Catholic community, but against the international Roman Catholic Church. "Indeed, because Palestine is the Holy Land for millions of Christians all over the world," it warned, "this gigantic injustice would rightfully be resented by them and by all men of good will."[136]

The submission of the CNEWA statement did not go unnoticed in UN circles. In short order, McMahon received the assurances of both Arab and Jewish leaders that Roman Catholic rights would be protected in a partitioned Palestine. On 16 June 1947, a week after issuing the statement, McMahon received a cable from Issa Nakleh, the New York representative of the Arab Higher Committee for Palestine, who assured him that UNSCOP "gave all assurances and guarantees the rights of Christians and access to the Holy

Places."[137] Nakleh, a Jerusalemite, Christian, and ardent anti-Zionist, reminded McMahon that the AHC had pledged guarantees for Christian rights and for access to the Holy Places in a memorandum submitted to the League of Nations in 1937, inferring that the Arab states could be relied upon as amicable partners in a partitioned Palestine. On 1 July 1947 this was followed by a personal visit from Nakleh, during which he again assured McMahon that the AHC was committed to protecting Christian rights in the territory.[138] Nakleh suggested, moreover, that Arabs and Catholics shared a common cause and a common foe in the territory, and that the Roman Catholic Church should "more openly come out against the Jews and proclaim itself for the Arabs."[139] McMahon offered no such assurances, emphasizing the purely apolitical nature of papal demands in Palestine, and didn't hesitate to express his concerns on the "disabilities under which Christians labour in the countries of the Arab league" – evidence of the Vatican's enduring skepticism of Arab nationalism.[140] In closing, he informed Nakleh that the CNEWA would "stand by [its] appeal to the United Nations until its committee on Palestine submits its report."[141]

In the autumn of 1947, McMahon received similar assurances from two prominent Zionists, Rabbi Wolf Gold of the Jewish Agency for Palestine (and future signatory of the Israeli Declaration of Independence) and Rabbi Bernard Lander, noted sociologist and future adviser to the Kennedy and Johnson administrations. In a visit to the CNEWA offices, they thanked the Catholic Church for its aid to Jews during the darkest days of the war and pledged unconditional Jewish support for Christian rights in a partitioned Palestine. "In a Jewish state," Gold confided to McMahon, Roman Catholics could expect "far greater security than they could ever expect from the Arabs."[142] McMahon's guests, however, expressed the "impression that Catholics [in the United States] were opposed to the creation of a Jewish state," and asked if "the powerful Catholic Church in America could help the cause in an unofficial way by letting leaders, especially in government, know her sympathy with the majority report."[143] McMahon's response revealed the apprehension that the church continued to harbor toward Zionism, and he challenged the rabbis to provide evidence of official Catholic reticence to the creation of a Jewish state, asking his guests to apprise him of "any Catholic organ" that might prove that "the Church was on either side of the present Arab-Jewish conflict."[144] The meeting affirmed that neither Jewish nor Arab nationalism would be embraced by the Vatican, and that only UN-brokered guarantees for the territory would be acceptable to Rome and the international church.

Such guarantees would be ensconced in the November 1947 partition plan (Resolution 181), which, in creating separate Israeli and Palestinian states, also established Jerusalem and its environs as a *corpus separatum*, a genuinely international regime to be administered by the UN. The area was to encompass not only Jerusalem but its surrounding hinterland, including southern Bethlehem and Nazareth, and other regions of spiritual and historical importance to the Roman Catholic Church. Other provisions, such as freedoms guaranteed to charitable and educational institutions, pledges not to tax (in posterity) or deny access to any churches or houses of worship, and freedoms of the press and of conscience, also appeared to appease Roman Catholic concerns.[145] The plan also established that a UN-appointed governor would be established for Jerusalem, who would be chosen "without regard to nationality" but who would "not be a citizen of either state in Palestine," a provision that appeared to protect the genuinely international character of the city.

Evidence does suggest that Vatican pressure through 1947, and particularly American Catholic advocacy, was a factor in securing these ends. American officials, on their part, seemed particularly reticent to raise the ire of the Christian churches. State Department officials Gordon Merriam (head of the Near East desk) and Fraser Wilkins (head of the Palestine desk) opposed entreaties to limit the internationalization of Jerusalem to the Old City, believing that many sites sacred to Christians fell outside this area. This led them to conclude that "the majority of Christian establishments would fall within the area of either Jewish or Arab states. Considerable Christian opposition to such a move could be expected."[146] Jewish Agency officials similarly revealed the significance of Vatican advocacy at the UN. Eliahu Elath, Israel's first ambassador to Washington and a leading participant in the discussions surrounding adoption of the partition plan, reflected on the influence of the Roman Catholic pressure at Lake Success, particularly on the question of Jerusalem. "The [Catholic] states were clearly determined to prevent the Jews or the Moslems from establishing their sovereignty over the city and to avoid this by according a special status to Jerusalem under the auspices of the UN," Elath noted. "Definition of the function of the Governor made it almost inevitable that a citizen of a *Christian* state would be appointed to this office, and this would afford him considerable leverage to turn Jerusalem into an independent political entity."[147]

Moshe Sharett, then head of the Political Department of the Jewish Agency, elaborated further on the specific influence of the Vatican and the Roman

Catholic lobby in securing a *corpus separatum*. "It became evident," the future Israeli prime minster wrote, "that the requisite majority for the Partition Plan could not be mustered if the internationalization of the Holy City was omitted from it … The Vatican regarded the latter measure as [one that would] … vest the Catholic Church with predominant influence … [thus] warranting acquiescence in the elevation of the Jewish people to the level of sovereign statehood."[148]

That the internationalization of Jerusalem and its environs was ensconced by UNSCOP's final resolution of November 1947, then, could only be considered a victory for the Vatican and for the American Catholic lobby at the UN. While acquiescing to the partition plan, the church had at least appeared to have preserved a base for continued influence in the region, free from the interference of a sovereign power, and had secured the rights of the Catholic minority and Catholic institutions throughout the territory. Just weeks before the official announcement of the partition plan, McMahon lauded American Catholic efforts to secure an internationalized zone for Jerusalem, reporting to Spellman that CNEWA efforts had "borne much fruit" and had "forced both Arab and Jewish leaders to approach us, and it has influenced [UNSCOP] in making its report."[149] Indeed, the advocacy of the NCWC's UN Office and the CNEWA represented the leading edge of the Roman Catholic lobby on the shape of postwar Palestine. These hard-won concessions, however, were about to be challenged by the brutal realities of implementing the partition plan amid the outbreak of war between Israel and the Arab League in May 1948.

CHAPTER 5

The Holy City Between Rome, Washington, and Tel Aviv

Though the Vatican and American Catholics considered the 1947 UN partition plan a victory insofar as it preserved Jerusalem and the Holy Places as an international *corpus separatum*, the outbreak of violence immediately following its ratification confirmed the fears long held in Catholic circles: namely, that newly formed Jewish and Arab states would seize through force what they could not obtain by international consensus. The instability in Palestine in early 1948, in fact, caused the Vatican to reconsider its very support for the partition plan. The nascent State of Israel challenged the UN's internationalization of Jerusalem, favoring a modified compact for the city that would see only the protection of specific sacred sites, a position buttressed by Israeli military victories. By December 1948, the increasingly intractable problem was referred to a UN body, the Palestine Conciliation Commission (PCC), which was tasked with devising a solution to the Jerusalem question. Throughout 1949, American Catholics remained at the forefront of the Vatican's efforts to steer the PCC, the American delegation at the UN, and President Harry Truman toward a Palestine solution that preserved the *corpus separatum* as it had been conceived in the 1947 partition plan. The American Catholic lobby, however, was confronted with a powerful American Zionist one comprised of Jewish and various Protestants groups sympathetic to Zionism and determined to secure a Jewish Jerusalem. That increasing numbers of American senators and congressmen, including President Truman himself, favored a modified agreement on Jerusalem (one unsatisfactory to the Vatican) only complicated American Catholic efforts. The survival of the *corpus separatum* after the December 1949 vote on the PCC proposal, following a frenetic year of conflict, diplomacy, and a spiraling refugee crisis, once again appeared to confirm the leadership of the American Catholic Church, and its various organs, in securing an outcome long sought by the Vatican.

DIES FATALIS: CATHOLICS AND THE BIRTH OF THE STATE OF ISRAEL

Despite deep and genuine cooperation on the challenge of communism and Soviet containment, Pope Pius XII and Washington drifted apart on the question of Palestine from the early winter of 1948 on. The Vatican continued to lend tentative support to UN Resolution 181 on the strict condition that Jerusalem and its environs be protected by an international mandate, preserving a crucial and symbolic base for Roman Catholic influence in the region and beyond. The outbreak of violence almost immediately following the December ratification of the partition plan, however, tested the Vatican's tentative support, confirming fears that the plan only facilitated open competition between Jewish and Arab nationalism, producing bloodshed and disorder. In the months that followed, tensions and outbreaks of violence between Jews and Arabs indeed intensified, compounded by the Jewish underground's continuing struggle against the British presence in the territory. The April 1948 capture of the Arab town of Deir Yassin by the Irgun, which resulted in the deaths of more than one hundred villagers, including women and children, followed by an Arab attack on a Jewish medical column just days later, resulting in the deaths of doctors, nurses, and patients, epitomized the vitriolic atmosphere in the territory on the very eve of Jewish statehood.

The escalation of violence caused the Vatican to question whether the functional internationalization of Jerusalem and its environs could be achieved. The establishment of a *corpus separatum*, and the guarantee of rights for Roman Catholic institutions and faithful, had, after all, constituted the very basis of Vatican support for partition. Added to this were Vatican fears that instability in the territory would lead to the spread of communism in Palestine and the wider area. The Holy See's diminishing support for partition was revealed to Myron Taylor's office in February 1948 by Domenico Tardini, Pope Pius XII's acting secretary of state. In a "brutally frank" discussion with Taylor's assistant, Graham Parsons, Tardini spoke of the "mistakes of the United States now replacing the mistakes of Britain [in Palestine]," suggesting that partition, as conceived in the UN plan, far from producing a lasting peace in the territory, would in fact bring about a chaotic situation in which only Moscow could profit.[1] In linking Zionism and Bolshevism, a connection long since posited by Vatican officials, he apprised Parsons of the observations of Monsignor Valerio Valeri, former apostolic delegate to Egypt, Palestine, and Cyprus, who had warned "twenty years ago [of] the existence of flourishing communist cells in Tel Aviv."[2]

Similar sentiments were echoed later in the same month by Monsignor Gustavo Testa, the recently appointed apostolic delegate to Palestine and Jerusalem.[3] The posting replaced the former nunciature in Egypt, Palestine, Jordan, and Cyprus, creating a structure where Egypt, Palestine, and Jordan received separate nuncios, reflective of the Holy See's desire to have a dedicated ambassador committed to the rapidly evolving situation in Palestine.[4] During a lengthy conversation with Parsons in late February, Testa reiterated Tardini's apprehensions on the partition plan, expressing frustration that the American government, and leading papers such as *The New York Times*, couldn't see that "only Russia would benefit from carrying through the tragedy of partition."[5] He continued that the full implementation of the partition plan would lead to deepening violence, and would require an occupying force of at least 100,000 troops to maintain order. Again linking partition to the threat of communist infiltration, Testa warned of Washington's willingness "to oppose Russia at the Dardanelles and yet promote conditions [in Palestine] which will place her so much nearer to important objectives."[6] "Once astride in the eastern Mediterranean," he warned, "Russia will not leave."

The conversation, in fact, hinted at a formal reversal of Vatican policy. Testa suggested a reconsideration of partition by the UN General Assembly as the only viable solution, detailing to Parsons his idea of a federated state with Swiss-style cantonal governments, akin to the proposal put forward by the Colombian delegation to the UN, which was already urging the General Assembly to repeal the partition plan. Throughout the conversation, Parsons reminded Testa of the growing public support for political Zionism in the United States, summarizing for him the points contained in a confidential January 1948 survey of American public opinion indicating that a full two-thirds of the American public now favored the partition plan, and alluding to the difficulties, both domestic and international, of an American reversal on the plan.[7] It was a reminder to the Vatican of the power of American domestic opinion on the question of Palestine. Parsons's conversations with these leading Vatican figures, in sum, confirmed that Washington and Rome were indeed drifting apart on Palestine, even if the Vatican maintained a stoic public silence on the issue. In his report to US Secretary of State George Marshall, Parsons noted the similarities between Testa's and Tardini's positions, observing that "however much they represented [Testa's] personal views, they also represented the official Vatican viewpoint."[8]

The Vatican's disenchantment with partition did not take long to register with a number of Latin American delegations at the UN, as dissatisfaction with the plan in the wider Roman Catholic firmament became quickly evident. In February 1948 the Colombian delegation, as noted, officially submitted a motion to reconsider the partition plan, on the grounds that subsequent strife had proven its futility. On 27 February 1948, a day after meeting with Testa, Parsons received Mauricio Nabuco, the Brazilian ambassador to the Holy See, who admitted that, should the Colombian resolution pass, and Resolution 181 were resubmitted to a vote, Brazil would reverse its position and vote against partition.[9] He continued that Brazil's vote in favor of the earlier plan in November 1947 was a "mistake," and that although Brazil had supported it in solidarity with Washington, "the real act of friendship was not to vote with the United States in this instance." He informed Parsons that, should the partition plan be revisited, Brazil would carry other South American states in voting against it, providing the necessary majority. Nabuco coyly denied that the Vatican was instructing South American states on the matter but hinted at the quasi-theological wellspring of his position. "As a good Catholic," he exclaimed to Parsons, "[I adhere] to the biblical prophesy that the Jews will be dispersed and not return to the land of Palestine."[10]

Vatican and wider Roman Catholic skepticism of the partition plan was, in fact, shared by large segments of the State Department and the American delegation to the UN, including its head, Warren Austin. This apprehension was centered on the thesis that immediate partition would lead to widescale conflict, requiring a UN peacekeeping force that would bring Soviet troops into Palestine and endanger American interests. As Michael Cohen has noted, this wariness on the implementation of the partition plan extended to Truman himself, who fretted that the imminent creation of Jewish and Arab states might threaten Marshall Plan objectives in the wider region, and sought instead to delay it until regional stability could be assured.[11] This was despite the president's well-known affection for the Zionist cause, which recent scholarship has attributed to a variety of factors: the influence of Jewish political and industrial advisers, the successes of American Zionist lobby groups (particularly the American Christian Palestine Committee) in shaping American policy, the importance of courting the "Jewish vote" in the 1948 federal elections, and Truman's own Baptist millenarianism, which envisioned the return of the Jews to Palestine as a presage to a final golden age.[12]

This general consensus led to Austin's 19 March resolution, announced to the Security Council, to revise the American position on the partition plan in favor of an international trusteeship for the territory. Stating that partition "cannot be implemented by peaceful means," the United States now sought UN trusteeship as a means "to afford the Jews and Arabs of Palestine ... further opportunity to reach an agreement regarding the future government of that country." Though the Vatican applauded Austin's announcement, it generated considerable exasperation among American Zionist organizations, who had come to accept Truman's support of imminent Jewish statehood as a certainty. The president privately lamented that the American position was announced just a day after he had met with Chaim Weizmann, whom he assured of his steadfast support for partition. Regardless, Austin's speech failed to turn the tide against the general UN consensus on Resolution 181, as the clock set in November 1947 continued to tick toward partition. Truman, perhaps sensing the inevitably of the partition plan, remained committed to supporting Jewish statehood through the winter and spring of 1948, a position clearly abetted by the powerful American Zionist lobby.

The success of this lobby was bolstered by a widely circulated and read press, which galvanized Jewish support for American Zionist organizations.[13] This efficacy impressed upon Catholic editors the need to counter this with a specifically Catholic viewpoint, particularly as it appeared that Zionist sympathies had spread among the American public and policymaking establishment, extending to Truman himself. The survey of American public opinion that Parsons had discussed with Testa only confirmed its influence on the Palestine question. That 1948 was an election year made the issue all the more pressing, as the Catholic vote could be tied to a Palestine solution acceptable to the Vatican and American Catholics. The urgency of shaping public opinion in the United States was impressed upon the American church by the Vatican itself. On several occasions in early 1948 Giovanni Montini, the Vatican's pro-secretary of state (and the future Pope Paul VI), expressed hopes that American Catholics, given their institutional strength and political organization, might exercise their power to gain an acceptable resolution, and he implored the NCWC to raise the issue of Palestine clearly and consistently in order to shape Catholic opinion for the ongoing struggle for the territory.[14]

In short order, Catholic editorials in the United States began to reflect the Vatican's growing dissatisfaction with the partition plan. Though Catholic journals had issued a tentative endorsement of the plan late in 1947, subsequent violence had quashed any remaining optimism, sparking renewed calls for an international trusteeship for Palestine. *America*, one journal that had considered partition "the best of many unsatisfactory alternatives," denounced the plan from February 1948 onward, observing that the violence it had prophesied for months had indeed come to pass.[15] While American Zionist groups continued to advocate for the implementation of the partition plan at all costs, including the use of American troops to secure it, *America* warned of the security risks of armed American intervention. Highlighting the State Department's own reservations on the plan, the journal chastised the Zionists and the UN for rushing to support a solution that was "too much wishful thinking."[16] The journal also flayed the Truman administration for "acting against its better judgement" and, in an ironic allusion to the American Zionist lobby, "bending to the will of a strong domestic pressure."[17]

The diocesan press largely echoed *America*'s stern disapproval of the partition plan, characterizing it as an unprincipled and unworkable scheme, implemented mainly to pander to American Zionist demands. In the spring of 1948, Catholic papers gave wide circulation to a series of declarations by the Christian Union, a provisional association of Christian leaders in the Middle East who denounced the partition plan in the strongest terms.[18] Issuing their statements directly to national governments and to the UN, and through Catherine Schaefer's UN Office, the Christian Union expressed "deep sorrow and strong indignation at the lamentable situation in which the Holy Land, cradle of peace, has been placed as a direct result of the erroneous policy which has been imposed on the country and which has culminated in the partition plan."[19] In June, just weeks after the formal establishment of the Israeli state, *The Brooklyn Tablet* published a manifesto issued by the Christian Union excoriating "armed Jews" for causing damage to Christian churches and sites, particularly in Jerusalem. Hardly a neutral statement, it proclaimed that "the largest part of the shells falling on the Holy Sepulchre and on churches, convents and Christian institutions are of Jewish origin … The Arabs have stated they respected the Holy Places, the convents, and the Red Cross institutions. In fact they have respected them up to the present time."[20] Diocesan papers such as *The Brooklyn Tablet*, *The Boston Pilot*, and *The Michigan Catholic* gave wide circulation to Christian Union statements, despite the fact that the Vatican did not officially endorse the group, and disregarding that Israeli officials at the UN had accurately identified the Christian Union as "a group of Christian-Arab clergymen with predominantly Arab congregations which has completely identified itself with the Arab Higher Committee."[21] *The New York Times*, which also published the Christian Union's manifesto of 31 May 1948, juxtaposed the group's claims with reports that Jewish shrines had, in fact, suffered a majority of the damage, and that "only a couple of bullet holes" had pierced the dome of the Holy Sepulchre.[22] Verity on all sides, it appeared, was a casualty in the larger battle for public opinion.

These reports coincided with the emergence of a public Vatican stance on the question of Palestine, a development indicative of the pope's desire to air the Vatican's views to the world on the very eve of Jewish statehood. The encyclical *Auspicia quaedam*, issued on 1 May 1948, lamented the ongoing war in the territory, and called upon Catholics worldwide to pray for an end to the conflict. Though not offering specific policy prescriptions, the plain language of the encyclical was evidence that the pope now intended to rouse international Catholic opinion on Palestine. This followed with an allocution several weeks later to the College of Cardinals in Rome in which he issued a plea to Roman Catholics everywhere. "How could the Christian world look on unconcernedly," he exhorted, "or in fruitless indignation, as that sacred ground which everyone approached with reverence most profound to kiss it with warmest affection, was being trampled by troops of war and bombed from the air? Reduce the 'Great Sepulchre' of Christ to a mass of rubble? God grant that the danger of so terrible a scourge may be finally dispelled!"[23] Pius XII signaled the Vatican's increasing displeasure with the partition plan, calling the Palestine situation "a political problem which still awaits an adequate solution." The allocution, forwarded to the NCWC in June and printed widely in the diocesan press, amounted to another call to action, to both the American bishops and ordinary Catholics, to raise the issue of Palestine clearly and consistently.[24]

The apprehension felt by both the Vatican and American Catholics on the expiration of the British Mandate for Palestine, set for 15 May 1948, was expressed succinctly by John J. O'Rourke, SJ, the American director of the Pontifical Biblical Institute in Jerusalem, who described that date as the *dies fatalis*, (the fateful day). "What is coming next, God only knows," he expressed in a letter to John LaFarge, SJ, the editor of *America*.[25] He further observed that, given the sacred character of Jerusalem to Christians, Muslims, and Jews alike, the fate of Jerusalem was "not merely an international problem but a supranational question."[26] His sentiments were echoed by Cardinal Spellman just a week before the expiration of the Mandate when he asserted that "War must not bloody the soil nor desecrate the scene of the sacrifice of the Prince of Peace, for if men and nations who profess to believe in God defile His Holy Homeland, how can they condemn godless barbarism in others?"[27] The archbishop's words, carried in an *America* article, were a clear allusion to Truman's firm commitment to Jewish statehood, despite the risks, and to the Roman Catholic imperative to protect the holy sites of Palestine.

The establishment of the State of Israel on 14 May 1948, and Washington's immediate diplomatic recognition of it, drew a predictably terse response from a wide cross section of the American Catholic press. *The Catholic World*'s editorial for July, penned by Monsignor Thomas McMahon, now national secretary of the CNEWA, was particularly acerbic. McMahon criticized the "unseemly haste" with which the United States recognized the fledgling state, abandoning political precedent and acting with "a cold-blooded disregard of ethical principle" in establishing relations with Tel Aviv before the cessation of conflict.[28] He further drew parallels between American and Soviet statecraft, suggesting that Washington had abandoned its strategic neutrality in the region in hastily recognizing Israel. "What Stalin had done in Czechoslovakia we did in Palestine," he charged. "We had blamed him for interference in the internal affairs of another nation, but when our turn came for trickery, we proved ourselves quicker and slicker than the master criminal."[29] In concluding, McMahon charged that the "breakneck speed" with which Tel Aviv was recognized could be traced to Truman's courting of the Jewish vote in the November elections, and he expressed doubts that either Zionist organizations or the Truman administration, both of which purported to act in the interests of humanitarian concern, would extend the same treatment to other groups. "Will they love humanity in December, after the elections, as they did in May?" he asked acidly. "We shall see."[30] Though his words were meant to galvanize American Catholic opinion, they also hinted at a growing frustration with Truman, whose open support for Israel compounded the challenge of the American Catholic lobby.

Following the establishment of Israel, and the summer of bitter struggle between the new state and its Arab neighbors, who invaded almost immediately, the American Catholic press shone a bright light on the desecration of Roman Catholic property in the territory, often laying blame for these transgressions at the feet of the newly formed Israel Defense Forces (IDF).[31] A majority of these articles were penned by Anthony Bruya, the NCWC's Jerusalem correspondent, and were based on the Vatican-commissioned reports of Monsignor Antonio Vergani, the Latin patriarchal vicar of Galilee, whose office had extensively cataloged alleged Israeli abuses against Catholic property and populations throughout the territory.[32] Channeled to the diocesan press by the NCWC's press office, which often relied on Bruya's articles as a sole source from the region, the articles detailed a host of atrocities perpetrated by the IDF in and around Jerusalem, which included the destruction and looting of churches, convents, and monasteries, as well as the desecration of relics, religious artworks, vestments, and books.[33] In September, Bruya drew from Vergani's latest report, which, in detailing damage to the Terra Sancta Hospice in Haifa, reported the discovery of broken crucifixes, an overturned altar, torn missals, and a smashed tabernacle. In the same report, Vergani expressed shock at "acts of profanation in the chapel," where he "surprised soldiers of both sexes dancing to the tune of the harmonium." "We have seen mattresses in the main chapel," he added. "Jewish soldiers must have slept there" – allusions to scandal meant to catalyze Catholic opinion.[34] Bruya's articles also refuted Israeli claims that acts against Catholic properties were merely "isolated transgressions by irresponsible individuals" who had already been brought to justice, intending to highlight, through lurid reportage, widespread Israeli complicity in the ongoing delay to fully internationalize Jerusalem and its environs.[35] That the Vatican shared this view of Israeli complicity was made evident in September when Montini, in explaining to Taylor's office why the Vatican would not recognize Israel diplomatically, offered that the decision was, in part, based on the fact that "unwarranted attacks on Catholic institutions and members of religious orders by irresponsible Jewish elements have caused a painful impression."[36] "Arabs," he continued, "have not attacked or molested Catholics, and have generally shown consideration and tolerance." While he expressed that the Vatican did not hold the Israeli government responsible for ordering the attacks, he concluded that it did expect Tel Aviv to exercise greater control over the IDF and other Jewish factions.[37]

Concrete action complemented press coverage. Charges of Jewish complicity in the desecration of Catholic property and violence against Catholic religious in the territory were formalized late in August, when McMahon, acting as national secretary of the CNEWA, put forward a request to the UN that alleged mistreatment of Catholics by Jews in Palestine, and the IDF's transgressions, be formally investigated by the world body. In a letter to Trygve Lie, secretary-general of the UN, McMahon highlighted "documented accusations" against the IDF in Jerusalem, citing Vergani's reports and the numerous articles in the Catholic and secular press as proof of Israeli violations.[38] McMahon lamented the lack of progress on the internationalization of Jerusalem since the partition plan of November 1947, and cited "authoritative sources" on "the criminal acts of Jewish forces against twelve Roman Catholic institutions in northern Palestine." In expressing the Vatican's anxiety on Israeli hegemony over Jerusalem (again underscoring his role as a primary Vatican emissary to the world body), McMahon expressed the fear that "the Jews might start a continued expropriation of ecclesiastical properties which may have no small repercussions in the Christian world."[39] In concluding, he warned that sustained Jewish transgressions would not be accepted by Christian leaders. "It is our considered opinion that if these overt acts continue or are explained by ascribing them constantly to irresponsible forces, then the entire Christian world is justified in its apprehension over the disregard of Christian spiritual and material interests in the new born State of Israel."[40] The letter, carried widely in the mainstream press, drew a terse response from American Zionist groups. In a visit to McMahon's New York office Eliahu Ben-Horin of the American Zionist Emergency Council (AZEC) accused his host of "atavistic anti-Semitism" in highlighting only Jewish transgressions in the territory. Ben-Horin, however, clearly sought to defuse the damaging potential of an American Catholic press campaign, admitting to McMahon that "the UN [was] weak," and pledging to raise the issue of placing CNEWA observers in Jerusalem with Israeli Foreign Minister Moshe Sharett.[41]

In the same month the Vatican, through the Latin Patriarchate of Jerusalem, requested the assistance of the American Knights of the Holy Sepulchre to contribute funds to the repair of Catholic property damaged in the 1948 Arab-Israeli War. This was another sign of Rome's cognizance of the leadership, and financial might, of the various organs of the American church.[42] The order, which included Spellman and Joseph P. Kennedy in its membership, represented a cross section of prominent American Catholics, including academics, jurists, industrialists, publishers, and politicians.[43] A statement issued through New York financier Luigi Criscuolo (who had been accused of antisemitism by several Jewish American newspapers), not only appealed to its membership to assist the church in Palestine, but called upon American Jewish groups to shoulder a significant burden for the damage, clearly implying Jewish culpability in the molestation of Catholic sites. In appealing, in general terms, to the "friendly relations" between

Catholic prelates and Jewish rabbis in the United States, it called upon Jewish groups to "cut the Gordian knot of diplomatic procedure and make a large donation out of Jewish relief funds to the restoration of Catholic Church properties which were destroyed."[44] The statement, which appeared in both the secular and Catholic press, was also forwarded to the heads of a number of prominent Jewish organizations, including Henry Morgenthau, chairman of the Jewish Appeal.

In October, Cicognani again urged the NCWC to do all it could, through the diocesan press and its capillary network of organizations, such as the National Council of Catholic Men (NCCM), the NCCW, and the CAIP, to promote the desire of the Vatican for a "just settlement on the Palestine conflict and for the internationalization of Jerusalem and the Holy Places."[45] Cicognani's letter was sent in conjunction with the October 1948 release of Pius XII's encyclical *In multiplicibus curis*, his second encyclical of the year to speak directly to the conflict in the Holy Land. The encyclical constituted an explicit call to action to Roman Catholics everywhere. "We do not believe that the Christian world could contemplate indifferently, or in sterile indignation," it proclaimed, "the spectacle of the sacred land … trampled over again by troops and stricken by aerial bombardments. We do not believe that it could permit the devastation of the Holy Places, the destruction of the great sepulchre of Christ."[46] As Silvio Ferrari has observed, the encyclical marked a decisive evolution in the papal stance on the Holy Land. Firstly, it announced in language clearer and more explicit than *Auspicia quaedam* the pope's own position on the future of the territory and the need for an immediate cessation of hostilities and aid to those displaced by the conflict. Secondly, it signaled the expansion of Vatican demands for Jerusalem and the wider territory, replacing previous requests for legal guarantees for the Holy Places (as expressed privately by a number of Vatican figures), with renewed calls for the complete internationalization of Jerusalem and "free access to the Holy Places scattered throughout Palestine."[47] The encyclical, in sum, insisted on a vigorous Catholic defense of the *corpus separatum*, extending beyond Jerusalem to Holy Places throughout the territory, echoing the expansive "zone of exclusion" Pacelli himself had presented to Nahum Sokolow thirty years earlier.

Throughout October and November, the American Catholic press continued to highlight IDF transgressions, giving prominence to Vergani's reports and Bruya's steady stream of dispatches from Jerusalem.[48] Catholic papers also gave wide coverage to the report of two American Franciscan priests stationed in Jerusalem, Patrick J. Coyle and Theophane Carroll, who had both served as wartime chaplains in Europe. Their statement, which was also broadcast on Palestine Radio on 22 October 1948, highlighted Israeli attempts to downplay damage to Catholic sites, and theorized more ominously on Tel Aviv's plans to supplant Christianity in the Holy Land altogether.[49] In stoking fears of Israeli efforts to erase Catholicism's institutional presence in the territory, it stated that "a further consideration causing anxiety to Christians in Jerusalem is that there seems to be an overall plan to gradually replace Christian institutions. Of various Catholic schools in the Jewish section of Jerusalem, four have been filled so far, one way or another, with Jews. At the time of this report, Jewish authorities are ready to move into the Terra Sancta College to make it a part of the Hebrew University." In underscoring the validity of Catholic reportage on Jerusalem, and the insincerity of Tel Aviv's claims to be acting to curtail these attacks, it continued that the "desecrations that have happened … [the Israeli government] wants to minimize, especially in the press. The well-founded suspicions of Christians must remain: that these acts reveal only too well the mentality of a section of the Jewish people."[50] As in Vergani's report, it also detailed Jewish expropriations of "Catholic homes looted by Jews," the harassment of Catholics by the IDF and other Jewish groups, and specific vandalizations of Christian relics, including a crucifix in the Benedictine Church of the Dormition, which had been shorn of its arms as well as its head. Undoubtedly, such details were intended to shock and to galvanize American Catholic support for the enforcement of the expanded *corpus separatum*.

In November, the American Catholic press gave wide circulation to the public appeal of Archbishop Arthur Hughes, the apostolic nuncio to Egypt, who charged that continued delays to the internationalization of Jerusalem, and the expanding refugee crisis in the region, were the result of "deliberate Jewish efforts to decimate the Arabs and destroy Christianity in Palestine."[51] Hughes declared himself "appalled by the callousness with which the world accepts the intention to expose to death and hardships the Arab refugees, in order to make room for 600,000 Jews." In citing the "particular hatred" that Jews had demonstrated against Catholic institutions, he urged Catholics worldwide to support relief efforts for Palestinian Christians, and to urge their governments to press for an imminent cessation to the violence. This was followed by the wide press circulation, in December, of a petition sent by the leaders of Iraq's Catholic community to Spellman decrying the "ravages caused by the war in Palestine on the part of a pitiless enemy devoid of respect for the Holy Places or for religious and charitable foundations."[52] It further lamented the "flagrant injustice and barbarous treatment meted out to the Christian and Moslem Arabs of Palestine," and expressed "alarm at the fate in store for Christians and Moslems in danger of becoming prey of intolerant and materialist Zionism." In closing, it urged Spellman to use his "great influence" to inform public opinion and shape Washington's views before the entrenched establishment of "a Zionist government which will be a permanent source of discord and trouble among the peoples of the Middle East."[53]

The Catholic press also gave increasing coverage to the refugee crisis that was becoming progressively grave in the latter half of 1948, with particular attention called to the Arab Catholic refugee problem, an issue that would now assume a central place in the Vatican's diplomacy. American Catholic newspapers highlighted the Christian refugee crisis with increasing regularity, cognizant that Zionist organizations had successfully leveraged the issue since the end of the war in increasing Jewish refugee admission quotas to both the United States and Palestine.[54] According to figures presented in the Catholic press, Roman Catholic refugees displaced by war in Europe were double the number of Jewish refugees, yet American Catholic demands for open-door immigration policies to the United States appeared to be consistently upstaged by American Jewish groups and their success in linking the Jewish refugee question to increased immigration quotas to Palestine.[55] By the summer of 1948, the Catholic press attempted to tie the Arab Christian refugee crisis into its general critique of Israeli incursions, and to use it as another argument in favor of the immediate internationalization of Jerusalem and its environs. Fed by a steady stream of reports from Schaefer and the NCWC's UN Office, the diocesan press gave wide coverage to the unfolding crisis.[56] Schaefer's reports generally traced the spread of the refugee problem to the "revised" Jewish state, which had expanded through war to encompass a larger territory than it had been allotted in the 1947 partition plan.[57] As a result of "Jewish imperialism," several Catholic papers noted, the number of Christian refugees in the Holy Land had risen to over 100,000 by October, "the vast majority of whom," the papers noted, "were Roman Catholic."[58]

In connection to the crisis, the CNEWA, designated by the Vatican as the official relief organization for Palestinian refugees (both Arab and Christian), established the American Appeal for Holy Land Refugees. Offertory collections at masses raised nearly $1 million for the initiative by the fall of 1949, further proof of the financial power wielded by the American faithful. The initiative, while providing essential aid to refugees, also kept the CNEWA at the forefront of the Vatican's efforts to press its demands on the nascent Israeli state. Given the growing importance of the refugee question in the Palestine equation, the initiative also ceded additional clout to both Spellman and McMahon in advocating for Catholic refugees in Washington and at the UN. Imploring its readers to support the new initiative through the offertory, *America* emphasized the connection between refugee aid and the Catholic stake in the territory. "The Catholic Church has been associated with all the problems of the Near East since the birth of Christ. The purposes of our Catholic personnel … are non-political. That Catholic missionaries remained through the fighting … is proof of their non-political purpose. It is proof, too, that they expect their rights to be protected and, where infringed, restored."[59] In closing, it hinted at Israeli complicity in the unfolding crisis. "There is scarcely a religious house in Palestine that is not sheltering refugees," it noted. "The officials at Tel Aviv know this."[60]

PRESS WARS: THE BATTLE FOR PUBLIC OPINION

Though a furor among American Catholics against IDF actions in Israel might have seemed relatively inconsequential, considering Israeli successes in first establishing a state and then expanding it during the 1948 war, evidence suggests that Tel Aviv in fact considered negative publicity, particularly from American Catholic circles, to be detrimental to its interests. This was particularly so as Israeli officials and American Zionist organizations such as the American Christian Palestine Committee lobbied the UN and the Truman administration for Israel's admission to the world body in the summer of 1948.[61] Wide publicity of IDF transgressions posed a clear danger to the country's candidacy, raising questions on the legitimacy of its application. A continued delay in the functional internationalization of Jerusalem, moreover, prolonged Tel Aviv's strained relationship with the Vatican, bringing international Catholic pressure to bear against the ambitions of the new state. David Ben-Gurion, Israel's first prime minister, greatly feared the negative impact of such publicity, and in July issued explicit instructions to Israeli officers: "It is your duty that the special force in charge of defending the Old City makes merciless use of machine guns against any Jews, and in particular Jewish soldiers, who tries [*sic*] to defile a Christian or Muslim Holy Place." He further instructed local Jewish leaders in Jerusalem to send a cable to the pope reporting that "all is well with the Christian communities, and the Holy Places have not been damaged."[62] Despite these precautions, damages ensued, prompting the aforementioned plethora of reportage in the Catholic press, which an Israeli official described as "a wave of poisonous propaganda directed against us in the Catholic world, based on stories of a campaign of desecration of churches allegedly conducted by the IDF … They are inflating each incident of damage – however slight – caused by a handful of uncultured and irresponsible people."[63] Yaacov Herzog, an attaché to the Israeli minister of religious affairs, sensed the significance of Catholic reportage on Jerusalem when he observed that "these incidents sowed seeds of suspicion in influential Vatican circles," thus piquing "the anxieties of Vatican policymakers" and generally creating challenges for Israeli statecraft vis-à-vis the United States, the UN, and the larger Catholic world.[64]

The Israeli provisional government considered the growing Catholic furor over fighting in Jerusalem and the wider territory sufficiently dangerous to dispatch a number of emissaries to quell these critiques. In September 1948 Moshe Tov, director of the Latin American desk of the Israeli Foreign Ministry, toured a series of South American capitals to discuss diplomatic and consular relations. As the apostolic delegate to Uruguay informed the Vatican, Tov's mission was also intended to disprove notions of Israeli abuses against Catholic populations and institutions, and to assure these governments that Israel was their most trusted partner in the protection of Catholic interests in the territory.[65] Several weeks later, Israel initiated a secret mission to the Holy See itself to discuss guarantees for Israel's Catholic minority, Catholic institutions, and the sacred sites. In late September, Herzog and Dr Chaim Wardie, a director in the Ministry of Religious Affairs, arrived in Rome to discuss such guarantees directly with leading members of the Vatican Secretariat. The mission was facilitated by James McDonald, Washington's special representative to Israel, Gustavo Testa, the apostolic delegate to Palestine, and Vergani, the Latin patriarchal vicar of Galilee, whose damning reports on IDF damages in the city had been so widely covered in the Catholic press.[66] Herzog was under no illusion that the mission would be considered a formal diplomatic visit, but he expressed hope that such a meeting "[could] help materially in preventing misunderstanding in a field in which the Catholic Church takes so keen an interest."[67]

While Montini himself assented to the meetings, neither he, Tardini, nor the pope, men who were clearly the most influential figures in the Vatican, met with Herzog and Wardie. Just three weeks earlier, on 3 September, the pope had suffered a seizure and had lay unconscious for thirty minutes, a fact known only to a small circle of curial officials.[68] Ascribed to extreme overwork, the pope's condition was met with the recommendation that papal audiences be curtailed for the remainder of the month. As such, meetings were granted with Enrico Galeazzi, personal physician and trusted adviser to Pius XII, Monsignor Pietro Sigismondi of the Secretariat of State, and Archbishop Valerio Valeri of the Congregation of the Oriental Churches.[69] Herzog described the mandate of the three-week mission as an attempt to "pay our respects to the Holy See, and to seek informal counsel on the manner in which the Catholic Church would wish Israel to define, in its legal and administrative machinery, the religious rights of the Catholic communities in its midst."[70] Given the "unique place which the Holy Land occupies in the religious sentiments of mankind," he assured Vatican representatives that "the question would be given the most careful consideration on the highest level."[71] In addition to ascertaining the legal, civil, and religious rights that the Catholic Church sought in Israel, the mission was also intended to initiate dialogue that would lead to the Vatican's formal recognition of Israel and the exchange of ambassadors.

Though Pius XII was encouraged by Israeli efforts to bring forth proposals directly to the Vatican itself, a stumbling block remained the full and effective internationalization of Jerusalem, upon which the Vatican Secretariat continued to insist. Just weeks after the departure of the Israeli delegates from Rome, Tardini forwarded to Taylor's office the pope's detailed position on Jerusalem, which continued to insist upon full internationalization as outlined in the 1947 partition plan.[72] The Vatican rejected proposals put forth by the UN that would give civil and judicial authorities the right to decide disputes pertaining to religious tribunals, as well as rights to determine cases at issue between religious groups and the civil courts. The Vatican was further concerned by the UN proposal's insistence that residency in Jerusalem would have to be proven for three uninterrupted years, meaning that Roman Catholics who had fled to the city since the outbreak of Arab-Jewish conflict would not be granted resident status. Such a regulation would clearly have limited the Roman Catholic presence in the city and hindered future Vatican claims for jurisdiction there. Only full and genuine internationalization, the document concluded, would protect the Roman Catholic presence in Palestine. Privately, moreover, Vatican officials expressed that the purpose of the Israeli mission had been to offset the international Catholic clamor over fighting in Jerusalem, which they maintained was legitimate, and which they agreed was detrimental to the prospect of Israel's admission to the UN.[73] Nonetheless, the Vatican agreed to study the Israeli proposals for a period of three months, despite its continued insistence on the full internationalization of Jerusalem.

Herzog and Wardie, by all indications, departed Rome in early October confident that their mission had at least begun to thaw the relationship between the Holy See and Tel Aviv, and even expressed the hope that it had laid the groundwork for the Vatican's full diplomatic recognition of Israel.[74] In alluding to the particular importance of blunting American Catholic criticisms of Israel, Wardie expressed to Taylor's office hopes "that Catholics in the United States might perhaps learn of this visit and thereby be reassured of Israel's feelings of respect and friendliness for the Holy See."[75]

Wardie correctly surmised that American Catholic criticisms were particularly damaging to Israeli objectives. American Jewish organizations and representatives of the Israeli provisional government in Washington, therefore, were anxious to quell Catholic anti-Israel sentiment in the United States, cognizant of the threat it posed to Tel Aviv's strengthening relationship with the American government. This initiative began in the summer of 1948 with a concerted effort in the Jewish press to emphasize Arab culpability in the destruction of Christian sites, in order to counter, as an AZEC press release put it, "the propaganda from Arab and pro-Arab sources on the question of the holy places in Jerusalem, which tends to present a distorted picture of the situation."[76] By August, a number of mainstream national papers such as *The New York Times*, *The New York Herald Tribune*, and *The Boston Globe* were also increasingly emphasizing Arab transgressions in the territory.

Jewish editors also rebuked Catholic journals directly for what they regarded as an ongoing campaign of misrepresentation on the fighting in Jerusalem. Philip Slomowitz, editor of the influential papers *The Jewish News* and *The Jewish Chronicle*, reproached the editorial board of *The Commonweal*, stating that as a reader and a former contributor to the journal, he had been "shocked in the past few months to read some of the biased and unfair comments you have made on the Jewish position in the State of Israel."[77] Slomowitz detailed a host of Arab damages to Christian sites, citing reports from both the Jewish and the mainstream press, and raised examples of Jewish-Catholic cooperation in the territory, which included Jewish troops providing access to Christians to the Tomb of David, a practice that had been forbidden under Ottoman rule. In concluding, he maintained that there was "a mass of evidence not only to disprove the charges of Jewish abuses, but to point on the contrary that while Arabs have destroyed Jewish and Christian holy places the Israelis have protected them. Surely Catholics ought to be the first to challenge libels against our people, and I am personally deeply grieved that the liberal *Commonweal* magazine should have fallen prey to the rumours instead of disproving falsehoods." Slomowitz forwarded copies of his correspondence with Catholic journals to officials in the Israeli provisional government in Washington and New York.[78]

Catholic editors were scarcely deterred by the disapproval of American Jewry, and relentlessly highlighted Israeli misdeeds in Jerusalem and the wider territory throughout the summer and fall. *The Commonweal*'s response to Slomowitz was indicative of the conviction of the Catholic press. Penned by Anne Fremantle, the British-born author, essayist, and noted convert to Catholicism, it defended, chapter and verse, the assertions made in the journal, and insisted that Catholic sources in the Holy Land were sound and unbiased.[79] "I do hope you print this letter on the front page of your journal," Fremantle curtly wrote to Slomowitz, "as it is doubtless the only way of informing your readers of the damage done by their co-religionists to a city that they also admit is holy." Catholic writers also challenged what they regarded to be fallacious reporting in the mainstream press. In November, *The New York Herald Tribune* carried an article by Howard Carroll, general secretary of the NCWC, challenging a series of articles in the same paper by Ruth Gruber, who claimed that the situation in Palestine was "idyllic."[80] Carroll sternly took Gruber's views to task and, in quoting Vergani's report liberally, laid out the full extent of Jewish abuses in the large-circulation daily.

Eliahu Elath, the special representative (and later ambassador) of the Israeli government to the United States, took pains to assure the NCWC News Service (the central clearing house of the national diocesan papers) that Tel Aviv took seriously the charges against Jewish elements in and around Jerusalem, and he drew attention to formal Israeli investigations into these misdemeanors.[81] In quoting the Israeli minister of religious affairs, Rabbi I.L. Fishman (who in August had ordered a formal investigation into charges against Jewish transgressions in Jerusalem), Elath assured the NCWC that "the suggestion that our state has or ever had any intention of expropriating Church property is wholly without foundation," and labeled coverage of the situation in Jerusalem as "fantastic slander typical of anti-Israeli propaganda."[82] He further assured the NCWC that he would seek immediate clarification from Tel Aviv of any future charges against Israeli elements in the territory. Similar assurances were forwarded to the NCWC and the apostolic delegate, Amleto Cicognani, by AZEC, in an attempt to mitigate the negative coverage so prevalent in the Catholic press.[83] Despite these pledges, Catholic coverage remained harshly critical of alleged Israeli transgressions, spurred by the Vatican's consistent message, issued through the apostolic delegate, to "raise the issue of Palestine clearly and consistently" in the American Catholic press.[84] Vatican and American Catholic leaders, increasingly aware of the power of public opinion on the issue of Palestine, were not about to allow the critiques of either American Zionists groups or representatives of the Israeli provisional government to derail an effective campaign. Just weeks after the Israeli and AZEC assurances of accountability, in fact, the diocesan press ran a series of damning articles by Father Raimond Naveau, a Belgian Benedictine stationed in Jerusalem, renewing charges of grave atrocities committed by Israeli forces in and around the city.[85]

This campaign was intended to underscore the need to create a genuine territorial internationalization for Jerusalem, as opposed to the various schemes for protecting access only to the Holy Places themselves suggested by the Israeli government. The establishment of a *corpus separatum*, as outlined in the 1947 partition plan, and the repatriation of Christian Arab refugees to Palestine, had become the clear focal points of Vatican efforts from the spring of 1948 onward, a policy that the Vatican had again communicated to Myron Taylor's office in November.[86] On these fronts, however, the Vatican was gradually losing the support of Washington. The Truman administration increasingly favored a modified condominium for Jerusalem, under which Israel, the now independent Hashemite Kingdom of Jordan (which controlled East Jerusalem), and the UN would share the administration of the city under a rotating chairmanship.[87] American plans would also have required a limited UN internationalization of individual scared sites, thus ensuring physical protection of their premises and guaranteeing access evenly to Christians, Jews, and Muslims.

The UN issued its own resolution in the September 1948 report submitted by Sweden's Folke Bernadotte, the UN mediator on Palestine. Bernadotte's plan called for an immediate cessation of war in the territory, repatriation and reparations for refugees displaced by the conflict, a revision of borders based on demographic factors, the merger of "Arab Palestine" with Jordan to create a "Greater Jordan," and the recognition of the *corpus separatum* for Jerusalem and its environs as outlined in the November 1947 partition plan. The report, while appearing to strike a judicious balance between Jewish and Arab interests in the territory, effectively rolled back some of the gains won by Israel on the battlefield, and further threatened Israeli sovereignty by calling for the repatriation of Arab refugees to the territory. Bernadotte's assassination in Jerusalem on 17 September 1948, shot point blank in his sedan at a roadblock by Lehi (or "Stern Gang") terrorists disguised as IDF soldiers, highlighted the deepening intractability of the Jerusalem question. On 11 December 1948, as had been suggested by Bernadotte himself, the UN established the Palestine Conciliation Commission, a body charged with mediating between the disputants in the Israeli-Arab conflict in order to reach a final settlement. The status of Jerusalem and the question of the refugees were the central issues of the PCC mandate. The General Assembly specifically instructed the PCC to present to its Fourth Session in the fall of 1949 "detailed proposals for a permanent international regime for the Jerusalem area."[88] The establishment of the PCC signaled to the Vatican another chance to shape a favorable solution on the fate of Jerusalem and its environs, despite flagging American support for full internationalization.

To the end of 1948, the Vatican remained unmoved in its insistence on full territorial internationalization for Jerusalem, the *corpus separatum* promised in November 1947. The October 1948 encyclical *In multiplicibus curis*, in terms starker than April's *Auspicia quaedam*, called for a genuine territorial internationalization for the city. In a key paragraph, Pope Pius XII implored those "in high quarters, where the problems of peace are discussed," to "give Jerusalem and its outskirts, where are found so many and such precious memories of the life and death of the Saviour, an international character which, in present circumstances, seems to offer a better guarantee for the protection of the sanctuaries."[89] The pontiff further called for "international guarantees for Holy Places throughout Palestine," and for the repatriation of Christian refugees to the Holy Land, reflecting Bernadotte's plan for Palestine's displaced peoples. As the new year dawned, the Vatican maintained a cautious optimism that the UN, given sufficient pressure from Catholic states and their allies at the world body, could still secure such an outcome.

"THE PAPAL REPRESENTATIVE" ARRIVES IN ISRAEL

The Vatican hardly placed all its faith in a UN-brokered resolution, as parameters for an authentic *corpus separatum* were also discussed directly with the Israeli government. Once again, the Vatican relied on the American church as a primary intermediary in relations with Israel. The first approach to Tel Aviv after the creation of the PCC was made by the CNEWA's Monsignor Thomas McMahon. His first mission, which lasted from December 1948 to

March 1949, was officially to manage Catholic aid efforts in Egypt, Lebanon, Israel, and Arab Palestine, given his chairmanship of the newly created American Appeal for Holy Land Refugees. In the territory he was officially tasked with coordinating relief efforts for refugees with Dr Bernard Joseph, the military governor of Israel. McMahon's agenda had a diplomatic assignment attached as well, however, to advocate for the repatriation of Christian Arab refugees to the territory and to campaign for the territorial internationalization of Jerusalem and its environs. Though McMahon had not been designated an official Vatican envoy, his private audiences with the pope both at the beginning and the end of his mission suggested such a role. James McDonald, the American special representative to Israel, noted that though McMahon "received his orders from his immediate supervisor, Cardinal Spellman, he is in fact so close to the Vatican in his work here that in reality, if not in form, he is the Papal representative."[90] McDonald's inference was later confirmed during an audience with Pius XII when, in praising the work McMahon had conducted for the Vatican, the pope "said in effect that he hoped McMahon could work out a settlement." This confirmed to McDonald "what [he] had long suspected – that Mgr McMahon, whose duties were officially charitable, had others besides."[91] Officials in the Israeli government, including Yaacov Herzog of the Ministry of Religious Affairs, concurred with this assessment, claiming that McMahon clearly "had wider powers as an unofficial representative of the Holy See on political matters," referring to him regularly as "the Vatican representative."[92]

Once in the territory, McMahon wasted little time in seeking out the power brokers on the Jerusalem question, despite an official and frenetic agenda of coordinating the distribution of relief aid in the entire region.[93] On the evening of 11 December 1948, McMahon had a lengthy discussion with Herzog, whose ministry dealt with the question of Jerusalem. McMahon's initial impressions were positive, describing the affable Herzog, "a young man, endowed with an Irish accent owing to his youth in Dublin," as "a pleasure to speak with."[94] On the question of the Holy City, Herzog actually suggested that McMahon's August memo to the UN "hadn't gone far enough" in insisting that church property, religious education, and Catholic marriages be protected. Herzog, in fact, expressed full agreement on the principle of a *corpus separatum*, but lamented "that he could not [speak] officially, especially since there were elections coming up here, and [citing] the matter of a constitution."[95] Herzog further hinted at a division between the civilian and military leadership in Israel, which complicated the Jerusalem question. "There is a definitive division of the victorious army from the political leaders," McMahon started in his report to Spellman, "and the former has its way." At the very outset of his mission, then, McMahon was made aware of the Israeli government's growing opposition, led by key figures in the IDF, to implementing the *corpus separatum* as conceived in Resolution 181. On the Catholic course going forward, McMahon was now unequivocal. "I think the party line in New York should be to press always for internationalization, including everything," he advised Spellman. "Acceptance of partition" was proof of the Vatican's good faith, "but the UN will have to devise some formidable way of implementing the internationality of the Holy Places, or all is lost."[96]

Two weeks later, McMahon took the Vatican's concerns to the Jordanians, who similarly opposed the idea of the *corpus separatum*, particularly in light the of Jordan's capture of Jerusalem's Old City during the 1948 Arab-Israeli War. The Vatican generally regarded the Hashemite Kingdom as sympathetic to Catholic interests given the rights and freedoms enjoyed by the church there. On the evening of 20 December 1948, McMahon was received at the winter home of King Abdullah in Shureh, where he chatted for nearly two hours with Abdullah and Dr Musa Husseini, a liaison officer for the monarchy.[97] McMahon remarked that Abdullah was "very cordial and paternal," growing "eloquent in his affirmations that Christians and Moslems are equal in his regime." On the subject of internationalization, however, the king was reticent, "especially since his soldiers had shed their blood to defend the Holy Places."[98] Upon the king's departure, McMahon continued on with Husseini, who assured him that although Abdullah didn't understand the Jerusalem question fully, he would take it up with him further. The monsignor reminded his host that Roman Catholics "had no more assurances from the Arabs than from the Jews that Christians could live [in Palestine] in peace," emphasizing that "the internationalization of Jerusalem would be proof from both sides that they respected Christian feelings." Though Husseini offered vague pledges to study the question in more depth, McMahon remained pessimistic. In his report to Spellman, he again urged a firm line on Jerusalem and alluded to the fragility of peace in the region, which underscored the need for action. "The present 'armistice' seems to be a prelude, but let us pray otherwise. This little world is not much further ahead – in fact, it has gone back. We must be loud on rightful claims."[99]

On 11 January 1949, McMahon held a two-hour meeting with James McDonald, the American special representative (and later ambassador) to Israel, at his home in Tel Aviv. The meeting was intended to dispel notions that the Vatican was prepared to accept a compromised solution to the Jerusalem question. While the protection of the Holy Places was important, he insisted that the "maintenance of the status quo" (meaning the full *corpus separatum* promised in 1947) was the only solution acceptable to the Vatican. Significantly, McMahon stressed the supreme importance of the repatriation of Catholic Arabs to Palestine, suggesting that the establishment of Jerusalem as a *corpus separatum* would facilitate the return of these refugees. The Vatican had long considered the maintenance of a Roman Catholic population in Palestine, the "living stones" of the region, as central to the legitimacy of its presence there. As such, McMahon informed McDonald that the Roman Catholic Church would prefer "that all of the [holy sites] be destroyed rather than the Christian population be eliminated," alluding to the importance the Vatican placed on the protection of Catholic populations in the territory.[100] He further suggested a benefit to Israel in the repatriation of Christians to Palestine: namely, as a buffer population between Jewish "liberals" and "excessive Rabbinical control or any tendency toward a theocracy."[101] McMahon's impression was that McDonald, and by extension Truman himself, were at least open to the Vatican's views, though the meeting was hardly conclusive. In recounting his dinner with "the President's man" to Spellman, a cautiously optimistic McMahon described his host as possessing a "courteous, kindly, and in fact princely personage." That he was "somewhat biased" by Israeli claims to Jerusalem, he concluded, should not dissuade Catholic efforts to demand internationalization.[102]

In February, McMahon presented similar points in a second meeting with Herzog, who could only offer his guest assurances that Israel, which was eager to negotiate a solution amenable to the Vatican, supported an international regime for the Holy Places specifically, and not the larger "zone of exclusion" encompassing Jerusalem and its environs proposed in 1947. Herzog's tone was decidedly less conciliatory than in early December, evidence that he was now acting on direct instructions from Tel Aviv. Growing Israeli obstinacy on the issue could be traced to plans for Jerusalem, which had always been considered the natural capital of Israel by the founding fathers of Zionism. Clearly sensing a growing upper hand in the struggle for Jerusalem's "New City," the Israeli cabinet had decided in January to terminate the military governorship of Jerusalem and replace it with a civilian government, an arrangement that would invoke the application of Israel's national civil law and further legitimize its claims there. Israel further declared that it would conduct municipal elections in the city in March, and made it known that it intended to hold the opening meeting of the First Knesset (constituent assembly) in Jerusalem on 14 February 1949.[103] Though Tel Aviv claimed that these measures were "administrative and not the annexation of Jerusalem," the demands put forth by the Vatican through McMahon were clearly incompatible with Israel's longer-term plans. The Jesuit journal *America*, which was kept apprised of McMahon's mission, observed accurately that, "despite protestations by Israeli officials that the [February Knesset meeting] was held in Jerusalem purely because of Israel's historical association with the Holy City, we have little doubt that they hoped to use the location of the Constituent Assembly as a weapon to strengthen their annexation plans."[104]

In early March, a frustrated McMahon discussed his mission in a private audience with Pope Pius XII, at which it was determined that a renewed pressure had to be applied both at the UN and in Washington. McMahon reiterated and expanded upon this plan in a lengthy memorandum on his mission for Spellman in which he warned of the difficulties in dealing with Israeli authorities particularly. "It is characteristic of the Jew," he noted, "that as soon as he feels his own position consolidated, he becomes less and less disposed to think of the rights of others."[105] McMahon decried Israel's emboldened opposition to the *corpus separatum*, claiming that Tel Aviv "spreads the rumor that the Vatican is willing to compromise, and in the meantime they will work with all the forces of their propaganda to erase the UN vote." He also reminded Spellman that the fight was also with Jordan, who similarly sought to ignore the *corpus separatum*, and "with the two great powers, the United States and Britain, which make possible the defiance of Israel and Jordan." McMahon's strategy was to apply Catholic pressure more directly to the UN and to the American government, and to expand the campaign of the Catholic press in the United States to call attention to Israeli and Jordanian transgressions in the territory. "Israel is sensitive to such pressure," McMahon suggested, "especially in the United States. I believe our Catholic press should not lose any opportunity to present … objectively the Palestine question, repeating the history of the UN's declarations and decisions, and also the declarations of the Holy Father, and remaining ever alert to the counter-propaganda in the secular press." His conclusion underscored the urgency of the moment. "This is not the time to remain quiet on the whole issue," he implored Spellman, "even though the passage of time has seemed to make this *fait accompli* acceptable to most of the world."[106]

Upon his return to New York McMahon wasted little time, penning his third open letter to UN General Secretary Trygve Lie on 21 March.[107] In stating that Roman Catholics "most understandably could not agree" with recent Israeli statements opposing the internationalization of Jerusalem (a clear reference to his recent meetings), he emphasized that "the Christian world has complete justification in requesting international status for the Holy City." The agreement of November 1947, he implored, assented to by the Catholic world, could not be simply undone by "Israeli military occupation." He further seethed at "certain officials" in the Israeli government who denied the repatriation of Catholic Arab refugees to their "ancestral homes, inhabited by their fathers for centuries, to which they, in the overwhelming majority, have always wished to return." "Who shall have the right," he asked, "to say they cannot or may not?" In closing, McMahon again raised the supranational character of the Jerusalem question and urged the PCC directly to find an amenable solution. "Jerusalem and the Holy Places engage not only the sentiments but the sacred interests of the great mass of mankind," he instructed. "We insist that your [Palestine] Conciliation Commission be motivated by these considerations of elementary justice."[108]

McMahon relayed a similar message in discussions with Jewish leaders in New York. In a private meeting on 20 April 1949 with the B'nai B'rith's Ben Epstein and Rabbi Bernard Lander, McMahon was unequivocal in championing Catholic interests in a partitioned Palestine. In a conversation he described to Spellman as "rather violent," he offered a spirited defense of Roman Catholic demands for an internationalized zone for Jerusalem as outlined in 1947. When Lander suggested that the church was pro-Arab, McMahon countered that it was in fact "pro-Arab *refugees*, interested in human rights and justice for the downtrodden," and tersely brushed aside suggestions that the Jews had not been responsible for the displacement of Arab populations. "This is present Jewish propaganda," McMahon informed his guests. "There are many instances where Arabs were driven out by Israeli soldiers," he declared, quoting examples to his guests.[109] McMahon similarly dismissed suggestions that the pope had "asked Catholics to play politics" in the encyclical *Auspecia quaedam*, countering that Pius XII had merely asked "Catholics in free nations to exercise their democratic rights to protect Christian claims in Palestine."[110] On the question of Jerusalem, McMahon excoriated his guests for their suggestion that Roman Catholic rights could be negotiated in a Jewish-controlled territory. "There is nothing to talk over – the Jews have stolen what is not theirs," McMahon charged, reminding his guests of Israel's defiance of the 1947 partition plan. "Talking things over is like taking my coat and leaving me the sleeve."[111]

In the same month, McMahon issued an impassioned plea for Palestine during an address at his alma mater, New York's Fordham University. In a speech entitled "Rites and Rights in the Homeland of Our Saviour," he referred to Jerusalem as a "capital of Christianity," clearly challenging Israel's own designs for the city as a national capital.[112] The speech, however, centered squarely on the rights of displaced Arab Catholic refugees, an emerging cornerstone of McMahon's diplomacy. Insisting that he "wished the State of Israel well, because the footsteps of returning Jews bear traces of bloody persecution," McMahon nonetheless claimed to "have come back here with my eyes full of the misery of homeless human beings, and my heart even more sensitive to the rights of Christendom." As in his UN letter, he again referred to the supranational character of Jerusalem, calling it "a microcosm, the crossroads of the world and the capital of three religions, whose rights make it imperative that the land can never be exclusionist and that no solution will be lasting that will obscure these indigenous rights." He further linked outstanding Roman Catholic grievances to the debate on Israeli UN membership, which had begun in April, warning Washington that American Catholics would be watching these talks closely. "During the next week the admission of the State of Israel to the UN will be discussed and voted on. During the same time, the Conciliation Commission will be discussing the internationalization of Jerusalem and the repatriation of refugees. Millions of Christians in this country will be wondering and will have a right to wonder what will be the policy of our government in the face of the assertion of Christian rights."[113] The speech, carried widely in the diocesan press, was a clear signal to Truman and the Democrats that American Catholics would be closely monitoring developments on Jerusalem, accepting nothing less than the full *corpus separatum* promised in 1947.

McMahon's Fordham address initiated a more vocal and public Catholic lobby on Palestine that extended through the spring and summer of 1949. Vatican demands were again laid out in the 15 April 1949 encyclical *Redemptoris nostri*, Pope Pius XII's third consecutive encyclical on Palestine, a clear sign of the priority with which the Vatican viewed the Jerusalem question. The document again called for the internationalization of the Holy City, citing the damages to ancient sites, "not a few [of which have] suffered serious loss and damage owing to the upheaval of war."[114] The "piteous appeals" of refugees, "prey to destitution, contagious diseases and perils of every sort," was heard clearly by the Vatican, which continued to link the maintenance of the *corpus separatum* with the repatriation of Arab Christian refugees. The encyclical, in no uncertain terms, urged global Catholics to action. "Let [Catholics], wherever they are living, use every legitimate means to persuade rulers of nations and those whose duty it is to settle this important question." It instructed religious to "encourage the faithful committed to your charge to be ever more concerned about the conditions in Palestine and have them make their lawful requests known, positively and unequivocally."[115]

Throughout the spring of 1949 the Vatican urged the American bishops "to make known among Catholics and the general public, in a truly effective manner, the desire and the will of the Catholic Church to defend and protect the sacred and centuries-old rights which She has had in Palestine."[116] The bishops were called upon to encourage their faithful to "make their voices heard by the responsible government authorities" and to further "do whatever may be in your power … to create a strong movement of your faithful and to undertake the necessary steps with the civil authorities for the purpose of obtaining the desired goal."[117] It was an appeal of uncommon directness, speaking both to the immediacy with which the Vatican regarded the issue, and to the credence it placed in the political clout of the American church.

On 27 April a pastoral letter, composed by the most influential figures in the American episcopate, was issued after the spring meeting of the NCWC in Washington. Titled "The Internationalization of Jerusalem and Its Environs," the letter, carried widely by both the Catholic and the mainstream press, and read from thousands of pulpits nationwide, characterized the urgency with which the American bishops regarded the future of Jerusalem.[118] The statement mirrored the demands made in the papal encyclical, and emphasized that American Catholics "had the right to expect that these sentiments, firmly rooted in the decisions of the United Nations, will now be respected by those [to] whom we should all appeal for their continuous affirmation." Like McMahon's address, it sought to politicize the Jerusalem issue among American Catholics, whom it exhorted "to use their democratic privileges in this free nation to obtain from those in our government and in the United Nations continued assurances that the original commitments as to Christian rights in Palestine will be carried out."[119]

While McMahon labored tirelessly on the Palestine question, he was steadfastly backed by Spellman, the de facto leader of the American church. In early April, Spellman hosted Israeli President Chaim Weizmann and Abba Eban,

Israel's representative for UN affairs, at his Madison Avenue residence. He quickly ascertained, to his dismay, that Israel was walking back its commitment to the full *corpus separatum* in favor of what Spellman described as a "mitigated, so-called indirect internationalization," which would give sovereignty over Jerusalem to both Israel and Jordan, a policy severely at odds with that sought by the Vatican and the international church.[120] Spellman's concerns were similarly piqued when he pressed his guests on the refugee question, specifically a recent statement of Israeli Prime Minister David Ben-Gurion, published in *The New York Times*, that Israel was not amenable to the repatriation of Arab Christian refugees to Israel, another policy wholly at odds with Vatican demands. Despite assurances from both Weizmann and Eban that Ben-Gurion was sensitive to Catholic concerns, and had already modified his position, the meeting clearly underscored for Spellman the need for a sustained Catholic campaign both in Washington and at the UN.

On 29 April, Spellman initiated a correspondence with President Truman that would extend through the spring and summer of 1949. In his first letter, he reiterated the details of his meeting with Weizmann and Eban, seeking assurances that the American government remained committed to the full *corpus separatum* as outlined in November 1947, and reconfirmed by the UN in 1948. In sum, he urged Truman to take a stronger tack against the "*fait accompli* policies of Israel, which disregards United Nations decrees," and to honor the "Christian stake" in the Palestine question. The president's response, however, both in tone and in content, suggested that he was now leaning in Israel's direction, favoring a modified solution that would grant Israel and Jordan governing responsibility in Jerusalem, but under UN supervision. Truman cited the proposed cost for a UN police force for Jerusalem, estimated at $30 million annually, as an important factor in the evolving views on the *corpus separatum*. In closing, Truman assured Spellman that the United States remained committed to the resettlement of Arab refugees in Israel, considering it "essential to a lasting peace in Palestine."[121] The president's views were cold comfort to Spellman, as they confirmed that the United States was rapidly warming to the mitigated internationalization plan now sought by Israel. This impression was only deepened by the late April release of the first PCC "Progress Report," which suggested a diluted international regime for Jerusalem reflective of the rapidly evolving situation in the city.[122]

In early May, just a week before the UN was set to vote on Israel's membership, the NCWC produced an eight-page memorandum titled "The Christian

Factor in the Palestine Equation" that sought, with legal precision, to outline the demands made by the Vatican and the American bishops on the status of Jerusalem.[123] The memo traced the historical aspects of the question from the medieval period through the twentieth century, and focused specifically on the form of internationalization agreed upon in Resolution 181. The document stated that Catholic and wider Christian assent to the 1947 partition plan had hinged upon assurances made by the UN on Jerusalem, quoting the agreement that "the safeguarding of the Holy Places, buildings and sites located in Palestine should be *a condition to the grant of independence*." It reminded delegates that the solution to the Palestine problem was "not merely bipartite, but tripartite," suggesting that Christian concerns were an essential factor in a lasting solution. The memo expressed concern over Israel's "gradual annexation" of Jerusalem, asserting that "military or civil conquest does not liquidate or neutralize the previous decisions of the General Assembly," and that "if '*force majeur*' is thus recognized and legitimated, there can be little effectiveness attributed to United Nations activities." It further warned that there remained a significant gulf between the form of internationalization acceptable to Israel (protection of the Holy Places only), and that insisted upon by the Vatican (the *corpus separatum* comprising Jerusalem and its environs), despite the "chatter" in UN circles that suggested otherwise. In closing, it admonished the "mitigated internationalization" favored by Tel Aviv and suggested that diplomatic tact and malleability could only achieve so much, urging a firmer hand on Israel. "The necessity of good will is unquestionable," it concluded, "but something else is also necessary. Clear understandings make good friends."[124] The memo was clearly intended as a short handbook for legislators and UN delegates on the question, and was intended to raise the issue loudly just as the General Assembly was set to debate Israeli membership. Catherine Schaefer forwarded translations to Latin American, Arab, and "various other delegates" at the UN. The following day, copies were also distributed widely among members of the American, Canadian, and Australian delegations, as well as to a number of American legislators.[125]

In the same weeks, McMahon again pressed the case directly with the Israeli government. On 28 April 1949, he held a lengthy meeting in his New York office with Abba Eban, Israel's UN representative. In the brief exchange, Eban informed his host that Israeli Foreign Minister Moshe Sharett and Prime Minister Ben Gurion both now definitively favored a modified *corpus separatum* that would see Israel maintain juridical sovereignty in the "New City" while ceding control and access to the Holy Places to the UN.[126] Eban further expressed his hopes that the Vatican would not actively impede Israel's admission to the UN, suggesting that Catholic interests could be better protected with Israel as a member of the world body. He concluded by informing McMahon that Catholic pressure was indeed having an impact at the highest levels, as President Truman had recently informed Israel's UN delegation that "not only was the Catholic Church universally disturbed over Israeli actions," but that the president also feared "a deterioration in Catholic-Jewish relations in the United States."[127]

In summarizing the meeting for Spellman, McMahon suggested an intensification of the existing strategy – namely, maintaining diplomatic pressure vis-à-vis both the American government and the UN, as well as expanding the campaign of the Catholic press in pressuring governing bodies to respect the integrity of preexisting agreements. It was crucial, McMahon said, for Catholic bodies to remind the pertinent authorities of the deadly potential of allowing the force of arms to shape the Jerusalem question, citing particular danger to Catholic interests in such a scenario. "The politics of the *fait accompli*," warned McMahon, "will inspire the Jews and Abdullah to whatever extremes [Catholic] opposition may permit them to go."[128] McMahon also stressed that it was "most essential that the Jews do not triumph with what is the professed Ben Gurion [*sic*] policy" – the moving of Israel's capital to Jerusalem – as this would signal conclusive defeat, both real and symbolic, of the Vatican's Palestine policy. McMahon identified here the two key focal points for Catholic efforts moving forward, which he identified to Spellman as "the party line": the full internationalization of Jerusalem and its environs, and the repatriation of Arab refugees to Israel, intertwined objectives that had to be pursued in unison. In closing, McMahon stressed the need for an orchestrated and transnational Catholic effort, requesting that the Holy See "keep us completely informed of any approaches made by Jews or Arabs to Rome on these issues," and citing the importance of remaining "in complete accord, since the United States government will form the prevailing policy of the United Nations on these matters."[129]

In early May, McMahon released a short pamphlet through the CNEWA, *Only the Meek*, which summarized the points he had outlined for Spellman.[130] Distributed to American Catholic organizations, UN delegates, and members of the American and Israeli governments, the pamphlet outlined the imprescriptible rights of Christians in the territory, stating that no lasting solution could be found by ignoring the "indigenous rights" of Christianity in Palestine. McMahon lamented that Catholics were again called upon to "protest against the present over-extension of Israeli rights," and vowed that, "as the sons of the Crusaders, we cannot bow down to the sons of Israel, because we cannot let go by default rights shared by 700 million Christians throughout the world." McMahon further cautioned Tel Aviv not to interfere in the return of "indigenous Arabs" to Israel. "It is not within the compass of the authority of Israel," he affirmed, "to say that the refugees may not return." The pamphlet concluded by reminding readers that "when Hitler was persecuting the Jews, it was Pope Pius XII who made the Vatican itself a refuge for these persecuted ones."[131]

The scope of his mandate to advocate for Arab refugees was revealed on 9 May 1949, when Spellman announced that McMahon would be returning to the territory in his capacity as head of the CNEWA to coordinate Catholic relief efforts in Israel, Jordan, Syria, and Egypt, a role that placed him in charge of disbursing nearly $2 million in aid relief from American Catholic sources. On 27 May 1949, as McMahon was at the Vatican in preparation for the mission, Pope Pius XII named him president of the newly created Pontifical Mission for Palestine (PMP), an organization created to coordinate the administration of dozens of Catholic organizations and associations working in the region, as well as to coordinate Catholic relief efforts with non-Catholic organizations.[132] As Maria Chari Rioli has noted, humanitarian action in support of refugees was emerging as the central locus of intervention for the Vatican in the region.[133] In short order, the PMP would assume control of a network of parishes, refugee camps, religious institutions, schools, and hospitals, and would direct the relief efforts of long-established French, Swiss, and Belgian Catholic organizations.[134] The PMP would also function as the liaison of the Holy See with the International Red Cross and UN agencies in the region, a role that gave McMahon additional leverage. Between 1949 and 1955, the New York–based CNEWA would be the leading source of funding for the PMP. Though the fiscal might of American Catholics was undoubtedly a factor in McMahon's nomination, it could also be ascribed to the high regard in which he was held by curial officials as a diplomat and strategist, and it maintained him at the forefront of Catholic efforts to shape the Jerusalem question.

"WHATEVER THE CONSEQUENCES": THE BROADENING OF AMERICAN CATHOLIC PRESSURE

That the Vatican was in complete accord with McMahon's strategy was made clear in a 15 May 1949 memo sent by Amleto Cicognani, the apostolic delegate in Washington, to the American bishops. Cicognani urged the bishops to instigate a wider program of public advocacy on the question of Jerusalem to make known to relevant authorities Pope Pius XII's "grave concern in regard to the question of Palestine, and especially Jerusalem and the Holy Places, insofar as they have been affected by the new political situation."[135] Cicognani identified the specific points to be advocated by American Catholics – namely, the full internationalization of Jerusalem and its environs and the repatriation of displaced refugees. The bishops were given ample autonomy in crafting this campaign, as Cicognani implored them to "do whatever may be in your power to create a strong movement of your faithful, and to undertake the necessary steps with the civil authorities for the purpose of attaining the desired goal." Though the Vatican had long valued the role of the American diocesan press in shaping Catholic opinion, it made pointed appeals to Catholic editors in the spring of 1949 to highlight papal and wider Roman Catholic demands for the Holy Land. Requests for intensified Catholic coverage were often issued through the apostolic delegation to the NCWC News Service.[136] Though the Vatican also began to forward reports of damage to Roman Catholic shrines to the same body "to offset the false statements made in recent months by the representatives of Israel," the apostolic delegate urged the diocesan papers "not to mention the Holy See as a source," cognizant of the challenges this might create for dialogue with Tel Aviv.[137]

Diocesan papers, hardly needing the prodding of Rome, gave unprecedentedly wide coverage to the situation in the territory. Anthony Bruya, who remained the NCWC's correspondent in Jerusalem, penned a long series of articles that amplified familiar themes: the desperate plight of displaced Arab refugees, Arab-Christian strife at the hands of the IDF and other Jewish elements, Catholic aid in the refugee camps, and continued Jewish agitations against Christian rights in Palestine.[138] The emphasis of these themes was not limited to the diocesan press. Catholic journals such as the Jesuit weekly *America*, the Paulist weekly *The Catholic World*, the independent lay *The Commonweal*, and *The Sign*, among others, echoed these demands, producing a largely unitary and coherent public voice on these issues.[139] On several occasions the Vatican also requested that American Catholic journals reprint relevant articles from papal organs such as the *L'Osservatore Romano* and *La Civiltà Cattolica* to harmonize demands put forth by Catholics and clearly inform American Catholic laity of the Vatican's position.[140]

So anxious was the Vatican to cultivate this uniformity that it monitored the American Catholic press closely, calling attention to articles that did not accord with papal views on Palestine. The Vatican Secretariat was keen to avoid a repeat of the Archbishop Rummel incident, in which the New Orleans prelate was rebuked for expressing views on Palestine that did not accord with those of Rome. In May, for example, Cicognani wrote the NCWC News Service, calling attention to a March article quoting a British Labour MP, Dr Samuel Segal, who had cast doubt on the feasibility on internationalizing Jerusalem. Cicognani wrote that the Vatican had "expressed wonderment at the fact that the NCWC News Service had given prominence to such remarks," and the apostolic delegate implored Frank Hall, director of the service, to prevent such articles from appearing again.[141] In his response, Hall explained that the piece had appeared in the diocesan press "before the intensive Catholic campaign for internationalization had started," but assured that the NCWC would "be alert to prevent a recurrence."[142]

Once again, intensified American Catholic critiques of Israeli policies and actions drew a terse response from American Zionist groups and from the Jewish press, a situation the NCWC appeared to have anticipated. In January, the NCWC News Service produced a series of form letters, to be used by editors of the Catholic diocesan weeklies, to refute the potential criticisms that might be leveled against the Catholic press over its coverage of events in Israel and the wider region.[143] In response to what was becoming "a considerable number of communications and visits from Israeli, Zionist, and Jewish agencies, organizations and individuals expressing much concern over [NCWC] dispatches from the Holy Land," the letters were intended to present a unitary American Catholic response to inevitable Jewish critiques.[144]

Despite this preparedness, such critiques were indeed forthcoming, as Zionist agencies continued to grasp the potential dangers of an ongoing American Catholic propaganda campaign against Israel. In a February memorandum, AZEC encouraged its members to counter negative Catholic reporting whenever possible, observing that reports in the press "had an unfavourable effect on Jewish-Catholic relations in the United States and the world over. If left unchecked, this development could have the most undesirable results both for the State of Israel and for Jewish communities in many lands."[145] Leading Jewish American commentators surmised the fairly direct links between Vatican policy on Palestine and American Catholic activism. Eliahu Ben-Horin, former Irgun member and now a journalist, and adviser to AZEC on Middle Eastern affairs, observed in July that "the Catholic propaganda machine is at the moment engaged in a campaign directed against Israel. The campaign derives its inspiration from the Vatican, and its main slogan is the internationalization of Jerusalem."[146] Judd L. Teller, director of the Office of Information for the American Jewish Congress, observed that his "familiarity with the religio-imperialist designs of the Vatican in the Middle East" had apprised him of the wider Roman Catholic campaign to undermine Israel.[147] This extended to the American Catholic press, where he discerned a "Catholic campaign of intimidation [that] has gone to the length of attempting to intimidate American Jews into siding with the Vatican against Israel."[148] Criticisms of Catholic press coverage, in fact, emanated from the Israeli government itself, with Foreign Minister Moshe Sharett condemning what he called "the growing propaganda with regard to the holy places" and urging that "His Holiness, the Pope ... will deem it good to examine the facts and inform everyone concerned of the truth in order that ... the question of the holy places should not serve as a source of libellous propaganda against us."[149]

Throughout the spring and summer of 1949, Jewish papers in the United States such as *The American Hebrew*, *The Detroit Jewish News*, *The National Jewish Monthly*, *The Reconstructionist*, and *The Rubicon* consistently defended Israel's claim to Jerusalem, and its right to regulate the entry of dispossessed Arab refugees, articles clearly refuting Catholic designs for the territory.[150] In August, an *American Hebrew* editorial identified a clear hardening in American Catholic attitudes toward Israel just weeks after the Vatican had asked American bishops to intensify their campaign for Jerusalem and the refugees. It identified a shift in Catholic attitudes in May, when "distinguished Catholic prelates and numerous Catholic periodicals began to direct particular vigorous criticism at Israel," at which point American Catholics "were no longer negotiating for limited objectives" as much as indulging in "attacks upon Israel which were immoderate, and ... permeated with a feeling of hostility to the very existence of the new State,"[151] The editorial rhetorically asked why it appeared that leading figures in Washington, including Acheson and Truman himself, appeared to be gradually aligning with Rome on the Palestine question, suggesting a Vatican-Washington axis at play. "Is it the newly strengthened opposition of Catholic circles to Israel that provides an explanation," it asked, "or has the Catholic Church itself been persuaded by the old opponents of Israel in Washington and London to join the opposition?"[152] Though no such axis existed – the Truman administration was in fact lending increasing support to Tel Aviv's ambitions – such reportage was successful in eliciting sympathy and political support from American Jewry.

The Jewish press buttressed the strident and largely successful American Zionist lobby, where the advocacy of groups such as AZEC, the AJC, and the ZOA, merged with Truman's well-documented sympathy for Zionism, were generally able to steer Washington's Israel policy in directions amenable to Tel Aviv's interests. Added to this was the support and lobbying of the American Christian Palestine Committee (ACPC), the largely Protestant body and proponent of Israel that had, as recent scholarship contends, played a significant role in Washington's diplomatic recognition of Israel in 1948, and which continued to advocate for the nascent state.[153] Formed in 1942, the bipartisan ACPC included among its early members then-Senator Harry Truman, Secretary of the Interior Harold Ickes, 1940 Republican presidential nominee Wendell Willkie, and New York Senator Robert F. Wagner. By the later 1940s, the ACPC had emerged as a leading voice of Christian Zionism in the United States, advocating for the right of Israel's existence on humanitarian, geopolitical, and theological grounds.[154] The existence of a vocal Christian Zionist lobby (primarily Protestant), in addition to robust Jewish Zionist advocacy, served to place American Catholics at odds with this emerging consensus, and highlighted the clear parallels between the Vatican's Palestine policy and the political demands of its faithful in the United States.

In spite of the intensive and growing activism of the American Zionist lobby, and indeed partly because of it, Catholic advocacy on Palestine continued to broaden throughout the summer of 1949. The admission of Israel to the UN in May, a decision that was supported by the American delegation, only roused the Catholic lobby further. McMahon, regarding the outcome as a severe setback to papal efforts to shape the Jerusalem question, penned a trenchant memo to Spellman critiquing the Zionist lobby in the United States. Citing American Zionist pressure as having had a strong effect on the Truman administration's Israel policy, McMahon suggested a vigorous airing of Catholic concerns. "It is no longer the time to fear the counter charges of American Jewry as to antisemitism. Catholic sympathy for the persecuted Jews and for the establishment of their homeland has been manifest enough. Catholic criticism of the political State of Israel is objective and inspired by consternation over the complete disregard of our Christian claims, not only by the little state but also by the government of the United States."[155] To McMahon, it was clear that the decisive moment had arrived. "Whatever the consequences," he concluded, "and not the least of these consequences may be an all-out fight with American Jewry and a constant attack on presidential policy, the Catholic body will pursue this battle till the bitter end." In a memo to Spellman issued just a few days later, McMahon recommended that the bishops raise their voices even further as a means to counter the American Zionist lobby. "It will be good for the 'other side' to know," he suggested, "that the bishops speak in the name of nearly thirty million people in this country and that we are confident our views are shared by many other millions of Christians."[156]

Catholic ire was also aroused by tensions between Jewish authorities and Catholics in Jerusalem, where ongoing disputes over church property only served to inflame fragile relations. The barring of American Franciscans from praying in the Cenacle (the building that purportedly contained the room in which the Last Supper was held) on Holy Thursday of 1949 struck a particularly raw nerve. Moshe Dayan, the military commander of the Jewish-controlled portion of Jerusalem, refused the request, citing security concerns, despite the fact that Jewish pilgrims were permitted to visit the Tomb of David – located in the same complex on Mount Zion.[157] The Cenacle incident appeared to spark the very expansion of public advocacy that McMahon had suggested to Spellman.

At the request of Cardinal Richard Cushing, Boston's Holy Name Society planned a massive rally to call wider attention to the situation in Jerusalem. On the evening of 6 June 1949, nearly fifty thousand faithful attended a Rally for the Holy Land at Fenway Park, where Cushing led a dramatic ceremony from "a majestic high altar, bedecked in white gold and decorated with palms, rhododendrons and tall white lilies" – a spectacle "heightened by the rich robes of the prelates, the Monsignori, and the contrasting colours of the various religious communities."[158] The pageantry reached a crescendo when the lights of the stadium were shut off, and nearly four thousand men formed a "living rosary" on the playing field, carrying torches and colored flashlights, "illuminating the crucifix and the Our Father beads in red, the Hail Mary beads in green, and the links between in gold," and leading a solemn rendition of the Lord's Prayer as the mysteries were enacted on the tableaux. At the conclusion of the rosary, described by *The Brooklyn Tablet* as "one of the most impressive religious pageantries ever witnessed," Cushing returned to the altar to address the question of the Holy Places. Referring specifically to the Cenacle incident, Cushing led an impassioned plea for the internationalization of Jerusalem. "How can Christendom, how can universal Catholicism," he thundered, "fail to take a prayerful but passionate interest in the future fate of these sacred places? We pray that those who determine the permanent status of Jerusalem and the sacred shrines of Palestine will be conscious that they are not merely the agents of men, but they are also instruments in the hands of God."[159] Cushing underscored the Christian stake in the Jerusalem question, urging Catholics never to abandon their "traditional rights, as venerable and inviolable as those of any others." In emphasizing the spiritual, rather than political, imperatives for internationalization, he delivered a barely concealed censure of Washington's growing alignment with Israel. "Please God will they put aside the cynicism and the callous indifference to spiritual values shamelessly revealed in some recent declarations by political spokesmen of so-called 'Christian nations.'" Cushing also invoked ancestral Roman Catholic tenets in demanding action on Palestine. "I make this plea as we seek the blessing of the God of Abraham and Isaac and Jacob through the sacrament which Christ left us the night before he died when his disciples gathered in Jerusalem to receive his testament of love, the charter of his peace," he intoned. "Surely the sublime events of that night have given Jerusalem an international character which no political convention should attempt to annul."[160] The Fenway rally represented only the most stirring of a number of demands from Catholic laity for an international Jerusalem. In August, the Catholic War Veterans of America presented a petition outlining similar demands to Truman, Trygve Lie, George Marshall, the American delegation to the UN, and representatives of all of the UN member states, bringing the combat veterans' unique clout to bear on the Palestine question.[161] Similar demands were presented by a range of national Catholic organizations such as the NCCM, the Knights of Columbus, and the Catholic Central Verein of America.

The Cenacle incident also prompted another exchange of letters between Truman and Spellman. On 10 June 1949, Spellman expressed disappointment that the admission of Israel into the UN, "due in no small degree to the attitude and influence of the United States delegation," was passed without a resolution on Jerusalem, which was now to be determined "at a later date" by the PCC, which had relocated to Lausanne.[162] In imploring the president to defend "the spiritual heritage of millions and millions of American Christians," he reminded Truman that "the 'later date' and, in fact, the last date that will affect the Christians of this country and of the world is now, and the place is Lausanne." The Roman Catholic Church, Spellman continued, sought full territorial internationalization "to prevent ... the sacred scenes of Christ's life from becoming secularized, confiscated, taxed out of existence and rendered inaccessible." To the point that such concerns might be "alarmist," Spellman referred specifically to "recent, authentic reports received from Jerusalem which showed an adverse Israelistic attitude, based on alleged provisions of security, which denied Christians – several of them Americans – access to the scene of the Last Supper in the Jewish 'New City' during Holy Week … while Jews were permitted to visit the tomb of David in the same area."[163] Given the precariousness of Catholic interests in Jerusalem, Spellman urged action from Truman. "The traditions and interests of millions of Christians in the United States and of the entire world, who look to Palestine also as their Holy Land, must be articulated at Lausanne by your representative, if the United States is not to be regarded by the whole Christian community as having failed them by default."[164]

Truman's response, penned on 22 June, sought to assuage Spellman's concerns by assuring the archbishop that he "firmly believe[d] in the necessity for the international guarantee of free access and protection of the Holy Places."[165] It was clear, however, that Truman's interpretation of the evolving debate leaned decidedly toward a guarantee of access to the sacred sites themselves, and not the territorial internationalization sought by the Vatican. On this score, Truman reiterated the potential cost of policing such an international city, with a figure "in excess of thirty million dollars" estimated by "competent officials in this government."[166] Truman concluded that he was in complete agreement with Spellman that "it is essential that Christians of the whole world be permitted freely to visit the Holy Places in Jerusalem, as soon as normal conditions are restored in Palestine. The United States government, through the PCC and the UN, will work for the establishment of a regime in Jerusalem which will assure this right."[167] The president's final response to Spellman, on 26 July, clearly suggested that he had accepted the reality of Jerusalem as a partitioned city, and even hinted at a millenarian view of the city as Israel's historic and biblical center. "Jerusalem is widely regarded among Jews not only as constituting an integral part of Zionist aspirations," he wrote to Spellman, "but as being the very heart and centre of the Zionist movement. Israel now treats the New City as *integrally* a part of Israel and it is doubtful if any Israeli government would be permitted, even if it wished to do so, to relinquish the New City to a direct international regime."[168]

Truman's responses underscored the urgent need to continue raising awareness among Catholic laity so as to bring maximum public pressure to bear on the issue. To this end, a number of eminent American bishops rallied to the cause throughout the summer, bolstering their public calls for an international Jerusalem with appeals to the faithful to make their voices heard. The archbishop of Philadelphia, Dennis Cardinal Dougherty, implored every adult Catholic in the United States to write to their political representatives on Capitol Hill and urge them to support "the points proposed by our Holy Father."[169] Dougherty's call was echoed by Mooney, Cushing, McNicholas, O'Boyle, and a number of other bishops in dioceses nationwide. In July, New Orleans Archbishop Rummel, who had been censured by the Vatican for his support of Jewish immigration to Palestine during the war, urged "every congregation [to] appeal by letter or telegram to the UN offices in New York" and demand that Catholic views be heeded, lest the Holy Places "become objects of profanation or converted into dust and ashes."[170] The episcopate's call for action, the NCWC reported to Cicognani, resulted in legislators and congressmen being "flooded with letters from Catholic citizens."[171]

The growing public agitation of Catholics on the Jerusalem question was appearing to pay some dividends. On 22 June 1949, New York Congressman Franklin Roosevelt Jr, who had recently completed a tour of Palestine, arranged a meeting between the NCWC's Monsignor James Griffiths and a group of New York congressmen "to discuss the real issues of the Palestine problem."[172] Clearly sensing an ally in Roosevelt and the gathered legislators, Griffiths reported to the apostolic delegation his "success in supplementing Mr Roosevelt's impressions at [our] off the record discussions this afternoon." By early July, Myron Taylor had added his name to those openly advocating for the full internationalization of Jerusalem. In a letter to Truman, he advised strenuously that the city "not be divided but placed in international control under the United Nations."[173] Stressing the purely strategic and political advantages of such a move, and echoing the views of the French and Italian ambassadors to the Holy See, he counseled Truman that "any further segregation of populations not friendly within the sacred sections of Palestine will lead to unending strife and constant problems for the nations to wrestle with."[174] Taylor's support for internationalization was echoed at the highest levels of the State Department. George F. Kennan, the chief architect of American postwar foreign policy, had expressed reservations on the partition plan from its origins, fearing that it only aided Soviet strategy, and regarded the *corpus separatum* as a final means of preventing open warfare between Israel and its Arab neighbors. Far from a fait accompli, it was clear that by the late summer of 1949 the question of Jerusalem was emerging as an increasing thorny issue, dividing American and world opinion along defined lines.

THE TRANSNATIONAL "CATHOLIC ORBIT" AND THE JERUSALEM QUESTION

American Catholic activism came at the head of a growing international Catholic campaign for a full *corpus separatum*, sparked in part by the pope's call to action outlined in *Redemptoris nostri*. In May, the Lebanese, French, Brazilian, and Argentinian episcopates followed the American lead in issuing formal requests, both to their own governments and to the UN, for a settlement protecting Catholic interests in the territory.[175] In June, similar demands were expressed to the British government by the Catholic hierarchies of England and Wales. British Catholic demands were echoed in the same month by the Anglican bishop in Jerusalem, Reverend Weston Henry Stewart, whose open letter to Trygve Lie and the PCC was cosigned by Luigi Barlassina, the Catholic auxiliary bishop of Jerusalem.[176] Sir Eric Drummond, former secretary-general of the League of Nations and a Catholic member of the House of Lords, similarly pledged support for an internationalized Jerusalem, calling for an expanded *corpus separatum* in line with that which Pope Pius XII "considered necessary."

In early spring, The Hague–based International Union of Catholic Women (IUCW), through its New York secretariat, issued a detailed memorandum to the PCC demanding an internationalized Jerusalem and the repatriation of Arab refugees.[177] Speaking for "36 million women and girls in 65 countries and 5 continents," the petition raised specifically female concerns on the Palestine question, connecting delays in the repatriation of the refugees to the psychological and sexual abuse of women and children languishing in the refugee camps of Egypt and southern Palestine.[178] On Jerusalem, IUCW demands echoed a familiar refrain: that the city was a uniquely historical crossroads of three faiths, a "spiritual home" in which Roman Catholics held "imprescriptible rights." The statement also referenced the recently adopted Universal Declaration of Human Rights, linking access to the Holy Places to the freedom of worship ensconced in it. The demands of Christians in the Holy Land, it concluded, could not be ignored "without impairing democratic principles in all civilized countries."[179]

In August, in an address before the Irish parliament (the Dáil), Irish Foreign Minister Sean MacBride made a "special appeal to the government of Israel" for the internationalization of Jerusalem. He invoked the history of persecution endured by both Irish and Jews, declaring that "our common suffering from persecution and certain similarities in the history of the two races create a special bond of sympathy and understanding between the Irish and the Jewish peoples."[180] To MacBride, this historical parallel lent particular gravitas to Ireland's request. "Speaking from that point of view," he continued, "I venture to make a special appeal to the government of Israel to meet the just claims of the Christian world for an international regime guaranteeing the safety of the Holy Places and freedom of access to them." He later confirmed that Irish diplomats in London and Washington were pursuing this end, and assured that his plea was shared by the Irish government, which "strongly supported" calls for the "internationalization of the whole area of Jerusalem."[181] As Shulamit Eliash has noted, Irish relations with Israel in this period were deeply influenced by the Vatican's demands on the *corpus separatum*, as the drive for internationalization, led by the Irish bishops and embraced by the laity, was a factor in Ireland's withholding of full diplomatic relations with Tel Aviv.[182]

In the same month, the official organ of Spanish Catholic Action, *Ecclesia*, announced that the Spanish episcopate, on an appeal directly from the Vatican, would be applying renewed pressure on Madrid over the Holy Places. Spanish bishops also implored the American and Canadian bishops to "interpose [their] good offices with [their] own governments" so that "all of the nations of the Christian orbit could carry out the will of Rome."[183] Despite historical tensions between anglophone and francophone Catholics in Canada, a remarkable unanimity existed on the question of Jerusalem. Bishops across the nation, as well as national Catholic societies, heeded the 9 May 1949 call of the apostolic delegate, Ildebrando Antoniutti, to "insist that the government of Canada – which has given proof of its special interest in the new Israeli State – ensure that Catholic rights in the Holy Land be respected."[184] Italian Catholics, deeply connected to the Vatican both historically and culturally, exerted their own pressure on their national government. Through the spring and summer of 1949, Catholic journals such as *L'Osservatore Romano*, *Civiltà Cattolica*, *L'Avvenire d'Italia*, and *Il Quotidiano* boldly insisted on Israeli adherence to the *corpus separatum* and the repatriation of Arab refugees, demands that the bishops carried to officials in the Chamber of Deputies.[185]

Calls to action also emanated from more obscure corners of the Catholic world. In July, the Catholic associations of Sindh and Baluchistan, two of Pakistan's five provinces, issued a memo to the government in Karachi to pressure the PCC and the UN for a solution to the Jerusalem question amenable to Catholic interests. In early fall John Francis Norton, the bishop of the Diocese of Bathurst, Australia, led a rally in the tiny gold rush town of Gulgong demanding the internationalization of Jerusalem, placing the issue within the context of the Crusaders' battles to win back the Holy Land from the infidels. In the October rally, he denounced "the Zionist state backed by international finance," which had "profaned churches, smashed crucifixes and statues … and ill-treated religious people."[186]

This transnational "Catholic orbit" had already functioned to curtail Tel Aviv's ambitions when Israel's May bid for UN membership was accepted with conditions attached by a clutch of Central and South American states.[187] Key among these demands was the strict Israeli adherence to the principles outlined in the 1947 partition plan, as well as the repatriation of refugees displaced by the subsequent conflict, both conditions conforming to the Vatican's own demands. The Chilean delegation insisted that the resolution to admit Israel explicitly mention its obligations to the November 1947 resolution, and an Argentinian motion suggested that Israel and the PCC formally "take into account the views of the Holy See" when deciding on the form and extent of an internationalized Jerusalem.[188] Argentinian delegates, in fact, pressed Israeli representative Abba Eban over his assurances that the papal encyclicals would be used as a guide for Israeli policymakers, taking "careful note" of all of Eban's pledges.[189] On the importance, and imperative, of Israel's and the UN's fulfillment of all of these vows, Catholic representatives were unequivocal. The Lebanese ambassador to the UN, Dr Charles Malik, expressed the gravity of the issue to the Vatican and the global church. "What is at stake is not Jerusalem, not the Arabs, not the Jews," he declared on 18 May 1949, "but the quality of Western statesmanship itself."[190]

This mounting international Catholic pressure precipitated a concentrated effort by Israel, in the spring and summer of 1949, to establish direct diplomatic relations with the Holy See, part of an attempt to mitigate the effects of transnational Catholic pressure by negotiating directly with the Vatican Secretariat. In early August Israeli Foreign Minister Moshe Sharett, clearly bending to the pressure applied to Israel, forwarded Myron Taylor's office a range of proposals for Jerusalem.[191] If the Vatican was only interested in the full internationalization negotiated in 1947, it was not possible, claimed Sharett, as this would place 100,000 Jews under an ambiguous international regime, and at risk of Arab attacks. He did, however, offer some conciliatory positions: international control and supervision of the Holy Places both in Jerusalem and in the rest of the territory (including sites in Jewish-controlled sections of West Jerusalem) and the internationalization of the Old City, with Israel providing for its economic and political stability.[192] The Vatican, sensing momentum in the dispute, rejected Sharett's proposals. Tardini explained to

James Dunn (American ambassador to Italy) that the Vatican "was always cautious and slow in all matters involving recognition of any newly created state," calling the immediate exchange of ambassadors "quite premature," but he suggested a deeper rationale for rejecting both Sharett's proposals and the diplomatic recognition of Israel.[193] He stressed that the position of the Vatican remained unchanged from that revealed in the encyclicals of 1948 and 1949, which proposed a full *corpus separatum*, an "international buffer" for the city "which neither Jew nor Arab could violate." Tardini asserted that "no other solution could be considered adequate by the Holy See," since the present status of Jerusalem teetered on the edge of a renewed Jewish-Arab war.[194] He suggested that as a pretext to "serious negotiations," Israel would "do well to settle grave unwarranted war damages suffered by Catholic institutions in the Holy Land."

On 12 August 1949, Tardini forwarded to Taylor a six-page memo under the title "The Present Situation in Jerusalem," a "compendium of *de facto* and *de jure* considerations which according to the Holy See were essential in the just resolution of the Palestine question."[195] These proposals, in short, dismissed any possibility of a compromise on the Vatican's part, amounting to a loquacious restatement of long-held positions. The memo outlined factors beyond Catholic interests for the internationalization of Jerusalem. These included the notion that the city was a crucial dividing line between Arabs and Jews, and that international control would greatly reduce the chances of a war sparked by either for absolute control of it. Tardini also surmised that an internationalized Jerusalem would be more economically self-sufficient, not least because its stability would draw Catholic pilgrims from around the world, generating significant revenues.[196] On the question of recognizing Israel and entertaining Israeli proposals for Jerusalem, Tardini insisted on the establishment of a *corpus separatum* as a precondition to any exchange of ministers. The Vatican clearly preferred allowing Tel Aviv to twist in the wind of international Catholic pressure to providing a direct line of communication for resolving disputes.

Though the Vatican refused to extend formal recognition to Israel, it continued to use McMahon as an unofficial envoy in the territory. At the request of Pius XII, the American prelate had returned in June 1949 as the president of the PMP to coordinate the distribution of aid in the refugee camps strewn through the territory. Though the Vatican refused to confirm or deny rumors that McMahon's aid mission had a political agenda attached, his meetings with high-ranking Israeli officials confirmed that he indeed functioned as a papal envoy. At any rate, the Israeli government continued to regard him as the pope's de facto representative. McMahon's August meetings with Yaacov Herzog and Chaim Wardie, of the Ministry of Religious Affairs, and Moshe Sharett revealed a growing entrenchment of both Vatican and Israeli positions. In a meeting with Sharett that the latter described as "long and grim," McMahon informed his host that nothing short of a "full blooded international regime" would satisfy the Vatican. The growing intractability of the Jerusalem question was evident in Sharett's notes. "What he obviously meant to convey," he recorded, "was that the Catholics had not originally objected to one portion of the Holy Land being given to the Jews and another to the Arabs provided they themselves got Jerusalem, but as things had now turned out, they found themselves cheated out of their rightful heritage."[197]

In another meeting just days later, Herzog asked McMahon how Israel could effectively open dialogue with the Vatican on Jerusalem and the refugees, particularly in advance of the UN debate on the PCC's resolutions, set to begin in September. Herzog also discussed with McMahon the Israeli interpretation of the encyclicals of 1948 and 1949, claiming that he "did not read in them the UN partition plan of 1947."[198] McMahon, again revealing the leadership of the American church on the issue, replied that "the Vatican is not a member of the UN, but the United States bishops and our own CNEWA have been demanding implementation of the 1947 plan, and have never been told by our Holy Father to do otherwise."[199] Clearly sensing the upper hand, he yielded to none of the earlier suggestions, already floated by Sharett and again put forward by Herzog. "I gather that the Jews are anxious to get to the Vatican before the September troubles, and to present some compromise … all of which will naturally be in their favour," he reported back to the NCWC. "My own idea is that we should not be taken in, for it is certainly a policy of '*divide et impera*.' However it is good to know what they are up to. I already indicated that they have promised nothing, and that the most critical moment in the whole period comes in the September Assembly."[200] Spellman's most trusted monsignor had surmised correctly. As the fall 1949 session of the UN General Assembly was set to begin, the Jerusalem question was about to reach a high boil, and American Catholic advocacy would witness its most crucial days.

CHAPTER 6

Chimeras of Triumph

In the fall of 1949, the American bishops orchestrated a frenetic and final campaign to shape the Jerusalem question. At the UN, numerous compromise solutions were debated and discarded, lending credence to Catholic hopes that the full *corpus separatum* could yet be reimposed. Catholic diplomacy at the world body was conducted by two remarkable laywomen, Catherine Schaefer and Alba Zizzamia, who acted as skillful intermediaries between Vatican, American, Israeli, and Jordanian interests. Israel, which clearly considered American Catholic political pressure a threat to its visions for Jerusalem, organized its own campaign to countervail the NCWC's narrative. From December 1949 to December 1950, it appeared that the transnational Catholic lobby, led by the American church, had scored a definitive and implausible triumph in steering the Palestine Conciliation Commission to preserve the *corpus separatum* as it had been conceived in the 1947 partition plan. The implausibility of implementing the *corpus separatum* on Jerusalem, however, given the mounting tensions in the Holy City, soon rendered these UN resolutions a dead letter. From 1951 onward, the papal curia relied increasingly on the CNEWA's irrepressible Monsignor Thomas McMahon to spearhead the Vatican's final attempts to wrest a victory from the looming jaws of defeat.

THE PALESTINE CONCILIATION COMMISSION AND THE FATE OF THE HOLY CITY

The PCC's initial proposals for the city, which were contained in the twenty-five-article "Jerusalem Statute," were completed by the committee on 29 August 1949, and were forwarded to the UN to be debated in the General Assembly's Fourth Session, set to open in September. Its recommendations amounted to a compromise between proponents and opponents of a *corpus separatum* for the city, shaped by American desires to offend neither camp too severely. Though French PCC delegates were claiming that Vatican and French Catholic pressure was making it difficult to agree to anything less than full internationalization, they were eventually persuaded to adopt a middle-of-the-road approach that still appeared to fulfill the spirit and letter of the 1947 partition plan.[1] The PCC statute called for the establishment of a "permanent international zone" for Greater Jerusalem (the territory that was to be a *corpus separatum*), which also encompassed Bethlehem and predominantly Arab villages on the outskirts of Jerusalem, including Ein Karim, Shuafat, and Abu Dis. Though it recognized Jerusalem as one entity, it recommended the division of the city into Arab and Jewish zones. It delegated civic jurisdiction to the "responsible authorities of the two zones," essentially recognizing Israeli and Jordanian sovereignty in the city. It limited administrative bodies to the provision of public services and forbade the establishment of national and governmental institutions there, a clear challenge to Israel, which had already located some of these in the city, including the Supreme Court. Immigration quotas were also imposed in an effort to preserve the "demographic equilibrium of the area of Jerusalem."[2] A fourteen-member General Council was established to govern the city; Jewish and Arab zones would elect five members each, and the UN commissioner would select an additional four members deemed representative "of distinctive minority groups in the Jerusalem area." On the Holy Places, the statute proposed the appointment of a neutral (neither Israeli nor Arab) commissioner who would ensure free access to sites sacred to Christians, Jews, and Muslims, and who was authorized to station guards outside of them.[3] This UN official was also granted the authority to arbitrate disputes over access to sacred sites, and was instructed to defer to the rights and practices of each as they existed in May 1948, ensconced as they were by the 1757 Status Quo agreement.[4] In essence, the PCC's Jerusalem Statute was a hybrid scheme intended both to establish a quasi-international character for the city, reflective of the 1947 partition plan, and to recognize the reality on the ground, where the Israeli and Jordanian presence had become well entrenched.

Though the State Department, whose guidelines constituted the essence of the PCC recommendations, believed that the statute represented "a last chance to achieve any degree of internationalization," the plan was not well received by the Vatican. In early September, advance copies of the PCC statute were forwarded to the Vatican and the American hierarchy, under strict confidence, by Catherine Schaefer's NCWC UN Office. Domenico Tardini, the Vatican's acting secretary of state, immediately surmised that the PCC formula amounted to a significant watering down of previous pledges. His memo to Schaefer expressed skepticism that a UN commissioner could effectively arbitrate disputes between Arab and Jewish interests or protect access to the Holy Places. Tardini further posited that neither Israelis nor Jordanians should be appointed to governing bodies in the PCC scheme, arguing that this would only legitimize the forceful seizure of the city. The Vatican continued to insist upon a full *corpus separatum* for Jerusalem and its environs. A day after receiving the report, he requested that Schaefer's office redistribute a NCWC pamphlet, *The Rights of Christians in the Holy Land*, to delegates at the General Assembly.[5] In her reply, Schaefer agreed that it made a powerful case for the Roman Catholic position, adding that the "historical aspects of the pamphlet will be particularly valuable, since the long story of the vicissitudes of the Holy Places is proof that their control by single nations has never insured either their real freedom or protection."[6]

Within days, the Vatican again turned to the assistance of the NCWC UN Office. On 16 September 1949, Tardini forwarded Schaefer a second memo outlining the Vatican's questions and concerns on a large number of the twenty-five points in the PCC's Jerusalem Statute.[7] The Vatican's concerns centered on the danger of renewed conflict between Jewish and Arab factions in the city, threatening access to and the security of the Holy Places, and on the impossibility of impartiality in appointing a UN General Council. Tardini again instructed Schaefer to distribute these Vatican observations to the UN "to make known the mind of the Holy See on this delicate and complex problem." He emphasized the need to target those whose views were amenable to the Vatican's, "delegates likely to make their own contributions toward an equitable solution of the question."[8] To this end, he suggested Catholic delegates such as Charles Malik of Lebanon, Father Anand Souza of India, and Dr Emil Castro of El Salvador.

Tardini's urgency was motivated by the Vatican's growing apprehension that various interests were conspiring against papal designs, and that some Catholic allies in the struggle for Palestine were wavering, believing that the PCC recommendations were reflective of papal policy. The specter of Moscow also loomed. In early September, Tardini informed the NCWC of his concern about certain PCC members whom he suspected of harboring hardened anti-Catholic sentiments. He specifically identified Dr Pablo de Azcárate, principal secretary of the PCC, whom he deemed "an active Red in the Spanish Civil War," with "an anti-Catholic record."[9] He asked the NCWC UN Office to keep tabs on PCC members and to forward any relevant information to Rome. Catholic apprehensions were heightened further on 16 September 1949 when, during an off-the-record UN luncheon for press correspondents, Secretary-General Trygve Lie expressed to Schaefer little hope that "the obstacles in the Jerusalem question would be overcome or bypassed by the General Assembly," hinting at the difficulty in imposing an international regime in a city already controlled by Israel and Jordan.[10] Lie further suggested that the Arab refugee problem would likely be "settled by dollars," suggesting monetary incentives for neighboring Arab states taking in refugees, in lieu of resettlement in Palestine.

In the same week, Schaefer also surmised that several Central and South American delegates were warming to the PCC's compromise statute for Jerusalem, in addition to the American and British delegations, which were prepared to support PCC proposals "as a basis of discussion." She reported to Carroll that the Dutch delegation, which "included several Catholic members," and which had supported the *corpus separatum* concept since its inception, was now considering "introducing a resolution which would in effect scrap the whole idea of true and proper internationalization, leaving Jerusalem partitioned as it is now, merely providing for some sort of mixed commission" to guarantee protection of and access to the Holy Places.[11] She considered the Dutch position particularly important for its effect on the positions of Belgium and Luxembourg, both Catholic-majority states. As "the Benelux countries have a habit of consulting on these matters," she stated to Carroll, she would provide him with "urgent clarification" of the Dutch position.[12]

Schaefer's efforts were also buffeted by a robust, vocal, and transnational pro-Israel lobby that included the largest and most powerful American Zionist groups such as AZEC, the AJC, and the ZOA. It also included American Protestant groups such as the ACPC, which favored Israeli sovereignty in Jerusalem, and which generally supported Israeli positions vis-à-vis the Arab world and the UN. Members of the ACPC, which included both evangelical and mainline Protestant churches, had grown strident in their calls for defending the Israeli state. While mainline Protestants regarded Israel as a liberal democratic outpost of Western civilization, and saw the protection of the Jews as a humanitarian imperative, evangelicals additionally regarded the creation of Israel as a sign of biblical prophecy, presaging the return of Christ and the "end of days."[13] These groups largely mirrored the position of the Israeli government itself, which had dismissed the PCC plan before the September General Assembly session had even begun. Israeli Foreign Minister Moshe Sharett referred to the plan as "anachronistic," "incongruous," and "illusory," rejecting any scheme that did not recognize Jerusalem as the rightful capital of Israel. Richard Ford, the American chargé d'affaires in Tel Aviv, confirmed this sentiment in a letter to the State Department. Israelis had "become so closely identified with the proposition that Jerusalem must be and practically already is the capital," he wrote on 9 September 1949, "that any thought of retrogression at this late date appears out of the question."[14]

In mid-September, AZEC issued an appeal to Truman demanding the right of Israel to use Jerusalem as its rightful capital. *Palestine*, AZEC's bulletin, voiced the opinion of a majority of Jewish organizations in stating that "the Jews of Jerusalem and their political life are not the concern of religious mankind; the Holy Places and their security are," a position that clearly challenged the Vatican's stand.[15] On 3 November 1949, AZEC and smaller Zionist groups staged a large "Save Jerusalem" rally at New York's Manhattan Center, with leaders unanimously going on record to call for the rejection of the PCC plan for Jerusalem, and to "accord the Jews of the Holy City the right to participate in the government of Israel and share in its problems and responsibilities."[16] Speakers included Republican Congressman Jacob K. Javits, Democratic Congressman Emanuel Celler, and prominent Zionist leaders such as Nahum Goldmann and Louis Lipsky. In turn, speakers emphasized the feasibility of protecting the sacred sites within a Jewish Jerusalem, echoing Tel Aviv's rationale. Passionate evocations of Israel's historic claims to the city, however, were also invoked. A reading of Psalm 137 of the Hebrew Bible, a lament on the Jewish exile in Babylon, deepened the solemnity of the gathering. "If I forget thee, O Jerusalem," read its fifth and sixth verses, "let my right hand forget her cunning. If I do not remember thee, let my tongue cleave to the roof of my mouth; if I prefer not Jerusalem above my chief joy." In closing, Lipsky, chairman of the American Zionist Council, asserted, "without Jerusalem, Israel would be deprived of its spiritual significance."[17] Virtually the whole spectrum of American Jewry was mobilized in the Save Jerusalem campaign, as Zionist leaders, encouraged by a powerful grassroots support among the faithful, organized a focused bid to convince the American UN delegation to "reject any plan which would sever the New City of Jerusalem from Israel."[18]

To this was added the support of the ACPC, represented by influential theologians such as Reinhold Niebuhr and Carl Voss, who, despite earlier hesitations, had become firm supporters of Israeli sovereignty.[19] In a letter to Truman on 19 October 1949, 101 members of the ACPC attacked the PCC proposals as "neither desirable nor practicable." The letter specifically recognized Jerusalem's "New City" (the section controlled by Israel) as "the natural capital of the State of Israel," adding that "the realization of the universal interest in Jerusalem and the fulfillment of the national aspirations of the people of Israel are in no way incompatible."[20] On 3 November 1949, the same day as the ACPC rally in New York, fifteen prominent Protestant and labour leaders forwarded a letter to General Carlos P. Romulo, president of the UN General Assembly, and Secretary-General Trygve Lie, demanding an "international curatorship" for the Holy Places, with an administering commission composed of representatives from the Protestant, Greek Orthodox, Roman Catholic, Jewish, and Muslim faiths, and responsible to the UN Security Council. The letter advocated strongly for a Jewish Jerusalem, echoing the demands of American Zionist groups, and was clearly intended to downplay the Vatican's stake in the Holy City by making a Catholic representative only one of five representatives on the commission. Among the signatories, which included no Roman Catholics, were Niebuhr, G. Bromley Oxnam, Methodist bishop of New York, Norman B. Nash, Episcopalian bishop of Massachusetts, James Patton, president of the Farmers Educational and Cooperative Union, and Walter P. Reuther, president of the United Automobile Workers of America.[21]

Leading American Catholic figures were well aware of the threat that the vociferous and focused Save Jerusalem lobby presented to the Vatican's interests on the Jerusalem question, and the diocesan press wasted little time in pointing up not only Israeli transgressions in the territory, but also the powerful Zionist lobby at work in the United States. Throughout September and early October 1949, *The Brooklyn Tablet* reported on an American Zionist pressure campaign, coordinated "by several thousand orthodox rabbis," that had resulted in a flood of telegrams, letters, and cards being dispatched to Truman and to American UN delegates from synagogues and Jewish organizations.[22] On 15 October, the paper further reported that a "crusade" was about to be organized, and called on American Jewry to take a biblical oath

(Psalm 137) whereby they would "bind themselves in relentless opposition to the internationalization of Jerusalem."[23] "In 1947," the paper observed wryly, "we found no Zionists calling on American Jewry or on world Jewry for a 'Biblical Oath' to repudiate the internationalization of Jerusalem and its environs. At that time, when the viability of a Jewish state hung in the balance, there was no mystical invocation of the phrase, 'If I forget thee, O Jerusalem.'"[24] *The Brooklyn Tablet* mused openly on the potential of American Zionism's campaign to "mislead officials of the United States and the United Nations into thinking that there was only one point of view on the future of Jerusalem."[25] "It is possible that officials will get that impression," it warned, "if the position of Catholics is not expressed with comparable vigour and volume." It reminded readers that Psalm 137 was "as much a challenge to the multiple millions of Christians throughout the world as it is to Jewry and Islam," and it implored Catholics not to "forget Jerusalem, even in this latest hour of struggle between Isaac and Ishmael."[26]

In early November, Catherine Schaefer expressed similar, if less grandiloquent, sentiments to Howard Carroll, general secretary of the NCWC, urging that the American bishops make the struggle for Jerusalem their highest priority until the matter was settled at the UN. In alluding to the powerful American Zionist lobby, she observed that "the present position of the United States is in favour of the PCC report, but is subject to constructive influence. You will remember that the United States position showed itself to be quite susceptible to strong representations of public opinion on previous occasions when the Palestine question was discussed."[27] Observing that this position "would be influential, if not decisive to the outcome," she advised Carroll that a high-level representation from the American hierarchy to the US government was imperative. "A personal visit to President Truman by one of these officials," she added, "would also help tremendously." She also urged representations from lay Catholic organizations, in line with the Pope Pius XII's call to action in *Redemptoris nostri*. She cited the recent examples of the French Women's Catholic Action, which had submitted a petition to the Quai d'Orsay demanding internationalization, and the Catholic Women's League of Canada, which had passed and published a resolution on the question. In closing, she emphasized to Carroll the urgency of the matter. "If anything is to be done by Catholics," she stressed, "it is imperative it be done soon. The Delegation of Israel is cultivating and consulting with members of various delegations, including those from Catholic countries, and giving the impression that its plan, which would not provide for the internationalization of Jerusalem, has the support and tacit approval of the Vatican. A clear and unequivocal statement of Catholic aims and desires in the matter is needed."[28]

The NCWC wasted little time in intensifying its own campaign. The day after receiving Schaefer's letter, Carroll wrote to Dean Acheson, reminding the secretary of state of the American bishop's April statement, which contended that only the creation of a genuine *corpus separatum* "could guarantee the security and preservation of the Holy City, which is venerated by the whole civilized world, and which has been contested in blood by Jews and Arabs."[29] The letter, which was also forwarded to Warren Austin and other key members of the American UN delegation, was clearly intended to highlight American Catholicism's continued insistence on full *corpus separatum*, and to counter impressions that the PCC's proposals were acceptable to the Vatican, as some American Zionist groups had inferred. The next week, Carroll cabled the letter directly to the White House.[30] On 20 November 1949, Archbishop Timothy McNicholas of Cincinnati, chairman of the administrative board of the NCWC, made his own representation to Truman, asking the president for American intervention at this crucial juncture.[31] Stating that he spoke "for the vast majority of American citizens," he expressed hope that the United States "would remain true to its glorious traditions of deep respect for religion and decency, and exercise its powerful influence in this matter." On the lay Catholic front, the NCCM and the NCCW also sent telegrams to Truman, Acheson, and Austin urging American support for genuine internationalization.[32]

The role that Schaefer's UN Office played in the crucial weeks leading to the decision on Jerusalem can hardly be overstated. In early November, Schafer and her assistant, Alba Zizzamia, were asked by Carroll, on instructions directly from the Vatican, to "draft a memorandum or statement on the Catholic position on Jerusalem" to be used by the bishops at their upcoming annual meeting for 1949.[33] Tardini, in fact, suggested that Schaefer's eventual memorandum, which would be formulated from the principles gleaned from confidential Vatican memoranda on Jerusalem and the papal encyclicals, be used as a guide for UN delegates from Catholic states. Tardini was concerned that there was "a good deal of confusion among UN delegates as to the precise position of the Church on the question," a situation exacerbated by Israeli delegates who claimed that Tel Aviv's proposals were amenable to the pope.[34] To this end, Carroll forwarded Schaefer a confidential Vatican memorandum outlining Pope Pius XII's continued insistence on nothing short of genuine internationalization.[35] Schaefer and Zizzamia's familiarity with both papal positions and the PCC proposals made them, in Carroll's view, ideal candidates to draft "an accurate statement of our position in the present stage of negotiations." Just five days later, Schaefer returned a pithy yet comprehensive statement, which she admitted she and Zizzamia had "torn their hair out over, separately and collectively."[36] Schafer also included, for the "strictly confidential information of the bishops," a copy of the Israeli draft proposal for Jerusalem, allowing the NCWC to anticipate Tel Aviv's position before formulating their own statement. The bishop's annual statement for 1949, issued on 21 November, bore the indelible mark of both the Vatican's memoranda and of Schaefer and Zizzamia's draft.[37] Carried widely in the diocesan press, it was also forwarded to Truman, Austin, and members of the American UN delegation.

Schaefer's office was similarly crucial in surmising where support for the Vatican's position did and did not exist among UN delegates, and for the dissemination of a range of memoranda and position papers from the NCWC and Vatican sources to these delegates, an effort that required a close monitoring of South American and European voting intentions. By mid-November, with a vote just weeks away, Schaefer perceived support from the Brazilian, Peruvian, Cuban, Lebanese, and Soviet delegations, along with the support of a clutch of Arab states, who supported a *corpus separatum* primarily to curb Jordanian ambitions in the region.[38] On 15 November, however, she reported that a number of delegations, "even those sympathetic to the Catholic point of view," were warming to the compromise solution proposed by the PCC. "Some have said they are starting on the basis of the PCC plan without much enthusiasm for it," she reported to Carroll, "in the hope that by insisting on as much as possible, some form of satisfactory compromise can be restored."[39] Schafer was referring to Catholic states, such as Mexico, Venezuela, and Chile, whose positions had modified steadily since the late summer. Their positions were likely shaped by the growing skepticism on the feasibility of a *corpus separatum*, and their desire to remain onside with the United States on such a key vote. Axel Serup, legal adviser for the PCC, confirmed Schaefer's growing apprehension during an off-the-record luncheon when he announced that UN priorities were focused squarely on the protection of the holy sites themselves, as well as peace between Arab and Jewish factions. The UN "had no interest," he revealed to her, "in the exercise of sovereignty of civil administration."[40]

In the midst of sagging support, and just weeks before a UN decision on Jerusalem, the efforts of the Vatican and the American church reached a fever pitch. On 14 November, the Vatican issued an apostolic exhortation by Pope Pius XII calling upon Catholics worldwide to pray for a just settlement for Jerusalem, "a status in accordance with the norms of true justice that will remove the dangers of war and will preserve the sacred character of those places."[41] The following day, Cicognani urged the American bishops "to call upon your pastors, priests, religious and laity to organize and to participate in public and solemn prayers for this intention." "I am sure that your Excellency," he continued, "will find for your diocese the means best calculated to acquaint your priests and people with the purpose and meaning of this crusade, and to carry out the ardent desire of the Holy Father" – a clear attempt to rouse American Catholics on the eve of the UN vote.[42] In the final two weeks of November, various archdiocesan associations, including those in Los Angeles, Dallas, Chicago, Cleveland, Detroit, and Buffalo, engaged in letter-writing campaigns urging federal representatives to adopt a solution amenable to the Vatican and the global church.[43]

Further evidence of American Catholic leadership at this crucial juncture was highlighted by Vittorio Veronese, president of Italian Catholic Action, when he requested that the NCWC present his organization's petition demanding the full internationalization of Jerusalem and its environs to the UN.[44] "It is my personal conviction," Veronese stated, "that at this time American Catholics, being closest to the high international assembly and, as free citizens of a great country, able to make themselves heard, can do so much so that the rights of Christendom may be neither ignored nor go unrecognized. I take leave, therefore, in the name of Italian Catholic Action, to ask ... the NCWC to be the authoritative interpreter of our ardent desire to see the problem of the Land of Jesus solved according to justice."[45] In alluding to the fact that Italy was not a UN member state, and again to the preeminent position of American Catholics among national branches of the church, he concluded that "Since Italy is not allowed to express, together with other free nations, its opinion on the Palestinian problem, may the American Catholics be our spokesmen in this cause, which is common to us all."[46] In mid-November, Schaefer presented the petition to numerous PCC delegates. In early December, just days before the UN vote on Jerusalem, Carroll forwarded copies of the letter to Truman, Acheson, and Austin, as well as dozens more copies to Schaefer for distribution to additional UN delegates.[47] The statement was also given wide exposure in the diocesan press. In his letter to Truman, NCWC General Secretary Howard Carroll informed the president that he spoke "for the Catholics of Italy, as well as of the rest of the world," emphasizing the universality and unanimity of Catholic demands on the Jerusalem question.[48]

The Ad Hoc Political Committee's debate on the PCC report began on 24 November 1949. In short order, three new plans emerged to challenge it, evidence that Catholic pressure was having some effect. The first alternative, supported by some American UN delegates, advocated for the limited internationalization suggested in the PCC plan, with some modifications designed to accommodate Israeli and Jordanian concerns. A second view, proposed by Israel, pledged the protection of the Holy Places themselves, but limited mainly to the Jordanian-controlled Old City, in line with similar proposals that Yaacov Herzog had earlier presented to the Vatican directly. The third proposal, put forward by the Australian delegation, favored a full *corpus separatum* as originally proposed by the November 1947 General Assembly resolution. This view, which rejected the compromises proposed in the PCC plan, was supported by a number of Latin American states, the Arab League, and the Soviet Bloc. As Chanan Reich has demonstrated, the Australian resolution was driven by domestic Catholic pressure in the form of bishops instigating a widespread campaign to maintain the full *corpus separatum* promised in 1947. With a December election looming, nearly half the sitting cabinet being Roman Catholic, and the Australian Labor Party having committed to defending the 1947 partition plan, Foreign Minister Herbert Evatt had little choice but to support the full internationalization proffered by the Australian delegation to the UN.[49]

In the midst of the General Assembly deliberations on Jerusalem, another persuasive advocate for the Catholic position emerged: Charles Malik, Lebanon's ambassador to the UN. A powerful proponent of the Vatican's perspective at the world body, Malik, whom Schaefer considered "a sincere Catholic and ally on the question of Jerusalem," indeed wielded particular esteem in UN circles. He had served as a rapporteur for the Commission on Human Rights, president of the Economic and Social Council, and Lebanon's ambassador to the United States from 1945 to 1955. In 1948, Eleanor Roosevelt appointed Malik to the drafting committee that produced the Universal Declaration of Human Rights, a document that bore some of the hallmarks of his philosophical and theological views. These included his rejection of authoritarian systems that violated the dignity and rights of the individual, a position that created some friction between Malik and Soviet Bloc delegates. As a Levantine-born diplomat, philosopher, scholar, theologian, and Christian, he exerted a definitive influence on both Arab delegations and representatives of Catholic-majority states at the UN.

On the question of Jerusalem, Malik ardently supported a full *corpus separatum* for both Jerusalem and its environs, positing that the sanctity and security of the Holy Places could only be secured through a UN regime, as

Israeli-Jordanian sovereignty in the city portended further conflict and destabilization. On 26 November, in coordination with Schaefer, Malik delivered a powerful statement on Jerusalem to the General Assembly.[50] Reading liberally from the recent statement of the American bishops, a document crafted by Schaefer and Zizzamia, Malik delivered a bold defense of a fully internationalized Jerusalem. He reminded delegates that Christians had "held the Holy Places in Palestine as a sacred trust" for centuries, and that Catholic orders such as the Franciscans had suffered martyrdom in defense of them. Malik dismissed the PCC plan as "pretending internationalization of the Jerusalem area, but by no means achieving it," clearly contrasting the full internationalization sought by the Vatican and outlined in Pope Pius XII's recent encyclicals with the "mere control or curatorship" proffered by the PCC scheme. In concluding, Malik warned that anything short of a *corpus separatum* would mean the subordination of the sacred character of Jerusalem and the Holy Places, to the detriment of Christians, Jews, and Muslims alike.

At this stage of the negotiations, a palpable American ambivalence on the Jerusalem question set in, a hesitancy that can be traced to two factors. The first was Washington's desire to offend neither opponents nor supporters of a full *corpus separatum* – that is, Jews and a majority of American Protestant groups on one side, and American Catholics on the other. The debate on Jerusalem had taken a bitterly divisive turn since support for the PCC scheme had weakened in September, and the American delegation became progressively wary of the increasingly polarized issue. The second factor in Washington's vacillation was an underestimation of the Vatican's ability to galvanize Catholic-majority states into support for internationalization, as evidenced by a growing support for the *corpus separatum* from a number of Central and South American delegations.[51] On 29 November, a seventeen-country subcommittee was formed to study the various proposals, and given three days to propose a draft resolution of its own. That the American delegation was not included in this committee is further evidence of Washington's efforts to distance itself from the increasingly thorny Jerusalem question.

The subcommittee, composed primarily of Soviet Bloc, Arab, and Catholic-majority states, and which included Malik's Lebanese delegation, wasted little time in proposing a solution. On 2 December it adopted, with only minor amendments, the Australian draft resolution proposing full internationalization in accord with the 1947 partition plan. Three days later, the Ad Hoc Political Committee resumed its debate on the Jerusalem question. With support for the PCC plan collapsing, and backing for full internationalization once again resurgent, a last-ditch compromise was jointly offered by the Swedish and Dutch delegations. This proposal, designed to break the logjam between proponents and opponents of the full *corpus separatum*, suggested a fundamental internationalization of the Holy Places throughout Israel and Jordan, a demilitarization of Jerusalem, and a ban on the establishment of administrative organs in the city by either state. The plan included the appointment of a UN commissioner who would be empowered to assure Israeli and Jordanian compliance. Though the American delegation saw merit in the Swedish-Dutch resolution, it remained hesitant to become embroiled in the polarized question, particularly considering the domestic implications of adopting a visibly partisan stance. The lack of American support for the Swedish-Dutch proposal virtually guaranteed the acceptance of the Australian resolution. On 7 December, in an open vote, the Ad Hoc Political Committee affirmed the Australian draft resolution by a vote of 35 to 13, with 11 abstentions. The result meant that the resolution most favored by the Vatican and its allies was about to be placed back on the agenda of the General Assembly for a vote on 9 December 1949.

As such, the voting intentions of Catholic-majority states assumed prime importance. Schaefer, who had monitored such intentions closely for both the American bishops and the Vatican, expressed concern over the leanings of several Latin American delegations on the final ballot. Cuba, Haiti, and Bolivia, she apprised Tardini, appeared to be lukewarm on the Australian resolution, while Guatemala, Uruguay, Chile, and the Dominican Republic were preparing to reject it altogether. Just days before the vote, Tardini wired a number of these delegations, urging them to support a resolution that was in line with the papal encyclicals and which the Vatican had officially endorsed. At this crucial stage, Spellman's far-reaching influence once again became manifest as he engaged in an urgent campaign of personal diplomacy as the final vote loomed.[52] From New York, he called papal nuncios in Latin American capitals to make vigorous representations to their governments to stand in line with the Vatican on Jerusalem.[53] The cardinal's intervention appeared to account for a shift in the voting intentions of at least four delegations (those of Mexico, Venezuela, Haiti, and Chile) that had either voted against the Australian resolution in the deliberations of the subcommittee or had abstained during a 7 December preliminary ballot. Spellman similarly wired the head of the Philippine delegation, Carlos Romulo, upon learning that it was preparing to cast a "no" vote. Spellman was, in the end, able to secure the support of the Philippines on the final ballot. Despite widespread skepticism of the feasibility of complete internationalization, and the desire to remain aligned with the United States on a key vote, the pressure exerted by Tardini, Spellman, and Schaefer in the final days of deliberations appeared to be decisive. As a member of the Haitian delegation explained, voting for a Jerusalem free from the sovereignty of Israel or Jordan was "in keeping with the wishes of the Catholic countries."[54]

On 9 December 1949, after ten hours of debate marked by tension and disagreement, the committee voted 35 to 14 to adopt the Australian resolution to internationalize the Jerusalem area as outlined in the 1947 partition plan, with support coming from what the NCWC described as "an unusual alignment of Latin American, Arab and Soviet bloc states."[55] As Avi Shlaim has noted, Soviet support for internationalization was a sign of Moscow's disenchantment with Israel's progressive alignment with the United States, despite the nascent state's earlier policy of nonalignment.[56] Notable supporters also included the Philippines (which Spellman had aggressively courted), Brazil, France, Belgium, and Luxembourg (which had wavered up to the last minute), two-thirds of the Latin American delegations, and a number of Arab states.[57] Though the United States, Britain, and Canada opposed the resolution, the outcome was a clear victory for the Vatican and the American bishops, who had coordinated and cultivated the "Catholic vote" at the UN to the final hours.[58] An amendment introduced by El Salvador (which had assured Schaefer of its support) defined the internationalized area as Jerusalem and its environs, including Bethlehem and other towns, while another amendment, sponsored by the Soviets and Lebanon, urged "immediate implementation."[59] Though the outcome was everything the Vatican could have realistically hoped for, a Colombian delegate to the PCC, who had cited the solidarity of Catholic states as crucial to the outcome, presciently observed that "now [was] not the time to stop praying," an allusion to the difficulties of implementing the plan.[60]

Despite obvious challenges, the result was a clear triumph. Just days after the vote, Schaefer composed a short memo outlining the factors that had contributed to the success of the Vatican and the international church in securing the full *corpus separatum*.[61] The prime factor, she suggested, was the solidarity of Catholic delegations in the final tally. She noted that though the chatter at Lake Success and reportage in the American mainstream press had focused on "Vatican pressure and Roman Catholic opinion on Latin American governments," less noticed was the support of Catholic-majority European states in the final vote. France, Belgium, and Luxembourg, "none of which were openly committed to full internationalization at the outset," voted in the affirmative, with the Netherlands, another state with a large Catholic population, abstaining. European "no" votes were registered by predominantly Protestant-majority states, including Britain, Denmark, Norway, and Sweden. Schaefer also credited the solidarity of Arab states, citing Charles Malik's efforts, whom she lauded for "spearheading" the Arab vote, describing him as "insistent and articulate in stressing the religious interests and in presenting the views of religious leaders, twice referring to the papal encyclicals and reading into the record the statement of the Catholic hierarchy of the United States." His "exposition of the thesis of Israel's expansionist aims to encompass all of Jerusalem, and of the United States' consistent support of Israel," she observed, "had its effect."[62] Schaefer further proposed that Israeli intransigence had also contributed to the results of the final vote by raising fears that the General Assembly could be coerced into bending to the will of one member and accepting "the dangerous precedent of recognizing de facto situations achieved by force of arms, or be led by fait accompli tactics."[63] Her reflection on the vote also shed an interesting light on Spellman's role, noting as she did that Manila's UN representative voted in the affirmative even though Elpidio Quirino, president of the Philippines, was "known to be opposed to the full internationalization resolution."[64] Finally, Schaefer credited Soviet Bloc votes, which came from the Soviet Union, Poland, Czechoslovakia, and Byelorussia, as also having carried the day.

The intense horse trading that had produced the Jerusalem resolution had indeed frayed the nerves of delegates, as Schaefer surmised in the days after the vote. On 16 December, at a post–General Assembly meeting convened by the UN for observers and NGOs, she noted that most attendees shared "a marked reluctance to comment on the internationalization vote," despite attempts by American officials to draw out reactions.[65] She observed, however, that there was "less sympathy for the Israeli stand than the [secular] American and Jewish press would imply." Predictably, reactions from Tel Aviv and Israeli-friendly press organs were severely critical of the UN verdict. *The New York Post*, which had been an opponent of internationalization, opined that, "In moral terms, the UN decision is shabby beyond belief … its religious mask shows through, its legal garments are skimpy, its moral grounds non-existent, it unsettles rather than settles the peace, and it lacks any method of enforcement."[66] James McDonald, now the American ambassador in Tel Aviv, concurred that Vatican influence played a key role in the final vote. Though he attributed part of Israel's defeat to overconfidence, he opined that "the single greatest factor in its failure was the Vatican, which used its diplomatic influence in favor of internationalization of the Holy City. That influence was sufficient to carry the day."[67] Israeli Prime Minister David Ben-Gurion reflected on the international influence exerted by the Vatican against Israel. "On this occasion," he observed, "the power of the Vatican and the Catholic Church has been manifest as it has probably not been since the Reformation."[68] Foreign Minister Moshe Sharett, for his part, called 9 December 1949 a "dark day" for the UN, and stormed that "Israel [was] aligned against the whole world," charging that "three powerful forces have joined hands against us – the Arab world, the Communist world and the Catholic world."[69] "The 'Catholic attitude' manifested," Sharett thundered – in a clear allusion to deicide – "a fanatical religious dogma, the desire to seek revenge for a nation's sin and to settle an account of 1900 years standing."[70] Protestant groups such as the ACPC, which had also warned against a *corpus separatum*, joined the chorus of denunciation, criticizing the plan as "dangerous and unnecessary."[71] *The Nation*, a leading liberal-progressive journal, expressed its own hypothesis on Israel's defeat. On 17 December 1949, Lillie Schultz, an administrator for the American Jewish Congress, a UN observer, and a staff writer and editor at *The Nation*, penned an article tracing the voting patterns to the Vatican's pervasive influence. "The immediate problem the UN faces," she concluded, "is to destroy the Vatican's power of coercion."[72]

In the immediate aftermath of the vote, congratulations abounded in American Catholic circles. The NCWC's Howard Carroll praised the "masterful and effective championing of Christian interests" shown by Dr Charles Malik, head of the Lebanese legation to the UN, who had read sections of the American bishop's statement for 1949 into his speech to the General Assembly.[73] Malik was assured that his efforts had "elicited widespread admiration and was a source of deep gratification." On 3 January 1950, the Vatican, through Cicognani, voiced its thanks for the activism of the American Catholic Church. "I am directed to express the sentiments of profound gratitude of the Secretariat of State," he wrote, "for the cooperation which the entire Episcopate of the United States gave in courageously making known and repeating the words of the Supreme Pontiff for the defence of the rights of the Church in the land of Our Blessed Saviour."[74] The Vatican reserved special praise for the NCWC and the advocacy of Schaefer's UN Office. "In a special manner I have been asked to express appreciation for the cooperation of the staff of the National Catholic Welfare Conference in supplying timely information to the

Secretariat of State regarding this question, and for the success they attained in their contacts with persons useful in the task of making known the point of view of the Holy See."[75]

Despite the Vatican's diplomatic triumph on the Jerusalem question, however, there remained the difficult task of implementing such a scheme in the midst of a region still locked in bitter struggle. Israel and Jordan, in short order, unequivocally rejected a plan that would eliminate their sovereignty over the Holy City. Israel quickly moved to establish a more permanent national presence there, clearly intended to demonstrate its rejection of the UN's verdict. In December 1949, Ben-Gurion had already driven home the point that Israel would refuse to comply with the UN's resolution for an internationalized Jerusalem when he declared that a "Jewish Jerusalem [was] an organic and inseparable part of the State of Israel," and that, if forced to, Jews would "sacrifice themselves for [it] no less than Englishmen for London, Russians for Moscow or Americans for Washington."[76] An Israeli government memorandum later explained its position in equally definitive terms. "The suggestion that Israel is nothing to Jerusalem and Jerusalem is nothing to Israel may appear fantastic, yet this bewildering thesis is explicitly held up by the [*corpus separatum*]. One cannot have it both ways. It is an axiom that Israel cannot be regarded as a factor in the implementation of a regime based on the disappearance of its own authority."[77] As such, Tel Aviv wasted little time in preparing to make Ben-Gurion's sentiments a concrete reality. Just a week after the vote, he set 1 January 1950 as the deadline to transfer Israel's government ministries to Jerusalem, effectively establishing the city as the national capital, despite its uncertain legal status. Jordan's King Abdullah similarly flouted calls to internationalize the city, and he ordered permanent Friday prayers to be held there, which he attended personally.

Israeli and Jordanian intractability came at the head of a growing list of factors that soon militated against Vatican and American Catholic designs for Jerusalem. This included the effective end of the Myron Taylor mission in January 1950, a signal that the Truman administration did not see the enduring utility of a Vatican envoy. The termination of the Taylor mission, in large part due to Protestant pressure, was coupled with surging support for a Jewish Jerusalem from a number of mainline American Protestant groups, a factor that complicated any possible American acquiescence on the internationalization of Jerusalem. Finally, and perhaps most troubling to the Vatican, were signs of a breakdown in international Catholic solidarity on the Jerusalem question, with some states coming to regard the pursuit of territorial internationalization as perhaps just but ultimately unfeasible.

The Jerusalem question was reexamined by the UN's Trusteeship Council in January, when a committee was convened at Geneva to hammer out a functioning resolution that would suffice in the face of Israeli and Jordanian intransigence. On 5 January 1950 the NCWC's Howard Carroll pressed the American delegation at Geneva on its Jerusalem policy, anxious to secure assurances that the United States would seek to uphold the majority decision of December 1949.[78] The delegation's response confirmed Carroll's concerns that American support for the status quo at Geneva (i.e., the *corpus separatum*) would not be forthcoming. The delegation would verify only that the United States would seek a "workable resolution" that would guarantee the protection of the Holy Places, be acceptable to Israel and Jordan, and satisfy the international community's desire for peace and stability in the region.[79] Once again, the American church would be called upon to assume the lead in advocating for papal policy at the UN.

MS ZIZZAMIA GOES TO GENEVA

As it became evident that American support for the Jerusalem resolution could not be counted upon, the importance of making known the Catholic viewpoint at the UN, and of fomenting support among the various delegations there, became increasingly essential. To this end, the NCWC's UN Office dispatched Alba Zizzamia, assistant director to Catherine Schaefer, to the Trusteeship Council's Geneva session in January 1950. Zizzamia held a doctoral degree in literature from the University of Rome and had served as a professor of Italian and French at Trinity College in Washington, DC. A scholar of Christian history and experienced in the cut and thrust of UN diplomacy, Zizzamia was uniquely suited for the task. Her mandate was threefold: to keep the American bishops and the Vatican apprised of developments on the Jerusalem question, to supply the diocesan press with reports, and, where possible, to disseminate the Roman Catholic position among the various delegations. Before arriving in Geneva, Zizzamia was received in a private audience by Pope Pius XII, where they discussed her mandate. The pope thanked the NCWC for its efforts on Jerusalem, an issue that remained "a most serious question," both to him personally and to the international church, a sentiment he repeated to his guest throughout the short audience.[80]

At Geneva, Zizzamia soon confirmed that the *corpus separatum* scheme for Jerusalem, which had been passed by a UN majority resolution just a month previous, was under attack from a number of quarters. Most notably, she sensed the willingness of American delegates to support a revised and diminished statute, consistent with the response that the NCWC had received earlier in the month. Though the United States had not supported the December 1949 agreement, the NCWC had hoped that American delegates, in following their own precedent, would support the majority decision. Francis Sayre, head of the US delegation, however, expressed to Zizzamia the "unrealizable" nature of the *corpus separatum*, a solution that could not be imposed without force. "It will not mean peace," opined Sayre, "and it is not Christian," a clear challenge to the Roman Catholic Church, which remained the most powerful international advocate of full internationalization.[81] Sayre also informed Zizzamia that the United States could not support any action on Jerusalem that might require the deployment of American troops to the city, a concern that Truman had previously communicated to Spellman.[82] By late January, Zizzamia reported that American support in maintaining any semblance of full internationalization was unlikely. From this point forward, it was evident that Washington sought a compromise solution for Jerusalem, one amenable to Israel, despite the vague assurances that Truman and officials in the American government had offered Catholic leaders the previous year.

In another report, Zizzamia noted the "unwholesome" atmosphere at Geneva, where "the preponderance of sentiment is not favourable to the Catholic viewpoint, which is regarded as unrealistic if not unjust."[83] She noted several Central and South American delegates who appeared to favor a revised statute on Jerusalem. The Philippines, which Spellman had notably swayed in the final hours of the December vote, also appeared to be moving toward support for a compromise solution. She further noted that Pierre Ryckmans, head of the Belgian delegation, "made no attempt to hide his irritation" at Catholic attempts to maintain the *corpus separatum* against all evidence that it could succeed. "Why stick to the Assembly resolution of December 9," he told Zizzamia, "when there is no way at all to implement it?"[84] In confidence, a French delegate echoed Ryckmans, informing Zizzamia that "if it were not for religious fanaticisms in Jerusalem, the question could be settled. The Catholic Church and Catholic organizations are very stupid, because if a [compromise solution] is not accepted, there will be nothing."[85] Only among Arab delegations did she find unanimous support in maintaining the *corpus separatum*. Iraq's Dr Fadhel Jamali assured her that Arab states would not accept a watered-down solution. "If the Arabs and the Catholics stick together," he observed, "we can block any other plan," though he admitted that such a statute "would probably remain a dead letter."[86]

The revised statute that emerged from the Trusteeship Council's Geneva session did reflect the prevailing spirit among delegates there in the form of a compromise statute reflective of the realities on the ground. The so-called Garreau Plan, tabled by French representative Roger Garreau, proposed that as the area defined by the General Assembly resolution was too extensive to be administered by the UN, extraterritoriality should be applied only in the area regarded as "absolutely essential" to the "protection of the Holy Places and freedom of movement for pilgrims."[87] In essence, the Garreau Plan called for the division of the territory of Jerusalem into three parts: an Israeli zone under the authority and administration of Israel, a Jordanian zone under the authority and administration of Jordan, and an "International City" under the sole authority and responsibility of a UN-appointed "Governor of the Holy Places."[88]

The Garreau Plan appeared to garner the support of a majority of the delegations that opposed the December 1949 resolution, including the United States, and that generally favored a revised scheme acceptable to both Israel and Jordan. The plan also received the endorsement of the powerful ACPC, the prominent Christian Zionist organization, which had dispatched a fact-finding mission to Jerusalem in December and January. At a January 1950 press conference in New York, the ACPC discussed its "findings on the feasibility of the internationalization plan for Jerusalem," concluding that the *corpus separatum* idea was "dangerous and unnecessary."[89] The statement closely mirrored Sayre's position in recommending a UN commissioner for the Holy Places, but not territorial internationalization, which might necessitate the deployment of American troops. That the report was forwarded specifically to Sayre, Secretary of State Dean Acheson, and Trusteeship Council President Roger Garreau suggests that it was clearly intended to influence American policy at Geneva.

A concerned Zizzamia noted to Carroll that not only were ACPC observers active in Geneva, they also "seemed to be on very good terms with members of the U.S. delegation."[90] Its observers, her report continued, were creating the impression among delegates that Roman Catholic groups, both in Palestine and abroad, accepted the Garreau Plan as a realistic compromise. In private conversation, Garreau himself noted that Cardinal Spellman "had been shown the plan," suggesting that the de facto head of the American Catholic

Church was not opposed to it. Garreau further suggested that he had received no protest from the Vatican, despite Zizzamia's insistence that papal policy remained unchanged.[91] The inclusion of the ACPC report as an enclosure to the Garreau Plan, submitted on 13 January 1950, and the reading of the report to a session of the Trusteeship Council by Samuel Guy Inman, a member of the ACPC's mission, was evidence of the influence the organization wielded at Geneva.[92] Inman's authority was buttressed by his background as an academic and consultant to the State Department, where he was credited with shaping Washington's "Good Neighbor" policy with Central and South American states. During his address before the council on 11 February 1950, Inman suggested that his organization's view was representative of global Christian interests generally, and he mentioned "two or three times that the ACPC includes in its membership Catholic laymen."[93] "Mr Inman seems to be creating the impression," Zizzamia reported to Carroll, "that he is speaking for Catholic opinion." Though Iraq's delegate, Fadhel Jamali, questioned the political slant of the ACPC, charging that it "wore Zionist glasses," the organization was nonetheless successful in shaping the view that Christians, including Roman Catholics, were accepting of revisions to the 1949 *corpus separatum* agreement.[94] Given that the Vatican did not have its own representative at the Trusteeship Council's meeting, the task of correcting that impression fell largely to Zizzamia.[95]

The Vatican indeed rejected the revised scheme, a position based on drafts of it forwarded to Rome by Zizzamia. At the end of January, on the very eve of Garreau's tabling of the plan, the Vatican issued a memorandum outlining its unequivocal position on Jerusalem "as clearly set forth in the papal encyclicals."[96] It insisted that the Holy See "had expressed its position, and did not accept or approve any compromises," a statement intended to scuttle the idea that Rome was softening its stand. It demanded adherence to the status quo, fearing that a plan such as Garreau's would create more turmoil than it would resolve.[97] This was followed by a *pro memoria* in early February, which more strenuously outlined Vatican objections to the plan. It specifically criticized Garreau's notion of creating "zones" in Jerusalem, charging that it "was not clear how a boundary can be viable which crosses the narrow streets and alleys of the Old City, nor how these little international islands can escape damage in case of an armed conflict."[98] It concluded that the Holy See, in rejecting the plan, "could not share in the responsibility for its acceptance on the part of the Trusteeship Council." In early February, as the council prepared to debate the Garreau Plan, Zizzamia actively disseminated the Vatican's stand among various delegations, making clear that any suggestion of a moderated Roman Catholic stance was categorically false.

Archival evidence suggests that, in the crucial days of debate on the Garreau Plan before the Trusteeship Council, Roman Catholic pressure again shaped the responses of a number of delegations, including that of the United States. Yossi Feintuch has observed that the American delegation's position on the Garreau Plan became increasingly ambiguous and incoherent, reflective of a desire to maintain a distance from the thorny question it was meant to address.[99] In confidence, delegates revealed to Zizzamia that domestic politics continued to play a role in American policy. American Catholic and Jewish pressure, specifically, appeared to shape Washington's indeterminate stance. This was expressed by France's Pierre de Leusse, who confided that, despite "the formidable propaganda campaign sponsored by Israel, the money used on the press (and some say among the delegates), and the pressure put on the American government, attention will have to be paid to Catholic strength in the U.S. Mr Truman will have to take into account the Catholic votes, which are far more numerous than the Jewish votes, although the Jews have more money."[100] As such, he predicted that Sayre's eventual stance would be one of "passing the buck" to avoid political entanglement in the United States.[101] Australia's John Hood offered similar sentiments, citing "opposing parties" as being central to the UN's lack of resolve on the Jerusalem question. "This was notably true for the United States," he offered, "which is, after all, 'the kingpin' in this."[102]

Indeed, American vacillation would render the Garreau Plan a dead letter. On 10 February, the Trusteeship Council shelved the proposal in favor of a draft resolution calling for the immediate reconsideration of the 1948 Jerusalem Statute, which had called for the complete territorial internationalization of the city. A Belgian amendment provided for the implementation of the statute at a date to be determined later and made its enactment subject to the approval of Israel and Jordan. Secretary of State Acheson instructed Sayre to vote for the statute, provided the Belgian amendments were carried, but to follow up his vote with a statement affirming to the council that it would have to pass muster with Israel and Jordan before implementation. It was a stance perfectly crafted to offend neither camp of the *corpus separatum* debate, and bore clear signs of being influenced, at least in part, by American domestic politics. That Sayre was instructed to abstain on the final vote, for fear of creating an impression that the United States had reversed its position against internationalization, epitomized Washington's sensitivity to the Jerusalem question.

Though the defeat of the Garreau Plan could most visibly be traced to the resolute stand of Arab delegations at Geneva, most notably those of Iraq and Syria, the influence wielded by the Vatican through Catholic delegates and observers was noted in a number of quarters. The ACPC's Samuel Inman, who had presented the Trusteeship Council his organization's report on the feasibility of internationalization, held a late-February press conference at Lake Success at which he bemoaned the revival of the *corpus separatum*, charging that it would "make Jerusalem a centre of international intrigue and disorder."[103] Though Inman claimed that American public opinion was solidly behind his conclusions, he suggested larger forces were at play in Geneva. "It is no secret," he exclaimed, "that the Vatican wants to create a sub-capital at Jerusalem."[104] Similar sentiments were expressed to Zizzamia earlier in the month, when an Israeli correspondent whose wife was attached to Israel's embassy in Washington echoed Inman's view. "It is no secret the [pope] wants a Vatican City in Jerusalem. Since he did not get control as he wished when the commission under the old mandate failed to be set up, he hopes to get Catholic control there now through the Catholic countries at the UN."[105] "The Jerusalem question," he admitted to Zizzamia, "is a bone in our throat."[106]

The Trusteeship Council's adoption of the Jerusalem Statute on 4 April 1950, barely altered from the December 1949 resolution, appeared to be another example of Catholic pressure snatching victory from the jaws of defeat. It was again, however, a largely illusory triumph, as its practical implementation proved much more difficult than its adoption. The Jordanian election of April 1950 created further barriers, as its results confirmed the unity of the eastern and western banks of the Jordan River and their merging into one unified state, the expanded Hashemite Kingdom of Jordan. The following day, Jordan notified the UN that it had formally annexed central Palestine and East Jerusalem (which it had already occupied).[107] Just five days after the incorporation of East Jerusalem into Jordan, the Soviet envoy to the UN informed Secretary-General Trygve Lie that, in light of developments in Jerusalem, Moscow considered the Jerusalem Statute unfeasible and thus would not continue to support it. It was a development that marked the end of the curious and short-lived Catholic-Arab-Soviet consensus on the *corpus separatum*, placing greater pressure on "Catholic" delegations to deliver a Jerusalem solution amenable to the Vatican.

From April onward, given the rapid evolution of circumstances, Zizzamia noted a definitive waning of support for carrying out the Jerusalem Statute. Though the United States had remained theoretically neutral on the April vote, abstaining along with the United Kingdom, evidence suggests that the American delegation's impatience with the old formula was growing. "It is increasingly evident that the U.S. delegation," she confirmed, "has no interest whatsoever with the total internationalization plan."[108] Sayre, head of the American mission, confided to Zizzamia that he "would be willing to cooperate if anyone will show us how internationalization can be put into effect, but we feel it is turning back history."[109]

Flagging enthusiasm for internationalization extended beyond the American delegation. "Many delegates, in private conversation, admit that internationalization was the best, long-run solution," Zizzamia noted to Carroll in May, "but they professed utter helplessness as to the possibility of realizing it."[110] She also noted that Australia's John Hood, who had introduced his country's favorable resolution regarding internationalization at the December 1949 General Assembly session, and who "upheld it with a skilled diplomacy," was to become Australian ambassador to Indonesia. The defeat of Australia's Labor Party in the December 1949 elections, where domestic Catholic pressure played a role in Herbert Evatt's support of the *corpus separatum*, signaled the potential loss of another ally. Hood's "successor on the Trusteeship Council could, without embarrassment," Zizzamia explained, "express a change in the Australian position."[111] In addition, she revealed uncertainty on the part of a number of South American delegations who could not be counted on if the question, as it appeared it would, was returned to the General Assembly. In late April, in a moment of candor, she bluntly assessed the situation for Carroll. "The fact that there is a diminishing interest in the internationalization of Jerusalem, even among the nations that originally voted for it, should be recognized. If the Statute elaborated by the Trusteeship Council is not implemented, which does not at the moment seem at all likely, it should be decided whether it is advisable from the viewpoint of Catholic interests to keep the question open and before the United Nations."[112] The view from Geneva clearly confirmed that support for the Vatican's vision for Jerusalem was withering on numerous fronts.

JERUSALEM CALLING: ISRAEL, ITS ALLIES, AND THE "CATHOLIC PROBLEM"

From the early spring of 1950 onward, the notion of a *corpus separatum* was also countered by a generously funded and well-orchestrated propaganda campaign by the Israeli Foreign Ministry, an effort Uri Bialer considers unique in the history of the ministry.[113] A special division, established in April 1950, was allocated considerable funds, recruited leading experts, and was active on the international scene. Its objective was to present Jewish Jerusalem to the world as a vital, modern city and an inseparable part of the State of Israel. It was also intended to emphasize Judaism's historic stake in the city, and to emphasize the justice and practicality of Israel's proposals for a solution.[114] To this end, the division commissioned numerous pamphlets and books for wide distribution to buttress Tel Aviv's position. Special emissaries were also sent to the capitals of several Latin American states to disseminate the Israeli perspective among nominally pro-Vatican UN members, an initiative clearly intended to break up the transnational Catholic "bloc" that had functioned to keep the *corpus separatum* alive. Bialer notes, however, that Israeli efforts were careful not to engage in open polemics against the Vatican "so as not to provoke the other side to launch a vocal attack on us," evidence that Tel Aviv continued to regard the Vatican, and its international allies, as a viable threat.

Sensing a growing momentum, Israel's ambassador to the UN, Abba Eban, tabled a new proposal in May that signaled some flexibility on the Jerusalem question.[115] The proposal essentially suggested the internationalization of a zone immediately surrounding the sacred sites in the Old City to be administered by an autonomous UN commissioner. In the United States, wider public opinion appeared to be growing in favor of a compromise solution along the lines of that proposed by Israel. The ACPC offered its endorsement of Eban's proposal on 28 May, and just days before, Truman and Acheson received petitions, signed by almost three hundred prominent Americans, urging the United States to back the recent Israeli proposals. Signatories included a cross section of Protestant leaders, including bishops of the Episcopal Church (led by New York's Episcopalian bishop, Charles K. Gilbert), as well as Methodist, Unitarian, and United Brethren leaders. Other signatories included college presidents, academics, and Nobel Prize laureates. In June, Eleanor Roosevelt added her own support to the petition, a symbolic endorsement given President Roosevelt's close relationship with American Catholic leaders.[116] Also in support were several leading newspapers such as *The New York Times* and *The Washington Post*, which provided positive editorials on the Israeli proposals. The following week, Carroll assured Cicognani that the NCWC was preparing to counter the statement, but his response indicated a growing pessimism in American Catholic circles. "The NCWC is, of course, preparing a critique of the statement for the press," he informed the apostolic delegate, "but is too much to expect, even with our best efforts, that the attitude of the United States government will change radically. From our point of view it seems that only the steadfast and continuing support of Catholic nations which are members of the UN can assure the acceptance of the position of the Holy See."[117]

Carroll's dour appraisal, however, did little to modify the Vatican line on Jerusalem. Nor did the growing consensus on a compromise to the *corpus separatum*, bolstered by Eban's recent proposal, alter the Vatican's insistence on the original formula. To underscore this, Cicognani reissued the *pro memoria* of February to the NCWC the day after Eban's proposal was circulated at Geneva. On 31 May, the Vatican's insistence on the original plan was outlined in *The New York Times*.[118] Quoting "well informed Vatican circles," the article outlined papal opposition to the notion of Israeli or Jordanian sovereignty in Jerusalem, which, given the existing proposal, "could be broken in the event that hostilities were resumed," an outcome the Vatican thought likely. In essence, the Vatican considered the problem juridical, and not political, given that a circumscribed *corpus separatum* would create an international zone within a city that was not legitimately Israeli or Jordanian to begin with. The December 1949 agreement, it concluded, "did not affect the principle of the nationality of Jerusalem, since no one disputes that principle. The question is one of administration and not of nationality."[119]

In June, the Trusteeship Council began its seventh session in an effort to formulate a definitive report to the General Assembly recommending a solution to the Jerusalem question. Zizzamia noted that the session was held "in an atmosphere created by an extremely skilful Israeli propaganda and pressure campaign."[120] In light of this, Zizzamia suggested a two-pronged strategy in defense of the Vatican's interests. She advised "concerted action on the part of the Catholic press in UN member states before the [December] General Assembly to counteract Israeli propaganda. One tactic must be a critical attitude … on the compromise plans." She also advised, despite flagging support for the *corpus separatum*, "political pressure in the various countries, and especially in the United States."[121] Within days of the session opening, it appeared that Zizzamia's suggested strategies would have some time to germinate. On 14 June, just two days after convening, the Trusteeship Council resolved unanimously to inform the General Assembly of its inability to ensure the implementation of the Jerusalem Statute "either by force" or by "moral authority."[122] Garreau, as the council president, admitted that "the results of his mission had proved disappointing and that the implementation of the statute would seem to be seriously compromised under present conditions."[123] "In other words," Zizzamia's report noted wryly, "the Trusteeship Council has accomplished virtually nothing."[124]

The failure of the Trusteeship Council to resolve the Jerusalem conundrum did, ultimately, allow crucial time for the American church to shape Catholic and wider opinion on the question, as well as to mount a more coherent pressure campaign in advance of the December meeting of the General Assembly. Optimism at the NCWC, however, remained muted through the summer of 1950. In June, at Cicognani's behest, Carroll ordered a critique of the ACPC statement in support of a Jewish Jerusalem, though he cautioned the apostolic delegate that "it is too much to expect, even with our best efforts, that the attitude of the United States government will change radically."[125] Carroll placed greater hope in Roman Catholic delegates at the UN, advising Cicognani that, "from our point of view, it seems that only the steadfast and continuing support of Catholic nations which are members of the UN can assure the acceptance of the position of the Holy See."[126] On this score, the Vatican requested regular appraisals of developments both at the UN and in the United States, which the NCWC forwarded throughout the summer.[127]

On the issue of shaping public discourse, the NCWC continued to defend the integrity of the *corpus separatum*, despite the deferral of debate on the question at the UN. Throughout the summer, the diocesan press, fed by reports from Schaefer and Zizzamia, highlighted the merits of full internationalization as well as the potential pitfalls of the various compromise schemes that surfaced in the first half of 1950.[128] In June, Carroll ensured that the views of the Armenian patriarch of Jerusalem, Bishop Tiran Nersoyan, who had penned an eloquent and persuasive defense of the Vatican's position on Jerusalem, were given ample coverage in the diocesan papers. In order to balance what Catholics perceived as one-sided coverage in the mainstream secular press (which generally favored a compromise solution), Carroll also advocated for Catholic views to be aired in mainstream papers. On 4 June 1950, *The New York Herald Tribune* carried Nersoyan's statement, which had been forwarded to the paper by Carroll.[129]

In a bid to shape elite opinion, and to underscore the juridical legitimacy of the *corpus separatum*, Catholic academic journals also highlighted the imperative for an internationalized Jerusalem. The March 1950 issue of *Thought*, a quarterly published by Fordham University, featured an article by Constantine Rauckaskas, a professor of international law at the school, carefully outlining the historical evolution of the Jerusalem question.[130] Rauckaskas argued that the purpose of internationalization was not merely to protect the Holy Places from destruction and to guarantee access to them, as compromise solutions had suggested, but also to "preserve the future peace in granting such places an administration which would be above the interest of any church or religion and above the particular interest of any nation or state."[131] In essence, Rauckaskas posited that the Jerusalem question was international, not simply national, and that the interests of Israel and Jordan in the city were superseded by the superior rights of the international community and the three global faith groups that cherished Jerusalem as a Holy City. Rauckaskas opined that the preservation of the full *corpus separatum* was essential to the maintenance of regional peace, which, he concluded, should be the UN's primary motive. In July *The Jurist*, published by the Catholic University of America's Faculty of Law, carried an article by law professor Peter Berger in which he similarly delineated the case for internationalization.[132] Presenting a detailed history of the city, Berger posited that imperial or national sovereignty in Jerusalem had almost always produced conflict, and often imperiled the rights of Christian, Muslim, and Jewish pilgrims. Given the growing tensions since 1947, he continued, the only feasible resolution was a *corpus separatum* safeguarded by a UN presence in the city; only this, he concluded, would "form a *cordon sanitaire* against the excess of nationalism. If they [a UN peacekeeping force in Jerusalem] do not form a serious military obstacle against a well-equipped army, they will be a moral hindrance at least against aggression." The piece was clearly intended to reassert the case for a genuine *corpus separatum* amid the muddying waters of the various compromise solutions floated in the spring of 1950. It was also intended to confirm that the Vatican and American Catholics accepted nothing less than what was pledged in December 1949, despite chatter that a practical compromise was acceptable in Roman Catholic circles. At Carroll's behest, Schaefer distributed Berger's article to all the UN delegations as a reiteration of the Vatican's stand.[133]

As the December General Assembly session drew nearer, however, American Catholic optimism was clearly waning in the face of a number of headwinds. The first of these was Israeli intransigence in claiming the city as its de facto capital, despite its indeterminate legal status. In September, Schaefer noted the "fait accompli" attitude of Israeli delegates and officials at the UN, who "assumed that Jerusalem will be, and for all practical purposes was, a part of Israel."[134] Abba Eban, Israel's ambassador to the UN, confirmed Schaefer's sentiment in the September issue of *United Nations World*, the body's semi-official journal.[135] In it, Eban outlined the inherent historic and moral righteousness of a Jewish Jerusalem, whose negation, he claimed, would be antidemocratic and against the wishes of the city's own residents. The *corpus separatum*, which he charged was "conceived in disregard of the wishes and interests of Jerusalem's population," was "courageously discarded by the Trusteeship Council and returned to the General Assembly unimplemented." Eban concluded that "democratic principles, which had a compulsion of their own, could least of all be set aside in the city of Jerusalem, in which the ideal of government by consent is expressed in the daily practice of a proud and constructive national life."[136] That Eban's notions were steadily garnering acceptance among UN delegates was, by September, clear to leading figures in the NCWC.

Another emerging challenge faced by the American Catholic lobby came in the form of pointed critiques of that lobby itself by figures in the American liberal and academic establishment. The appearance of Paul Blanshard's *American Freedom and Catholic Power* late in 1949 sparked a growing critique of American Catholic political power, and of the Vatican's attempts to shape Washington's policies through its American faithful.[137] In the book Blanshard, a lawyer and contributing editor at *The Nation*, asserted that the United States had a "Catholic problem" in that the American Catholic Church represented "an undemocratic system of alien control." This "Catholic problem" was not a question of religion, wrote Blanchard, but "an institutional and political problem," and the American church, in this view, had to be "reckoned with as an organ of political and cultural power." Blanchard's implication was clear: the American hierarchy leveraged "the political power of some twenty-six million American Catholics to bring American foreign policy into line with Vatican temporal interests."[138] Though presented as a manifesto for the separation of church and state, the work often revealed a nativist, anti-Catholic bent. That it received acclaim from a number of leading public intellectuals, including John Dewey, Albert Einstein, and Bertrand Russell, only broadened its influence. Far from an obscure polemic, the work sold nearly 300,000 copies in its first year, remaining on *The New York Times* bestseller list for seven months, making it, as John T. McGreevy has noted, "one of the most unusual bestsellers of 1950."[139] Though several leading Catholic figures, including John Courtney Murray, Robert C. Hartnett, and James M. O'Neill, offered rebuttals to Blanshard's charges, none of these responses could undo the disrepute and sense of suspicion being draped over American Catholic political activism.[140]

Blanshard's thesis was buttressed later in 1950 by Pierre Van Paassen, a journalist and Unitarian minister whose book *Jerusalem Calling* leveled specific charges against the Vatican and the American Catholic lobby on the Jerusalem question.[141] Apart from surveying the history of Catholic antisemitism, Van Paassen "illuminated" American Catholicism's attempts to "subvert the triumph of Zionism through international political activism."[142] He charged that "the struggle of Rome against Israel goes on, and will be intensified as papal nuncios negotiate with Arab princes, and General Franco, to devise ways and means to prevent the new community of Israel from assuming a position and playing a role of importance in the international concert."[143] Van Paassen also claimed to unveil the "machinations" of the American Catholic political lobby, including Spellman's eleventh-hour intervention on the Jerusalem vote.[144] Though a number of Van Paassen's claims bordered on the fantastical, including that he was told directly by Vatican officials that Israel was "obviously an outpost of the Soviet Union in the Near East," and that its very existence "was a threat to peace in that part of the world," Catherine Schaefer cautioned the NCWC that the book would likely "stir up considerable anti-Catholic sentiment, particularly among the Jews."[145] "The charge of official anti-Semitism by the church will be thrown around a lot, I imagine," she warned. "We should be prepared to meet the attacks that will come."[146]

The third headwind faced by American Catholic efforts was the growing consensus between American Jews, Protestants, and liberals for a Jewish Jerusalem. It was a development that essentially pitted Catholics against a majority of their fellow citizens on the *corpus separatum*, highlighting the papal inspiration of the American Catholic position. Bolstering this consensus was Truman's steadfast desire for a pragmatic solution for Jerusalem, reflective of the reality of Israeli and Jordanian claims to the city, and consistent with Truman's position as outlined to Spellman the previous summer. Truman's support for Israel and for a Jewish Jerusalem, shaped in part by his own Baptist eschatology, was primarily driven by national interests and the pressures of domestic politics.[147]

In October, in a confidential memorandum to the NCWC, Schaefer noted this confluence of forces ranged against the Vatican and American Catholics. Chief among these challenges, she noted, was Washington's insistence on a compromise solution amenable to Israel and Jordan, a policy that produced "the weak and vacillating positions of other countries" on the Jerusalem question.[148] She highlighted the influence of domestic factors on Washington's stance, stating that "American policy on this question is undoubtedly made at the White House … it is strictly political in a domestic sense," and noted Truman's "responsiveness to the cohesive vote and pressure of five million Jews."[149] "This policy," she continued, "is helped along by the constant lobbying of Israeli and American Jews, and by the attitude of the [Protestant] World Council of Churches, and by the press in the United States which constantly infers that the Vatican has changed its point of view and is willing to 'settle' for less than full internationalization." "To correct this impression," she concluded to Carroll, "the first responsibility lies on Catholics in the United States."[150]

"MAXIMUM EXPOSURE": CATHERINE SCHAEFER'S UN OFFICE ORCHESTRATES A FINAL PUSH

Schaefer's memo suggested a vigorous campaign prior to the upcoming UN session, given that the Jerusalem question was weeks away from appearing on the General Assembly's agenda. She continued to believe that pressure on the US government, which was a linchpin on the Jerusalem question, remained the most viable strategy. Even down to this late stage, she intimated that pressure on Washington and the American delegation to the UN might yet bear fruit. "If, through United States pressure Israel could still be made willing to yield that portion of the Jerusalem area it now occupies, the task of persuading Jordan … to yield the Old City to international control would be simplified."[151] To Schaefer, the key to exerting pressure on Israel was to exert pressure on Washington, which exercised more financial and diplomatic clout in Tel Aviv than any other power.

Schaefer proposed a multipronged strategy. She recommended that organizations such as the NCCW and the NCCM pass resolutions demanding that the Truman administration defend the *corpus separatum* "as was promised in the Democratic Party platform of 1948."[152] Such resolutions, she instructed, "should be utilized on the local and state scale, as well as nationally, by means of group and individual letter writing to political figures, newspapers, etc." Maintaining awareness of the Jerusalem question among Catholic parishioners, particularly as the November 1950 midterm elections approached, was another priority. As she lamented to Carroll, however, "the Catholic public remains somewhat ignorant of the Palestine problem and the problem of Jerusalem. Could there not be some sermons very soon in every diocese followed by prayers particularly for Jerusalem? The question will come up in the General Assembly in two weeks. Time is of the essence."[153]

Within days of Schaefer's call to action, the various organs of the American church again began to mobilize. The NCCW, at its annual convention in October, produced another resolution calling for the full internationalization of Jerusalem. The statement demanded that the UN honor its pledge on the Holy City, which had, until then, been "flouted and ignored."[154] It urged the world body to implement its 1949 resolution "so that history may not accuse it of using its pledge to further special political and territorial aims." It specifically called on Washington to "respect not only the deep convictions and desires which so many of its citizens hold in common with peoples throughout the world, but also to respect the decisions and honour the UN and cooperate actively in the UN to this end."[155] The NCCW, founded specifically to "give Catholic women of the country a common voice and an instrument for collective action," also heeded Schaefer's call to write to local and state representatives to press for a favorable resolution. On 6 November 1950, copies of the NCCW resolution were forwarded to President Truman, Secretary of State Dean Acheson, and Warren Austin, head of the American delegation at the UN.[156] On the same day, the diocesan press reported on the urgent appeal of the Paris-based Comité de Sauvegarde des Lieux Saints (Committee for the Safeguarding of the Holy Places) for the immediate implementation of the *corpus separatum* in an attempt to highlight the international scope of Catholic appeals for Jerusalem.[157] The next week, Schaefer ordered translations of the French statement to be distributed to every delegation at the UN.[158]

The American bishops, through the coordination of the NCWC, also intensified their campaign in the fall of 1950. In October, the NCWC augmented its tack on internationalization by demanding that any loan from Washington to Tel Aviv be contingent upon Israel's acquiescence on the Jerusalem question. Based on information from Alessandro Mombelli, the NCWC's correspondent in Jerusalem, that the Israeli state was "near bankruptcy," and that the American government was about to release a "multi-million dollar loan" to Tel Aviv, the bishops demanded that "the UN's plan for internationalization be a condition of American financial aid to the Israeli government."[159] The statement continued that "American Catholics do not want to be a party to an agreement which would thwart their deep interests in safeguarding the holiest Christian sites." On 11 October 1950, the statement was forwarded to Truman and to the American delegation at the UN.[160]

The American bishops also sought to raise the issue as widely as possible throughout the dioceses as the General Assembly session drew near. In early November, the NCWC ordered the immediate distribution of a memo, composed by Schaefer, to the entire episcopate.[161] The document outlined the history of the Jerusalem question at the UN, emphasizing the Holy See's unchanged position on internationalization, and was intended to serve as a template for sermons on the issue for the remaining Sundays of the month.[162] This was augmented the same week by the translation and distribution, at the behest of Chicago's Cardinal Samuel Stritch, of an *Osservatore Romano* editorial restating the Holy See's resolute position on the issue. Stritch wanted "the mind of the Holy See to be known in as many quarters as possible," and urged the bishops to send copies to all diocesan priests.[163] He also requested that the NCWC "forward the piece to the secular press at the earliest moment" in an effort to make known "the authentic position of the Vatican with regard to the internationalization of the Jerusalem area."[164] Carroll further urged "their Excellencies to use whatever resources available to them to have the position of the Holy See widely and accurately understood."[165]

Despite this frenetic campaign, Schaefer sensed a distinct loss of momentum. An off-the-record conversation with John Ross, the American representative to the Ad Hoc Political Committee, confirmed her fears that the United States regarded the full *corpus separatum* as infeasible, and would only back a plan amenable to Israel and Jordan. "I never liked that scheme anyway," Ross confided to Schaefer, as it contained "that fancy Latin phrase."[166] Given the diminishing hope of American support, Schaefer attempted to determine any remaining pockets of support. On 13 November 1950, she was informed by Iraq's Dr Fadhel Jamali that the Arab nations that had firmly backed the scheme in 1949 would continue to do so. On the same day, Cuba's Francisco Ichaso confirmed that the Latin American delegations that had already supported the plan remained firm in their support. He added, confidentially, that "even Uruguay, which had campaigned violently against the resolution last year, would stand for territorial internationalization this year."[167] Specifically, Ichaso assured Schaefer that the Holy See could expect the support of Cuba, Bolivia, Brazil, Colombia, and El Salvador. Though the Soviet-Arab-Catholic bloc that had delivered the *corpus separatum* in 1949 was no longer, it appeared that core support among Arab and Catholic states remained firm. On 15 November 1950, Schaefer apprised Carroll of these developments in comments that were forwarded to the apostolic delegate the following day.[168]

On 7 December 1950, as the General Assembly's Ad Hoc Political Committee began its review of the Jerusalem question, it was clear that a compromise was sought by a majority of representatives. In short order, Sweden's Erik Boheman introduced a Swedish-Dutch proposal that amounted to a repudiation of the *corpus separatum*, proposing provisions to instead "ensure the international protection of the spiritual and religious interests of the world community."[169] In addition, it called for a UN-appointed commissioner to administer the Holy Places, though one who would be under the authority of the Israeli and Jordanian governments, a plan that clearly repudiated the Vatican's stance.

In the tense but crucial days leading to a vote, American Catholic efforts to secure a *corpus separatum* now reached an apex, spurred further by the submission, on 29 November 1950, of a petition from over one thousand American educators and Protestant seminary professors "instructing" the Truman administration, and the American delegation at the UN, to "take the initiative in settling the problem by international supervision of the Holy Places, leaving political sovereignty in the hands of the Israeli and Jordanian governments."[170] In response, Schaefer ordered the translation and distribution of a statement from Italian Catholic Action to UN delegations, as a means of both countering the "Protestant statement" and reiterating the Roman Catholic position on the question. She further assured the association's president, Vittorio Veronese, that the statement would receive "maximum exposure" in the American diocesan press, which carried it widely during the first week of December.[171] The statement, along with that of the French Committee for the Safeguarding of the Holy Places, was also carried on NCWC radio broadcasts in a bid to emphasize the international character of Roman Catholic demands for Jerusalem. In the same week Martin Work, national secretary of the NCCM, forwarded his organization's petition to Dean Acheson and Warren Austin.[172] In speaking for the "deepest interests and sentiment for the Holy Places shared by millions of co-religionists in the United States," it linked clearly, if implicitly, the potential voting power of thirty million American Catholics with demands to preserve the *corpus separatum* for Jerusalem.[173]

By 11 December 1950, as the General Assembly entered the crucial week in which the fate of Jerusalem would be decided, open disproval of the Swedish-Dutch resolution quickly emerged. Arab and "Catholic" delegations, in particular, rightly regarded the plan as the death knell of the December 1949 agreement. Lebanon's Dr Charles Malik, who had carried the torch for Catholic interests on the floor of the General Assembly in 1949, again advocated for the preservation of past resolutions on Jerusalem. On that Monday, Malik, at the request of his delegation, made two interventions against the Swedish-Dutch proposal, arguing that it essentially discarded the majority resolutions passed by the same assembly in 1947, 1948, and 1949. He was rebutted by Israel's Abba Eban, who urged delegates to accept the Swedish-Dutch proposal lest "the opportunity for any form of internationalization might pass."[174] The following day Malik, who had assured Schaefer that he had a strategy "up his sleeve" for the General Assembly session, read into the record a number of statements that Schaefer had previously distributed to delegates through her office. These included the statements of the French Committee for the Safeguarding of the Holy Places as well as the *Osservatore Romano* editorial of late November.[175] He further requested that the French statement be distributed as an official document of the General Assembly. In addition, Malik read into the record an *America* editorial of June 1950 that had forcefully argued for a *corpus separatum* as the only means to preserve peace and stability in the region. In stressing that "religious interests had been overlooked in the political and national rivalries" roiling the city, he lamented the resulting "uneasy peace prevailing in Jerusalem and the whole of Palestine."[176] Eban, who had emerged as Malik's adversary in these final days, offered a stern rebuttal, highlighting a multitude of Christian leaders who backed a "realistic approach" on Jerusalem. Eban specifically read into the record a statement from the Greek Orthodox patriarch of Jerusalem, who favored the Swedish-Dutch proposal, as well as the recent "Protestant statement."[177] He cautioned "those who were interested in religious peace … [to] consider that [full internationalization] might well lead to religious schism and division." He further deemed Malik's position "wishful thinking," and unreflective of "a general shift of opinion since 1948 and 1949." "Let it be forever recorded that a practical solution [Sweden's] came before the General Assembly in 1950 and Israel gave it support," he concluded. "Historians will regard it as a turning point in history."[178]

Wrangling over the Swedish-Dutch resolution produced a Belgian resolution that again sought to appease the opposed factions. Submitted on 12 December 1950, the resolution called for the appointment of a four-person panel to consult with Israel, Jordan, and other interested parties to ascertain "the conditions of settlement capable of ensuring the effective protection of the Holy Places."[179] The committee was to report its findings at the General Assembly's

Sixth Session the following year. Belgium also accepted, at the insistence of Malik and other members of the Lebanese delegation, an amendment urging the committee to keep in mind the UN's three successive resolutions on Jerusalem (all of which preserved territorial internationalization). Though the Belgian proposal didn't assure the survival of the *corpus separatum*, it kept alive the possibility of its implementation at a later date, enough to give it support from Catholic delegates. On 13 December 1950, the Ad Hoc Political Committee voted to adopt the Belgian proposal. As State Department files have revealed, Cardinal Spellman again played a role in last-minute negotiations, urging a number of delegations to back the Belgian scheme, and "exerting a decisive influence against the Swedish draft resolution."[180]

The General Assembly voted on the Belgian resolution on 15 December 1950. The results of the vote, which failed to produce the two-thirds majority required for adoption, revealed the deep chasm between those supporting and opposing the *corpus separatum*. In the end, a majority of South American states (Chile, Colombia, Ecuador, Paraguay, Peru, and Venezuela) supported the proposal, evidence of the durability of the transnational "Catholic bloc." France, which appeared noncommittal in the final days, also supported the Belgian proposal. Though the American delegation voted against the resolution, its position was clearly tempered by passions aroused by the question in the United States. As a result, it was reluctant to overtly back any plan "on a matter of such religious and emotional value," fearing the domestic repercussions of any such stand. Acheson himself instructed John Ross to make no efforts either to persuade other members to follow the American course "or to discourage a possible shift in the voting for the Belgian resolution."[181] If American Catholic pressure had not succeeded in securing American support for the Belgian proposal, it did appear to have dissuaded Washington's support of the Swedish-Dutch alternative. At the very least, it seemed that Catholic pressure had again assured the survival of the *corpus separatum*.

MCMAHON'S FINAL MISSION TO ISRAEL

The survival of the *corpus separatum* as a concept, however, did little to alter the reality of a Jerusalem now firmly divided between Israeli and Jordanian interests. The defeat of the Belgian resolution signaled a growing acceptance of the status quo by a number of prominent UN delegations, including that of the United States. Though Washington continued to support the principle of an internationalized Jerusalem, its practical implementation now appeared hopelessly futile. As such, UN debate on the status of the city declined significantly for the remainder of the decade. As Elihu Lauterpacht has observed, after the December 1950 vote, "the question of Jerusalem was conspicuous only by its absence from discussion at the UN."[182]

Despite increasingly diminishing odds, American Catholics continued to play a central role in pressing the Vatican line in Washington and at the UN. In July 1951, the indefatigable Monsignor Thomas McMahon, in his role as head of the Pontifical Mission for Palestine, appeared before the House Committee on Foreign Affairs to advocate for a just resolution to the Jerusalem question and the Arab refugee problem.[183] McMahon, in fact, connected the two issues, and posited that the repatriation of Palestinian Arabs displaced by war, and the implementation of the UN resolution on Jerusalem, were also crucial to American strategic interests in the wider Middle East. "You have the friendship of Israel," he reminded the committee, "but you must also get the friendship of the Arab states, and you cannot get it by delaying tactics."[184] McMahon suggested that an American policy aligned with that of the Vatican would solidify Washington's relations with the Arab League states, expanding American influence in the region at a key moment in the unfolding Cold War. Finally, McMahon urged the congressmen not to forget the Christian stake in Palestine. In reminding the committee that he "speaks for the Catholic Church, at least in my capacity as head of her relief efforts in the Middle East," he implored Congress to respect Vatican claims, arguing that "one is not anti-Semitic when he urges the Christian right in Palestine."[185]

Despite McMahon's contention that the *corpus separatum* served both American and Vatican interests, evidence of Washington's de facto acceptance of the status quo was soon laid bare. At the opening of the Sixth Session of the UN General Assembly in November 1951, the American delegation's reticence to broach the Jerusalem question was palpable. Though McMahon decried this abdication, accusing delegates of "trying to disembarrass themselves of their own resolutions and their own votes," the stalemate on Jerusalem appeared firm. It was against this backdrop that the Israeli government, in May 1952, announced that its Foreign Ministry would be moved to Jerusalem "as soon as the necessary technical arrangements were completed."[186] In July, an Israeli spokesman confirmed Tel Aviv's designs for the city, stating that Jerusalem "was, is and always will be the capital of Israel," calling the *corpus separatum* "impractical and unrealistic" and, for all intents and purposes, a "dead issue."[187] In November, upon the death of President Chaim Weizmann, the official residence of the Israeli president was also moved to Jerusalem, prompting Prime Minister Ben-Gurion to declare that "the status of Jerusalem now remains as settled as that of Rome or London."[188]

The Seventh Session of the UN General Assembly, which opened in October 1952, again confirmed that the moment of consensus for a genuine internationalization of Jerusalem had long since passed. Though a number of Latin American states and the Philippines again formally protested the fait accompli policy pursued by both Israel and Jordan, and despite Washington's official support for the *corpus separatum*, the notion remained a dead letter. The May 1953 tour of Israel by President Eisenhower's new secretary of state, John Foster Dulles, appeared to formalize American acquiescence to Israeli plans for the city. In Jerusalem, Dulles pressed Foreign Minister Moshe Sharett to respect the international status of the Holy Places, though the meeting was regarded as a de facto American recognition of Israel's claims. In July, the Foreign Ministry offices were formally relocated to the city. McMahon reflected bitterly on the Israeli move, and on Washington's feeble response, which he considered "formal recognition by the United States that Jerusalem can be considered Israeli property and the seed of the Israeli government."[189] He suggested to Spellman a bold campaign to expose Israeli abuses against personal and property rights in Jerusalem, "showing that the non-Jewish inhabitants of the city have been betrayed, as has the world at large." *L'Osservatore Romano* echoed McMahon's frustration when it commented wryly that "it is not every day that a state elects as its capital a city divided in two by a line of armistice that, at least legally, has no legitimacy."[190]

By the spring of 1953, McMahon's strategy increasingly centered on advocating for the repatriation of Arab refugees to the territory and highlighting Israeli transgressions against Catholic properties and institutions in Jerusalem and throughout the state. The funds that McMahon was responsible for distributing, as head of the PMP, were considerable.[191] Henceforth $20 million in clothing, food, medicine, and financial aid were to be dispersed to Palestinian refugees in the territory, the majority raised through American Catholic sources.[192] That the PMP's refugee program posed a distinct threat to Israel was revealed during a visit by Sharett to Washington in April. During a meeting with State Department officials, Sharett denied Israel's capacity to "absorb" the 800,000 Arabs who had fled or were exiled from Israel, and who he said had "no claim to the land."[193] McMahon coupled this refugee advocacy with a campaign in the Catholic press to shed light on Israeli infringements on Christian rights. These incidences included, most notably, the IDF's destruction of the Palestinian Christian village of Iqrit on Christmas Day 1951 (after the Israeli Supreme Court had ruled that its inhabitants could return), and the seizure of numerous properties in Jerusalem, including the Benedictine Abbey of the Dormition. In urging a broad-based press campaign, McMahon reminded the NCWC News Service that such an effort would only strengthen his hand in dealing with both Israeli and American officials. "We can get along by approaching the Israeli government directly and by telling them that we shall publish any difficulties right back here," he advised in July, urging Catholics to bolster critiques of Israel already appearing in the mainstream secular press. "It was very good to see the difficulties over the Benedictine Lands published in the *New York Times*. This gets us further."[194]

McMahon would get his chance to present the Vatican's policy directly to Israeli officials on what would be his final diplomatic mission to the Middle East in the fall of 1953. In a tour that lasted through October and November, he visited Lebanon, Syria, Egypt, Gaza, Jordan, and Israel. Though officially a mission to direct Catholic aid efforts in the region, his mandate also included a distinctly political agenda centering on the question of Jerusalem. Israeli aggression against Arab villages appeared to intensify around the time of McMahon's visit. On 16 September the Maronite Christian village of Kafr Bir'im, whose majority Arab population was expelled in 1948, was leveled by the Israeli Air Force, preventing the return of its inhabitants.[195] On 4 November, just prior to entering Jerusalem, McMahon toured the West Bank village of Qibya. Only a few weeks prior, the village had been attacked by Israeli forces under the command of Ariel Sharon, a reprisal for Arab fedayeen raids against Israeli villages and civilians. The nighttime raid, which resulted in the deaths of nearly forty women and children, was condemned by the State Department as "shocking." McMahon assured the Vatican that he would protest these attacks to Israeli officials and "let the world know what Palestine is like."[196] The Vatican was also concerned that the dispossession of Arabs in Israel would lead to their support of the Israeli Communist Party (Maki). Antonio Vergani, the vicar general for Galilee, warned Tardini that "politically, these poor people now vote communist in the hopes that Moscow might be their salvation!"[197] In the wake of this increasing instability, McMahon described "an air of great tension" among Israeli and Jordanian officials, an atmosphere that undoubtedly still gripped him as he crossed through the Mandelbaum Gate into Jerusalem just a few days later.

Upon entering the Old City, McMahon was greeted by Avraham Biran, the noted archeologist and commissioner of the Jewish-held quarter of Jerusalem.

Though Israeli officials had suggested that McMahon visit the Foreign Ministry, he politely informed Biran that he did not recognize the presence of the Israeli government there. Biran, with whom McMahon had always been on good terms, inquired about the "campaign of defamation of Israel" in the Catholic press, including the "nasty" comments attributed to McMahon himself. McMahon refuted his host's narrative, outlining Israel's consistent flouting of the Vatican's legitimate and juridically sound claims, in line with the UN resolutions of 1947 and 1948. He further dismissed suggestions that antisemitism or anti-Zionism had shaped papal policy, reminding Biran (rather disingenuously) that "the Church had not opposed the creation of Israel, or its nomination as the fifty-ninth flag in the United Nations."[198] Later that evening, McMahon dined with Biran and the American consul in Jerusalem, Roger Tyler, who regarded internationalization as "impractical," and who queried McMahon on "how it could be done, with Jordan digging in on one side and Israel very much here on the other." The Vatican, McMahon informed Tyler, was only concerned with the implementation of the resolution agreed upon in 1948. "How it should be done," he concluded, "was up to the United Nations."[199]

The following day, McMahon met again with Yaacov Herzog, special adviser on Jerusalem for the Israeli Ministry of Religious Affairs. Though not formally attached to the Foreign Ministry, the young Herzog, only thirty-two, was highly regarded by both Ben-Gurion and Sharett and wielded an influence beyond the confines of his official mandate. Herzog's role was to liaise with the various Christian communities in Old Jerusalem, safeguarding the Israeli position in the city and managing Catholic, Protestant, and Orthodox Christian claims.[200] An ordained rabbi and a skilled diplomat, well-connected in both religious and secular circles, Herzog was a formidable match for the irascible McMahon. Though McMahon had been offered a meeting with Ben-Gurion, he refused, revealing his growing exasperation with the Israeli government. He was convinced, in any case, that his meeting with Herzog "would be relayed anyway," and that he "could learn anything he wanted from him – an immature, budding statesman, not worth talking to except for his value as a contact and channel."[201] McMahon's estimation of the young diplomat had clearly declined since the time of their previous meetings, as it had become increasingly obvious that Herzog's diplomacy represented nothing more than the hard line of Ben-Gurion and Sharett.

During a tense meeting at the Terra Sancta College, the pair clashed on the status of the city. Herzog immediately pressed McMahon on why the Catholic

Church opposed direct negotiations between Israel and Jordan on Jerusalem. The monsignor responded that such negotiations, "intended by Jews as the way to throw over every United Nations commitment of the past," would negate the world body's established resolution on the issue. McMahon then interrogated Herzog on the treatment of Christian minorities by Israel, highlighting the IDF's September 1953 destruction of Kafr Bir'im. Though Herzog blamed the incident on "the trigger-happy military," he offered assurances that Israel "would be treating its Christian minority correctly in the future."[202] The brief exchange, lasting less than thirty minutes, clearly underscored the chasm between Vatican demands and Israeli intentions.

Just days later, McMahon held a second meeting with Herzog in Haifa, at the residence of George Hakim, the Melkite Catholic archbishop of Galilee. McMahon regarded Hakim as a valued ally in his diplomatic work in the territory, a figure he described as "young, vital and intelligent," and whose "abilities are presently providential." McMahon further extolled the archbishop's role as a source of intelligence. It was Hakim who had notified the Vatican of IDF transgressions in the Christian villages of Iqrit and Kafr Bir'im, and who lobbied the Israeli government for the right of return for displaced Arabs. McMahon particularly admired Hakim's "bold use of his diocesan monthly to attack any adverse government actions."[203] During dinner, the question of Jerusalem again sparked a heated exchange. McMahon charged that "Zionist agents" had functioned to thwart the UN resolutions of 1947 and 1948, that Israeli lobbyists had pressured Washington's UN delegation on the issue, and that "Zionist propaganda" had actively worked to foment uncertainty and confusion among Catholic UN delegations.[204] He reminded Herzog of the political power of thirty million American Catholics, who continued to exert considerable influence on Washington. Herzog was resolute, refuting the monsignor's charges one by one. "By now, McMahon's face was very red," he later recalled, "his gaze wandering and violent, his fists clenched." Herzog firmly reminded McMahon that, being familiar with history, he must have been aware of Jewish suffering through the ages. "We paid for our admission to the family of nations with blood and tears. The State of Israel represents the consolation of Providence to our tormented people," Herzog concluded, alluding to the biblical covenant that promised the land to the people of Abraham. "Why [can't you] leave us in peace?"[205]

Though McMahon's report on the mission exhibited the requisite optimism, stating that the Israeli government "remains exasperated over the constant, logical, unflagging policy of the Holy See on the Holy Places, the international city of Jerusalem, and the refugees," it was clear that momentum was shifting away from the Vatican and the international church. In January 1954, Sharett succeeded Ben-Gurion as prime minister, placing an implacable foe of Vatican policy at the very center of Israeli state power. Sharett, who as foreign minster had already rejected calls for the repatriation of Arab refugees, declared that "No encroachment of any land will be permitted on the sovereignty of Israel over the New City or on the present status of Jerusalem, capital of Israel."[206] Within weeks of Sharett's accession a number of embassies, including those of France, Britain, Italy, Brazil, Sweden, and Belgium, began accepting invitations from the Israeli Foreign Ministry in Jerusalem, a clear sign that the international consensus on the *corpus separatum* had crumbled. Though Washington officially adhered to the UN resolution on Jerusalem, and its ambassadors would still conduct affairs from the embassy in Tel Aviv, the State Department relaxed its position in May 1954, acknowledging "the need for ready access" for some diplomatic officials to conduct business directly with the Foreign Ministry in Jerusalem.[207] By November, the newly appointed American ambassador to Israel, Edward B. Lawson, presented his credentials to President Yitzhak Ben-Zvi in Jerusalem. Though McMahon immediately cabled Eisenhower, asking the president for assurance that the move was not "the opening wedge in recognizing New Jerusalem as the Israeli capital," it was clear that American policy had adjusted to the realities of the divided city.[208]

By early 1955, the strain of nearly a dozen years of frenetic politicking on the Palestine question had taken its toll on McMahon. On 16 March 1955, he tendered a brief resignation letter to Spellman and Pope Pius XII. Cardinal Eugene Tissèrant, secretary of the Vatican's Congregation for the Oriental Churches and a curial official with a detailed knowledge of the monsignor's diplomatic activity, praised McMahon's fervor and tenacity in a letter to Spellman, who, in his stead, nominated Monsignor Peter Tuohy, who had assisted McMahon since 1951, as the national secretary of the CNEWA. McMahon was assigned as pastor to Park Avenue's Church of Our Savior, just blocks away from Spellman's Madison Avenue residence. Though he continued to write and speak on the Jerusalem question, it was clear that the Vatican's policy, aided by his tireless diplomacy, had ultimately been thwarted. Just prior to resigning, he likened his failure to secure the *corpus separatum* to "a man looking into the windows of his home to be told by intruders that he could have any compensation except possession" – a prophetic analogy that revealed the ultimate defeat of Vatican efforts to shape the Jerusalem question.[209]

On 6 December 1956, McMahon died of a heart attack at age forty-seven. His death signaled the effective end of American Catholic efforts to actively shape the Jerusalem question. Though the CNEWA continued its work in the region, pressing the Israeli government on the issue, and the NCWC remained firm in its policy on the Holy City, the effects of a decade of war, strife, and bitter struggle between Israel and Jordan had produced an implacable stalemate. In May 1958, on the tenth anniversary of Israeli statehood, and as Jewish organizations prepared celebrations across the United States, the Jesuit weekly *America* mused plaintively. Israel "has sown bitterness in the Middle East," the editorial declared, the triumph of Zionism having been "counterbalanced by the tragic fate of an equal number of Arab refugees whom they have replaced in Palestine. In open defiance of the UN, the very organization which gave birth to the new nation, Israel made Jerusalem her capital."[210] On the question of a reconciliation of Catholic and Israeli interests, the journal was clear. "When the Holy City is internationalized according to the wishes of the world community, when some sensible revision of boundaries in the Middle East is effected, and when the Palestine refugees receive their due, perhaps more fulsome congratulations will be in order."[211] For the remainder of the decade, the American bishops were resigned to defending the rights of Roman Catholic access to holy sites in the territory. A modest triumph concerned Haifa's Stella Maris monastery, the cradle of the Carmelite order, which had been seized and occupied by the Israeli Navy since 1951. Following "repeated rude rebuffs by the Israelis to the local superior," the NCWC's Legal Department took up the case in 1958 on behalf of the Vatican. Several months of intense negotiations, both with the State Department and with the Israeli government, yielded the withdrawal of the naval offices and an indemnification paid to the Carmelites.[212] It was a small victory in a decade of rebuffs for the Vatican and the American church.

Conclusion

On 30 April 1964, nearly one thousand delegates gathered at New York's Hilton Hotel for the annual meeting of the American Jewish Committee. By this time, the AJC had become a leading American voice for civil liberties and social equality for both Jews and non-Jews alike, and its annual meeting drew attendees from across the political, religious, and social spectrums. During the dinner session, at which Secretary of State Dean Rusk was awarded the AJC's American Liberties Medallion, a senior member of the American Catholic hierarchy rose to deliver the keynote speech. The speaker was Cardinal Francis Spellman, and his words represented nothing short of a historic repudiation of Roman Catholic antipathy to Jews and to Judaism. The cardinal asserted that antisemitism could "never find a basis in the Catholic religion," and that, "far from emphasizing the differences which divide Jews and Christians, our faith stresses our common origins and the ties which bind us together."[1] Beyond general platitudes on Judaeo-Christian fellowship, however, Spellman addressed a specific theological question that had arisen in response to a recent B'nai B'rith survey revealing that a majority of Catholics continued to regard Jewish complicity in the crucifixion as a barrier to dialogue and kinship. Speaking to the ancestral notion of deicide, the cardinal was unequivocal: "Responsibility for the crucifixion of Jesus as an event of history belongs only to those who were present at the time and responsible for His death," he declared. "It is simply absurd to maintain that there is some kind of continuing guilt which is transferred to any group of people and rests upon them as a curse they must suffer ... It is one of those distorted and terribly harmful notions which somehow gains currency and like a cancer, spreads among certain people who wish to justify their own bigotry."[2] President Lyndon Johnson, greeting the dinner, noted the significance of Spellman's participation when he praised "the growing spirit of Christian-Jewish understanding which has been a most important part of the AJC's work."[3]

The slow and winding path to reconciliation between Roman Catholicism and Judaism did not happen suddenly, nor was it complete by the time of Spellman's speech. Even the 1993 establishment of diplomatic relations between the Vatican and the State of Israel, as Karma Ben-Johanan's recent work makes evident, was but another step in a long road to reconciliation between the faiths – a process that continues still.[4] It is undeniable, however, that the last ninety years have witnessed a gradual, if at times staggered and uneven, process of Catholic reckoning and dialogue with Judaism. As John Connelly has demonstrated, the origins of this theological and social rapprochement stretches back to the 1930s, and was shaped by a diverse and international group of theologians and scholars, many of them converts to Catholicism from Judaism and Protestantism.[5] In tracing the theological evolution of figures such as Johannes Oesterreicher, Karl Thieme, Jacques and Raissa Maritain, and others, Connelly charts the gradual and sometimes torpid move away from the "theology of contempt" described by Jules Isaac and toward the interfaith vision described by Spellman. The theological key to this evolution, argues Connelly, was a rigorous reappraisal of the letters of Saint Paul, which referred never to the conversion of the Jews, and which emphasized the immutably Jewish roots of Christianity and the enduring validity of the Abrahamic Covenant. The historical key to this evolution was the Holocaust itself, which forced Catholics to confront their relationship to Judaism in the aftermath of the murder of six million Jews, including a million children.

In the United States, the roots of this theological rapprochement could also be traced back to the 1930s, originating in American Catholic denunciations of Kristallnacht in 1938.[6] Catholic condemnations of antisemitism continued throughout the war itself, and featured a range of American theologians, scholars, and bishops including John Courtney Murray, John Ryan, Fulton Sheen, Maurice Sheehy, John Mitty, and Edward Mooney. The Jewish source of Christianity was underscored by Ryan before the war itself, when he reminded Catholics that antisemitism was "contrary to Christianity" and that "followers of Christ cannot believe that He would hate the race from which He sprang."[7] In 1944, as the horrors of the Holocaust steadily came to light, Mooney reminded Detroit's faithful that Catholic teaching exalted "the historic and religious role of the Jewish people, and glories in the heritage of Judaism which is an essential element of Christianity."[8] Following Oesterreicher's arrival in the United States in 1940, his establishment of the Institute for Judaeo-Christian Studies at Seton Hall University in 1953 provided a scholarly nerve center for the exploration of theological and historical bridges between the faiths. The institute produced a series of leading scholars in the field, including Father Edward H. Flannery, whose seminal 1965 work *The Anguish of the Jews* was the first systematic study of Catholic antisemitism by a member of the hierarchy, and another testament to the growing interfaith spirit fomenting within the church.[9] "The sin of anti-Semitism is many things," Flannery wrote in his conclusion, "but in the end it is a denial of the Christian faith, a failure of Christian hope, and a malady of Christian love. Nor is it the least of sins."[10]

This zeitgeist of Catholic-Jewish fraternity loomed large as the Second Vatican Council opened its fourth session in September 1965. Called in 1959 by Pope John XXIII as a wide-ranging project of consultation, reform, and renewal, the council was intended, as Pope John announced in his opening speech in 1962, to allow the faith "to be studied afresh and reformulated in contemporary terms."[11] The pope's vision was indeed embraced in the council's debates. A number of American bishops and theologians took active roles in its sessions, embracing its reformist zeal as evidenced by the promulgation of *Dignitatis humanae*, a declaration on religious freedom conceived by John Courtney Murray and tabled by Archbishops Albert Meyer of Chicago and Joseph Ritter of St Louis. In calling for interfaith cooperation between the major religions in the face of rising secularism and materialism, *Dignitatis humanae* signaled a retreat from the triumphal isolationism of previous eras and a move toward a spirit of dialogue. In addition to Meyer and Ritter, there emerged in Rome a growing faction of reformist American bishops, including Detroit's John Dearden, Kansas City's John Patrick Cody, Baltimore's Lawrence Shehan, Washington's Patrick O'Boyle, and San Antonio's Stephen Leven, who more openly took up the council's mandate of revival and renewal.

The council's fourth session was most remembered, perhaps, for the promulgation of *Nostra aetate*, a declaration on the relationship of the Roman Catholic Church to non-Christian religions. Notable was the declaration's fourth section, which dealt specifically with Judaism. Drafted with the assistance of Oesterreicher, and moved forward with the encouragement and support of both Spellman and Cushing, it repudiated the centuries-old charge of deicide against the Jews and denounced the notion that the Jews bore a collective and enduring guilt (as had Spellman's speech of the previous year).[12] It further stressed the religious and spiritual bonds shared by the faiths, reaffirming the eternal covenant between God and the people of Israel. It also dismissed the Catholic objective of trying to convert the Jews, acknowledging the salvific legitimacy of Judaism, a symbolic turning point if juxtaposed with Pope Pius X's 1904 warning to Theodor Herzl that, should the Jews return to Palestine, there would be "Catholic priests waiting there to baptize them all." *Nostra aetate*, for the first time in history, called for Catholics and Jews to engage in friendly dialogue and theological discussion so as to better understand each other's faiths. After intense debate, the declaration was adopted by the world's cardinals and bishops on 28 November 1965, a definitive turning point in the history of Catholic-Jewish relations.

The drafting and promulgation of *Nostra aetate* did not immediately settle the question of land, as Pope Paul VI's January 1964 pilgrimage to the Holy Places made clear. During the two-day visit, the State of Israel was never mentioned by the pope, and he spent much of his time in Jordanian-controlled Jerusalem. His brief visit with Israeli President Zalman Shazar and Prime Minister Levi Eshkol was held in Megiddo, underscoring the Vatican's refusal to acknowledge Jerusalem as Israel's capital. During the meeting, Paul VI did not address Shazar as president, and according to Foreign Minister Golda Meir, his meetings with Eshkol and a number of ministers was tense, owing to the Vatican's perceived silence on the recent bombings, by Palestinian commandos, of Israeli targets such as the Tomb of the Patriarchs in Hebron and the Mahane Yehuda Market in Jerusalem. The Sephardic chief rabbi of Israel, Yitzhak Nissim, boycotted the papal visit, accusing the pope of waging "a total war against the country that God had given to His people."[13] Though the Israeli government moved to contain the potential fallout of Nissim's statement, it was clear that the papal visit had done little to improve Israeli-Vatican relations.

Indeed, notwithstanding the spirit of interfaith dialogue at the council that preceded Paul VI's visit, the brief pilgrimage revealed the enduring gulf between Israel and the Vatican on the Jerusalem question. In the immediate aftermath of the Six-Day War of June 1967, when Israel captured Jordanian-held Old Jerusalem and effectively claimed control over all of the Holy Places, the Vatican again insisted on the internationalization formula of 1947. Just days after the armistice, *L'Osservatore Romano* ran a front-page editorial insisting on a full *corpus separatum*, positing that while no one contested "the strength of the spiritual and historical bonds which bind Jerusalem to Judaism and Islam, neither can it be forgotten that the Christian world looks upon Zion as a unique and great holy place."[14] Nor did the postwar settling of dust, when Israel consolidated its control over the entirety of Jerusalem, convince the Vatican otherwise. In October 1969, during the first visit of an Israeli foreign minster to the Vatican, Paul VI again insisted, during an hour-long meeting with Abba Eban, on the necessity of the city's full internationalization as the key to peace and stability in the region and the wider world.[15]

While *Nostra aetate*, then, did not immediately move the Vatican's longstanding Palestine policy, its acknowledgment of the explicitly Jewish origins of Christianity ("the beginnings of her faith are found already among the Patriarchs, Moses and the prophets"), as well as its recognition of the validity of the Abrahamic Covenant ("she received the revelation of the Old Testament through the people with whom God … concluded the Ancient Covenant"), did appear to provide the theological framework for a dialogue with the Israeli state. And as with the gradual rapprochement between Judaism and Catholicism, led as it was by some formative American Catholic thinkers, some of the earliest expressions of a Catholic Zionism also emanated from within the American church. In 1965, Father Edward Flannery, in his *Anguish of the Jews*, posited that anti-Zionism was often a form of unconscious antisemitism, one that stemmed from a refusal to accept the covenantal bond between the Jews and Israel. In 1967, he warned Catholics to be wary of again being accused of "silence" in the face of Jewish suffering when Israel was attacked by its Arab neighbors during the Six-Day War. In January 1968, as Israel consolidated control over Jerusalem in the aftermath of the conflict, Seton Hall's Institute of Judaeo-Christian Studies offered Catholic support for a Jewish Jerusalem. A "Statement of Conscience," authored by Flannery and Oesterreicher, declared that "Jerusalem as a unified city is a demand of history, as well as of Jewish consciousness," and that Israel would be a faithful guardian of the Holy Places.[16] In 1974, when Jordan's King Hussein decried the "capture" of Jerusalem, Oesterreicher again made a claim for the historical and biblical legitimacy of Jewish sovereignty over the city. "The Jerusalem of today is not a city in captivity, as the King likes to think," he declared. "It is free, as it has never been before … Biblically speaking, Jerusalem is God's city, as the land is God's land. Men are but tenants. The glory of the Israelis is to have been good stewards, to have been worthy of His trust … The people whom God made His own out of sheer love, have gathered in Zion; the divided city is one again!" Oesterreicher concluded by quoting Matthew 19:6, alluding to the prophecy of the Zionist triumph: "What God has joined together, man must not separate."[17]

The publication in 1977 of *Honor the Promise: America's Commitment to Israel* by Robert F. Drinan, SJ, was emblematic of the sea change in American Catholic attitudes toward Zionism and the State of Israel in the decades after the intense campaign for Jerusalem's internationalization wound down in the later 1950s.[18] The weight of Christian responsibility and guilt for the Holocaust, argued Drinan, necessitated a new understanding between Christians and Jews and a reparation both "moral and material." This reparation, however, should not be motivated by feelings of guilt, since this alone "would be an unhelpful basis for Christian-Jewish understanding." What was first required of all Christians, Drinan urged, "was a recognition of the righteousness of Zionism as the basis for the Jewish democratic state."[19] Drinan, a Jesuit priest, Georgetown law professor, and congressman, had, in fact, been expressing such notions publicly for over a decade. On the need for Roman Catholic acceptance of Zionism, he was unequivocal:

> There is no doubt that Zionism as the basis for the establishment of a nation is unique in the annals of mankind. But so is the whole history of the Jewish people. Consequently, it is improper to adopt a procrustean attitude to insist that Israel conform to the usual model of a contemporary state … From the beginning, Judaism was conceived as the interlinking of a people, a Torah, a land. The Hebrew Scriptures, medieval and modern Jewish literature, the Talmud, and the Jewish liturgy is replete with the idea of a return to Zion … Zionism and Judaism have always been integral parts of each other. Since the Holocaust and the founding of Israel the inseparability of Judaism and Zionism has never been clearer.[20]

Though Drinan did not speak for the Vatican or for the American episcopate on the issue, the lack of public rebuke from either body did signal the demise of the activist and near-monolithic Roman Catholic transnationalism that had characterized earlier periods. By the 1970s, it was evident that the ideological solidarity that had made the American Catholic Church such a valuable ally to Rome in the struggle for Palestine had run its course. Though many American bishops continued to adhere to the Vatican line on Israel and the Jerusalem question, the consensus of previous decades had been replaced by a plurality of nuanced views, which included outright support for Zionism and for the State of Israel.

For nearly four decades between the 1920s and the early 1960s, however, the Vatican could faithfully rely on the American Catholic Church, and particularly its bishops, to transmit uniquely Roman Catholic ideologies and policies within the most powerful nation in the world. As Peter D'Agostino has skilfully demonstrated, this Roman Catholic transnationalism manifested itself in the 1920s in the attitudes and opinions of American Catholics on the Roman Question (where American Catholics supported the creation of a sovereign territory for the papacy in Italy), and on Mussolini's Fascist regime. In the 1930s, this transnational relationship between the papacy and American Catholics congealed into a defined political lobby, when the American bishops, organized through the National Catholic Welfare Conference, represented papal interests vis-à-vis Washington on Mexican anticlericalism and the Spanish Civil War. As in the case of American Catholic sympathy for Mussolini and Italian Fascism, these positions created frictions with non-Catholics, and clearly delineated the Roman sources of American Catholic beliefs. Also emerging in the 1930s was a rising chorus of American Catholic opposition to political Zionism, another position that appeared to take its inspiration directly from papal Rome, and which placed Catholics at odds with their fellow citizens.

The growing political stridency of the American bishops, as outlined in chapter 2, was girded by a number of factors in the interwar decades. The organization of an episcopal conference in 1920, the NCWC, undoubtedly provided an organizational nerve center through which the bishops could more concertedly, and forcefully, express a collective political will. The exponential growth of the church, owing to migration and high birthrates, particularly in the Northeast, facilitated a rapid institutional expansion in the interwar years, when Catholic schools, hospitals, and colleges, as well as a plethora of new parishes, were built to accommodate this burgeoning population. The genuinely warm relationship between President Roosevelt and leading American bishops was further evidence of the growing clout of American Catholics. The Vatican, for its part, was clearly cognizant of the growing power of the American church, and from the early 1920s on sought to strengthen its ties with the American episcopate. In addition to its growing political influence, the Vatican was aware of the significant financial clout of the American church, as evidenced by the vast sums raised in the United States for the Papal Relief Mission to Moscow between 1922 and 1924. The ceding of perpetual control over the CNEWA to the archbishop of New York in 1931 can be clearly traced to the fundraising capacity and the political clout of American Catholics. Roosevelt's appointment of Myron Taylor as his personal representative to the Holy See on the eve of the Second World War appeared to cement the informal, yet ideologically cohesive, alliance between the Vatican, American Catholics, and Washington.

Upon the United States' entry into the war in 1941, American Catholics heeded the call to duty issued by the bishops, who had abandoned isolationist leanings to wholly endorse the war effort. The course of the conflict, however, revealed the extent to which the bishops continued to "toe the Roman line" – actively in their protests of the Allied bombing of Rome, and passively in their adherence to the established Vatican position on Zionism. Both from the Vatican and from the various organs of the American Catholic Church there emerged a distinctly dual response to the tragedy of Europe's Jews. On the one hand, expressions of sympathy for the Jewish plight were expressed by Rome and the American bishops alike. American Catholics, in fact, expressed their revulsion at the Nazi persecution of Jews in particularly poignant and clear language, surpassing the Vatican's restrained expressions of sympathy and solidarity. On the other hand, however, faced with the substantive question of Jewish emigration to Palestine, and the creation of a Jewish national home there, the American bishops remained resolutely in line with Rome. It was a policy that withstood the full airing of the tragedy of the Holocaust, and which stood firm against the rising tide of sympathy for Zionism in the United States, not just among Jews but among a growing segment of American Protestant churches, Congress, and even President Harry Truman himself. Open expressions of sympathy for Zionism from the American bishops, in contrast, were virtually nonexistent. When nonconformity did surface, as the case of New Orleans Archbishop Joseph Rummel illustrated, it was quickly suppressed, further evidence of the unanimity the Vatican expected from the American episcopate.

In the postwar years, as the Palestine question reached its most crucial phase, the American bishops adhered staunchly to papal opposition to the creation of a Jewish home in the Holy Land. At the root of this stance remained an ancestral Roman Catholic refusal to yield the territory of Christ's birth, life, and death to a faith and a people that it continued to hold responsible for deicide, an idea expressed clearly and consistently by American Catholics after 1945. Catholic leaders in the United States, in fact, emerged as committed opponents of Zionism in an atmosphere of rising sympathy for that very cause. On this question the bishops, the diocesan press, independent Catholic journals, religious orders, and a range of lay Catholic organizations exhibited a remarkable consensus, evidence of a resilient position on the Palestine question that clearly took its inspiration from the Vatican. The dearth of dissenting voices in the American Catholic Church only underscored the monolithic unanimity of American Catholic attitudes.

As I have argued in this study, not only did the various organs of the American Catholic Church support the papal position on Palestine, but Catholic leaders in the United States also emerged as the primary advocates of this Vatican policy in the first decade of the Cold War. A number of factors placed American Catholics at the forefront of this Roman Catholic transnational lobby attempting to shape developments on postwar Palestine. The withering of the British Mandate for the territory after 1945 and the passing of the question to the UN made the United States the hub of the debate on the future of Palestine. The close ties of leading American bishops to the American government, the Vatican surmised, endowed them with a unique ability to transmit papal policy to the most powerful capital in the world. As both patriotic Americans and loyal Roman Catholics, and as leaders of a faith group that had valiantly responded to the nation's call to arms during the Second World War, these figures brought a distinctive pressure to bear on Washington. Ideological affinities between Washington and the Vatican in the early postwar years, moreover, also raised hopes that the efforts of the American bishops on Palestine would bear fruit.

That this transnational lobby was unable, ultimately, to secure its demands spoke volumes on the limits of Vatican diplomacy in the early Cold War. Despite musings on the nefarious politicking of the Holy See and its international network of bishops by polemicists such as Paul Blanshard and Avro Manhattan, the Roman Catholic lobby was not able to claim any definitive victories on Palestine. From a policy of opposing the very creation of a Jewish state in the Holy Land, to strenuously advocating for an internationalized zone encompassing Jerusalem, Bethlehem, and Nazareth, to finally demanding the working establishment of a circumscribed *corpus separatum* for Jerusalem's Old City, Roman Catholic labors came to naught.

Several factors militated against these efforts. The Vatican and American Catholics were met by a well-orchestrated and well-funded American Zionist lobby, which gradually gained the support of a number of mainstream Protestant churches. The Holocaust itself, though not altering the Vatican's position, had also created a compelling logic for a Jewish state, and created a significant groundswell of public support for Zionism among non-Catholics. Even Vatican demands for a functioning internationalization of Jerusalem, promised by three successive UN resolutions, met the reticence of the Truman administration. American troops needed to secure the city, along with the funds required to maintain such a force, was enough to give Truman and the American delegation to the UN pause. Finally, the fickle support of a number of majority-Catholic states at the UN, eager to remain onside with the United States on Israel, ultimately stalled the implementation of a *corpus separatum* for Jerusalem.

The American Catholic lobby on Palestine could, in retrospect, be credited with some modest victories. As this study has outlined, the nascent Israeli state did consider the Vatican's efforts, and particularly those of American Catholics, as threatening to its interests. As a result, Israeli policymakers tried earnestly to forge a solution to the Jerusalem question acceptable to the Vatican. Tel Aviv also encouraged, and funded, an American Zionist counter-lobby to blunt criticisms of Israel in the American diocesan press, which were considered detrimental to its reputation at the UN. Intense American Catholic lobbying also shaped the guarded and prudent Jerusalem policy of Warren Austin and the American delegation to the UN. Though Austin's delegation never cast a vote in favor of territorial internationalization, it was instructed not to counsel other delegations on the question, or to trumpet its policy too loudly. The divisiveness of the question in the United States, documents reveal, was at the root of this circumspection. Vocal disapproval of the scheme from Austin might have sunk the *corpus separatum* much sooner, but intense Catholic lobbying managed to make the question politically volatile for Truman. As a result of American discretion, then, the Jerusalem question remained theoretically "in play" at the UN into the 1950s.

In the final analysis, however, it was, as Peter C. Kent has expressed, a "lonely Cold War" for the Vatican, as the case of Palestine illustrated. Though the transnational consensus on Palestine between Rome and the American church remained firm, the American bishops and the various organs of American Catholicism could not even secure the most modest of the Vatican's demands. The ideological transnationalism observed by Peter D'Agostino on the Roman Question and Italian Fascism remained vigorous through the first decade of the Cold War, as the robust American Catholic campaign on Palestine attested. It was, however, to be the last stand of such a monolithic Catholic lobby. The Second Vatican Council, and its promulgation of *Nostra aetate*, would herald the beginning of a new era in relations between Catholicism and Judaism and, by extension, between the Vatican and Israel. The council, moreover, would unleash a plurality of views in the church that would preclude the survival of such a monolithic stand. Growing consensus on issues such as disarmament, civil rights, economic justice, peace, ecumenism, and interfaith dialogue only served to draw the Vatican and the international Catholic diaspora closer to other faith groups, including Jews, who sought similar ends.

Notes

INTRODUCTION

1 As a result of these negotiations, the Vatican named Andrea Cordero Lanza di Montezemolo its first apostolic nuncio to Israel in 1994. While the original agreement settled the property rights of the Roman Catholic Church in Israel, the issue of Jerusalem was not raised in the document, despite the fact that the Vatican continues, down to the present, to hold the official position that the city should be internationalized. For a fuller analysis of the accords, see Marshall J. Breger, ed., *The Vatican-Israel Accords: Political, Legal and Theological Contexts* (University of Notre Dame Press, 2004).

2 A *corpus separatum* (Latin for "separated body") was the phrase used to describe Jerusalem's theoretical extraterritoriality during the debates on the partition of Palestine at the UN. The UN's 1947 partition plan, in fact, proposed a *corpus separatum* for Jerusalem and its surrounding territory, which encompassed the towns of Bethlehem, Ein Karem, and Abu Dis.

3 Sergio Minerbi's *The Vatican and Zionism: Conflict in the Holy Land, 1895–1925* (Oxford University Press, 1990) provides a comprehensive analysis of the historical roots of the Vatican's position on political Zionism in the early years of that movement. Minerbi traces the Vatican's anxiety toward the potential of Jewish sovereignty over the holy sites of Palestine, as well as the active, and often frenetic, diplomacy of papal nuncios in opposing the Balfour Declaration of 1917. The failure of the Vatican to secure even the most modest of its demands, as Minerbi skilfully delineates, was but a prelude to setbacks of the following decades. George Irani's *The Papacy and the Middle East: The Role of the Holy See in the Arab-Israeli Conflict, 1962–1984* (University of Notre Dame Press, 1986) complements Minerbi's analysis, with a par-

ticular focus on papal policy in the region after the Second Vatican Council (1962–65). On relations between the Vatican, the Jewish Yishuv, and the Israeli state, see Agathe Mayeres-Rebernik's comprehensive *Le Saint-Siège face à la « Question de Palestine »: De la Déclaration Balfour à la création de l'État d'Israël* (Honoré Champion, 2015). Andrej Kreutz's *Vatican Policy on the Palestinian-Israeli Conflict* (Greenwood Press, 1990), explores the evolution of papal policy on the Palestine question, but also examines the Vatican's relationship with the Palestinian national movement through the twentieth century. A number of articles by Silvio Ferrari have more specifically examined the Vatican's quest to secure access to the holy sites of Palestine in the postwar years, as well as delineating failed papal attempts to secure an internationalized Jerusalem in the same period. Uri Bialer's *Cross on the Star of David: The Christian World in Israel's Foreign Policy, 1948–1967* (Indiana University Press, 2005) examines Israeli perspectives on the relationship with the Vatican in the post-1948 period, revealing the extent to which Tel Aviv considered the Vatican a genuine threat to the interests of the nascent state.

4 Transnational perspectives have been employed by historians in various forms throughout the twentieth century. *Annales* historian Fernand Braudel's *The Mediterranean and the Mediterranean World in the Age of Phillip II* (Colin, 1949) could be considered a forerunner of the transnational genre, as he explored geographic, economic, and demographic influences while "great power" politics, and specifically the role of European sovereigns, were considered marginal to this narrative. Political scientists Joseph Nye and Robert Keohane edited a collection of essays on transnational politics, *Transnational Relations and World Politics* (Harvard University Press, 1971), that further defined the field and that included an essay by sociologist Ivan Vallier on the Roman Catholic Church as a transnational actor.

5 See, for example, Akira Iriye and Petra Goedde, *International History: A Cultural Approach* (Bloomsbury Press, 2022). See also Ian Tyrell's *Transnational Nation: United States History in Global Perspective since 1789* (Palgrave Macmillan, 2015), and Iriye's essay, "The Making of a Transnational World," in Iriye, ed., *Global Interdependence: The World since 1945* (Belknap Press, 2014), 681–847.

6 The study of the Vatican as a transnational actor in international affairs was pioneered by sociologist Ivan Vallier His foundational 1972 essay, "The Roman Catholic Church: A Transnational Actor," delineated the multifaceted organization of the international church, which pursued its objectives not only through the Vatican Secretariat and its network of papal diplomats,

but also through a global nexus of religious and lay Catholic organizations. Vallier's focus, however, remained contemporary, and did not explore the historical dimensions of Vatican transnationalism. See Vallier's chapter in Keohane and Nye, *Transnational Relations and World Politics.*

7 For an overview of the Vatican's global diplomatic structure, see Thomas J. Reese, *Inside the Vatican: The Politics and Organization of the Catholic Church* (Harvard University Press, 2003).

8 Chappel's *Catholic Modern: The Challenge of Totalitarianism and the Remaking of the Church* (Harvard University Press, 2018) examines the church's gradual embrace of modernity as it negotiated its place in a secularizing twentieth-century global society. Chappel traced this evolution through the work of theologians and Catholic intellectuals in Austria, France, and Germany who turned away from the lure of totalitarianism systems of the Right and the Left to embrace the democratic and rights-based regimes of postwar Europe.

9 Robert A. Graham, SJ's *Vatican Diplomacy: A Study of Church and State on the International Plane* (Princeton University Press, 1959) remains a forceful examination of the structure and method of the Vatican's diplomatic activities. More recently, essays in Peter C. Kent and John Pollard's *Papal Diplomacy in the Modern Age* (Praeger, 1994) have explored papal diplomacy in a range of twentieth-century contexts.

10 The terms "Holy See," "papacy," and "the Vatican" are used interchangeably in this book in reference to the central government of the Roman Catholic Church.

11 See Byrnes's "Sovereignty, Supranationalism, and Soft Power: The Holy See in International Relations," *Review of Faith and International Affairs* 15, no. 4 (2017): 6–20.

12 See Katharina McLarren and Bernhard Stahl, "The Holy See as Hybrid Actor: Religion in International, Transnational and World Society," in *The Pope, the Public and International Relations: Post-secular Transformations*, ed. Mariano P. Barbato (Springer, 2020), 189–201. See also Jodok Troy, "The Pope's Own Hand Outstretched: Holy See Diplomacy as a Hybrid Mode of Diplomatic Agency," *British Journal of Politics and International Relations* 20, no. 3 (2018): 521–39.

13 See Lisa L. Ferrari's "The Vatican as a Transnational Actor," in *The Catholic Church and the Nation State: Comparative Perspectives*, ed. Paul Christopher Manuel, Lawrence Reardon, and Clyde Wilcox (Georgetown University Press 2006), 33–50.

14 See Barbato's "A State, a Diplomat, and a Transnational Church: The Multilayered Actorness of the Holy See," *Central European Review of International Affairs* 21, no. 2 (2013): 27–48; Ryall's "How Many Divisions? The Modern Development of Catholic International Relations," *International Relations* 14, no. 2 (1998): 21–34; and Beittinger-Lee's "Catholicism at the United Nations in New York," in *Religion, NGOs and the United Nations: Visible and Invisible Actors in Power*, ed. Jeremy Carrette and Hugh Miall (Bloomsbury, 2017), 177–94. Other recent studies that have considered transnational aspects of the church's global influence include Stephen J.C. Andes and Julia C. Young, eds, *Local Church, Global Church: Catholic Activism in Latin America from Rerum Novarum to Vatican II* (Catholic University of America Press, 2016); Colin Barr, *Ireland's Empire: The Roman Catholic Church in the English-Speaking World, 1829–1914* (Cambridge University Press, 2020); Luca Codignola, *Blurred Nationalities across the North Atlantic: Traders, Priests and Their Kin Travelling between North America and the Italian Peninsula, 1763–1846* (University of Toronto Press, 2020); Patrick J. Houlihan, *Catholicism and the Great War: Religion and Everyday Life in Germany and Austria-Hungary, 1914–1922* (Cambridge University Press, 2015); John T. McGreevy, *American Jesuits and the World: How an Embattled Religious Order Made Modern Catholicism Global* (Princeton University Press, 2016); John T. McGreevy, *Catholicism: A Global History from the French Revolution to Pope Francis* (Norton, 2022); Sarah Shortall, *Soldiers of God in a Secular World: Catholic Theology and Twentieth-Century French Politics* (Harvard University Press, 2021); Albert Monshan Wu, *From Christ to Confucius: German Missionaries, Chinese Christians, and the Globalization of Christianity* (Yale University Press, 2016).

15 Chamedes contends that after 1918, the Vatican sought to forge a postwar order that steered away from both Bolshevism and secular Wilsonian liberalism. Though directed from papal Rome, it was a project that called upon the support of local hierarchies, lay associations, and the Catholic media. See her *A Twentieth Century Crusade: The Vatican's Battle to Remake Christian Europe* (Harvard University Press, 2019).

16 Peter D'Agostino, *Rome in America: Transnational Catholic Ideology from the Risorgimento to Fascism* (University of North Carolina Press, 2005).

17 Ibid., 7.

18 The Americanist controversy, at its core, was precipitated by a belief in papal circles that a number of American bishops endorsed a separation of church and state (where the Vatican preferred closer church-state cooperation akin to European tradition). The Vatican feared that the American episcopate,

functioning in a pluralistic and rapidly industrializing society, would adopt a relativistic approach to church doctrine and theology. Pope Leo XIII's 1899 encyclical, *Testem benevolentiae*, was specifically issued to suppress the Americanist heresy.

19 See John F. Pollard, *Money and the Rise of the Modern Papacy: Financing the Vatican, 1850–1950* (Cambridge University Press, 2005), 136–8.

CHAPTER ONE

1 Genesis 15:18.

2 See Harry M. Orlinsky, "The Biblical Concept of the Land of Israel: Cornerstone of the Covenant between God and Israel," in *The Land of Israel: Jewish Perspectives*, ed. Lawrence A. Hoffman (University of Notre Dame Press, 1986), 27. For Orlinsky, the Hebrew Bible, as it referred to the connection between the Jewish people and Palestine, was essentially a lawbook, dedicated to the explication of the covenant, or contract, between God and the Jewish people, and the land itself was the covenant. The noted theologian and biblical scholar W.D. Davies has also written on the centrality of land to the covenant, observing that there is "a kind of umbilical cord between Israel and the Land." See his *The Gospel and the Land: Early Christianity and Jewish Territorial Doctrine* (University of California Press, 1974), and *The Territorial Dimensions of Judaism* (University of California Press, 1982).

3 See Gershon Cohen, "Zion in Rabbinic Literature," in *Zion in Jewish Literature*, ed. Abraham Halkin (Herzl Press, 1961), 52.

4 Though Christianity, Judaism, and Islam all consider Palestine sacred, the term "Holy Land" was used increasingly by Christians as their pilgrimages there increased after the fourth century. For a brief examination of the history of the term, see Kirsten Hoffgren Pedersen, "The Holy Land: History and Reality of the Term," in *People, Land and the State of Israel: Jewish and Christian Perspectives*, ed. Malcolm Lowe (Ecumenical Theological Research Fraternity in Israel, 1989).

5 Matthew 19:29. Quoted in Carole Monica Burnett, "Early Christians: Belonging Everywhere and Nowhere," in *Zionism through Christian Lenses: Ecumenical Perspectives on the Promised Land* (Pickwick, 2013), 75. For a brief overview of the gospels and their presentation of Judaism, see Philip A. Cunningham's *Seeking Shalom: The Journey to Right Relationship between Catholics and Jews* (Eerdmans, 2015), 80–108.

6 Luke 9:57–62.

7 John 4:20–21. Quoted in Pedersen, "The Holy Land," 36.

8 On the universality of Paul's ministry and epistles, see Mark Strom, "From Promised Land to Reconciled Cosmos: Paul's Translation of 'Worldview,' 'Worldstory' and 'Worldperson,'" in *The Gospel and the Land of Promise: Christian Approaches to the Land of the Bible*, ed. Philip Church (Pickwick, 2011), 14–27.

9 See Mark Keown, "Paul's Answer to the Threats of Jerusalem and Rome," in Church, *The Gospel and the Land*, 43.

10 Ibid. For a fuller examination of the place of land and the covenant in the Pauline Epistles, see Church, *The Gospel and the Land*, 164–220.

11 Quoted in Pedersen, "The Holy Land," 36.

12 Ibid.

13 For Jerome's second letter to Paulinus of Nola, dissuading him from making a pilgrimage to the Holy Land, see "Letter 58," *New Advent*, accessed 6 November 2024, http://www.newadvent.org/fathers/3001058.htm.

14 See Ronald Teske, SJ, ed., *The Works of Saint Augustine: A Translation for the 21st Century* (New City Press, 2001), 303.

15 Quoted in Carole Monica Burnett, *Zionism through Christian Lenses*, 99.

16 See Robert Andrew Everett, "The Land: Israel and the Middle East in Jewish-Christian Dialogue," in *Introduction to Christian-Jewish Relations*, ed. Michael Shermis and Arthur E. Zannoni (Paulist Press, 1991), 96.

17 Robert Michael, *Holy Hatred: Christianity, Anti-Semitism and the Holocaust* (Palgrave, 2006), 17.

18 See Everett, "The Land," 96.

19 Magda Teter contends that Augustine's repeated use of the "language of servitude, slavery and submission in reference to the Jews" forged a political order in which Jews were rendered a perpetual underclass in Christian societies. See her *Christian Supremacy: Reckoning with the Roots of Antisemitism and Racism* (Princeton University Press, 2023), 19–31. Lindsay Kaplan reveals that the proto-racism of figures such as Augustine, which foisted a "cursed inferiority" upon the Jews and condemned them to a position of everlasting servitude (*servitus Judaeorum*), created a template for the intensifying anti-Judaic repressions of the medieval centuries. See her *Figuring Racism in Medieval Christianity* (Oxford University Press, 2019), 19–56.

20 For a succinct overview of the relationship between early Christianity and Judaism, see Edward Kessler, *An Introduction to Jewish-Christian Relations* (Cambridge University Press, 2010), 1–64; Michael, *Holy Hatred*, 1–104. On the historical development of Christian anti-Judaism and antisemitism, see

Marvin Perry and Frederick Schweitzer, *Anti-Semitism: Myth and Hate from Antiquity to the Present* (Palgrave, 2002).

21 See Jules Isaac, *The Teaching of Contempt: The Christian Roots of Anti-Semitism* (Rinehart and Winston, 1964).

22 On the enduring connection between Judaism and Christianity in this period, and the attraction of Christians to Judaism, see Robert L. Wilken, *John Chrysostom and the Jews: Rhetoric and Reality in the Late 4th Century* (University of California Press, 1983), 66–94.

23 Edward H. Flannery, *The Anguish of the Jews: Twenty-Three Centuries of Antisemitism* (Paulist Press, 2004), 51.

24 Ibid.

25 Ibid.

26 On the persecution of Christians under Al-Hakim, see John Joseph Saunders, *A History of Medieval Islam* (Routledge, 1990), 137–9.

27 Quoted in Norman Housley, "Holy Land or Holy Lands? Palestine and the Catholic West in the Late Middle Ages and Renaissance," in *The Holy Land, Holy Lands and Christian History*, ed. R.N. Swanson (Boydell and Brewer, 2000), 230.

28 Quoted in Walter Zander, *Israel and the Holy Places of Christendom* (Praeger, 1971), 17.

29 Ibid., 15.

30 Ibid., 19.

31 On this emerging historiographical view of the Crusades as an essentially penitential undertaking, see Norman Housely, *Fighting for the Cross: Crusading to the Holy Land* (Yale University Press, 2008); Jonathan Riley-Smith, *The Crusades: A History* (Yale University Press, 2005); William J. Purkis, *Crusading Spirituality in the Holy Land and Iberia* (Boydell Press, 2008).

32 Jonathan Riley-Smith, *What Were the Crusades?* (Palgrave, 2002), 56.

33 Ibid., 62–3.

34 Relics, of course, played a significant role in medieval theology and popular devotion, and were connected to the expanding veneration of saints increasingly central to Christian piety. For a brief discussion of the place of relics and the veneration of saints in the medieval church, see Kevin Madigan, *Medieval Christianity: A New History* (Yale University Press, 2015), 320–42.

35 Quoted in Zander, *Israel and the Holy Places of Christendom*, 20.

36 Ibid.

37 Britain adopted the 1757 "Status Quo" edict into its Palestine Mandate in 1920, and United Nations representatives on the Palestine Conciliation Commission

referred to the "Status Quo" agreement between 1947 and 1949 in determining the validity of claims made by Orthodox churchmen in Palestine. See "United Nations Conciliation Commission for Palestine, Committee on Jerusalem – The Holy Places: Note on the History of the Status Quo, Working Paper Prepared by the Secretariat," 8 April 1949, National Catholic Welfare Conference (hereafter NCWC), Office of the General Secretary (hereafter OGS), archives of the Catholic University of America (hereafter ACUA), Box 44, File 22.

38 Although the Roman Catholic hierarchy had not functioned in Palestine since the end of the thirteenth century, the church had always maintained a presence there. After 1333, it was represented by the Franciscan order's Custody of the Holy Land. See F. Michael Perko, SJ, "Toward a 'Sound and Lasting Basis': Relations between the Holy See, the Zionist Movement and Israel, 1896–1996," *Israel Studies* 2 no. 1 (Spring 1997): 3. On the growth and development of the Palestinian Christian presence in Palestine from 1800 until the creation of the Israeli state in 1948, see Anthony O'Mahony, ed., *Palestinian Christians: Religion, Politics and Society in the Holy Land* (Melisende, 1999), 9–55.

39 Kreutz, *Vatican Policy on the Palestinian-Israeli Conflict*, 31.

40 Vatican reticence toward political Zionism was tied to papal fears of modern nationalism in general. The papacy's nineteenth-century clash with Italian liberal nationalism, which resulted in a complete loss of the pope's temporal authority, had created a deep and lasting Vatican mistrust of modernist ideologies (including socialism, secularism, and nationalism), which had only functioned to limit papal power and autonomy.

41 See Michael Brenner, *Zionism: A Brief History* (Markus Wiener Publishers, 2003), 8.

42 Martin Gilbert, *Israel: A History* (Harper, 2008), 4. For a succinct examination of Herzl's disenchantment with Jewish assimilation and his embrace of Zionism, see Derek Penslar, *Theodor Herzl: The Charismatic Leader* (Yale University Press, 2020), 47–84.

43 Quoted in Simon Sebag Montefiore, *Jerusalem: The Biography* (Knopf, 2011), 392.

44 For a survey of the origins and development of the Zionist movement, see Walter Laqueur's *A History of Zionism from the French Revolution to the Establishment of the State of Israel* (Knopf, 2003).

45 Raphael Patai, ed., *The Complete Diaries of Theodor Herzl*, vol. 1 (Herzl Press, 1960), 352–4.

46 Ibid.

47 Ibid. Herzl's skepticism of papal support deepened in August and September of 1896 as Italian newspapers, echoing *L'Osservatore Romano*, reported that the Vatican was attempting to make a protest against the occupation of Palestine by the Jews. When his attempt to meet Agliardi's successor as papal nunio to Vienna, Cardinal Emidio Taliani, was rejected, it confirmed to Herzl the growing obstinacy in Vatican circles to the Zionist project.

48 The Basel Program, passed at the congress, confirmed that "Zionism aims to create a home for the Jewish people in Palestine secured by public law."

49 *La Civiltà Cattolica*, 1 May 1897. Quoted in Livia Rokach, *The Catholic Church and the Question of Palestine* (Saqi Books, 1987), 11.

50 On this antisemitic turn in the Catholic press, see Nina Valbousquet, "Race and Faith: The Catholic Church, Clerical Fascism, and the Shaping of Italian Anti-Semitism and Racism," *Modern Italy* 23, no. 4 (2018): 355–71; David Leibovitch Dahl, "Normalisation of Antisemitism, 1880–1900: The Case of a Jesuit Community in Rome," *Patterns of Prejudice* 48, no. 1 (2014): 47–66.

51 Patai, *The Complete Diaries of Theodor Herzl*, 1:1593–5.

52 Ibid.

53 Ibid.

54 Ibid.

55 See Andrew M. Canepa, "Pius X and the Jews: A Reappraisal," *Church History* 61, no. 3 (1992): 362–72. On responses to Zionism among Italian Jews, see Riccardo di Segni, *Le Origini del Sionismo in Italia* (Centro Giovanile Ebraico di Firenze, 1972).

56 Patai, *The Complete Diaries of Theodor Herzl*, 4:1601–6.

57 Ibid. In the early 1890s, Herzl himself had entertained the idea of the mass conversion of European Jews to Catholicism, on the grounds that the pope would call a campaign to end antisemitism. See Penslar, *Theodor Herzl*, 62–3.

58 Patai, *The Complete Diaries of Theodor Herzl*, 4: 1601–6.

59 *Die Welt*, 1 April 1904. Quoted in Minerbi, *The Vatican and Zionism*, 101. (*Die Welt*, which was edited by Herzl, is not to be confused with the German national daily newspaper of the same name, which was launched in 1946.)

60 Leonard Stein, *The Balfour Declaration* (Simon and Schuster, 1961), 407.

61 On the rapid growth of international Zionism after 1904, see Laqueur, *A History of Zionism*, 136–208.

62 On Sykes's growing commitment to the Zionist cause, and on the origins and development of the Sykes-Picot Agreement over the winter of 1915–16, see Stein's classic study, *The Balfour Declaration*, 233–69.

63 At the time, Pacelli was secretary of state for extraordinary ecclesiastical affairs in the Vatican Secretariat, a position second only to Gasparri's in the development of Vatican foreign policy.

64 Minerbi, *The Vatican and Zionism*, 107.

65 Stein, *The Balfour Declaration*, 405.

66 Sokolow was apprised of this by the pro-British Zionist Felix Pinkus, who, quoting from a 25 April article in the *Journal de Genéve*, discussed a Catholic plan to prevent British control of the areas around Bethlehem, Nazareth, and Jerusalem, instead creating an enclave under Vatican jurisdiction. See Chaim Weizmann to Sir Ronald Graham, 4 May 1917, in Barnett Litvinoff, ed., *The Letters and Papers of Chaim Weizmann*, ser. A, vol. 7 (Oxford University Press, 1977), 395.

67 Stein, *The Balfour Declaration*, 406.

68 Quoted in Minerbi, *The Vatican and Zionism*, 108.

69 Kreutz, *Vatican Policy on the Palestinian-Israeli Conflict*, 35.

70 On the Vatican's application of concordat diplomacy to thwart the emergence of either a Wilsonian global order or a Bolshevistic order, see Chamedes, *A Twentieth-Century Crusade*, 17–68.

71 Minerbi, *The Vatican and Zionism*, 110. In closing, Sokolow assured Gasparri that the Zionists did not wish to establish a "kingdom," but merely an autonomous home. The secretary of state assured his guest that his reference was a figure of speech, but that the Zionists could count on the support of the church: "You may count on our sympathy. We shall be glad to see the land of Israel … You will certainly need priority in acquiring lands and for the immigrants … I wish you full success" (110). On Sokolow's meetings with Pacelli, Gasparri, and Benedict XV, see also Isaiah Friedman, *The Question of Palestine, 1914–1918: British-Jewish-Arab Relations* (Schocken, 1973), 151–6.

72 Kreutz, *Vatican Policy on the Palestinian-Israeli Conflict*, 35.

73 Ibid., 111.

74 Pinchas E. Lapide, *Three Popes and the Jews* (Hawthorn, 1967), 84.

75 Stein, *The Balfour Declaration*, 408.

76 Chaim Weizmann, *Trial and Error: The Autobiography of Chaim Weizmann* (Harper, 1949), 240.

77 An alternative thesis has been presented by Agnes de Dreuzy, who contends that Benedict XV's diplomacy on the question of Palestine signaled a break from the Vatican's traditional anti-Zionist line. She contends that instead of being fixed on immutable theological positions, Benedict's Palestine policy was based on a more nuanced appreciation of international diplomacy on the

Near East, and a desire to balance Zionist and Vatican aspirations in Palestine. See her *The Holy See and the Emergence of the Modern Middle East: Benedict XV's Diplomacy in Greater Syria, 1914–1922* (Catholic University of America Press, 2016), 222–58.

78 Though secondary literature on the Balfour Declaration is fairly extensive, a splendid study of its origins and implementation is Ronald Sanders's *The High Walls of Jerusalem: A History of the Balfour Declaration and the Birth of the British Mandate for Palestine* (Holt, Rinehart and Winston, 1983).

79 Kreutz, *Vatican Policy on the Palestinian-Israeli Conflict*, 36. The Vatican considered itself the protector of the Arab Christian population in Palestine, who were seen as the "living stones" of the faith in the Holy Land.

80 On the reactions of the American Catholic press, see Esther Yolles Feldblum's *The American Catholic Press and the Jewish State, 1917–1959* (Ktav, 1977), 17–28.

81 Charles Loiseau, "Ma mission auprès de Vatican," *Revue d'histoire diplomatique*, no. 74 (1960): 105.

82 Sergio Minerbi, *L'Italie e le Palestine, 1914–1920* (Presses Universitaires de France, 1970), 69.

83 See Nina Valbousquet, "Transnational Antisemitic Networks and Political Christianity: The Catholic Participation in The Protocols of the Elders of Zion," in *Religion, Ethnonationalism and Antisemitism in the Era of the Two World Wars*, ed. Kevin P. Spicer and Rebecca Carter-Chand (McGill-Queen's University Press, 2022), 48–71. For a general survey of the myth of Judeo-Bolshevism, see Paul Hanebrink, *A Specter Haunting Europe: The Myth of Judeo-Bolshevism* (Harvard University Press, 2018).

84 Valbousquet, "Transnational Antisemitic Networks," 48–71.

85 Constantine Rackauskas, "The Internationalization of Jerusalem," NCWC/OGS/ACUA, Box 44, File 30.

86 Quoted in Chamedes, *A Twentieth-Century Crusade*, 53.

87 The Catholic press, for its part, similarly trumpeted the Vatican's anti-Zionist stance in the postwar period. The British Catholic *Tablet*, for example, dispelled any notion of Vatican support for Zionism in March 1919, calling the idea of papal support for Zionism "quite untrue." See "Zionism," *Tablet*, 1 March 1919, 248.

88 See Rohan Butler and J.P.T. Bury, eds, *Documents in British Foreign Policy, 1919–1939*, ser. 1, vol. 8 (London: HMSO, 1966), 164.

89 Litvinoff, *The Letters and Papers of Chaim Weizmann*, 9:297.

90 Ibid., 11:96.

91 Ibid.

92 According to Weizmann's letters, an audience with Benedict XV was not arranged due to a prior visit to the pope by the British Zionist Sir Herbert Samuel, who had allegedly made false promises to limit Jewish immigration to Palestine. See ibid., 11:348.

93 Ibid. Chaim Weizmann to Nahum Sokolow, 24 May 1922, 11:97–8.

94 Ibid.

95 Ibid. Chaim Weizmann to Albert Einstein, 2 June 1922.

96 Ibid., 11:77.

97 Pietro Cardinal Gasparri to John Francis Charles de Salis (British minister to the Holy See), 6 March 1922, NCWC/OGS/ACUA, Box 18, File 44.

98 Ibid.

99 Kreutz, *Vatican Policy on the Palestinian-Israeli Conflict*, 41–2.

100 Aide-mémoire to the League of Nations, 4 June 1922, NCWC/OGS/ACUA, Box 18, File 44.

101 Quoted in Manlio Graziano, *In Rome We Trust: The Rise of Catholics in American Political Life* (Stanford University Press, 2017), 70. Pius XI issued the encyclical *Ubi arcano Dei consilio* (On the peace of Christ in His kingdon) in December 1922.

CHAPTER TWO

1 Several excellent surveys outline the rise of the American Catholic Church from its origins to the middle of the twentieth century. See James M. O'Toole, *The Faithful: A History of Catholics in America* (Harvard University Press, 2009); Charles R. Morris *American Catholic: The Saints and Sinners Who Built America's Most Powerful Church* (Times Books, 1997); James Hennessey *American Catholics: A History of the Roman Catholic Community in the United States* (Oxford University Press, 1981); Jay P. Dolan *The American Catholic Experience: A History from Colonial Times to Present* (Doubleday, 1985).

2 On the American Catholic war effort and the establishment of the National Catholic War Council, see Elizabeth McKeown, *War and Welfare: American Catholics and World War I* (Garland, 1988). *The Catholic World* was created in 1865 by Father Isaac Hecker, an American convert to Catholicism who founded the Paulist fathers in New York City in 1858. Hecker was closely associated with the Americanist movement and was a vocal proponent of the deeper assimilation of Catholics into American secular and political culture.

3 *Handbook of the National Catholic War Council*, December 1918, NCWC/OGS/ACUA, Box 18, File 44.

4 Though Catholics comprised about 16 percent of the population in 1917, their enlistment rate was nearly 21 percent. See *Handbook of the National Catholic War Council*, December 1918, NCWC/OGS/ACUA, Box 18, File 44.

5 "Report of the Chairman of the NCWC Administration Committee," 23 September 1920, NCWC/OGS/ACUA, Box 22, File 44.

6 Elizabeth McKeown, "The National Bishops' Conference: An Analysis of Its Origins," *Catholic Historical Review*, no. 66 (1980): 574.

7 The NCWC was also opposed from within the American hierarchy. Cardinals William O'Connell and Dennis Dougherty, who would both later serve on the board of the CNEWA, advocated for disbandment, fearing a reduction of their own clout within the American church. Edmund Walsh to Edward Hanna, 6 March 1922, NCWC/OGS/ACUA, Box 22, File 44.

8 For a fuller examination of the political campaign of American Catholics on Mexican anticlericalism, see Matthew A. Redinger's *American Catholics and the Mexican Revolution, 1924–1936* (Notre Dame University Press, 2005).

9 Raphael M. Huber, ed., *Our Bishops Speak: National Pastorals and Annual Statements of the Hierarchy of the United States* (Bruce Publishing, 1952), 188–9.

10 Ibid., 68–70. A pastoral letter (sometimes referred to simply as a "pastoral)" is an open letter addressed from a bishop to his faithful and is generally considered to represent the official position of the Roman Catholic Church on a particular matter. The pastoral issued by the bishops on Mexico was a joint pastoral, intended to emphasize the importance of the Mexican crisis to the entire American Catholic community.

11 The bishops emphasized that the statement "is no interposition of our influence either as Bishops or as citizens to reach those who possess political power anywhere on earth, and least of all in our own country, to the end that they should intervene with armed force in the internal affairs of Mexico for the protection of the Church." Ibid., 94. Direct political pressure would, in short order, be discreetly applied by members of the hierarchy directly to figures in the American government.

12 The Knights of Columbus, an order founded in Connecticut in 1882, coordinated its own campaign to resist the anticlerical Mexican state during the Cristero War (1926–29). See Julia G. Young, "Knights and *Caballeros*: Cross-Border Catholic Activism during Mexico's Cristero War," *Mexican Studies/Estudios Mexicanos* 33, no. 2 (Summer 2017): 245–71.

13 "Statement of Appeal from the NCWC to NCCM and NCCW Councils," August 1926, NCWC/OGS/ACUA, Box 5, File 44.

14 Redinger, *American Catholics and the Mexican Revolution*, 24.

15 Circulation figures for Catholic papers and periodicals for 1937 indicate a circulation of 2,396,516 for diocesan newspapers and 4,604,141 for magazines. Though circulation rose in the 1930s, these figures still infer a wide readership in 1926. See "National Catholic Welfare Conference News Service: Circulation Figures," 7 June 1937, NCWC/OGS/ACUA, Box 21, File 2.

16 For excellent synopses of Burke's diplomacy during the Mexican crisis, see Stephen J.C. Andes, *The Vatican and Catholic Activism in Mexico and Chile: The Politics of Transnational Catholicism, 1920–1940* (Oxford University Press, 2014), 74–99; Redinger, *American Catholics and the Mexican Revolution*, 65–99.

17 Despite the 1929 agreement, frictions between the church in Mexico and the Calles regime persisted. The election of Franklin Delano Roosevelt in 1933 appeared to hearken a renewed isolationism in Washington, as the president was hesitant to disturb the American "Good Neighbor Policy," which pledged noninterference in the domestic affairs of neighboring states. Roosevelt's desires to cultivate ties with American Catholics, however, eventually drew him into the Mexican situation. In the summer of 1934 Amleto Cicognani, the new apostolic delegate to Washington, asked Burke to lobby the president for a resolution. An intensive campaign of public awareness coordinated by the NCWC, as well as Burke's advocacy with the president, created the impetus for action. Though the "Borah Resolution," which threatened Calles with sanctions and the breaking of diplomatic relations, eventually stalled in Congress, the episode signaled an increasingly closer relationship between the White House and American Catholics. See Richard Gribble, "Roman Catholicism and US Foreign Policy, 1919–1935: A Clash of Policies," *Journal of Church and State* 51, no. 1 (Winter 2008): 92–8; David B. Woolner and Richard Kurial, eds, *FDR, The Vatican and the Roman Catholic Church in America, 1933–1945* (Palgrave Macmillan, 2003).

18 Pope Pius XI to William O'Connell, Dennis Dougherty, George Mundelein, and Patrick Hayes, 10 August 1927, NCWC/OGS/ACUA, Box 44, File 5.

19 Walsh, a Jesuit priest and academic, would achieve notoriety as an envoy and diplomat for much of his career. Like Burke, he was involved in negotiations with Calles on the Mexican crisis, and he negotiated with the Iraqi government to establish the American College at Baghdad in 1931. He would establish a reputation as a stern anticommunist. It was alleged that it was Walsh who first suggested that Senator Joseph McCarthy use the issue to gain political prominence. On Walsh's remarkable career, and particularly on his anticommunist activities, see Patrick McNamara, *A Catholic Cold War: Edmund A*

Walsh, S.J., and the Politics of American Anticommunism (Fordham University Press, 2005).

20 Hansjakob Stehle, *Eastern Politics of the Vatican, 1917–1979* (Ohio University Press, 1980), 49.

21 This program included the construction of a School of Christian Archaeology, an Ethiopian College in the Vatican, a new palace in the square facing Santa Maria Maggiore, the building of a palace that would house the governor of the Vatican City State after 1929, and the construction of a new propaganda college for the training of missionary priests, among other projects. See John F. Pollard, *Money and the Rise of the Modern Papacy: Financing the Vatican, 1850–1950* (Cambridge University Press, 2005), 134.

22 Ibid., 223.

23 Sir Odo Russell to Austen Chamberlain, 9 March 1924. Quoted in Thomas E. Hachey, *Anglo-Vatican Relations, 1914–1939: Confidential Annual Reports of the British Ministers to the Holy See* (G.K. Hall, 1972), 71.

24 Ibid., 70.

25 Ibid., 88–9.

26 "Annual Report – Russian Papal Relief Mission, 1924," Georgetown University Archives, Special Collections (hereafter GUA-SC), Edmund Walsh Papers, Box 6, File 392.

27 "Catholic Near East Welfare Association Annual – 1927," NCWC/OGS/ACUA, Box 122, File 2.

28 Pietro Cardinal Gasparri to Edmund Walsh, 13 March 1926, GUA-SC, Edmund Walsh Papers, Box 6, File 392.

29 Edmund Walsh to Reverend Stephen Donahue, secretary of the archbishop of New York, 28 September 1926, GUA-SC, Edmund Walsh Papers, Box 6, File 392.

30 "Catholic Near East Welfare Association Annual – 1927," NCWC/OGS/ACUA, Box 122, File 2. The "annual" implored Catholics to join the association. "Once more the Vicar of Christ is looking to our annual roll-call to maintain his works of mercy. If you are already enrolled as a member, renew your membership NOW. If, by any chance, you are not one of those who have already responded to the Holy Father's appeal, enrol TODAY."

31 "Catholic Near East Welfare Association – Board of Directors," April 1926, GUA-SC, Edmund Walsh Papers, Box 6, File 391.

32 Cardinal Luigi Sincero to Pietro Cardinal Gasparri, 10 March 1926, GUA-SC, Edmund Walsh Papers, Box 6, File 388.

33 Ibid.

34 The appeal, which was launched on 23 January, achieved its target in just four

months. The leading archdioceses and dioceses, by contribution, were New York ($96,074), Philadelphia ($90,256), Boston ($58,449), Springfield ($53,649), and Hartford ($46,227), underscoring the power and fundraising capacity of the church in the Northeast. "CNEWA Appeal," 31 May 1927, GUA-SC, Edmund Walsh Papers, Box 6, File 391.

35 A number of mainstream secular newspapers echoed Hoover's sentiments. See "Press Comment," 1 January 1927, GUA-SC, Edmund Walsh Papers, File 6, Box 388. Papers such as *The Evening Globe* (Boston), *The Democrat* (Waterbury, Connecticut), *The Daily American Tribune* (Dubuque, Iowa), and *The Telegram* (Worcester, Massachusetts) commented favorably on the work of the CNEWA.

36 "Pope Pius XI to the Archbishops and Bishops of the United States," 30 July 1927, GUA-SC, Edmund Walsh Papers, Box 6, File 392.

37 "The Papal Annual: A Review of the International Welfare Activities of the Holy See," January 1928, GUA-SC, Edmund Walsh Papers, Box 6, File 392.

38 "Pope Pius XI to the Archbishops and Bishops of the United States," 23 October 1928, GUA-SC, Edmund Walsh Papers, Box 6, File 391.

39 Ibid.

40 Ibid.

41 In a short span, the Holy See completed concordats with Latvia (1922), Poland (1925), Lithuania (1927), Romania (1927), and the German states of Rhineland, Westphalia, and Saarland (1929).

42 See Peter C. Kent, *The Pope and the Duce: The International Impact of the Lateran Agreements* (St Martin's Press, 1981), 2. For Mussolini, the accords cemented his seizure of power, completing the matrix of institutional structures supporting his regime. He based his dictatorship on a series of compromises with the traditional institutions of the Italian state: the monarchy, the armed forces, the industrial community, and the church. The Lateran Accords completed this process, putting to rest the longest-standing grievance of Italian unification, and providing Mussolini and the Fascist state an enhanced international prestige. See Adrian Lyttleton, *The Seizure of Power: Fascism in Italy, 1919–1929* (Scribner's, 1973), 429–32.

43 See Peter C. Kent, "A Tale of Two Popes," *Journal of Contemporary History* 23, no. 4 (1988): 589–608.

44 Hennessey, *American Catholics*, 285. On Spellman's life and career, see James Cooney's *The American Pope: The Life and Times of Francis Cardinal Spellman* (Times Books, 1984).

45 On the career of Mundelein, see Edward Kantowicz, *Corporation Sole: Cardinal Mundelein and Chicago Catholicism* (Notre Dame University Press, 1983).

46 Ibid.

47 Hachey, *Anglo-Vatican Relations*, 399.

48 Pacelli's tour served American purposes as well, by helping to censor the anti-Roosevelt and antisemitic "radio priest," Father Charles Coughlin. It also gave Pacelli the opportunity to propose diplomatic relations between Washington and the Vatican, a sign that the papacy could no longer depend solely on its European network, particularly as the clouds of war gathered over the continent. His itinerary included a two-week tour of the nation, a stay in New York City as the guest of Myron C. Taylor (Roosevelt's future "personal representative" to the Holy See), and, finally, a luncheon with the recently reelected Roosevelt at Hyde Park. For a fuller treatment of the Pacelli visit, see G. D'Alessio, "The United States and the Vatican (1936–1939): From Eugenio Pacelli's Visit to the US to Myron Taylor's Mission to the Holy See," in *Pius XI and America*, ed. C.R. Gallagher, D. Kertzer, and A. Melloni (Lit Verlag, 2012), 129–54.

49 Several members of the American hierarchy, including Mundelein, O'Connell, and Hayes, were vexed by Spellman's close control of Pacelli's visit, a result of his friendship with Pacelli and his Roman contacts. John J. Burke, the NCWC's general secretary, expressed frustrations over Spellman's diffidence toward the conference during Pacelli's tour, and criticized the bishop's treatment of Amleto Cicognani, the apostolic delegate, who had been frustrated in his own efforts to manage Pacelli's agenda. Burke considered Spellman's disregard for the NCWC a rebuff not to the organization alone, but also to the bishops it represented – in effect a snub of the American hierarchy itself. See John J. Burke to Edward Mooney, 26 October 1936, NCWC/OGS/ACUA, Box 152, File 27.

50 Coughlin's popularity and demagoguery presented no idle threat. As Charles Gallagher has illustrated, Coughlin's incessant references to Judeo-Bolshevism through the decade abetted the rise of groups such as the Christian Front, a right-wing militant organization that aimed to purge the nation of atheism, communism, and rapacious capitalism, and whose leaders were finally arrested as they plotted an armed coup against the federal government. See Gallagher's *Nazis of Copley Square: The Forgotten Story of the Christian Front* (Harvard University Press, 2021). See also Warren I. Donald, *Radio Priest: Charles Coughlin, the Father of Hate Radio* (Free Press, 2005) and Mary

Christine Athans, *The Coughlin-Fahey Connection: Father Charles E. Coughlin, Father Denis Fahey and Religious Anti-Semitism in the United States, 1938–1954* (Peter Lang, 1991).

51 Francis Spellman to John Burke, 8 November 1936, NCWC/OGS/ACUA, Box 152, File 29.

52 Peter C. Kent, *The Lonely Cold War of Pope Pius XII: The Roman Catholic Church and the Division of Europe, 1943–1950* (McGill-Queen's University Press, 2002), 64.

53 George Q. Flynn, *Roosevelt and Romanism: Catholics and American Diplomacy, 1937–1945* (Greenwood Press, 1976), 99.

54 From 1933 to 1936, Spellman would discuss the virtues of formal Vatican-American diplomatic ties with both Kennedy and James Roosevelt, the president's son, a message he would later take to the president himself during Pacelli's visit.

55 "Press Release," Franklin Folsom (executive secretary, League of American Writers), 9 October 1937, NCWC/OGS/ACUA, Box 22, File 50.

56 See Flynn, *Roosevelt and Romanism*, 40.

57 Ready expressed indignation that the "duly elected representatives of our American democracy, sworn to uphold the right of religious liberty, could place themselves on record as sympathetic with a government which has absolutely proscribed the exercise of religion in the territory which it governs." See "Statement of the Right Rev. Monsignor Michael J. Ready, General Secretary of the National Catholic Welfare Conference, on the 'Good Will' Message of Certain Senators and Congressmen to the Barcelona Spanish Regime," 31 January 1938, NCWC/OGS/ACUA, Box 23, File 50.

58 The American bishops' statement was issued in support of the Spanish bishops' statement of July 1937, which amounted to a global appeal for support in the face of republican anticlericalism. See "Joint Letter of the Spanish Bishops to the Bishops of the Whole World Concerning the War in Spain," 1 July 1937, NCWC/OGS/ACUA, Box 22, File 50.

59 Resolutions were issued by the National Council of Catholic Men, the National Council of Catholic Women, the Knights of Columbus, and the Catholic Daughters of America, who issued a telegram directly to Hull demanding that the United States formally protest against religious persecution in Spain. In addition, Dennis Cardinal Dougherty, archbishop of Philadelphia, instructed his parishioners to petition Congress the keep the embargo, a plea that resulted in ten thousand telegrams arriving on Capitol Hill in two weeks.

60 Flynn, *Roosevelt and Romanism*, 43.

61 Fred Israel, *Nevada's Key Pittman* (University of Nebraska Press, 1963), 157.

62 See Flynn, *Roosevelt and Romanism*, 47–55.

63 "Jerusalem's Capture," *Catholic Telegraph*, 27 December 1917.

64 "Christ's Attitude towards the Politico-Religious Attitude of the Jews," *American Catholic Quarterly Review* 43, no. 170 (April 1918): 177–204.

65 Ibid., 178–9.

66 "Jewish State in Palestine," *Catholic Telegraph*, 9 May 1918.

67 See, for examples, *Tidings*, 23 April 1920, which expressed the "general international determination that Jerusalem in the future must be under the rule of a Christian power."

68 "Interest Aroused by Audience Granted High Commissioner to Palestine," *Catholic Telegraph*, 8 July 1920.

69 "Patriarch of Jerusalem Says Internationalized Palestine Would Be Better than a Zionist State," *Catholic Telegraph*, 23 September 1920.

70 "Division of Jews Over Zion State Growing Larger," *Catholic Columbian*, 31 March 1922.

71 Churchill's "White Paper" of 1922 offered a "clarification" of Britain's position on Palestine, which warned Zionists not to place "exaggerated expectations" on the imminent creation of a Jewish state, and appeared to limit the Balfour Declaration to a promise of a home for both Jews and Arabs in the territory, and that all citizens of the territory would be regarded as Palestinians. Zionists considered the White Paper a severe check on the creation of a Jewish state, which it essentially was.

72 "Joint Resolution Favouring the Establishment in Palestine of a National Home for the Jewish People," 21 September 1922, GUA-SC, Robert F. Wagner Papers, Box 1, File 4. The resolution favored a home for the Jews in Palestine, but it asserted that it was "clearly understood that nothing shall be done that may prejudice the civil and religious rights of Christians and all other non-Jewish communities in Palestine, and that the Holy Places and religious buildings and sites in Palestine shall be adequately protected."

73 On this rapprochement between Catholics and Jews in 1920s America, see Egal Feldman, *Catholics and Jews in Twentieth-Century America* (University of Illinois Press, 2001), 45–64.

74 Kreutz, *Vatican Policy on the Palestinian-Israeli Conflict*, 46.

75 "Time Table for the Staying in Jerusalem of His Eminence, William Cardinal O'Connell, Archbishop of Boston," archives of the Archdiocese of Boston, Cardinal O'Connell Papers, Box 16, Folder 10.

76 See *Crusader's Almanac*, 1 October 1929, 29.

77 *America*, 14 February 1925, 432. Quoted in Kreutz, *Vatican Policy on the Palestinian-Israeli Conflict*, 45.

78 Ibid., 46. The movement was also bolstered by the vibrancy of American Zionist organizations, which provided both financial assistance and political pressure on Washington. On the growth of American Zionism, see Naomi W. Cohen, *The Americanization of Zionism, 1897–1948* (Brandeis University Press, 2003); Mark A. Raider, *The Emergence of American Zionism* (New York University Press, 1998).

79 The Emirate of Transjordan, for example, which had existed as an autonomous political unit under the Balfour Declaration, was granted full independence from Britain in 1928, though the British maintained a military presence and controlled the territory's foreign affairs. The creation of Transjordan, which limited the geographic extent of an eventual Jewish state, served as a paradigm for Palestinian Arab nationalists, who sought a similar outcome for Palestine.

80 Feldblum, *The American Catholic Press and a Jewish State*, 38. As mentioned in chapter 1, the "Status Quo" on Palestine was a 1757 agreement between the Ottoman Empire and various Christian groups in Palestine guaranteeing access and stewardship of their various holy sites.

81 Ibid. For detailed accounts of the riots, see Bernard Wasserstein, *The British in Palestine: The Mandatory Government and the Arab-Jewish Conflict, 1917–1929* (Royal Historical Society, 1978), 217–35.

82 William B. Ziff, *The Rape of Palestine* (Longmans, 1938), 128. Christian Arabs, for their part, played no significant role in the unrest, a fact that was confirmed by the British high commissioner in his report on the attacks.

83 Livia Rokach, *The Catholic Church and the Question of Palestine* (Saqi Books, 1987), 17.

84 In February 1929, in response to rising Arab-Jewish tensions, the Vatican created an autonomous apostolic delegation that included Palestine, Transjordan, and Cyprus, and which was entrusted to the delegate in Cairo, Valerio Valeri.

85 On the effects of this expanded apostolic delegation on the Vatican's policies in Palestine, see Paolo Zanini, "The Establishment of the Apostolic Delegation to Palestine, Cyprus and Transjordan (1929): Cause or Effect of Changes in Vatican Middle East Policy?," *Church History* 87, no. 3, (2018): 797–822.

86 On Valeri's diplomacy in the wake of the 1929 riots, see Paolo Zanini, "The Holy See, Italian Catholics and Palestine under the British Mandate: Two

Turning Points," *Journal of Ecclesiastical History* 67, no. 4, (October 2016): 799–818.

87 *Commonweal*, 11 September 1929. Quoted in Feldblum, *The American Catholic Press and the Jewish State*, 39.

88 Ibid.

89 Mombelli's reports were carried by some of the largest-circulation diocesan papers in the United States, including *The Brooklyn Tablet*, *The Commonweal*, *The Michigan Catholic*, *The New World*, and *Our Sunday Visitor*.

90 *Brooklyn Tablet*, 12 October 1929, 7. Mombelli elaborated on the purely political nature of Zionism in a later article, where he reported on the visit of Captain Robert Gordon-Canning, an English lawyer who visited Palestine on a fact-finding mission for the British government. Gordon-Canning praised the "indomitable spirit" of Muslims in the Holy Land, who presented a "solid front" against the Zionist movement, as well as the "determination of Arabs never to accept the Balfour Declaration." The article amounted to a panegyric to Arab resistance and a very thinly veiled censure of Zionism. See "Disturbances in Palestine Political and not Religious," 6 January 1930, NCWC/OGS/ACUA, Box 44, File 18.

91 See, for example, Mombelli's "Palestine: Catholics Affirm Principles of Their Rights," 7 December 1935, NCWC/OGS/ACUA, Box 51, File 10.

92 "Work Is the Only Religion of the Communist Colonies of Zionism," *Catholic Telegraph*, 18 September 1930.

93 On the struggle between moderate and militant Zionism in the United States, see Rafael Medoff, *Militant Zionism in America: The Rise and Impact of the Jabotinsky Movement in the United States, 1926–1948* (University of Alabama Press, 2002).

94 "Communists Open Propaganda Drive in the Near East," *Catholic Transcript*, 5 March 1931.

95 *Brooklyn Tablet*, 12 October 1929, 7.

96 Morris Lazaron to John J. Burke, 12 January 1930, NCWC/OGS/ACUA, Box 44, File 18.

97 John J. Burke to Morris Lazaron, 17 January 1930, NCWC/OGS/ACUA, Box 44, File 18.

98 Ibid.

99 "An Outburst of Zionism," *Month*, November 1930, 456–7.

100 "Justice for Jew and Arab," *Month*, December 1930, 547–8.

101 "Palestine Problems," *Commonweal*, 29 January 1930, 360; "Palestine," *Commonweal*, 3 September 1930, 433.

102 *America*, 1 November 1930, 75.

103 *New World*, 13 September 1929, 4.

104 *Brooklyn Tablet*, 7 September 1929, 9. Quoted in Feldblum, *The American Catholic Press and the Jewish State*, 40. The association of Jews with deicide was made on occasion in the Catholic press throughout the interwar period. See, for example, "Did the Jews or the Roman Put Christ to Death?," *Brooklyn Tablet*, 10 April 1937, 6.

105 These limits were never strictly enforced by British officials, and they became effectively impossible to enforce after 1933, when Hitler's rise in Germany created a steady stream of Jewish immigrants to Palestine.

106 Martin Sicker, *The Middle East in the Twentieth Century* (Praeger, 2001), 47.

107 "Seven Christians among Killed in Palestine Riots: Zionism Given Blow," *Brooklyn Tablet*, 12 October 1929, 1.

108 "Palestine Trouble Is Political: Noted English Lawyer Calls Balfour Guilty of the Unrest," *Brooklyn Tablet*, 18 January 1930, 2.

109 "Jews Are Caught Smuggling Arms into Palestine," *New World*, 27 December 1929, 4. American Catholic leaders also linked Bolshevism and Zionism in the United States, but they remained cautious not to present their critiques of Zionism and Bolshevism as a form of anti-Judaism, despite that very implication. See "Criticizes Jews Who Backs Reds," *Brooklyn Tablet*, 19 June 1937, 3.

110 The journal, published four times annually from the 1920s to the 1950s, appeared also in German-, Polish-, and Italian-language editions to broaden fundraising potential among the major ethnic groups in the American Catholic Church.

111 See, for example, "Catholic Rights in the Holy Land Imperiled," *Crusader's Almanac*, 1 October 1932, 34; "News of the Holy Land," *Crusader's Almanac*, 1 October 1933, 58–9.

112 *Crusader's Almanac*, 1 April 1934, 1. The journal encouraged donations of twelve dollars, which secured one's status as a "perpetual crusader."

113 *Crusader's Almanac*, 1 October 1932, 1.

114 See, for example, "What of Palestine," *Commonweal*, 19 June 1936, 201–3; "Palestine and Zionism," *Sign*, July 1936, 741–3.

115 See, for example, "Christian Arabs Issue Protest: Strongly Attack Holy Land Policy of British," *Brooklyn Tablet*, 5 September 1936, 4; "Palestine and Zionism," *Catholic World*, October 1937, 12–18; "Clergy Quoted in Arab Appeal: Ask Christian America to be Neutral on Palestine," *Brooklyn Tablet*, 22 October 1938, 1.

116 In response to intensifying insurrection from Arab nationalists in 1936 and 1937, known as the "Great Arab Revolt," the Mandatory government created a

Royal Commission to investigate the unrest and propose a solution. Headed by Lord Peel, the Palestine Royal Commission's report (also known as the "Peel Plan") recommended that the Mandate, having essentially become untenable, be replaced by a partition of the territory between the Arabs and the Jews. The Peel Plan became the basis of the UN's postwar partition plan.

117 "The Jewish National Home," *Sign*, October 1936, 132–3.

118 "The Riots in Palestine," *Sign*, July 1936, 108.

119 See "While Jew and Arab Battle for Control of Palestine," *America*, 17 December 1938, 244–7; "England Is Perplexed by Jew and Arab in Palestine," *America*, 24 December 1938, 272–4; "Palestine Homeland," *America*, 3 June 1939, 180; "The White Paper for Jews and Arabs," *America*, 10 June 1939, 199–200.

120 "While Jew and Arab Battle for Control of Palestine," *America*, 17 December 1938, 245.

121 Ibid.

122 "England Is Perplexed by Jew and Arab in Palestine," *America*, 24 December 1938, 273.

123 Ibid.

124 "Palestine Homeland," *America*, 3 June 1939, 180.

125 On the ZOA and its successes both before and during the Second World War, see Aaron Berman, *Nazism, the Jews and American Zionism, 1933–1948* (Wayne State University Press, 1990), 41–124.

126 "Palestine Homeland," *America*, 3 June 1939, 180.

127 "Sets Forth Arab Side of Conflict: Palestine Situation Has More than One Angle," *Brooklyn Tablet*, 24 December 1938, 3.

128 Ibid. In this article, *The Brooklyn Tablet* presented segments of the radio broadcast of Fuad Mufarrij, academic and general secretary of the Arab National Bureau in Damascus. The paper's frequent reprinting of the speeches, statements, and articles of leading Arab nationalists and scholars revealed its implicitly anti-Zionist editorial line, maintained both before and after the Second World War.

129 "Arabs Set Forth Their Viewpoint: Palestine Problem Is Shown to Have Another Side," *Brooklyn Tablet*, 18 February 1939, 4.

CHAPTER THREE

1 For a succinct survey of American-Vatican relations in the interwar years, see Luca Castagna, *A Bridge across the Ocean: The United States and the Holy See between the Two World Wars* (Catholic University of America Press, 2014).

2 For a brief examination of the New Deal–era alliance between American

Catholics and Roosevelt's Democratic Party, see Manlio Graziano, *In Rome We Trust: The Rise of Catholics in American Political Life* (Stanford University Press, 2017), 81–90.

3 On the details of Taylor's appointment, see Gerald Fogarty, *The Vatican and the American Catholic Hierarchy*, (Hiersemann, 1982) 259–69.

4 During the meeting, Roosevelt assured Spellman that the appointment of Taylor was a preliminary step toward the establishment of full diplomatic relations between the United States and the Vatican. See Francis Spellman to Luigi Maglione, 25 October 1939, Archives of the Archdiocese of New York, Cardinal Spellman Papers, Box 2, File 15.

5 Kent, *The Lonely Cold War*, 64.

6 On this transatlantic transfer of Vatican assets, see Patricia McGoldrick, "New Perspectives on Pius XII and Vatican Financial Transactions during the Second World War," *Historical Journal*, no. 55 (2012): 1029–48.

7 Kent, *The Lonely Cold War*, 64. For a fuller examination of Spellman's wartime role as a conduit for Vatican-American relations during the Second World War, see Fogarty's *The Vatican and the American Catholic Hierarchy*, 259–312. So highly esteemed was Spellman in Roman circles, in fact, that there was speculation, as the war drew to a close, that the archbishop of New York would be named the Vatican's secretary of state, a position made vacant upon the death of Cardinal Luigi Maglione in August 1944. Upon reflection, Spellman concluded that as archbishop of New York, he could operate free of Vatican strictures, forcing Pius XII to rely on him as a political linchpin between Rome and Washington. Though Spellman ultimately rebuffed Pius's offer, he was careful not spark a row between himself and the pope. He later informed friends that he had never wanted the job as secretary of state, but that he had diplomatically informed Pacelli that he was indifferent to remaining in the United States, and that he "would leave New York, family or anything if the Holy Father thought [he] could serve in any place for the church." See John Cooney, *The American Pope: The Life and Times of Francis Cardinal Spellman* (Times Books, 1984), 140–3.

8 Edward Mooney to Franklin D. Roosevelt, 22 December 1941, NCWC/OGS/ACUA, Box 123, File 4.

9 Ibid.

10 Francis Spellman, *The Road to Victory* (Scribner's, 1942), 101.

11 Prior to August 1941, American Catholic support for the war effort was not unanimous. Some German American bishops were reticent to openly support a war against their ancestral homeland, and some Irish American bishops saw

only a threat to Britain, not Nazi barbarity. Lend-Lease also gave some American bishops pause, as it appeared that the United States was finding common cause with Soviet Russia (whom many American Catholics had vilified throughout the Spanish Civil War). This ambiguity was reflected in the Catholic press as well. See Fogarty, *The Vatican and the American Hierarchy*, 269–73.

12 Amleto Cicognani to Michael Ready, 12 January 1941, NCWC/OGS/ACUA, Box 44, File 18.

13 "Catholic Bishops Hail Will to Win," *New York Times*, 25 December 1941.

14 Franklin D. Roosevelt to Edward Mooney, 24 December 1941, NCWC/OGS/ACUA, Box 123, File 4.

15 Myron C. Taylor to Pope Pius XII, 19 September 1942, *Actes et Documents du Saint Siege relatifs a la Seconde Guerre Mondiale* (Libreria editrice Vaticana, 1975), 5:681–4. Hereafter *Actes et Documents*.

16 Ibid. Quoted in Fogarty, *The Vatican and the American Hierarchy*, 284–5.

17 "Victory and Peace: Annual Statement Issued by the NCWC Administrative Board in the Name of the Bishops of the United States," 14 November 1942, NCWC/OGS/ACUA, Box 44, File 19.

18 "Confidential Memorandum," Roosevelt to Pope Pius XII, 2 September 1942, NCWC/OGS/ACUA, Box 11, File 1. In the same memo, the president pleaded with the Vatican not to accept a negotiated peace with the Axis, a move that would have severely jeopardized American and Allied military strategy in Europe, as well as plans for postwar settlements.

19 Ibid.

20 In a letter to the apostolic delegate in Washington, Amleto Cicognani, Detroit's archbishop, Edward Mooney, reflected on the difficulties of maintaining American Catholic morale on the war effort as the bombing of Rome intensified, and in containing "that relatively small but noisome sector of our Catholic population which has been outstanding in its political opposition to the domestic and foreign policies of President Roosevelt." Edward Mooney to Amleto Cicognani, 27 August 1943, archives of the Archdiocese of Detroit (hereafter AAD), Edward Mooney Papers, Box 18, File 2.

21 Michael Ready to Franklin D. Roosevelt, 15 September 1943, NCWC/OGS/ACUA, Box 21, File 7. In this letter, the bishops reaffirmed their "deep patriotic devotion" to the president and to the American war effort.

22 See Gerald Fogarty, "Archbishop Francis J. Spellman's Visit to Wartime Rome," *Catholic Historical Review* 100, no. 1 (Winter 2014): 84.

23 Ibid., 84–5. Fogarty contends that the wartime Vatican was growing

increasingly skeptical of Britain's ability to restrain the Allied bombings of Rome, a fact that deepened the pope's reliance on Spellman's connection to Roosevelt and the American government.

24 Mooney, Spellman, and Stritch to Roosevelt, 21 September 1943, *Actes et Documents*, 7:648–50.

25 Ibid.

26 "The Essentials of a Good Peace: A Statement Issued by the NCWC Administrative Board in the Name of the Bishops of the United States," 11 November 1943, NCWC/OGS/ACUA, Box 44, File 18.

27 Britain's 1939 White Paper on Palestine, issued on 17 May, limited Jewish immigration to Palestine to seventy-five thousand for a five-year period and was due to be stopped completely on 31 March 1944.

28 A volume of scholarly attention has been focused on the question of Vatican assistance to European Jews during the Holocaust. The debate was initiated by the 1963 publication of Rolf Hochhuth's *The Deputy*, a play that accused Pius XII of not acting forcefully enough in denouncing Nazi crimes against the Jews, and that set the tone for future discussions on the role of the wartime pope in assisting persecuted Jews. An extensive scholarship has emerged seeking to refute accusations against the Vatican's wartime inaction on the Holocaust. Particularly since the appearance of John Cornwell's critical *Hitler's Pope* (Penguin, 1999), numerous scholars have produced works defending Pacelli's wartime record. These include Jose Sanchez's *Pius XII and the Holocaust: Understanding the Controversy* (Catholic University of America Press, 2002), Joseph Bottum and David Dalin's *The Pius War: Responses to the Critics of Pius XII* (Lexington Books, 2004), and Dalin's *The Myth of Hitler's Pope: How Pius XII Rescued Jews from the Nazis* (Regnery, 2005).

29 Suzanne Brown-Fleming notes that the Vatican's neutrality during the Second World War prioritized the protection of the institutional church and Catholic populations and abnegated the "right of exercising its moral and spiritual power" as granted in the 1929 Lateran Accords. As a result, Pius XII operated more as chief Vatican diplomat and strategist than spiritual and moral exemplar and leader. See her "Pope Pius XII, Vatican Neutrality and the Holocaust: Case Studies from the Newly Opened Vatican Archives" in *The Vatican and Permanent Neutrality*, ed. Marshall J. Breger and Herbert R. Reginbogin (Lexington Books, 2022), 105–18.

30 On papal neutrality in the First World War, see Adrian Ciani, "Vatican Neutrality and the Great War," in *The Routledge History of the First World War*, ed. Paul R. Bartrop (Routledge, 2025), 712–23.

31 Quoted in Robert A. Ventresca, *Soldier of Christ: The Life of Pope Pius XII* (Harvard University Press, 2013), 173.

32 On the Vatican as a wartime neutral power, see Adrian Ciani, "Apolitical Arbiter? The Vatican as a Neutral during the Second World War," in *The Routledge History of the Second World War*, ed. Paul R. Bartrop (Routledge, 2022), 576–90.

33 Andrea Riccardi contends that the Vatican's diplomatic isolation in Europe, particularly as the Nazi empire expanded, only deepened the pope's circumspection and caution. See his *La guerra del silenzio: Pio XII, il nazismo, gli ebrei* (Laterza, 2022), 3–64. On papal responses to the persecution of Eastern and Central European Catholics, see Ventresca, *Soldier of Christ*, 170–6, 207–18.

34 On the papacy's relations with Europe's Jews since the Enlightenment, see Adrian Ciani, "The Papacy and the Jews since the French Revolution," in *The Cambridge History of the Papacy*, vol. 1, Joëlle Rollo-Koster, Robert A. Ventresca, Melodie H. Eichbauer, and Miles Pattenden (Cambridge University Press, 2025), 770–92.

35 On the extent to which racial antisemitism had permeated the Vatican Secretariat and wider Catholic circles in Italy, leading to a view of a "Jewish race" considered foreign to the Fascist regime, see Nina Valbousquet, "Race and Faith: The Catholic Church, Clerical Fascism, and the Shaping of Italian Anti-Semitism and Racism," *Modern Italy* 23, no. 4 (2018): 355–71.

36 Ventresca, *Soldier of Christ*, 178.

37 On the Vatican's distinction between racial and theological antisemitism, see Hubert Wolf, *Pope and Devil: The Vatican's Archives and the Third Reich* (Harvard University Press, 2010), 110–12.

38 Pinchas Lapide, a postwar Israeli diplomat and scholar of the wartime papacy, contended that racial laws were never fully implemented in Italy due in part to the ceaseless interventions of the papal nuncio to Italy, Francesco Borgongini-Duca, on behalf of Italian Jews. See Lapide's, *Three Popes and the Jews* (Hawthorn, 1967), 127.

39 Ibid., 128–38.

40 Jacques Kornberg has argued that the Vatican adopted a decentralized approach to opposing Nazi persecutions in various belligerent states, leaving it to the local bishops to decide whether or not to protest. See his *The Pope's Dilemma: Pius XII Faces Atrocities and Genocide in the Second World War* (University of Toronto Press, 2018), 75–155. On Vatican diplomatic efforts to mitigate antisemitic laws in Nazi-occupied states, see also John F. Morley,

"Pope Pius XII, Roman Catholic Policy and the Holocaust in Hungary," in *Pope Pius XII and the Holocaust*, ed. Carol Rittner and John K. Roth (Bloomsbury, 2018), 154–74. On Catholics efforts to rescue persecuted Jews in Croatia, see Esther Gitman, "Archbishop Alojzije Stepinac of Zagreb and the Rescue of Jews, 1941–45," *Catholic Historical Review* 101, no. 3 (Summer 2015): 488–529.

41 For a survey of the "Brazilian Visa Project," see Jeffrey Lesser, *Welcoming the Undesirables: Brazil and the Jewish Question* (University of California Press, 1995).

42 DELASEM continued its work in the postwar period, with the assistance of the Vatican, in facilitating the emigration of Italian and European Jews to Palestine, the United States, and South America. For a short history of the organization, see Sandro Antonini, *DELASEM: Storia della più grande organizzazione ebraica italiana di soccorso durante la seconda guerra mondiale* (De Ferrari, 2000). Susan Zuccotti has argued that the Vatican's contribution to the DELASEM project was cynical and insincere, as it contributed little of its own funds to the project, instead redistributing donations from Jewish and American Catholic sources. See her *Under His Very Windows: The Vatican and the Holocaust in Italy* (Yale University Press, 2000), 71–81, 150–70, 181–8.

43 In April 1944, for example, President Roosevelt, through the office of Myron Taylor, asked if the Holy See could transmit financial aid to Polish Jewish refugees in Rome and to the Jewish Children's Aid Society in Rome. In its reply, the Vatican agreed, stating it would "continue, as it has in the past, to work for all victims of persecution." See Lapide, *Three Popes and the Jews*, 128.

44 See Owen Chadwick, "Weizsacker, the Vatican and the Jews of Rome," *Journal of Ecclesiastical History* 28, no. 2 (April 1977): 179–99.

45 John Connelly, *From Enemy to Brother: The Revolution in Catholic Teaching on the Jews, 1933–1965* (Harvard University Press, 2012), 147–73.

46 Ibid., 170.

47 Memorandum by Monsignor Domenico Tardini, Vatican, 7 April 1943, *Actes et documents*, 9:233.

48 Quoted in David Kertzer, *The Pope at War: The Secret History of Pius XII, Mussolini, and Hitler* (Random House, 2022), 275.

49 Notes de la Secretaire d'Etat, Vatican, 5 May 1943, *Actes et Documents*, 9:274.

50 Luigi Maglione to William Godfrey, 3 March 1943, *Actes et Documents*, 9:184.

51 Ibid.

52 "Notes on the Persecution of Jews, Particularly Slovakian, and the Actions of the Holy See," Luigi Maglione, 7 April 1943, *Actes et Documents*, 9:233.

53 Luigi Maglione to Amleto Cicognani, 18 May 1943, *Actes et Documents*, 9:300.

54 Ibid.

55 See Maria Mazzenga, "Toward an American Catholic Response to the Holocaust: Catholic Americanism and Kristallnacht," in *American Religious Responses to Kristallnacht*, ed. Maria Mazzenga (Palgrave, 2009), 85–144. Coughlin's broadcast, titled "Persecution – Jewish and Christian," was delivered on 20 November 1938, and presented a wide array of accusations against German Jews, linking them to both finance and communism, and implicitly suggesting that brutality against them was the only option left to Hitler and the Nazi Party. On the issue of persecution, Coughlin suggested that Roman Catholics should more properly focus their attentions on the maltreatment of Catholics around the world, using the recent examples from Spain and Mexico. See "Address by Father CE Coughlin," 20 November 1938, NCWC/OGS/ACUA, Folder 1, Box 16.

56 Christopher J. Kaufmann, *Faith and Fraternalism: The History of the Knights of Columbus, 1882–1982* (Harper and Row, 1982), 335–6.

57 Mazzenga, *American Religious Responses to Kristallnact*, 93.

58 "Mgr Ryan Raps Nazi Persecution of Jews," *Michigan Catholic*, 14 July 1938, 3–4.

59 Ibid.

60 Ibid.

61 Ibid.

62 For a transcript of the broadcast, see "Catholic University Anti-Nazi Broadcast, November 16, 1938," Catholic University of America Digital Collections, accessed 7 December 2024, http://hdl.handle.net/1961/cuislandora:296582.

63 Mazzenga, *American Religious Responses to Kristallnacht*, 96.

64 On the emerging Jewish-Catholic "front" against totalitarian persecutions in the United States, which had taken root in the 1930s, see Nina Valbousquet, "Jewish-Catholic Diplomacy, Humanitarianism, and Transatlantic Responses to Persecutions, 1930s–1940s," in *La Santa Sede, gli Stati Uniti e le relazioni internazionali durante il pontificato di Pio XII*, ed. Roberto Regoli and Matteo Sanfillipo (Studium, 2022), 143–63.

65 Under Skillin's direction (which lasted to 1967), the journal became a leading voice of liberal Catholicism in the United States, publishing a range of seminal essays by figures, both Catholic and non-Catholic, such as Hanna Arendt, Luigi Sturzo, G.K. Chesterton, Evelyn Waugh, Hilaire Belloc, and others. He was unafraid to challenge preponderant views in the American church. In 1938, Skillin penned an editorial deploring the widespread tendency of American Catholics to conflate Franco's anticommunism with the cause of

the faith, a position that placed him at odds with a number of leading figures in the American church. On *The Commonweal*'s role in shaping liberal Catholicism in the United States, see Rodger Van Allen, *The Commonweal and American Catholicism: The Magazine, the Movement, the Meaning* (Fortress Press, 1974).

66 "The Lindbergh Speech," *Commonweal*, 26 September 1941, 532. By the late 1930s, Lindbergh had become a chief spokesman of the ardently isolationist "America First" movement.

67 Ibid.

68 "On Anti-Semitism," *Commonweal*, 25 September 1942, 534–7; "Racist Law and the True Meaning of Racism," *Commonweal*, 4 June 1943, 181–8. For a fuller treatment of Maritain's complex views on Judaism and Nazi antisemitism, see Richard Francis Crane, "Jacques Maritain, the Mystery of Israel, and the Holocaust," *Catholic Historical Review* 95, no. 1 (Spring 2009): 25–56.

69 Samuel Moyn contends that the modern concept of human rights was not solely (or even primarily) a product of secular, liberal ideologies, but rather emerged in Christian conceptions of liberty (and particularly religious liberty) and provided a blueprint for post-1945 conceptions of universal rights. See his *Christian Human Rights* (University of Pennsylvania Press, 2015).

70 James Chappel, "Explaining the Catholic Turn to Human Rights in the 1930s," in *Christianity and Human Rights Reconsidered*, ed. Sarah Shortall and Daniel Steinmetz-Jenkins (Cambridge University Press, 2020), 79.

71 "Racist Law and the Meaning of Racism," *Commonweal*, 4 June 1943, 181.

72 *America*'s wartime circulation hovered around sixty thousand copies.

73 "Persecution Stalks the Jews across the Face of Europe," *America*, 19 September 1942, 654–5.

74 "The Mass Murder of Jews," *America*, 12 June 1943, 266.

75 Ibid.

76 Ibid. In this vein, see also "Persecution Stalks the Jews across the Face of Europe," *America*, 19 September 1942, 654–5; "Fulton Sheen on Anti-Semitism," *America*, 28 November 1942, 200; "The Massacred Jews," *America*, 13 March 1943, 630; "The Church on the Jews," *America*, 15 May 1943; "The Murder of a Race," *America*, 6 October 1945.

77 "Anti-Semitism Would End in General Bigotry," *Catholic Action of the South*, May 1939, 2.

78 "Catholics and Anti-Semitism," *Catholic World*, October 1939, 175.

79 See, for example, "We Pray for All Victims of Persecution," *Brooklyn Tablet*, 19 November 1938; "Day of Prayer for Racial Victims Is Asked by Prelates,"

Our Sunday Visitor, 20 November 1938, 14; "Germany," *New World*, 25 November 1938, 2; "Father Coughlin Denounces All Persecutions," *Brooklyn Tablet*, 26 November 1938; "Msgr Ryan Raps Nazi Persecution of Jews," *Michigan Catholic*, 7 July 1938; "Anti-Semitism," *Catholic Mind*, March–April 1944, 356–9; "Jews Thank Pope for Aid Given Them: Pius XII Reiterates Stand of Vatican against Persecution and Hatred," *Michigan Catholic*, 6 December 1945.

80 *The Brooklyn Tablet*, edited by the "Coughlinite" Patrick Scanlan, did present reportage and opinion that was often anti-Judaic in its slant, but on the question of Nazi persecutions of European Jews, the paper did fall into line with the expressions of solidarity found in most of the Catholic press. There were exceptions to this, however. In December 1938, for example, *The Brooklyn Tablet* suggested that Catholic sympathy for Jewish persecution had actually intensified the persecution of the church in Germany, sharpening "the vilification of the Church in the Nazi press directed particularly against His Holiness Pope Pius XI and the German hierarchy." It was an implicit suggestion that sympathy for the Jewish plight was detrimental to Catholic interests. See "Sympathy for Jews Is Resented: Catholics Assailed in Germany for Christian Spirit," *Brooklyn Tablet*, 3 December 1938, 2.

81 Official pronouncements and statements from the various Christian denominations, including Roman Catholics, against the policy of antisemitism were compiled in 1943 by the National Conference of Christians and Jews and published and widely distributed in a pamphlet entitled *Christians Protest Persecutions*. The pamphlet was a compilation of the denunciations of a number of Christian groups on Nazi persecution of European Jewry. Though a majority of the denominations quoted were under the umbrella of the (Protestant) Federal Council of Churches of Christ in America, the pamphlet included the American Catholic bishops' annual statement for 1942, "Victory and Peace," which denounced the persecution of both Christians and Jews in Nazi-occupied Europe.

82 "Archbishop Scores Attack on Jews," *Michigan Catholic*, 8 June 1944, 1. See also "Archbishop Mooney Speech," June 1944, AAD, Edward Mooney Papers, Box 42, File 2.

83 Ibid.

84 Ibid. Mooney's sentiments, however, also implicitly alluded to Roman Catholic positions on Zionism, suggesting Poland and other locales as a potential postwar "haven" for displaced Jews. "In the heroism of Christians who have so often risked and not so infrequently given their lives to rescue their even more unfortunate Jewish brothers, may we not find an augury that when the

agony is over, Jews and Christians will work together to write a brighter page of history in liberated Europe, and particularly in Poland which has, at least, the historic glory of offering Jews a haven of refuge when they were driven out of other countries?"

85 Sheen's *The Catholic Hour*, which aired from 1930 to 1950, was followed in 1951 by the Catholic television program *Life Is Worth Living*, aired first by DuMont and later by ABC, and which attracted a wide viewership (estimated at nearly ten million by 1956), even earning Sheen an Emmy Award in 1952 as "Most Outstanding Television Personality."

86 Fulton Sheen, "The Thing We Are Fighting Against," *Catholic Hour*, 10 January 1943.

87 Ibid.

88 *America*, 28 November 1942, 200.

89 Saul E. Bronder *Social Justice and Church Authority: The Public Life of Archbishop Robert E. Lucey* (Temple University Press, 1982), 63.

90 See Hugh J. Nolan, ed., *Pastoral Letters of the United States Catholic Bishops, 1941–1961*, vol. 2 (National Conference of Catholic Bishops, 1984), 28–35.

91 "Archbishops and Bishops of the United States, *Statement on Victory and Peace*," 14 November 1942. See Raphael M. Huber, ed., *Our Bishops Speak: National Pastorals and Annual Statements of the Hierarchy of the United States* (Bruce Publishing, 1952), 110–14.

92 See John Morley, *Vatican Diplomacy and the Jews during the Holocaust* (Ktav, 1980), 205–8.

93 Roncalli's efforts to assist Jews during the war were extensive and were highlighted by several later scholars. Saul Friedlander notes that the Central Zionist Archives in Jerusalem contain a large number of documents detailing Roncalli's intercessions on behalf of persecuted Jews. See Friedlander's *Pius XII and the Third Reich: A Documentation* (Octagon, 1980), 222. On the distinction between Roncalli's anti-Zionism and his sympathy with the Jewish plight, see Paolo Zanini, "Angelo Roncalli, Nuncio to Paris, and the Establishment of the State of Israel," *Israel Studies* 22, no. 3, (Fall 2017): 102–24.

94 Roncalli (apostolic delegate to Istanbul) to Maglione, Vatican, 4 September 1943, *Actes et Documents*, 9:469.

95 "The Church and the Jews," *Catholic World*, 22 April 1942, 9.

96 "A Catholic Approach to the Jews," *Catholic World*, 8 September 1942, 8.

97 Ibid.

98 "Palestinian Question," *America*, 10 October 1944, 210.

99 Ibid. The editorial concluded, "They deserve justice and charity, but securing it for them brings up problems – one of which is the Palestinian question."

100 A large compendium of American congressional support for the Zionist cause, as well as a brief history of American Zionism, was published in 1944 by the American Zionist Emergency Council. See Reuben Fink, ed., *America and Palestine: The Attitude of Official America and of the American People toward the Rebuilding of Palestine as a Free and Democratic Jewish Commonwealth* (American Zionist Emergency Council, 1944).

101 On Thompson's embrace and eventual rejection of the Zionist cause, see Karine Walther, "Dorothy Thompson and American Zionism," *Diplomatic History* 46, no. 2 (2022): 263–91.

102 Ibid., 271.

103 As the prominent Zionist Abba Hillel Silver expressed at the Biltmore Conference, "what has been the basic fact in Jewish tragedy right through the ages is the fact of our national homelessness, of our abnormal political status in the world, and that now, after a second World War, in which Jews by the millions are already casualties … in a war in which Jews suffer doubly and trebly in relation to every other people, that … the ultimate solution of the Jewish problem must finally be sounded, and the ultimate solution is the establishment of a Jewish Nation in Palestine." See Aaron Berman, *Nazism, the Jews and American Zionism, 1933–1948* (Wayne State University Press, 1990), 89.

104 Maglione to Cicognani, 18 May 1943, *Actes et Documents*, 9:301–3. In this letter, Maglione outlined the Holy See's traditional opposition to the idea of a Jewish state in Palestine, which centered on Catholic fears of a loss of control of the Holy Places, concerns that Palestine had reached its "absorptive capacity," and that any granting of Jewish territorial rights in the territory may inspire Arab national movements as well, further complicating Catholic rights in Palestine.

105 See, for example, Amleto Cicognani to Luigi Maglione, 11 July 1944, NCWC/OGS/ACUA, Box 44, File 18. In correspondence with Cicognani, Bergson requested the support of the Holy See and the American church in the establishment of a "Hebrew Homeland" in Palestine, and informed the apostolic delegate that he would "take the liberty of calling, from time to time, on Your Excellency and on other representatives of the Holy to discuss various matters of concern to the Hebrew Nation in this time of its most desperate crisis." Cicognani offered no response. See also Peter Bergson to Amleto Cicognani, 27 June 1944, NCWC/OGS/ACUA, Box 44, File 18.

106 Amleto Cicognani to Luigi Maglione, 6 July 1944, NCWC/OGS/ACUA, Box 44, File 18. In his reports Cicognani noted, with only half-hearted relief, that mainstream Zionist organizations such as the ZOA and the American Zionist Emergency Council considered these new groups overtly aggressive and potentially disruptive, and sought to exclude them from serious negotiations on the future of Palestine. A *New York Times* article of 18 May 1944 quoted ZOA President Dr Israel Goldstein's characterization of the creation of Bergson's group as "buffoonery" and "comic opera drollery."

107 Amleto Cicognani to Michael Ready, 15 June 1943, NCWC/OGS/ACUA, Box 44, File 18.

108 Cardinal Luigi Maglione to the apostolic delegate in Washington, 18 January 1944, in *Actes et Documents*, 11:101.

109 Amleto Cicognani to Michael Ready, 19 May 1944, NCWC/OGS/ACUA, Box 44, File 18.

110 Amleto Cicognani to Michael Ready, 19 March 1941, NCWC/OGS/ACUA, Box 72, File 2.

111 "Wants Holy Land Open to Jews," *Michigan Catholic*, 9 February 1944, 1.

112 "Archbishop Deplores Closing of Palestine to Jewish Immigration," National Catholic News Service (NCNS), 2 February 1942, 6.

113 Ibid.

114 Amleto Cicognani to Joseph Rummel, 19 May 1944, NCWC/OGS/ACUA, Box 44, File 18.

115 Ibid.

116 Ibid.

117 Ibid.

118 Michael Ready to the ordinaries, titulars, auxiliaries, and administrators, 9 June 1944, NCWC/OGS/ACUA, Box 44, File 18.

119 Thomas McLaughlin to Michael Ready, 24 July 1944, NCWC/OGS/ACUA, Box 44, File 18. See also enclosure, 1–4.

120 Ibid., enclosure, 3.

121 Ibid., enclosure, 4.

122 Luigi Maglione to Michael Ready, 16 August 1943, NCWC/OGS/ACUA, Box 44, File 22.

123 "Zionists and Palestine," *America*, 13 October 1945, 39–40. The Anglo-American Committee of Inquiry did recommend an increase to Jewish immigration quotas to Palestine (to 100,000 annually), and did annul restrictions on land sales to Jewish immigrants, but it did not meet the demands of most leading

Zionists, who insisted that the emergency of Jewish displacement required an "open door" policy for Palestine.

124 For the full text of the 1946 AAIC report, see "Anglo-American Committee of Inquiry," Avalon Project: Documents in Law History and Diplomacy, Yale Law School, accessed 7 December 2024, https://avalon.law.yale.edu/subject_menus/angtoc.asp.

125 "Palestine," *America*, 1 December 1945, 239.

126 Ibid., 240.

127 "Solution of Palestine Is Allied Problem: Religious Attachment Is at the Root of Arab-Jewish Conflict," *Boston Pilot*, 1 December 1945, 1, 3; "Christian Rights in Holy Land Ignored in Arab-Jewish Dispute: Need Allied Decision to End Trouble," *Michigan Catholic*, 29 November 1945, 3. Assemani had spent most of his clerical career in the Near East, and served as the pastor of the Syrian-rite Church of the Sacred Heart, in Michigan City, Indiana, at the time of his appointment as representative of the Latin Patriarchate of Jerusalem. The latter was established by the crusaders in 1099 and endured until Muslim defeat in 1217. It was reestablished by Pope Pius IX in 1847, and the patriarch remained the most important Catholic administrator in Palestine into the twentieth century.

128 "Solution of Palestine Is Allied Problem," *Boston Pilot*, 1 December 1945, 3.

129 Ibid.

130 "Failure to Safeguard Christian Rights Will Prolong Solution of 'Palestine Question': Warns against Any Plan Which Would Ignore Sacred Character of Holy Places and Desecrate Homeland of the Saviour," 23 April 1945, NCWC/OGS/ACUA, Box 44, File 18.

131 See "Policy for Palestine," *Economist*, 29 September 1945, 450–1.

132 See, for example, *Michigan Catholic*, 29 November 1945; *Boston Pilot*, 1 December 1945; *Brooklyn Tablet*, 1 December 1945.

133 "Failure to Safeguard Christian Rights Will Prolong Solution of 'Palestine Question,'" 23 April 1945, NCWC/OGS/ACUA, Box 44, File 18.

CHAPTER FOUR

1 Charles Morris argues that the cultural and social influence of American Catholicism flowered in the decade beginning in 1945, as Catholic moral conservatism and anticommunism fused neatly with postwar American values. A flurry of Oscar-nominated, Catholic-themed films that painted American Catholicism in a particularly positive light, exemplified by *The Bells of St*

Mary's (1945), starring Bing Crosby and Ingrid Bergman, appeared to signal a new acceptance of the faith in American cultural, social, and political life. See Morris's *American Catholic: The Saints and Sinners Who Built America's Most Powerful Church* (Times Books, 1997), 196–254.

2 The 1940 federal census pegged the American population at 132 million, a figure that topped 150 million by the 1950 census. See Susan B. Carter, Scott Sigmund Carter, and Michael Haines, eds, *The Historical Statistics of the United States* (Cambridge University Press, 2006).

3 See Patrick Carey, *Catholics in America: A History* (Praeger, 2004), 93.

4 Rome erected archdioceses in Denver (1941), Indianapolis (1944), Omaha (1945), Washington, DC (1947), Seattle (1951), and Kansas City (1952). This was in addition to five new archdioceses erected in the late 1930s.

5 Harold Tittmann to Secretary of State (Byrnes), Vatican, 5 July 1945, National Archives and Record Administration (hereafter NARA), Record Group 59 (hereafter RG), Myron Taylor Papers, Box 28.

6 Harold Tittmann to Secretary of State (Byrnes), Vatican, 19 July 1945, NARA, RG 59, Myron Taylor Papers, Box 28.

7 By the end of 1945, Schaaf appointed another American Franciscan, Father Edmund J. Murphy, as commissary of the Holy Land. See Edmund J. Murphy to Paul F. Tanner, 22 January 1946, NCWC/OGS/ACUA, Box 18, File 44.

8 John Pollard, *Money and the Rise of the Modern Papacy: Financing the Vatican, 1850–1950* (Cambridge University Press, 2005), 225. On the intriguing career of Joseph P. Hurley, see Charles R. Gallagher, *Vatican Secret Diplomacy: Joseph P. Hurley and Pope Pius XII* (Yale University Press, 2008).

9 Peter C. Kent, *The Lonely Cold War of Pope Pius XII* (McGill-Queen's University Press, 2002): 157–8.

10 Ibid.

11 Spellman's candidacy was one of the worst-kept secrets of the period, as news of the potential appointment appeared in the Italian and American press by early 1946. Giovanni Capobianco, a wartime wireless operator for the Vatican, broke the story to the Italian press in January in Rome's *Il Giornale del Mattino*, much to the chagrin of Vatican officials. "An American Secretary of State of a universal Church," he reported, "would be acceptable to the whole world in view of the high prestige which the United States has gained for itself, during the last few years especially. Then, too, Mgr Spellman is an outstanding personality among American ecclesiastics, for aside from his highly charitable nature, he had throughout the war years pleaded for justice and universal brotherhood." Franklin Gowen to Secretary of State, Vatican, 21 January 1946,

NARA, RG 59, Myron Taylor Papers, Box 28. See also "Il Vaticano e gli Stati Uniti," *Il Giornale del Mattino*, 18 January 1946.

12 Gowen to Secretary of State, Vatican, 21 January 1946, NARA, RG 59, Myron Taylor Papers, Box 28.

13 Myron Taylor to Secretary of State, Vatican, 26 June 1945, NARA, RG 59, Myron Taylor Papers, Box 28.

14 "Relations with the Vatican," 12 February 1947, NCWC/OGS/ACUA, Box 11, File 1. Protestant groups had protested Taylor's appointment from 1939 forward, arguing that an American envoy to the pope violated notions of the separation of church and state. Opposition to a "personal representative" to the pope would remain persistent throughout the postwar years, forcing Truman to terminate the mission in 1951. On Taylor's mission during the Truman administration, see George J. Gill, "The Truman Administration and Vatican Relations," *Catholic Historical Review* 73, no. 3 (July 1987): 408–23.

15 Harry S. Truman to Pope Pius XII, 6 August 1947, NARA, RG 59, Myron Taylor Papers, Box 18, File 1; Pope Pius XII to Harry S. Truman, 26 August 1947, NARA, RG 59, Myron Taylor Papers, Box 18, File 1.

16 J. Graham Parsons to Walter C. Dowling, Vatican City, 5 December 1947, NARA, RG 59, Myron Taylor Papers, Box 18.

17 "Text of Statement 'Between War and Peace' Issued by Bishops of United States," 18 November 1945, NARA, RG 59, Myron Taylor Papers, Box 26. See also Raphael M. Huber, ed., *Our Bishops Speak: National Pastorals and Annual Statements of the Hierarchy of the United States* (Bruce Publishing, 1952), 126–30.

18 Franklin Gowen to Secretary of State, Vatican, 26 September 1946, NARA, RG 59, Myron Taylor Papers, Box 30. Tardini, though not secretary of state until 1958, worked closely with Pius XII and Giovanni Montini (the future Pope Paul VI) in the Vatican Secretariat. In this exchange with Franklin Gowen, an assistant to Taylor, Tardini expressed the Vatican's skepticism on Stalin's commitments to postwar peace, quoting the ancient maxim to "beware Greeks, even when they bring you gifts."

19 "Text of Statement 'Between War and Peace' Issued by Bishops of United States," 18 November 1945, NARA, RG 59, Myron Taylor Papers, Box 26.

20 See "U.S. Seen Adopting New Foreign Policy," *Boston Pilot*, 21 March 1947, 1, 5; "Pres. Truman's Message Lauded by Father Walsh," *Boston Pilot*, 28 March 1947, 4.

21 "Pres. Truman's Message Lauded by Father Walsh," *Boston Pilot*, 28 March 1947, 4. On Walsh's considerable efforts to promote anticommunism both

within Catholic circles and in wider American society, see Patrick McNamara's *A Catholic Cold War: Edmund A. Walsh and the Politics of American Anticommunism* (Fordham University Press, 2005).

22 "Memorandum of Conversation between Graham Parsons and Don Manuel Sotomayor Luna," 14 January 1948, NARA, RG 59, Myron Taylor Papers, Box 19.

23 "Memorandum of Conversation," 17 September 1948, NARA, RG 59, Myron Taylor Papers, Box 30. Montini assured Dunn strenuously that the Vatican considered the Marshall Plan "the most important contribution to the cause of peace, economic and moral rehabilitation of Europe and indirectly the whole world."

24 Ibid.

25 On the seminal 1948 Italian election, see Robert A. Ventresca, *From Fascism to Democracy: Culture and Politics in the Italian Election of 1948* (University of Toronto Press, 2004).

26 For a contemporary analysis of the letter-writing campaign, see C. Edda Martinez and Edward A. Suchman, "Letters from America and the 1948 Elections in Italy," *Public Opinion Quarterly* 14, no. 1 (Spring 1950): 111–25.

27 "Chicago, Cleveland Praying for Reds' Defeat in Italy," 12 April 1948, NCNS, 6.

28 See "Italians Warned of 'Red' Slavery," *New York Times*, 23 March 1948, 2.

29 Quoted in Kent, *The Lonely Cold War*, 198.

30 See aide-mémoire, Pietro Cardinal Gasparri, 4 June 1922, NCWC/OGS/ACUA, Box 18, File 44.

31 Pinchas Lapide, *Three Popes and the Jews* (Hawthorn, 1967), 277.

32 Ibid.

33 Paul Charles Merkley, *Christian Attitudes towards the State of Israel* (McGill-Queen's University Press, 2001), 138.

34 "Private Audience with Pope Pius XII at Castel Gandolfo," 11 September 1945, NARA, RG 59, Myron Taylor Papers, Box 28.

35 Ibid.

36 See aide-mémoire, Pietro Cardinal Gasparri, 4 June 1922, NCWC/OGS/ACUA, Box 18, File 44.

37 On the distribution of the aide-mémoire through the NCWC in June 1944, see Amleto Cicognani to Michael Ready, 19 May 1944, NCWC/OGS/ACUA, Box 44, File 14.

38 For an analysis of American public opinion on the Arab-Israeli struggle in these years, see Eytan Gilboa, *American Public Opinion toward Israel and the Arab-Israeli Conflict* (Lexington Books, 1987), 15–27.

39 On Truman's growing affinity with the American Zionist movement in the

United States in 1948 and 1949, and the influence of advisers such as David Niles and Max Lowenthal, see Michael A. Cohen, *Truman and Israel* (University of California Press, 2020), 59–86.

40 See, for example, "Failure to Safeguard Christian Rights Will Prolong Solution of the Palestine Question," 4 April 1945, NCWC/OGS/ACUA, Box 18, File 44. Bruya was also attached to the Washington-based Commissariat of the Holy Land, and was the editor of the association's quarterly review, *The Crusader's Almanac.*

41 "Christian Interests Must Be Protected in Plans for Holy Land's Future," 16 April 1945, NCNS.

42 Ibid.

43 Bruya's sentiments were echoed further in the Catholic press by Monsignor Michael Assemani, the representative of the Latin patriarch of Jerusalem to the United States, and also an NCWC correspondent in Palestine. In a series of articles in the fall of 1945, Assemani defended Christianity's ancient claims to the territory, arguing that any solution that handed political control of the territory to "either Jews or Mohammedans" would represent a violation of Christianity's stake in the territory. He similarly suggested a UN stewardship of Palestine and urged Allied governments to "put a stop to the religious and racial bickering" between Jew and Arab in the territory. See "Solution of Palestine Is Allied Problem: Religious Attachment at Root of Arab-Jewish Conflict," *Brooklyn Tablet*, 1 December 1945; "Christian Rights in Holy Land Ignored in Arab-Jewish Dispute," *Michigan Catholic*, 12 December 1945.

44 "Palestine," *America*, 1 December 1945, 2.

45 See, for example "Palestine Crisis: Arabs Must Be Considered," *America*, 29 June 1946, 262; "Zionists and Palestine," *America*, 6 July 1946, 290; "Refugees and Zionism," *America*, 13 July 1946, 319; "The Palestine Mandate," *America*, 20 July 1946, 111; "Tragedy in Palestine," *America*, 3 August 1946, 402.

46 "The Lesson of Palestine," *America*, 18 May 1946, 130–2.

47 "Refugees and Zionism," *America*, 13 July 1946, 319.

48 See, for example, "Palestine Crisis: Arabs Must Be Considered," *America*, 29 June 1946, 290; "Soviet Anti-Semitism?," *America*, 9 March 1946, 595. The latter editorial warned that, "while the British are blamed by the Zionists for exploiting Arab nationalism, Russia is showing quite as much interest in the six Arab states as Great Britain."

49 "The Palestine Reality," *Catholic World*, January 1946, 301–10.

50 Ibid. See also "Is America Fair to Islam?," *Catholic World*, February 1946, 396–402.

51 On the activities of these offices, see Daniel Rickenbacher, "The Arab League's Propaganda Campaign in the U.S. against the Establishment of a Jewish State (1944–1947)," *Israel Studies* 25, no. 1 (Spring 2020): 1–25.

52 "Tragedy in Palestine," *America*, 3 August 1946, 402.

53 Ibid.

54 "Zionist Impatience," *America*, 15 March 1947, 648. In this editorial, *America* urged the "political Zionists" to "reassess their course," given that the Arabs were strengthening their position at the UN, and political turmoil in the Holy Land was "progressively annoying" Britain, which needed to focus its energies elsewhere. It concluded that "even the UN will probably be unable to meet the insistent demands not only for a Jewish homeland but also for a state. Zionism is experiencing a crisis. The rest of the world can only hope that it does not endanger world peace."

55 On Catholic apprehension toward Arab nationalism, see Thomas J. McMahon, "Islands of Christianity in the Rising Moslem Sea," 4 March 1944, Archives of the Archdiocese of New York, Francis Spellman Papers, Thomas J. McMahon File.

56 "The Bomb in Jerusalem," *Commonweal*, 2 August 1946, 372.

57 Ibid. In the same issue, *The Commonweal* ran an article by J.L. Teller (a "Zionist observer") outlining the increasingly insidious campaign waged by Palestinian Zionists in their quest for a Jewish state. It dismissed parallels made in the American mainstream press that equated the Zionist struggle to that of eighteenth-century American revolutionaries, instead branding the Irgun and the Haganah as criminal terrorist organizations. In chiding Zionist arrogance, it charged that "the Jews are building Palestine as though it already were a Jewish state." See "The Tools of Jewish Resistance," *Commonweal*, 2 August 1946, 375–7.

58 See, for example, "Religion the Key to Conflict in Palestine," *Catholic Mind*, October 1946, 607–15; "Palestine and Murder," *Commonweal*, 13 December 1946, 222; "Britain and Palestine," *Commonweal*, 14 February 1947, 439–41; "Palestine Turmoil: Zionist Impatience," *America*, 15 March 1947, 647–8; "Palestine: A Solution," *Catholic World*, March 1947, 489–90.

59 Some historians contend that Britain's condition of a resolution that would satisfy both Arabs and Jews was, by design, a poison pill designed to render impossible the UN's intervention. Once control would be ceded back to Britain, it would be free to pursue its imperial interests in the territory. See, for example, Richie Ovendale, *Britain, the United States and the End of the Palestine Mandate, 1942–1948* (Royal Historical Society, 1989).

60 UNSCOP was comprised of representatives from eleven countries: Australia, Canada, Czechoslovakia, Guatemala, India, Iran, the Netherlands, Peru, Sweden, Uruguay, and Yugoslavia.

61 See "UN Committee on Palestine Proposes Strict Safeguards for Shrines, Religious Rights," NCWC News Service, 15 September 1947. During the course of UNSCOP's committee sessions, Catholic demands for the protection of Christian rights and the Holy Places in Palestine were presented by two American prelates; Monsignor Thomas McMahon, secretary of the CNEWA, and Bonaventure Simon, OFM, who spoke on behalf of the Franciscan Custody of the Holy Land.

62 Ibid.

63 Arthur Hughes to Domenico Tardini, 9 December 1947, Archivio Storico della Segrataria di Stato – Sezione per i Rapporti con gli Stati, Vatican City (hereafter ASRS), Popolazioni (hereafter pop.) 1948, Posizione (hereafter pos.) 113-3.

64 Ibid.

65 Myron Taylor to Cordell Hull, 14 March 1944, Ennio DiNolfo, *Vaticano e Stati Uniti dalle carte di Myron C. Taylor* (Angeli, 1978), 311. Taylor's concerns about a pan-Arab confederation were in reference to George Antonius's influential 1938 book *The Arab Awakening*, which called for a stronger political synthesis between the Arab peoples of the Middle East, and specifically proposed a "Greater Syria," which would encompass, among other territories, most of Palestine. The idea was as alarming to the Vatican as was the Zionist program, as both threatened the church in the region.

66 Shlomo Shafir, "Taylor and McDonald: Two Diverging Views on Zionism and the Emerging Jewish State," *Jewish Social Studies* 39, no. 4 (Autumn 1977): 331–2. Taylor's anti-Zionist views, which suggested an alternative "national home" for Europe's Jews, closely reflected those of the Vatican, and had been expressed to the State Department and the Oval Office since 1938, when Taylor was the American representative to the Évian Conference on the resettlement of Europe's Jews.

67 Thomas J. McMahon, "Threat to the Holy Places," *Sign*, June 1945. Archives, Catholic Near East Welfare Association (hereafter A-CNEWA), Monsignor Thomas McMahon Papers (hereafter TMP), Box 6, Folder 7.

68 The "Old City" is a one-square-kilometer area with the larger city that, until the mid-nineteenth century, constituted the entire city. It contains many of the sites sacred to Jews, Christians, and Muslims, including the Temple Mount and the Wailing Wall, the Church of the Holy Sepulchre, and the Dome of the Rock.

69 Kreutz, *Vatican Policy on the Palestinian-Israeli Conflict*, 93.

70 "Excerpt from the Democratic Platform for 1948," May 1948, NCWC/OGS/ACUA, Box 20, File 44. The same document also provides an excerpt from the Republican platform, which makes no mention of internationalization, and instead outlines a robust support for Israel from the Republican Party, which was "the first to call for the establishment of a free and independent Jewish Commonwealth."

71 On the origins and establishment of the NCWC, see Joseph M. McShane, *Sufficiently Radical: Catholicism, Progressivism and the Bishop's Program of 1919* (Catholic University of America Press, 1986).

72 On American Catholic pressure on the State Department regarding American policy vis-à-vis Mexico and Spain, as discussed briefly in chapter 2, see George Q. Flynn, *American Catholics and the Roosevelt Presidency, 1932–1936* (University of Kentucky Press, 1968), and Matthew Redinger, *American Catholics and the Mexican Revolution, 1924–1936* (University of Notre Dame Press, 2005).

73 Joseph Rossi, *Uncharted Territory: The American Catholic Church at the United Nations, 1946–1972* (Catholic University of America Press, 2006), xi.

74 On the pope's vision of a postwar order, see Rossi, *Uncharted Territory*, 27–65. This vision was largely outlined in the pope's Christmas messages for 1939, 1940, and 1941, as well as his Pentecost message of June 1941.

75 "Pope Urges Support of the United Nations," *America*, 15 November 1947, 171.

76 On the American bishops' statements, see Huber, *Our Bishops Speak*, 115–30.

77 Edward Conway to Howard Carroll, Washington, 31 May 1946, NCWC/OGS/ACUA, Box 1, File 11.

78 Samuel Stritch to Howard Carroll, 14 May 1946, NCWC/OGS/ACUA, Box 44, File 23.

79 Ross Hoffman to Howard Carroll, 3 June 1946, NCWC/OGS/ACUA, Box 53, File 22.

80 Rossi, *Uncharted Territory*, 4.

81 Jean Gartlan, *Barbara Ward: Her Life and Letters* (Bloomsbury, 2010), 16.

82 On the remarkable diplomacy of Schaefer, which included a tireless advocacy for international women's rights, and the work of her later assistant (and associate director of the NCWC "UN Office"), Alba Zizzamia, see Joseph Rossi, "The Status of Women: Two American Catholic Women at the UN," *Catholic Historical Review* 93, no. 2 (April 2007): 300–24.

83 "Report of the NCWC Office of UN Affairs: 1 October 1946–1 August 1947," NCWC/OGS/ACUA, Box 164, File 40.

84 "Report of the NCWC Office for UN Affairs: 1 October 1946–1 August 1947," 5, NCWC/OGS/ACUA, Box 164, File 40. Quoted in Rossi, *Uncharted Territory*, 8.

85 On Schaefer's attempts to build links between the various Catholic observer missions to the UN, see, for example, Catherine Schaefer to Howard Carroll [New York], "Status of Catholic Organizational Representation at the UN," 8 July 1947, NCWC/OGS/ACUA, Box 159, File 7.

86 See, for example, "Annual Report: 1950: NCWC Office for United Nations Affairs and Bureau of Information," 23, NCWC/OGS/ACUA, Box 164, File 40. Schaefer's monthly reports, organized as lengthy bulletins and entitled "Foreign Affairs: A Survey of Trends," were forwarded regularly to NCWC headquarters in Washington, where their contents were disseminated and debated by the bishops, the Catholic press, and the various departments and committees of the NCWC. See, for example, "Foreign Affairs: A Survey of Trends," December 1946, 2–3, NCWC/OGS/ACUA, Box 158, File 4; "Foreign Affairs," November 1947, 16–18, NCWC/OGS/ACUA, Box 158, File 5; "Foreign Affairs," December 1947, 17–18, NCWC/OGS/ACUA, Box 158, File 6.

87 These requests were normally channeled through the apostolic delegate in Washington, Amleto Cicognani, to the general secretary of the NCWC, Howard Carroll. See, for example, Amleto Cicognani to Howard Carroll, 20 November 1947, NCWC/OGS/ACUA, Box 160, File 7; Howard Carroll to Catherine Schaefer, 10 May 1948, NCWC/OGS/ACUA, Box 159, File 8; Howard Carroll to Amleto Cicognani, 17 May 1948, NCWC/OGS/ACUA, Box 127, File 10.

88 Pope Paul VI appointed Monsignor Alberto Giovanetti as the Holy See's first permanent observer to the UN in March 1964. See Joseph Rossi, "The Relation of the Apostolic Delegation to the United Nations: 1945–1964," *U.S. Catholic Historian* 12, no. 2 (Spring 1994): 91–105. Rossi contends that while the relationship between the apostolic delegation and the NCWC UN Office were sometimes strained during Amleto Cicognani's tenure (1938–58), it became more constructive during the tenure of Egidio Vagnozzi, apostolic delegate to the United States from 1958 to 1967.

89 Catherine Schaefer to Howard Carroll [New York], "Special Session on Palestine," 28 April–16 May 1947, NCWC/OGS/ACUA, Box 164, File 38.

90 Ibid., 4. According to the report, the CNEWA was denied a hearing on the grounds that "the request originated with [an] organization established outside Palestine and not directly [representing] the population of that country." The CNEWA was, however, heard by UNSCOP following the latter's formal creation in May 1947.

91 "Christian Rights in Holy Land Are Given Attention," *Brooklyn Tablet*, 17 May 1947, 1.

92 Catherine Schaefer to Howard Carroll, "Special Session on Palestine," NCWC/OGS/ACUA, Box 164, File 38, 6. For a detailed examination of the development of American policy on Jerusalem in this crucial period, see Yossi Feintuch, *U.S. Policy on Jerusalem* (Greenwood, 1987), 7–58.

93 "NCWC Resolution on the Holy Places," 19 May 1947, NCWC/OGS/ACUA, Box 44, File 18. The demands set forth by the NCWC in 1947 were taken up by Pius XII himself in April 1949, when his encyclical *Redemptoris nostri* repeated these demands, and called for the full internationalization of Jerusalem.

94 Griffiths would remain involved in the "UN Office" for the remainder of his career, being appointed by Pope John XXIII as the Holy See's observer at UN headquarters in 1958.

95 James H. Griffiths to Archbishop John T. McNicholas [New York], "Memorandum on the Christian Factor in the Palestine Equation," 17 April 1947, 1–6, NCWC/OGS/ACUA, Box 44, File 18.

96 Ibid., 3.

97 Ibid., 5.

98 See, for example, "Christian Rights in Holy Land Are Given Attention," *Brooklyn Tablet*, 17 May 1947, 1.

99 Catherine Schaefer to Howard Carroll, 2 May 1947, NCWC/OGS/ACUA, Box 159, File 6.

100 Ibid., 1–3.

101 Catherine Schaefer to Howard Carroll, 22 October 1947, NCWC/OGS/ACUA, Box 159, File 7. Marshall implored his guests that his comments were strictly off the record, though Schaefer relayed the information back to the NCWC that same afternoon. Marshall had never granted avid support to Zionism, and likely sympathized with Roman Catholic concerns for the future of the territory.

102 Catherine Schaefer to Howard Carroll, "Memorandum – Jerusalem," 26 April 1950, NCWC/OGS/ACUA, Box 159, File 26. Malik was a key figure at the UN in these years, eventually chairing the Social Committee and playing a central role in the formulation of the seminal 1948 UN Bill of Human Rights.

103 On Malik's key role and influence in the drafting and adoption of the Universal Declaration of Human Rights, see Mary Ann Glendon, *The Forum and the Tower: How Scholars and Politicians Have Imagined the World, from Plato to Eleanor Roosevelt* (Oxford University Press, 2011), 199–220.

104 On the Protestant churches and Palestine, see Hertzel Fishman, *American Protestantism and a Jewish State* (Wayne State University Press, 1973).

105 On the growth and development of evangelical Christian support of a Jewish

state in Palestine, see Caitlin Carenen, *The Fervent Embrace: Liberal Protestants, Evangelicals, and Israel* (New York University Press, 2012), 1–47.

106 "Back Christians in Holy Land," *Brooklyn Tablet*, 19 July 1947, 6.

107 "Freedom for Christians in Palestine Demanded," *Brooklyn Tablet*, 24 January 1948, 3.

108 Ibid.

109 Catherine Schaefer to Howard Carroll, "Stay in Paris: 19 September–2 October 1947," 3. NCWC/OGS/ACUA, Box 53, File 17. Schaefer mentioned specifically the inclusion of "God" in the 1947 human rights declaration, to which several Protestant groups had resisted.

110 On the Vatican's efforts to suppress evangelical Christian influence in Fascist Italy, see Kevin Madigan, *The Popes against the Protestants: The Vatican and Evangelical Christianity in Fascist Italy* (Yale University Press, 2021). On the Vatican's postwar efforts to confront the influence of Protestantism in Italy, see Paolo Zanini, *Il "pericolo protestante": Chiese e cattolici italiani di fronte alla questione delle libertà religiosa, 1922–1955* (Mondadori, 2019), 111-90.

111 Samuel Cavert to Howard Carroll, 10 April 1947, NCWC/OGS/ACUA, Box 44, File 18. Cavert had been approached by American Ambassador William Phillips, who had served on the 1946 AAIC, and who felt that a Catholic-Protestant joint statement might carry considerable clout.

112 Howard Carroll to Archbishop John McNicholas, 22 April 1947, NCWC/OGS/ACUA, Box 44, File 18.

113 Ibid.

114 See "End of Agitation on Myron Taylor Mission Is Asked: Former Under Secretary Welles Avers Peace and Unity Are Reasons for Assignment," *New York Herald Tribune*, 15 January 1947, 4.

115 "Deplores Protestant Attacks on Catholics: Harold E. Staasen Assails Baptist Convention for Rapping Supreme Court and Vatican Appointment," *Brooklyn Tablet*, 31 May 1947, 6.

116 "Taylor Mission to Vatican Defended," *Boston Pilot*, 25 January 1947, 1; "End of Agitation on Myron Taylor Mission Is Asked," *Brooklyn Tablet*, 18 January 1947, 3.

117 "Editorial Research Reports: Relations with the Vatican," 12 February 1947, NCWC/OGS/ACUA, Box 11, File 1.

118 See Harry S. Truman to Pius XII, 6 August 1947, 1–2, NARA, RG 59, Myron Taylor Papers, Box 18; Pius XII to Harry S. Truman, 26 August 1947, 1–3, NARA, RG 59, Myron Taylor Papers, Box 18. On American Catholic press coverage of the exchange of letters, see "U.S. and Vatican Stand Together for

World Peace," *Brooklyn Tablet*, 30 August 1947, 1; "Taylor's Mission to Vatican Seen as More Important," *Brooklyn Tablet*, 6 September 1947, 1.

119 "Biographical Data – Mgr Thomas J. McMahon," 1945, A-CNEWA, TMP, Box 6, Folder 7.

120 Ibid.

121 "Threat to the Holy Places," *Sign*, June 1945.

122 Silvio Ferrari, "The Holy See and the Postwar Palestine Issue: The Internationalization of Jerusalem and the Protection of the Holy Places," *International Affairs* 60, no. 2 (1984): 264. Italics added.

123 Francis Spellman to Warren Austin, 15 February 1947, A-CNEWA, TMP, Box 1, Folder 8.

124 Thomas McMahon to Francis Spellman, 21 February 1947, A-CNEWA, TMP, Box 1, Folder 8.

125 Ibid.

126 Thomas J. McMahon, "CNEWA Petition to the UN Political and Security Committee," 10 May 1947. See "Christian Rights in Holy Land Are Given Attention," *Brooklyn Tablet*, 17 May 1947, 1, 15–16.

127 Ibid., 16.

128 Though the CNEWA's request to present a verbal statement to UNSCOP was rejected (as were similar requests from a number of American Zionist organizations, including the ZOA), it did win the right to submit a written statement. See Andrew Cordier to Thomas McMahon, 13 May 1947, A-CNEWA, TMP, Box 3, File 19.

129 Thomas McMahon to the Special Committee on Palestine, 5 June 1947, AAD, Archbishop Edward Mooney Papers, Box 39, File 6, 1–4. See also *Letter to the United Nations Special Committee on Palestine*, 5 June 1947, in Constantine Rackauskas, *The Internationalization of Palestine* (Catholic Association for International Peace, 1951), 73–8.

130 For the text of Pius XII's address to the Arab Higher Committee, see enclosure to Amleto Cicognani to Howard Carroll [New York], 29 August 1946, NCWC/OGS/ACUA, Box 44, File 18.

131 Thomas McMahon to the Special Committee on Palestine, 5 June 1947, A-CNEWA, TMP, Box 8, File 2.

132 Ibid.

133 See *Palestine: A Study of Jewish, Arab and British Policies*, vol. 1 (Yale University Press, 1946), 534–6. The ESCO Foundation for Palestine was headed by Rose G. Jacobs, an activist with the Hadassah, the Women's Zionist Organiza-

tion of America. ESCO, which was comprised of American civic leaders and academics, favored a one-state solution for Palestine, but did not explicitly advocate for Jewish political dominion in the territory.

134 Thomas McMahon to the Special Committee on Palestine, 5 June 1947, A-CNEWA, TMP, Box 8, File 2.

135 Ibid., 75–6. The Latin patriarch of Jerusalem is the title possessed by the Latin Rite Roman Catholic archbishop of Jerusalem, who possesses jurisdiction over all Roman Catholics in Israel. Barlassina held the post from 1920 to 1947.

136 Ibid., 76.

137 Issa Nakhleh to Thomas McMahon, 16 June 1947, A-CNEWA, TMP, Box 1, File 8. Nakleh, who also served as the representative of the League of Arab States in Latin America, represented the Arab Committee for Palestine for nearly forty years, and presented more than fifty petitions during the UNSCOP hearings.

138 Thomas McMahon to Francis Spellman, 2 July 1947, A-CNEWA, TMP, Box 1, File 8.

139 Ibid.

140 Ibid.

141 Ibid.

142 Thomas McMahon to Francis Spellman, 10 October 1947, A-CNEWA, Box 1, File 8.

143 Ibid.

144 Ibid.

145 For a copy of the UNSCOP resolution on Jerusalem, which had been forwarded to the NCWC's press department, see enclosure to Eleanor Waters to William Fanning [New York], 25 November 1947, NCWC/OGS/ACUA, Box 23, File 44, 1–4.

146 *Foreign Relations of the United States* (Washington, DC: United States Government Publishing Office, 1947), 1:1143.

147 Shlomo Slonim, *Jerusalem in America's Foreign Policy, 1947–1997* (Kluwer, 1998), 15.

148 Ibid.

149 Thomas McMahon to Francis Spellman, 8 November 1947, A-CNEWA, TMP, Box 1, File 8.

CHAPTER FIVE

1 "Memorandum of Conversation," 13 February 1948, NARA, RG 59, Myron Taylor Papers, Box 19.

2 Ibid. Parsons was similarly warned of the dangers of partition, and the concomitant gains for the Soviet Union, by Mohammed Taher el Elmari, Egypt's ambassador to the Holy See, who warned Parsons that the prime beneficiary of partition would be Moscow, which was preparing to "pour Russian agents into Palestine to reap the whirlwind." See "Memorandum of Conversation," 14 January 1948, NARA, RG 59, Myron Taylor Papers, Box 19.

3 Testa was appointed on 22 February 1948, just days before his meeting with Parsons. In the interview, Parsons described his guest as "a pleasant Italian of about sixty" and "an easy conversationalist," someone who had traveled Palestine in 1913 by motorcycle and who "spoke admiringly of the work of the Jews, and although referring often to their fanaticism and to that of the Arabs, was essentially moderate and human without too much emphasis on the clerical viewpoint." See "Memorandum of Conversation," 26 February 1948, 1–2, NARA, RG 59, Myron Taylor Papers, Box 21.

4 On the reorganization of Vatican diplomatic posts in the region, see "Organization of the Catholic Church in Palestine, Transjordan and Cyprus," 25 February 1948, NARA, RG 59, Myron Taylor Papers, Box 20, 1–2.

5 Ibid., 2.

6 Graham Parsons to George Marshall [secretary of state], 26 February 1948, NARA, RG 59, Myron Taylor Papers, Box 30.

7 "Memorandum of Conversation," 26 February 1948, NARA, RG 59, Myron Taylor Papers, Box 20, 2. Though the document does not outline the full contents of the survey, the context of the conversation alludes to the idea that it outlined American public opinion leaning progressively in favor of partition, a position that the American government was finding increasingly difficult to oppose. On American public opinion and the partition plan, see Eytan Gilboa, *American Public Opinion toward Israel and the Arab-Israeli Conflict* (Lexington Books, 1987), 13–21.

8 Ibid.

9 "Memorandum of Conversation," 27 February 1948, NARA, RG 59, Myron Taylor Papers, Box 19.

10 Ibid.

11 See Michael J. Cohen, "Truman and the State Department: The Palestine Trusteeship Proposal, March 1948," *Jewish Social Studies* 43, no. 2 (Spring

1981): 165–78. See also Cohen's *Truman and Israel* (University of California Press, 2020), 345–90.

12 See, for example, Ronald Radosh and Alice Radosh, "Truman, Jews and Zionists," in *Harry S. Truman, the State of Israel and the Quest for Peace in the Middle East*, ed. Michael J. Devine (Truman State University Press, 2009), 95–118. In the same volume, see Michael J. Cohen's "Truman's Recognition of Israel: The Domestic Factor," 119–30. On postwar Christian Zionism, see Shalom Goldman, *Zeal for Zion: Christians, Jews and the Idea of the Promised Land* (University of North Carolina Press, 2010); Caitlin Carenen, "The American Christian Palestine Committee, the Holocaust, and Mainstream Protestant Zionism, 1938–1948," *Holocaust and Genocide Studies* 24, no. 2 (Fall 2010): 273–96. On the impact of Truman's own Christian faith in his conception of a peaceable and stable world order, see William Inboden, *Religion and American Foreign Policy: The Soul of Containment* (Cambridge University Press, 2008), 105–57.

13 Representative papers included *The American Zionist*, *The Congress Bulletin*, *The Jewish Herald*, *The Jewish News*, *The National Jewish Monthly*, and *The Rubicon*, among others.

14 Amleto Cicognani to Howard Carroll, 11 January 1948, NCWC/OGS/ACUA, Box 18, File 43.

15 "Palestine Steps," *America*, 6 March 1948, 622.

16 "Palestine Reversal," *America*, 3 April 1948, 733. The journal observed that, "on their part, the Zionists have seriously discredited their own cause by over-estimating their ability to maintain themselves in Palestine and by creating, through propaganda sometimes too powerful for their own good, an idealistic picture of the probability of avoiding the employment of outside armed forces. And the people of the world can hardly be blamed for conceiving a low opinion of the capacity of the United Nations to reach sound decisions, in view of the supposedly objective and mature consideration that went into the partition decision."

17 Ibid.

18 See, for example, "Christians Flay Partition Plan for Palestine," *Brooklyn Tablet*, 13 March 1948, 1; "Seizure of Holy Places Charged to Israeli Army," *Brooklyn Tablet*, 5 June 1948, 1; "Christian Holy Places Suffer in No Man's Land of Arab-Jewish Strife," *Michigan Catholic*, 1 April 1948, 4.

19 The Catholic representatives in the Christian Union were Reverend Albert Gori, custos of the Holy Land, Monsignor Ephrem Haddad, vicar in Jerusalem for the Syrian patriarch of Antioch, and Monsignor Robert Jacques, representative of the Armenian patriarch in Jerusalem.

20 "Seizure of Holy Places Charged to Israeli Army," *Brooklyn Tablet*, 5 June 1948, 1.

21 "Memorandum – Christian Union," 7 June 1948, Wayne State University Archives [hereafter WSUA], Walter P. Reuther Library of Labor and Urban Affairs [hereafter WRL], Philip Slomowitz Papers, File 65.

22 "Christian Leaders in Jerusalem Lay Damage of Shrines to Israel," *New York Times*, 1 June 1948, 12.

23 "Allocution of His Holiness Pius XII to the Sacred College," 2 June 1948, NARA, RG 59, Myron Taylor Papers, Box 30, 1–5.

24 Amleto Cicognani to Howard Carroll, 15 June 1948, NCWC/OGS/ACUA, Box 18, File 43.

25 John J. O'Rourke to John LaFarge, 9 April 1948, Georgetown University Archives, America Magazine Papers, File 18.

26 O'Rourke's letter was summarized in an article in *America*, "Fateful Hour for Jerusalem," on 24 April.

27 "The Holy City," *America*, 8 May 1948, 104.

28 "Israel and the Catholic Church," WSUA, WRL, Philip Slomowitz Papers, File 65. "Editorial Comment – Recognition of Israel," *Catholic World*, July 1948, 289–97.

29 Ibid., 290.

30 Ibid., 295.

31 Israel was invaded almost immediately after its founding on 18 May 1948 by Egypt, Iraq, Jordan, Lebanon, and Syria. The conflict, popularly known as the 1948 Arab-Israeli War, was concluded by separate armistice agreements signed between Israel and its warring neighbors in 1949.

32 See, for example, "Detailed Reports on Lootings in Palestine Holy Places Received from Jerusalem," NCWC News Service, 13 September 1948.

33 For a sampling of Bruya's articles on Jewish desecrations, see "Jerusalem Today: Where Christ Walked Now Strife Strides," *Michigan Catholic*, 25 March 1948, 6; "In Jittery Jerusalem: Christian Holy Places Suffer in No-Man's Land of Arab-Jew Strife," *Michigan Catholic*, 1 April 1948, 3; "Desecration of Jerusalem Surveyed during Truce," *Brooklyn Tablet*, 10 July 1948, 4; "Holy Land Strife Damages Shrines," *Brooklyn Tablet*, 24 July 1948, 3; "Holy Land Ruins Seen Work of UN: Christian Churches Appear to Be Main Targets," *Brooklyn Tablet*, 8 September 1948, 1; "Proof of Looting and Desecration in Haifa Is Cited," *Brooklyn Tablet*, 25 September 1948, 1.

34 "Proof of Looting and Desecration in Haifa Is Cited," *Brooklyn Tablet*, 25 September 1948.

35 See Uri Bialer, *The Cross on the Star of David: The Christian World in Israel's Foreign Policy, 1948–1967* (Indiana University Press, 2005), 7–10.

36 "Memo of Conversation," 17 September 1948, NARA, RG 59, Myron Taylor Papers, Box 30. Montini, in offering more details on the Vatican's nonrecognition of Israel, explained that the Vatican was "almost invariably the last to recognize new governments."

37 Ibid.

38 Thomas J. McMahon to Trygve Lie, 23 August 1948, AAD, Bishop Edward Mooney Papers, Box 39, File 6.

39 Ibid.

40 Ibid.

41 Thomas McMahon to Francis Spellman, 24 August 1948, A-CNEWA, TMP, Box 1, File 8.

42 "Israel and the Catholic Church," "Demands Israelis Rebuild Catholic Churches," August 1948, WSUA, WRL, Philip Slomowitz Papers, File 65.

43 Kennedy was nominated to the order in August 1946 by Archbishop Ricard Cushing of Boston. See Cushing to Luigi Barlassina, 27 August 1948, archives of the Archdiocese of Boston, Richard Cushing Papers, Box 29, File: "Order of the Holy Sepulchre."

44 "Israel and the Catholic Church," "Demands Israelis Rebuild Catholic Churches," August 1948, WSUA, WRL, Philip Slomowitz Papers, File 65.

45 Amleto Cicognani to Howard Carroll [Washington], 25 October 1948, NCWC/OGS/ACUA, Box 18, File 44.

46 The text of *In multiplicibus curis* is available at https://www.vatican.va/content/pius-xii/en/encyclicals/documents/hf_p-xii_enc_24101948_in-multiplicibus-curis.html.

47 See Ferrari, "The Holy See and the Postwar Palestine Issue," 267–8.

48 See, for example, "Jerusalem Still under Gunfire," *Brooklyn Tablet*, 9 October 1948, 2; "Israeli Troops Looted Shrines – US Priests Say," *Brooklyn Tablet*, 30 October 1948, 1; "Foresees Bethlehem Isolated at Christmas," *Brooklyn Tablet*, 30 October 1948, 4; "Victims of Holy Land War Rising," *Brooklyn Tablet*, 13 November 1948, 6; "Further Reports of Desecrations from Holy Land," *Brooklyn Tablet*, 11 December 1948, 1.

49 "Israeli Troops Looted Shrines – US Priests Say," *Brooklyn Tablet*, 30 October 1948, 1.

50 Ibid.

51 "Memo – Statement of Archbishop Arthur Hughes – Apostolic Nuncio to Egypt," 17 November 1948, NCWC/OGS/ACUA, Box 18, File 44.

52 Francis J. Murphy to Howard Carroll [Washington], 31 December 1948, NCWC/OGS/ACUA, Box 18, File 44; see attached telegram, 1–4. The signatories to the telegram were George Dallal, Syrian archbishop of Mosul, Yohanna Nissan, Chaldean archbishop of Zakho, Stephen Katcho, auxiliary bishop of Babylon, Raphael Rabban, Chaldean bishop of Amadia, and Paul Cheikho, Chaldean bishop of Agra.

53 Ibid., 4.

54 See Feldblum, *The American Catholic Press and a Jewish State*, 55–60.

55 See, for example, *Sign*, January 1946, 2; *Michigan Catholic*, 10 April 1947; *New World*, 11 July 1947, 1; *Our Sunday Visitor*, 18 April 1948, 4.

56 See, for example, Alba Zizzamia to Howard Carroll [Washington], and attached "Report on the Refugee Problem of Palestine," 2 September 1948, NCWC/OGS/ACUA, Box 44, File 31; Alba Zizzamia to Howard Carroll, "The Palestine Question," 2 November 1948, NCWC/OGS/ACUA, Box 38, File 156.

57 See, for example, "Palestine DP Problem Grave," *Brooklyn Tablet*, 18 September 1948, 15; "Jerusalem – Still under Gun Fire," *Brooklyn Tablet*, 9 October 1948, 2; "Arab Refugee Plight Serious," *Brooklyn Tablet*, 6 November 1948, 3; "Victims of Holy Land War Rising," *Brooklyn Tablet*, 13 November 1948, 2.

58 "Appeals to Americans for Holy Land Refugees," *Brooklyn Tablet*, 30 October 1948, 4.

59 "The Christian Stake in the Palestine Equation," *America*, 26 March 1949.

60 Ibid.

61 The ACPC, which was the most important Christian Zionist advocacy group in the United States, addressed Truman, Warren Austin (head of the American UN delegation), and Secretary of State George Marshall directly in June 1948 in support of Israel's admission to the UN. In the same month, the organization notified a range of US senators of its opposition to British support of Arab interests in Palestine, and of the use of European Recovery Program funds to support the Arab war against Israel. See "Israel and the Catholic Church," WSUA, WRL, Philip Slomowitz Papers, File 65; Karl Baehr, executive secretary (ACPC), to Truman, 22 June 1948, WSUA, WRL, Philip Slomowitz Papers, File 65; Karl Baehr to Alexander Cadogan (UK representative to the UN), 22 June 1948, WSUA, WRL, Philip Slomowitz Papers, File 65; Karl Baehr to Senator H. Styles Bridges, 22 June 1948, WSUA, WRL, Philip Slomowitz Papers, File 65.

62 Quoted in Bialer, *Cross on the Star of David*, 8.

63 Ibid.

64 Ibid.

65 Alberto Levame to Giovanni Montini, 5 September 1948, ASRS, pop. 1948, pos. 113-3.

66 Franklin C. Gowen to Giovanni Batista Montini, 23 September 1948, NARA, RG 59, Myron Taylor Papers, Box 20; Antonio Vergani to Montini, 24 September 1948, NARA, RG 59, Myron Taylor Papers, Box 20.

67 Yaacov Herzog to James McDonald, 20 August 1948, NARA, RG 59, Myron Taylor Papers, Box 20.

68 James Dunn to secretary of state, 7 October 1948, NARA, RG 59, Myron Taylor Papers, Box 20.

69 Yaacov Herzog to Franklin C Gowen, 7 October 1948, NARA, RG 59, Myron Taylor Papers, Box 20, 1–2. Valeri served as papal nuncio to France from 1936 until 1944, when his collaboration with the Vichy regime caused Charles de Gaulle to order his removal.

70 Ibid.

71 Ibid.

72 James Dunn to secretary of state [Washington], 12 November 1948, NARA, RG 59, Myron Taylor Papers, Box 30.

73 Franklin Gowen to secretary of state [Washington], "Secret Conversation between the Holy See and Israel on Catholic Interests in Israel," 2 November 1948, NARA, RG 59, Myron Taylor Papers, Box 20. Gowen reported to Marshall that various Vatican officials opined to him that the visit was "to offset the painful impression caused in Catholic circles by the bad treatment which several Catholic institutions and their members had suffered on various occasions at the hands of irresponsible Jewish elements in Israel and elsewhere in the Holy Land."

74 Yaacov Herzog to Franklin Gowen, 7 October 1948, NARA, RG 59, Myron Taylor Papers, Box 20. Herzog expressed to Gowan, as he prepared to leave Rome, that there "appeared to be ground for the feeling that the contacts which have been established should be viewed as a beginning of ultimately permanent relations of good will between the Holy See and Israel." It would be another forty-five years before the Holy See would recognize Israel diplomatically.

75 Franklin Gowen to secretary of state, NARA, RG 59, Myron Taylor Papers, Box 20, 2, November 1948.

76 "Israel and the Catholic Church – Memorandum – Desecration of the Holy Places in Palestine," 16 July 1948, WSUA, WRL, Philip Slomowitz Papers, File 65, 1–6. Jewish newspapers included *The American Zionist*, *The Congress Bulletin*, *The Detroit Jewish News*, *The Jewish Herald*, and others.

77 Philip Slomowitz to Editorial Board (*Commonweal* magazine), 26 July 1948, WSUA, WRL, Philip Slomowitz Papers, File 65, "Israel and the Catholic Church."

78 Slomowitz to I.L. Kenen, 10 August 1948, WSUA, WRL, Philip Slomowitz Papers, File 65; Slomowitz to Rita A. Grossman, 25 August 1948, WSUA, WRL, Philip Slomowitz Papers, File 65.

79 Anne Fremantle to Philip Slomowitz, 4 August 1948, WSUA, WRL, Philip Slomowitz Papers, File 65. One of the sources cited by Fremantle was the Christian Union, whose manifestos had been quoted liberally in the Catholic press, and which was regarded as a pro-Arab lobby by many in the State Department and the Israeli government.

80 See "Holy Places Touched by War," *New York Herald Tribune*, 12 November 1948, 4.

81 Eliahu Epstein to Archbishop John McNicholas, 24 August 1948, NCWC/OGS/ACUA, Box 44, File 31. Copies of Epstein's correspondence were also forwarded to Howard Carroll, Burke Walsh of the NCWC News Service, and Apostolic Delegate Amleto Cicognani.

82 "Press Release – Rabbi Fishman's Statement," August 1948, NCWC/OGS/ACUA, Box 44, File 31.

83 Eliahu Ben-Horin to Howard Carroll, 23 August 1948, NCWC/OGS/ACUA, Box 44, File 31.

84 See, for example, Amleto Cicognani to Howard Carroll, 29 August 1948, Box 43, File 31.

85 Howard Carroll to Amleto Cicognani, 19 October 1948, NCWC/OGS/ACUA, Box 44, File 18. See, for example, "Conditions in Nazareth Dismal, Says Belgian Priest," NCWC News Service, 27 December 1948. Among Naveau's claims were that "the Israelis [had] organized a large spy net and that Arabs are bribed to accuse each other at specially created offices."

86 James Dunn to secretary of state [Washington], 12 November 1948, NARA, RG 59, Myron Taylor Papers, Box 30.

87 On the details of Washington's evolving policy on Jerusalem in the last half of 1948, see Yossi Feintuch, *U.S. Policy on Jerusalem*, 51–7. American policy on the city was driven primarily by concerns over the creation of a UN police force for the divided city, which was estimated to cost $30 million annually, as well as fears that a constabulary consisting of American and Soviet personnel constituted a security threat to the United States, as well as a beachhead for Moscow in Palestine.

88 Ibid., 56.

89 See text of *In multiplicibus curis* at https://www.vatican.va/content/pius-xii/en/encyclicals/documents/hf_p-xii_enc_24101948_in-multiplicibus-curis.html.

90 James McDonald to secretary of state [Washington], 11 January 1949, NARA, RG 59, 867N/ 1-1149. See also enclosure.

91 Thomas McMahon to Francis Spellman, June 1951, A-CNEWA, TMP, Box 6, Folder 8.

92 Ibid.

93 McMahon's mission included the coordination of CNEWA aid relief in Egypt, Gaza, Lebanon, Syria, Jordan, and Israel.

94 Thomas McMahon to Francis Spellman, 10 December 1948, A-CNEWA, TMP, Box 6, Folder 7.

95 Ibid.

96 Ibid.

97 Thomas McMahon to Francis Spellman, 23 December 1948, A-CNEWA, TMP, Box 6, Folder 7.

98 Ibid.

99 Ibid.

100 See James McDonald, *My Mission in Israel, 1948–1951* (Simon and Schuster, 1951), 206. McMahon further insisted that the repatriation of refugees be carried out on a nonsectarian basis, stating that a Vatican plea solely for Catholic refugees would imperil its standing in the Arab world.

101 Feintuch, *U.S. Policy on Jerusalem*, 60–1.

102 Thomas McMahon to Francis Spellman, 3 March 1949, A-CNEWA, TMP, Box 6, Folder 7.

103 Ibid.

104 "What Fate Jerusalem?," *America*, 26 February 1949, 558.

105 "Confidential Report on Latest Journey," 20 March 1949, A-CNEWA, TMP, Box 6, File 8.

106 Ibid.

107 Thomas McMahon to Trygve Lie, 21 March 1949, AAD, Archbishop Edward Mooney Papers, Box 39, File 6.

108 Ibid.

109 Thomas McMahon to Francis Spellman, 20 April 1949, A-CNEWA, TMP, Box 1, File 8.

110 Ibid.

111 Ibid.

112 For the text of the speech, see "Pleads for Arab Refugee Exiled from Palestine," *Brooklyn Tablet*, 9 April 1949, 1.

113 Ibid.

114 The full text of *Redemptoris nostri cruciatus* is available at https://www.vatican.va/content/pius-xii/en/encyclicals/documents/hf_p-xii_enc_15041949_redemptoris-nostri-cruciatus.html.

115 Ibid.

116 Amleto Cicognani to the most reverend archbishops and bishops of the United States, 18 May 1949, NCWC/OGS/ACUA, Box 197, File 55. Signatories included Spellman, Mooney, Stritch, McNicholas, and Boston's archbishop, Richard Cushing.

117 Ibid.

118 See Huber, *Our Bishops Speak*, 364–5. The other signatories were Francis Keough, archbishop of Baltimore, Robert Lucey, archbishop of San Antonio, Patrick O' Boyle, archbishop of Washington, John Gannon, bishop of Erie, John Noll, bishop of Fort Wayne, Karl Alter, bishop of Toledo, and Michael Ready, bishop of Columbus.

119 Ibid.

120 Francis Spellman to Harry S. Truman, 29 April 1949, NARA, RG 59, N. O1/5-449.

121 Harry S. Truman to Francis Spellman, 19 May 1949, NARA, RG 59, N. 404/6-1449.

122 For a copy of the report, see "United Nations Conciliation Commission for Palestine: Progress Report," NCWC/OGS/ACUA, Box 23, File 44, 1–8. The report noted that Ben-Gurion, while accepting without reservation an international regime for the Holy Places, could not accept the full territorial internationalization of the city. "For historical, political and religious reasons," he is quoted, "the State of Israel could not accept the establishment of an international regime for the City of Jerusalem."

123 See Catherine Schaefer to Howard Carroll, 5 May 1949, NCWC/OGS/ACUA, Box 18, File 53. See also enclosure, "The Christian Factor in the Palestine Equation," 1–8.

124 Ibid., 8.

125 See James H. Griffiths to Paul F. Tanner, 6 May 1949, NCWC/OGS/ACUA, Box 44, File 23. Neither Schafer nor Griffiths disclosed lists of delegates or legislators to whom copies were sent.

126 Thomas McMahon to Francis Spellman, 28 April 1949, A-CNEWA, TMP, Box 6, File 7.

127 Ibid.

128 Ibid. Abdullah I was king of Jordan from May 1946 to July 1951.

129 Ibid.

130 For the text of this pamphlet, see Archives of the Library of Congress (hereafter ALC), Charles Habib Malik Papers (hereafter CMP), Box 93, File 4.

131 Ibid.

132 McMahon's appointment placed him in charge of the relief efforts of the CNEWA, the Sacred Congregation for the Oriental Churches, the Franciscan Custody of the Holy Land, and the Knights of the Holy Sepulchre, along with several national Catholic relief missions.

133 See Rioli's *A Liminal Church: Refugees, Conversions and the Latin Diocese of Jerusalem, 1946–1956* (Brill, 2020), 271–87.

134 Ibid., 146–65.

135 Amleto Cigognani to the bishops and ordinaries of the United States, 18 May 1949, NCWC/OGS/ACUA, Box 197, File 55.

136 See, for example, Antonio Samore to Howard Carroll, 15 January 1949, NCWC/OGS/ACUA, Box 22, File 44; Antonio Samore to Paul Tanner, 28 January 1949, NCWC/OGS/ACUA, Box 22, File 44.

137 Antonio Samore to Paul Tanner, 28 January 1949, NCWC/OGS/ACUA, Box 22, File 44.

138 See, for example, "Holy Land Relief Problem Studied," *Brooklyn Tablet*, 8 January 1949; "Tells of Plight of Arab Refugees," *Brooklyn Tablet*, 5 February 1949; "Describes How Mass Was Barred at Mount Zion," *Brooklyn Tablet*, 14 May 1949; "Sees Whittling Down of Pledges on Holy Places," *Brooklyn Tablet*, 13 August 1949.

139 See, for example, "Honor in Israel," *America*, 26 March 1949, 677; "Christian Rights in Jerusalem," *America*, 30 April 1949, 151; "No Peace in Palestine," *America*, 18 June 1949, 350.

140 See, for example, Amleto Cicognani to Howard Carroll, 17 July 1949, NCWC/OGS/ACUA, Box 23, File 44. In this letter, Cicognani requested that Carroll reprint a lengthy piece on Palestine by the Reverend A. Messineo, SJ, that had appeared in *La Civiltà Cattolica* the previous week.

141 Amleto Cicognani to Paul Tanner, 20 May 1949, NCWC/OGS/ACUA, Box 18, File 44.

142 Frank Hall to Amleto Cicognani, 23 May 1949, NCWC/OGS/ACUA, Box 18, File 44.

143 Howard Carroll to editors, "Memorandum – Editorial Information," 7 January 1949, NCWC/OGS/ACUA, Box 22, File 44, 1–7.

144 The NCWC News Service provided editors of diocesan papers three form letters with which to respond to critiques from Jewish editors and Zionist

figures. The first amounted to a defense of the reportage of Anthony Bruya, "an American religious with a remarkably fine record," as the letter described him. The NCWC letter vouched for the veracity of his reporting from the Holy Land, pointing up the fact that the Catholic press had given fair coverage to Tel Aviv's attempts to rectify the situation. The form letter concluded that, "If this reply seems strong, I call to your attention the fact that the accusations against this Service were palpably irresponsible." The next two letters provided more general refutations of charges that the Catholic press unfairly criticized Israeli transgressions. See Howard Carroll to editors, "Memorandum – Editorial Information," 7 January 1949, NCWC/OGS/ACUA, Box 22, File 44, 1–7.

145 Abe Tuvim to chairmen of the Local Emergency Committees, 17 February 1949, WSUA, Philip Slomowitz Papers, File 65, "Israel and the Catholic Church." See also attached memo, "Jewish-Catholic Relations in and Over Israel," 1–3.

146 "Israel and the Catholic Empire," *Congress Weekly*, 5–8, WSUA, Philip Slomowitz Papers, File 65.

147 "Campaign against Israel: Behind the Vatican's Plan to Internationalize," *Churchman*, 1 October 1949, 9. Teller's column was published in the evangelical *Churchman*, a journal that backed larger American Protestant support for Israel and for a Jewish Jerusalem.

148 Ibid.

149 "Israel, Attacking U.S. Stand, Bars Yielding of Territory," *New York Times*, 15 June 1949.

150 See, for example, "The British Catholic Press and Anti-Zionism," *Congress Bulletin*, 15 April 1949, 11; "The Problem of the Holy Places," *Reconstructionist*, 13 May 1949; "Catholic Charity and the Jews," *Rubicon*, June 1949; "Israel and the Catholic Empire," *Congress Weekly*, 25 July 1949; "Rome and Jerusalem: Vatican's Stand on Israel Has Been Unfriendly," *American Hebrew*, 5 August 1949; "The Church and Palestine in 1917," *National Jewish Monthly*, December 1949, 112–17.

151 "Memo – Excerpt from Article Appearing in the August 1949 Issue of the American Zionist," NCWC/OGS/ACUA, Box 153, File 10, 9 November 1949.

152 Ibid.

153 See, for example, Carenen, "The American Christian Palestine Committee, the Holocaust, and Mainstream Protestant Zionism." Though the ACPC's leadership consisted chiefly of mainline Protestant authorities, it did include one prominent Catholic, Senator Robert Wagner of New York, who had helped to found the group in 1941.

154 On the formation and development of the ACPC, see Carenen, *The Fervent Embrace*, 17–47. On the earlier history of Christian Zionism in the United States, see Samuel Goldman, *God's Country: Christian Zionism in America* (University of Pennsylvania Press, 2018).

155 "Memo: Israel's Open Disregard of Christian Claims in Palestine," 11 May 1949, A-CNEWA, TMP, Box 6, File 8.

156 Thomas McMahon to Francis Spellman, 18 May 1949, A-CNEWA, TMP, Box 6, File 8.

157 The diocesan press carried details of the Cenacle incident widely. See, for example, "Account Tells How Israelis Barred Franciscans from Cenacle on Mt Zion, but Let Jews Go," NCWC News Service, 9 May 1949, 5–7.

158 Though Fenway Park's official capacity was only 37,731, a majority of participants were assembled on the playing field, nearly doubling the number the venue could accommodate.

159 Ibid.

160 Ibid.

161 "Making Firm Plea for Jerusalem: Queens Catholic War Veterans Want Area Internationalized," *Brooklyn Tablet*, 20 August 1949.

162 Francis Spellman to Harry S. Truman, 10 June 1949, NARA, RG 59, Myron Taylor Papers, Box 26.

163 Ibid.

164 Ibid.

165 Harry S. Truman to Francis Spellman, 22 June 1949, NARA, RG 59, Myron Taylor Papers, Box 26.

166 Ibid.

167 Ibid

168 Harry S. Truman to Francis Spellman, 26 July 1949, NARA, RG 59, Myron Taylor Papers, Box 26.

169 *Catholic Standard and Times*, 10 June 1949.

170 "Prayers for Protection of Shrines in Holy Places Asked by Prelate," NCWC News Service, 11 July 1949.

171 Paul Tanner to Amleto Cicognani, 22 June 1949, NCWC/OGS/ACUA, Box 23, File 44.

172 Ibid.

173 Myron Taylor to Harry S. Truman, 2 July 1949, NARA, RG 59, Myron Taylor Papers, Box 26.

174 Ibid. Taylor also revealed his increasingly Arabist leanings to the president when he informed him that the "invasion and expropriation of Arab property without compensation which they have enjoyed throughout the

years, or centuries perhaps, is one of the crimes of the post-war period which time cannot efface."

175 "Demand Holy Shrines Be Internationalized," *Brooklyn Tablet*, 14 May 1949. On French Catholics and the Jerusalem question, see David Lazar, *L'opinion Française et la naissance de l'état d'Israël, 1945–1949* (Calmann-Lévy, 1972), 169–219.

176 "Internationalized Jerusalem Demanded," *Brooklyn Tablet*, 18 June 1949.

177 "Statement of the Delegates of the International Union of Catholic Women to the U.N. Conciliation Committee for Palestine," 24 March 1949, NCWC/OGS/ACUA, Box 175, File 10, 1–2.

178 The IUCW statement warned that "experience has taught us that in this field, time works against us. Waiting is condemning men to a degrading inaction, women and girls to the dangers of prolonged promiscuity, children to the wasting away of their physical, moral and intellectual powers, the family to a slow desegregation."

179 Ibid., 2.

180 "Cites Common Ties between Irish, Jews," *Brooklyn Tablet*, 13 August 1949.

181 Ibid.

182 Ireland extended only de facto recognition of Israel in 1948, and not de jure recognition, in large part to pressure Tel Aviv to implement the full internationalization of Jerusalem and its environs. On the connection between Irish foreign policy and the Vatican, see Shulamit Eliash's *The Harp and the Shield of David: Ireland, Zionism and the State of Israel* (Routledge, 2007), 73–97.

183 "Memorandum – Exchange of Communications between the Catholic Bishops of Spain and the Vatican Relative to the Internationalization of the Holy Places in Palestine," 9 August 1949, NARA, RG 59, Myron Taylor Papers, Box 26.

184 On Canadian Catholics and the Jerusalem question, see Paolo Zanini, "I cattolici canadesi e la questione palastinese: Aspetti locale di una mobilitazione transnazionale" (unpiblished manuscript shared with the author), 6.

185 On Italian Catholics and the Jerusalem question, see Paolo Zanini, *Aria Crociata: I cattolici italiani di fronte alla nascita dello Stato d'Israele, 1945–1951* (Unicopli, 2012), 167–230.

186 Quoted in Chanan Reich, "Religious Values and Political Expediency: Australia and the Question of Jerusalem, 1947–1950," *Jewish Political Studies Review* 6, nos 3–4 (Fall 1994): 149–50.

187 "Memorandum – Debate in the Third Session of the General Assembly on the Application of Israel for Admission to the UN," NCWC/OGS/ACUA, Box 20, File 53, 11 August 1949, 1–19.

188 "Memorandum on the Palestine Question," NCWC/OGS/ACUA, Box 159, File 10, 18 May 1949.

189 Ibid.

190 Ibid.

191 "Memorandum," 2 August 1949, NARA, RG 59, Myron Taylor Papers, Box 26.

192 Ibid. These proposals were forwarded to Taylor from Shlomo Ginossar, the Israeli ambassador to Italy.

193 James Dunn to George Marshall [Washington], 10 March 1949, NARA, RG 59, Myron Taylor Papers, Box 30.

194 Franklin Gowen to George Marshall [Washington], 12 August 1949, NARA, RG 59, Myron Taylor Papers, Box 30.

195 Franklin Gowen to George Marshall [Washington], "Memo – The Problem of Jerusalem: The Vatican's Latest Recommendations," 13 August 1949, NARA, RG 59, Myron Taylor Papers, Box 26. See attached Italian original, "Situazione presente di Gerusalemme."

196 Ibid. The document also disputed the costs of an international police force to secure the city's stability, a clear rejection of Truman's estimates on the cost of such a force.

197 Quoted in Slonim, *Jerusalem in America's Foreign Policy*, 143.

198 Amleto Cicognani to Howard Carroll [Washington], 26 August 1949, NCWC/OGS/ACUA, Box 44, File 23.

199 Ibid.

200 Ibid.

CHAPTER SIX

1 Yossi Feintuch, *U.S. Policy on Jerusalem* (Greenwood, 1987), 69.

2 "Palestine – Proposals for a Permanent International Regime for the Jerusalem Area" (PCC "Jerusalem Statute"), NCWC/OGS/ACUA, Box 44, File 23, 12 September 1949, 4.

3 Ibid. See also Feintuch, *U.S. Policy on Jerusalem*, 70.

4 Ibid., 10.

5 Catherine Schaefer to Howard Carroll, 12 September 1949, NCWC/OGS/ACUA, Box 159, File 11.

6 Catherine Schaefer to Domenico Tardini [Rome], 13 September 1949, NCWC/OGS/ACUA, Box 23, File 44.

7 Domenico Tardini to Catherine Schaefer [New York], 16 September 1949, NCWC/OGS/ACUA, Box 23, File 44. See attached memo, "Observations Generales," 1–2. Tardini's memo amounted to a restatement of the Vatican's

long-standing concerns. They also included skepticism that a commissioner for Jerusalem could guarantee a balance of the population between Arabs and Jews, skepticism that such a figure could impose authority on two sovereign powers, and doubts that a commissioner could guarantee universal access to the holy sites. Tardini also opined that the holy sites, also being ancient sites of world interest, could not simply be placed under the jurisdiction of foreign entities. In sum, the memo again demanded that the "status quo" of 1947 be implemented.

8 Ibid.

9 Catherine Schaefer to Howard Carroll [Washington], 1 September 1949, NCWC/OGS/ACUA, Box 159, File 11.

10 Catherine Schaefer to Howard Carroll [Washington], 16 September 1949, NCWC/OGS/ACUA, Box 53, File 20. See attached "Confidential Memorandum," 1–2.

11 Catherine Schaefer to Howard Carroll [Washington], 19 October 1949, NCWC/OGS/ACUA, Box 23, File 44.

12 "Confidential – Views of the Various Delegations and Groups Regarding the Holy Places," 20 October 1949, NCWC/OGS/ACUA, Box 23, File 44, 2.

13 Caitlin Carenen has traced the development of Protestant support of Israel from the later 1920s to Israeli statehood, noting that Jewish persecution under the Nazis served to shift long-standing anti-Judaic sentiments. See her *The Fervent Embrace: Liberal Protestants, Evangelicals, and Israel* (New York University Press, 2012), 18–42.

14 Feintuch, *U.S. Policy on Jerusalem*, 74.

15 *Palestine* editorial (Fall 1949), in ibid., 74.

16 "Parley Assails U.N. Jerusalem Plan," *New York Times*, 3 November 1949, 9.

17 Ibid.

18 Feintuch, *U.S. Policy on Jerusalem*, 75.

19 On the evolution of Niebuhr's support for Israeli statehood, see Samuel Goldman, *God's Country: Christian Zionism in America* (University of Pennsylvania Press, 2018), 107–19.

20 Feintuch, *U.S. Policy on Jerusalem*, 75.

21 Catherine Schaefer to Howard Carroll [Washington], 3 November 1949, NCWC/OGS/ACUA, Box 159, File 26. See attached memo, "15 Leaders Ask Jerusalem Split between Israel and Arab State."

22 "Freedom of Holy Land Threatened by Israeli Stand," *Brooklyn Tablet*, 8 October 1949, 1.

23 "If I Forget Thee, O Jerusalem," *Brooklyn Tablet*, 15 October 1949, 4. "In 1947,"

the paper observed wryly, "we found no Zionists calling on American Jewry or on world Jewry for a 'Biblical Oath' to repudiate the Internationalization of Jerusalem and its environs. At that time, when the viability of a Jewish State hung in the balance, there was no mystical invocation of the phrase, 'If I Forget Thee, O Jerusalem, Let my right hand forget her skill, Let my tongue cleave to the roof of my mouth …'"

24 Ibid.

25 "Freedom of Holy City Threatened by Israeli Stand," *Brooklyn Tablet*, 8 October 1949, 1.

26 Ibid.

27 Catherine Schaefer to Howard Carroll [Washington], 4 November 1949, NCWC/OGS/ACUA, Box 44, File 24.

28 Ibid.

29 Howard Carroll to Dean Acheson [Washington], 5 November 1949, NCWC/OGS/ACUA, Box 44, File 24.

30 Howard Carroll to Amleto Cicognani [Washington], 21 November 1949, NCWC/OGS/ACUA, Box 44, File 24.

31 Timothy McNicholas to Harry S. Truman [Washington], 20 November 1949, NCWC/OGS/ACUA, Box 197, File 55.

32 Howard Carroll to John T. McNicholas [Cincinnati], 7 December 1949, NCWC/OGS/ACUA, Box 197, File 55.

33 Howard Carroll to Catherine Schaefer, 8 November 1949, NCWC/OGS/ACUA, Box 159, File 26.

34 Howard Carroll to Samuel Cardinal Stritch [Chicago], 8 November 1949, NCWC/OGS/ACUA, Box 44, File 24.

35 Eleanor Leahy to Catherine Schaefer, 5 November 1949, NCWC/OGS/ACUA, Box 159, File 26. See attached memorandum, 3 November 1949.

36 Catherine Schaefer to Howard Carroll, 10 November 1949, NCWC/OGS/ACUA, Box 44, File 24. See attached memo, "Draft Statement on the Status of Jerusalem."

37 See Raphael M. Huber, ed., *Our Bishops Speak: National Pastorals and Annual Statements of the Hierarchy of the United States* (Bruce Publishing, 1952), 364–5.

38 "Confidential Memorandum – Jerusalem," 15 November 1949, NCWC/OGS/ACUA, Box 164, File 38. In a later memo, Schaefer provided some interesting insight into the rationale behind Soviet support for internationalization. She surmised that to Moscow, supporting a *corpus separatum* would assist in the defeat of that very end, as the Soviets felt they "merely had to

support a resolution to see it defeated." She also reasoned that Moscow hoped that its support would create insurrection in the region, allowing it to capitalize on the disorder and to utilize Jewish communists as political and imperial tools. See "Memorandum on the Status of Debate on Jerusalem," 1 December 1949, NCWC/OGS/ACUA, Box 24, File 44.

39 "Memorandum on the Status of Debate on Jerusalem," 1 December 1949, NCWC/OGS/ACUA, Box 24, File 44.

40 Ibid.

41 "Text of Apostolic Exhortation by Pius XII Ordering Worldwide Prayers for the Holy Places," 14 November 1949, NCWC/OGS/ACUA, Box 44, File 24. An apostolic exhortation is a communication from the pope to his global faithful encouraging corporate action on a certain issue or theme. It does not define church doctrine and carries less authority than an encyclical. It generally carries more urgency, however, than an ecclesiastical letter, and is usually issued when the church is facing a particular and/or time-sensitive crisis, such as the battle for the internationalization of Jerusalem.

42 Amleto Cicognani to the archbishops and bishops of the United States, 15 November 1949, NCWC/OGS/ACUA, Box 44, File 24.

43 See, for example, John Francis O'Hara (bishop of Buffalo) to Howard Carroll [Washington], 9 December 1949, NCWC/OGS/ACUA, Box 44, File 24.

44 Vittorio Veronese to Howard Carroll [Washington], 15 October 1949, NCWC/OGS/ACUA, Box 44, File 24.

45 Ibid.

46 Ibid.

47 See Howard Carroll to Harry S. Truman [Washington], 5 December 1949, NCWC/OGS/ACUA, Box 44, File 22. Facsimiles of this letter were also forwarded to Dean Acheson and Warren Austin.

48 Howard Carroll to Vittorio Vernonese [Rome], 6 December 1949, NCWC/OGS/ACUA, Box 44, File 24. To Veronese, Carroll expressed that the "joint efforts of the Catholics throughout the world may result in a decision which will satisfy our collective aspirations."

49 Chanan Reich, "Religious Values and Political Expediency: Australia and the Question of Jerusalem, 1947–1950," *Jewish Political Studies Review* 6, nos 3–4 (Fall 1994): 135–73. The Labor Party of Ben Chifley was defeated by Robert Menzies's Liberal-Country coalition in the 10 December federal election.

50 "Bishops' Statement on Jerusalem," ALC, CMP, Box 93, File 3, 18 November 1949.

51 On this growing American ambivalence, see Shlomo Slonim, *Jerusalem in America's Foreign Policy, 1947–1997* (Kluwer, 1998), 121–51.

52 In a conversation with General William A. Riley, head of the UN observers team, Spellman was warned that support for the *corpus separatum* came from an array of Arab and Soviet delegations whose interests lay not in protecting the Holy Places, but in undermining Israeli and Jordanian sovereignty, and ultimately in preparing for war against Israel. Riley later indicated to Ralph Bunche, the UN's chief mediator on the Arab-Israeli conflict, that Spellman was "utterly uninformed and unrealistic" on the issue of *corpus separatum*. See Slonim, *Jerusalem in America's Foreign Policy*, 142.

53 On Spellman's advocacy at this crucial juncture, see Edward B. Glick, "The Vatican, Latin America and Jerusalem," *International Organization* 11, no. 2 (Spring 1957): 213–19; Michael Brecher, "Jerusalem in Israel's Political Decisions, 1947–1977," *Middle East Journal* 32, no. 1 (1978): 25–6; Silvio Ferrari, "The Vatican, Israel and the Jerusalem Question, 1943–1984," *Middle East Journal* 39, no. 2 (1985): 316–31.

54 Glick, "The Vatican, Latin America and Jerusalem," 216.

55 "Jerusalem Internationalized by 38 to 14 Vote in General Assembly of United Nations," NCWC News Service, 12 December 1949, NCWC/OGS/ACUA, Box 24, File 44.

56 See Avi Shlaim, "Israel between East and West, 1948–56," *International Journal of Middle Eastern Studies* 36, no. 4 (2004): 659–60. On Israel's relations with the Soviet Union during its brief era of diplomatic nonalignment, see Laurent Rucker, "Moscow's Surprise: The Soviet-Israeli Alliance of 1947–1949," Working Paper No. 46 (Wilson Center, Cold War International History Project, July 2005), 1–36.

57 Other affirmative votes came from Afghanistan, Argentina, Australia, Bolivia, Burma, Byelorussia, China, Colombia, Cuba, Czechoslovakia, Ecuador, Egypt, El Salvador, Ethiopia, Greece, Haiti, India, Iran, Iraq, Liberia, Mexico, Nicaragua, Pakistan, Paraguay, Peru, Poland, Saudi Arabia, Syria, Ukraine, Venezuela, and Yemen. See "The Vote on Internationalization of Jerusalem by Nations," 12 December 1949, NCWC/OGS/ACUA, Box 24, File 44.

58 Others opposed included Israel, Jordan, Chile, Costa Rica, Denmark, Guatemala, Iceland, Norway, Sweden, Turkey, South Africa, Uruguay, and Yugoslavia. See "The Vote on Internationalization of Jerusalem by Nations," 12 December 1949, NCWC/OGS/ACUA, Box 24, File 44. Chile's abstention was later explained by Schaefer as a result of the pressure of Chilean Jews, who, "a week before the final vote, put the screws on the President to abstain from the Jerusalem question." Schaefer further described the "dangerous forces" of Masonry and Judaism in Chile. See "Memorandum – Background Information – Jerusalem," January 1950, NCWC/OGS/ACUA, Box 44, File 26.

59 "Jerusalem Internationalized by 38 to 14 Vote in General Assembly of United Nations," NCWC News Service, 12 December 1949, NCWC/OGS/ACUA, Box 24, File 44.

60 Ibid.

61 "Memo – Factors Contributing to the Final Adoption of the Resolution on the Internationalization of Jerusalem," 15 December 1949, NCWC/OGS/ACUA, Box 164, File 38.

62 Ibid.

63 Ibid., 2.

64 Ibid.

65 "Confidential Memorandum – Comments on the General Assembly Resolution on the Internationalization of Jerusalem," 16 December 1949, NCWC/OGS/ACUA, Box 164, File 38.

66 *New York Post*, 12 December 1949. Quoted in Feintuch, *U.S. Policy on Jerusalem*, 83.

67 "Memorandum – Vatican-Israel Relations," August 1951, A-CNEWA, TMP, Box 6, File 8.

68 Slonim, *Jerusalem in America's Foreign Policy*, 146.

69 "Israel Defies UN Decision to Make Jerusalem Free," *Brooklyn Tablet*, 17 December 1949, 1.

70 "Trygve Lie's New Year," *America*, 14 January 1950, 1.

71 Feintuch, *U.S. Policy on Jerusalem*, 84.

72 "The Jerusalem Story: A Victory for the Vatican," *Nation*, 17 December 1949.

73 Howard Carroll to Charles Malik, 28 December 1949, NCWC/OGS/ACUA, Box 25, File 44.

74 Amleto Cicognani to John T. McNicholas, 3 January 1950, NCWC/OGS/ACUA, Box 25, File 44.

75 Ibid.

76 See Feintuch, *U.S. Policy on Jerusalem*, 87–8.

77 "Israel Office of Information: Israel Submits a Jerusalem Plan," 28 May 1950, NCWC/OGS/ACUA, Box 26, File 44.

78 Howard Carroll to Porter McKeever, 2 January 1950, NCWC/OGS/ACUA, Box 25, File 44.

79 Porter McKeever to Howard Carroll, 6 January 1950, NCWC/OGS/ACUA, Box 25, File 44.

80 Alba Zizzamia to Catherine Schaefer, 15 January 1950, NCWC/OGS/ACUA, Box 159, File 12.

81 "Memorandum – Trusteeship Council – Jerusalem," 20 January 1950, NCWC/OGS/ACUA, Box 164, File 38.

82 Ibid.

83 "Memorandum – Trusteeship Council – Jerusalem," 6 February 1950, NCWC/OGS/ACUA, Box 164, File 38.

84 "Memorandum – Trusteeship Council – Jerusalem," 8 February 1950, NCWC/OGS/ACUA, Box 25, File 44.

85 "Memorandum – Trusteeship Council – Jerusalem," 6 February 1950, NCWC/OGS/ACUA, Box 164, File 38.

86 "Memorandum: Possible Statute for Jerusalem as Envisaged by Mr Roger Garreau, President of the Trusteeship Council," 31 January 1950, NCWC/OGS/ACUA, Box 169, File 30. In the same memo, Zizzamia mentioned that Fazali thought a "dead letter" might, at the very least, "teach the Jews a lesson," and provide a pretext to an Arab armed intervention in Israel.

87 Ibid.

88 See Feintuch, *U.S. Policy on Jerusalem*, 92–3.

89 "Report by Christian Fact-Finding Mission on Jerusalem: Rejects Internationalization Plan after 'Investigation' There, Press Release: American Christian Palestine Committee," 19 January 1950, NCWC/OGS/ACUA, Box 44, File 25. The report listed a number of factors supporting a revised statute for Jerusalem, including the fact that reports of Israeli desecration to shrines were exaggerated, the diminishment of tensions between Jews and Arabs in the territory, and the suitability of the Garreau Plan, which, according to the ACPC, was the most sensible and practical solution moving forward.

90 "Memorandum – Trusteeship Council – Jerusalem," 6 February 1950, NCWC/OGS/ACUA, Box 164, File 38.

91 "Memorandum – Trusteeship Council – Jerusalem," 20 January 1950, NCWC/OGS/ACUA, Box 164, File 38.

92 Inman was a noted authority on Latin American affairs, and was a pastor and academic of note, teaching at the University of Pennsylvania and lecturing at a wide range of leading American universities. He also served as Roosevelt's adviser at the Buenos Aires Conference (1936), where the United States reaffirmed the Monroe Doctrine.

93 "UN Group Votes to Start Immediately on Jerusalem Internationalization Vote," NCWC News Service, 13 February 1950, NCWC/OGS/ACUA, Box 25, File 44.

94 Ibid.

95 On 11 February 1950, a draft resolution by the delegate of the Dominican Republic to invite a Vatican representative to present its views was withdrawn. The council decided, without a vote, that communications with the Holy See could be made through regular diplomatic channels, since "some members had accredited diplomats posted there." "UN Group Votes to Start Immediately on Jerusalem Internationalization Statute," NCWC News Service, 13 February 1950, NCWC/OGS/ACUA, Box 25, File 44.

96 "Memorandum– Jerusalem," 30 January 1950, NCWC/OGS/ACUA, Box 164, File 38.

97 Ibid.

98 *Pro Memoria* – Jerusalem, 6 February 1950, NCWC/OGS/ACUA, Box 164, File 38.

99 Feintuch contends that while Francis Sayre, head of the American delegation at Geneva, favored the Garreau Plan, mixed signals from Washington precluded him taking a definitive stance on the proposal. See Feintuch's *U.S. Policy on Jerusalem*, 92–3.

100 "Memorandum – Jerusalem," 8 February 1950, NCWC/OGS/ACUA, Box 164, File 38.

101 Ibid. This was despite the fact that Sayre, from the start, regarded the Garreau Plan as the best possible solution to a perplexing problem. In early March, Zizzamia reported that Sayre "seemed to regret that the Garreau Plan had died," and that he regarded complete internationalization as "turning back history." See "Memorandum – Jerusalem," 3 March 1950, NCWC/OGS/ACUA, Box 44, File 25.

102 "Memorandum – Jerusalem," 9 February 1950, NCWC/OGS/ACUA, Box 164, File 38.

103 "Memorandum – Jerusalem," 17 February 1950, NCWC/OGS/ACUA, Box 44, File 25. Inman also raised the specter of Soviet infiltration of an internationalized Jerusalem, invoking a bogey that had been employed by all sides of the debate.

104 Ibid.

105 Ibid.

106 Ibid.

107 Feintuch, *U.S. Policy on Jerusalem*, 95.

108 "Memorandum – Jerusalem," 3 March 1950, NCWC/OGS/ACUA, Box 44, File 25.

109 Ibid.

110 "Memorandum – Sixth Session of the UN Trusteeship Council," 23 May 1950, NCWC/OGS/ACUA, Box 23, File 53.

111 "Memorandum – Jerusalem," 24 April 1950, NCWC/OGS/ACUA, Box 44, File 24.

112 "Memorandum – Jerusalem," 26 April 1950, NCWC/OGS/ACUA, Box 26, File 159.

113 See Uri Bialer, *The Cross on the Star of David: The Christian World in Israel's Foreign Policy, 1948–1967* (Indiana University Press, 2005), 44–9.

114 The Israeli Foreign Ministry produced thousands of copies of various publications, including *Jerusalem: Living City* and *The Jerusalem Affair*, translated into French and Spanish and distributed widely to UN delegations and foreign embassies. The ministry also produced a publication entitled *Christian News from Israel*, in English and French, intended to counter Vatican and wider Catholic narratives on the Holy Places. Ibid., 45.

115 The sixteen-page document outlined Tel Aviv's flexible new proposals for the city, which would have seen the internationalization of the immediate zone surrounding the Old City's sacred sites, and would allow for the establishment of a UN commissioner for the zone, who "would be wholly separate" from Israeli and Jordanian control, and who would enjoy "a certain degree of extraterritoriality so far as the Holy Places were concerned … [while] the authority of the occupying governments would be more or less withdrawn." It was an arrangement giving the UN full territorial control of the holy sites. While not the *corpus separatum* agreed upon in 1949, the proposals were evidence of Israeli attempts to negotiate a conciliatory, yet favorable, resolution. In Garreau's view, the proposals showed "an understanding and benevolent attitude towards the legitimate demands of all parties concerned," and represented "a considerable advance towards a settlement." See "Memorandum on the Question of Jerusalem: Analysis of the Statute for Jerusalem and a Proposal for a Solution," 26 May 1950, NCWC/OGS/ACUA, Box 44, File 26.

116 Ibid.

117 Howard Carroll to Amleto Cicognani, 8 June 1950, NCWC/OGS/ACUA, Box 44, File 26.

118 "Vatican Opposing Israel on Shrines," *New York Times*, 31 May 1950, 1.

119 Ibid.

120 "Memorandum – Jerusalem," 15 June 1950, NCWC/OGS/ACUA, Box 44, File 26.

121 Ibid.

122 Feintuch, *U.S. Policy on Jerusalem*, 98–9.

123 "Jerusalem Issue Returned to Assembly after Tepid Move to Internationalize," NCWC/OGS/ACUA, Box 44, File 26.

124 Ibid.

125 Howard Carroll to Amleto Cicognani, 8 June 1950, NCWC/OGS/ACUA, Box 44, File 26.

126 Ibid.

127 See, for example, Catherine Schaefer to Howard Carroll, 14 July 1950, NCWC/OGS/ACUA, Box 159, File 13; Howard Carroll to Amleto Cicognani, 28 July 1950, NCWC/OGS/ACUA, Box 159, File 13; Catherine Schaefer to Howard Carroll, 11 August 1950, NCWC/OGS/ACUA, Box 159, File 13.

128 See, for example, "Jerusalem in International Law," *America*, 15 April 1950, 33; "Internationalization Doomed," *America*, 27 May 1950, 231; "Therefore, Internationalize Jerusalem," *America*, 17 June 1950, 313.

129 Howard Carroll to John Butler, 12 June 1950, NCWC/OGS/ACUA, Box 44, File 26. Carroll's efforts with New York papers were intended to combat a perceived bias in the coverage in the mainstream press. An NCWC press report observed that "metropolitan newspaper comment in New York in general tends to regard internationalization as a dead issue and to favour the latest Israeli proposals. Lack of consent of the parties concerned is the main argument used against internationalization. Yet in favouring the Israeli proposals, the editorialists seemingly overlook the fact that Jordan has given no indication it will consent to these proposals either." See "Jerusalem Issue Returned to Assembly after Tepid Move to Internationalize," 19 June 1950, NCWC/OGS/ACUA, Box 44, File 26.

130 Constantine Rauckaskas, "The Jerusalem Problem: A Note on Legality," *Thought* 24, no. 96, (March 1950): 100–14.

131 Ibid., 113.

132 Peter Berger, "The Internationalization of Jerusalem," *Jurist* 10, no. 3 (July 1950): 8–41.

133 Howard Carroll to Catherine Schaefer, 28 July 1950, NCWC/OGS/ACUA, Box 44, File 26.

134 "Memorandum – Jerusalem," 21 September 1950, NCWC/OGS/ACUA, Box 23, File 53.

135 "Where Israel Stands," *United Nations World*, September 1950, 7–11.

136 Ibid., 11.

137 See Paul Blanshard, *American Freedom and Catholic Power* (Beacon Books, 1949).

138 Ibid., 3–4.

139 John T. McGreevy, *Catholicism and American Freedom: A History* (Norton, 2003), 166.

140 See, for example, John Courtney Murray's "Paul Blanshard and the New Nativism," *Month*, April 1951, 214–25; James M. O'Neill, *Catholicism and American Freedom* (Harper, 1952); Robert C. Hartnett, "My Debate with Mr Blanshard," *America*, 18 March 1950, 689–91. Also appearing in 1949 was Avro Manhattan's *The Vatican in World Politics*, another polemic that sought to "uncover" the Vatican's attempts to "spiritually conquer the United States, and ultimately Catholicize the world." See Manhattan, *The Vatican in World Politics* (Horizon, 1949), 10. On the distinctively religious impulses that informed Blanshard's critiques, and Murray's rebuttal, see Mark Massa, "Catholic-Protestant Tensions in Post-war America: Paul Blanshard, John Courtney Murray, and the Religious Imagination," *Harvard Theological Review* 95, no. 3 (July 2002): 319–39.

141 See Pierre Van Paassen, *Jerusalem Calling: A Frank Survey of the Chaotic International Scene* (Dial Press, 1950).

142 Ibid., 12.

143 Ibid., 190.

144 "That the Vatican is out to gain control of the Holy Places," Van Paassen claimed, "became evident during the debates on internationalization at the UN, when Cardinal Spellman of New York, throwing all restraint to the wind, telegraphed papal nuncios in various South American republics to insist to the governments to which they were accredited that they must take an uncompromising stand at Lake Success for the internationalization of the Holy City." Internationalization was implemented, he continued, "by an international commission, made up chiefly of Catholic South Americans, probably with a Monsignor at the head." Ibid., 215.

145 Van Paassen claimed to have been told this during a visit to the Vatican's Sacred Congregation of Extraordinary Affairs in June 1950. Cicognani denied that the author had ever been received at the congregation, and Carroll informed Schaefer to "seize any occasion to make this fact known." See Howard Carroll to Catherine Schaefer, 18 December 1950, NCWC/OGS/ACUA, Box 159, File 13.

146 Catherine Schaefer to Howard Carroll, 22 November 1950, NCWC/OGS/ACUA, Box 159, File 13. In order to blunt potential criticism, Schaefer ordered the reprinting and distribution of two pamphlets of the CAIP, *The Church and the Jews* and *Catholics and Jews*.

147 Michael J. Cohen contends that Truman's political pragmatism and proximity

to the American Zionist lobby, and not a theological affinity with Zionism, was the decisive factor in the shaping of his Palestine policy. See his *Truman and Israel* (University of California Press, 2020).

148 "Memorandum – Jerusalem," 22 October 1950, NCWC/OGS/ACUA, Box 164, File 38.

149 "Jerusalem – Prospects in the Present Session of the General Assembly," October 1950, NCWC/OGS/ACUA, Box 164, File 38.

150 "Memorandum – Jerusalem," 22 October 1950, NCWC/OGS/ACUA, Box 164, File 38.

151 "Jerusalem – Prospects in the Present Session of the General Assembly," October 1950, NCWC/OGS/ACUA, Box 164, File 38.

152 Ibid.

153 Ibid.

154 "National Council of Catholic Women Resolution: Internationalization of Jerusalem," October 1950, NCWC/OGS/ACUA, Box 44, File 26.

155 Ibid.

156 Howard Carroll to Margaret Mealey, 6 November 1950, NCWC/OGS/ACUA, Box 44, File 26; Margaret Mealey to Howard Carroll, 7 November 1950, NCWC/OGS/ACUA, Box 44, File 26.

157 "French Catholics Appeal to UN to Implement Its Jerusalem Stand," 6 November 1950, NCWC/OGS/ACUA, Box 44, File 26.

158 Catherine Schaefer to A. Vasnier, 10 November 1950, NCWC/OGS/ACUA, Box 44, File 26. In thanking Schaefer for her work, the committee's president, Comte de la Baume, assured her that the NCWC's efforts "were in perfect harmony with the appeal of the Catholics of France."

159 "Addendum – American Bishops Annual Statement for 1950," October 1950, NCWC/OGS/ACUA, Box 44, File 26.

160 Ibid.

161 "Memorandum – Jerusalem," 2 November 1950, NCWC/OGS/ACUA, Box 44, File 26.

162 On 17 November 1950, Domenico Tardini thanked Schaefer for her efforts, confident that "the memo will serve to enlighten North American Catholics regarding the present state of the question, and the grave motives for which the Holy See has pronounced itself in favour of the true and proper internationalization of the City as the only means to save Jerusalem and the Holy Places in the present violent conflict between Arabs and Jews." Domenico Tardini to Catherine Schaefer, 17 November 1950, NCWC/OGS/ACUA, Box 44, File 26.

163 Frank A. Hall to Howard Carroll, 27 November 1950, NCWC/OGS/ACUA, Box 44, File 26.

164 Ibid.

165 Howard Carroll to the cardinals, archbishops, bishops, co-adjutors and auxiliaries of the United States, 22 November 1950, NCWC/OGS/ACUA, Box 44, File 26. See also "I Cattolici per i Luoghi Santi," *L'Osservatore Romano*, 2 9 November 1950, 1.

166 "Memorandum – Jerusalem and the Arab Refugees," 9 November 1950, NCWC/OGS/ACUA, Box 164, File 38.

167 "Memorandum – Jerusalem," 13 November 1950, NCWC/OGS/ACUA, Box 164, File 38.

168 Howard Carroll to Amleto Cicognani, 18 November 1950, NCWC/OGS/ACUA, Box 44, File 23.

169 "United Nations General Assembly, 5th Session, Sweden: Draft Resolution," 5 December 1950, NCWC/OGS/ACUA, Box 44, File 26: 1-8.

170 "Memorandum – Jerusalem," 30 November 1950, NCWC/OGS/ACUA, Box 44, File 26.

171 Howard Carroll to Vittorio Veronese, 25 January 1951, NCWC/OGS/ACUA, Box 44, File 27. See also "International Jerusalem Stand Reaffirmed by Italian Catholics in Message to UN Assembly Head," 12 December 1950, NCWC/OGS/ACUA, Box 44, File 27.

172 Martin Work to Howard Carroll, 12 December 1950, NCWC/OGS/ACUA, Box 44, File 26.

173 Ibid.

174 "Memorandum – Jerusalem," 11 December 1950, NCWC/OGS/ACUA, Box 164, File 38.

175 "Memorandum – Jerusalem," 12 December 1950, NCWC/OGS/ACUA, Box 164, File 38.

176 Ibid.

177 Ibid.

178 Ibid.

179 Feintuch, *U.S. Policy on Jerusalem*, 100.

180 Ibid., 101.

181 Ibid., 102.

182 See Elihu Lauterpacht, *Jerusalem and the Holy Places* (Anglo-Israel Association, 1968), 31.

183 McMahon presented his views to a committee comprising of House Committee Chairman James P. Richards (D), John Martin Vorys (R), Walter Henry Judd (R), Jacob Javits (R), Frances Payne Bolton (R), and James G. Fulton (R).

184 "Remarks of Monsignor Thomas J. McMahon, Catholic Near East Welfare Association, before House Committee," 26 July 1951, A-CNEWA, TMP, Box 103, File 1.

185 The apostolic delegate in Washington, Amleto Cicognani, kept the Vatican Secretariat apprised of the details of McMahon's various appeals to the committee. See, for example, Amleto Cicognani to Giovanni Montini, 17 August 1951, ASRS, pop. 1948, Pos. 113-3.

186 Feintuch, *U.S. Policy on Jerusalem*, 105.

187 "Israel to Build a Capital City in Jerusalem – Memo – NCWC Office for UN Affairs," NCWC/OGS/ACUA, Box 44, File 28.

188 See "Catholics Opposed Plan Periling Internationalization of Jerusalem," *Chicago Daily News*, 29 December 1952, 4.

189 Thomas McMahon to Francis Spellman, 28 July 1953, A-CNEWA, TMP, Box 103, File 1.

190 "La Questione di Gerusalemme: Dopo un trasferimento," *L'Osservatore Romano*, 31 July 1953, ASRS, pop. 1948, pos. 113-3.

191 On McMahon's distribution of PMP funds, see Maria Chiara Rioli, *A Liminal Church: Refugees, Conversions and the Latin Diocese of Jerusalem, 1946–1956* (Brill, 2020), 271–87.

192 Sizeable contributions were received from the CNEWA, the NCWC's War Relief Services, the Franciscan Commissariat for the Holy Land, and the NCCW. See Peter Tuohy to Monsignor Angelo Dell'Aqua, 3 February 1955, ASRS, pop. 1950, pos. 90.

193 "Foreign Minister Indicates Israel Will Remain Adamant on Status of Jerusalem," NCWC News Service, 13 April 1953, 13.

194 Thomas McMahon to Howard Carroll, 15 July 1953, A-CNEWA, TMP, Box 103, File 1.

195 Just weeks before the bombing, the Israeli Supreme Court had ordered that the villagers had a right of return.

196 Silvio Oddi to Domenico Tardini, 22 January 1954, Archivio Apostolico Vaticano, Arch. Deleg. Gerusalemme e Palestina, fasc. 81, pos. 2.

197 Details of McMahon's mission were relayed to Rome by Silvio Oddi, who had been appointed as the apostolic delegate for Palestine, Jordan, and Cyprus in July 1953. See Silvio Oddi to Domenico Tardini, 15 May 1954, Archivio Apostolico Vaticano, Arch. Deleg. Gerusalemme e Palestina, fasc. 81, pos. 2.

198 "Report on Journey of Monsignor Thomas J. McMahon in the Middle East – October 18 through November 12," November 1953, A-CNEWA, TMP, 8–9.

199 In September, McMahon issued a letter to UN Secretary-General Dag Ham-

marskjöld critiquing Israel's move of its capital to Jerusalem, insisting that the UN support a full internationalization of the city and not the "functional" or "indirect" form that was taking shape. See Thomas McMahon to Dag Hammarskjöld, 16 September 1953, ASRS, pop. 1948, pos. 113-3, rf.

200 On Herzog's role in managing competing Christian claims to Jerusalem in this crucial period, see Michael Bar-Zohar's *Yaacov Herzog: A Biography* (Halban, 2005) 86–107.

201 Ibid.

202 "Report on Journey of Monsignor Thomas J. McMahon in the Middle East – October 18 through November 12," November 1953, A-CNEWA, TMP, 9.

203 Ibid., 12.

204 Bar-Zohar, *Yaacov Herzog*, 104.

205 Ibid.

206 "Internationalization of Jerusalem," 7 December 1953, A-CNEWA, TMP, Box 103, File 1.

207 Slonim, *Jerusalem in America's Foreign Policy*, 179. Until 1967, the United States maintained one consul general in Jerusalem, who was responsible for both the Israeli and Jordanian sectors of the city.

208 "President Asked to Reconsider Way U.S. Ambassador Presents Credentials to Israel," NCWC News Service, 8 November 1954.

209 Bialer, *Cross on the Star of David*, 29.

210 "Israel's First Decade," *America*, 3 May 1958, 156.

211 Ibid.

212 See Paul Tanner to Jacob Herzog, 7 April 1958, NCWC/OGS/ACUA, Box 21, File 44; Chaim Wardie to Harmon Burns, 25 August 1958, NCWC/OGS/ACUA, Box 21, File 44; Paul Tanner to Edward Mooney, 29 August 1958, NCWC/OGS/ACUA, Box 21, File 44; Paul Tanner to Francis Spellman, 1 October 1958, NCWC/OGS/ACUA, Box 21, File 44.

CONCLUSION

1 "Cardinal Scores Anti-Semitism," NCWC News Service, 5 May 1964, 1–2.

2 Ibid., 2.

3 "Cardinal Spellman Warns against Blaming Jews for Crucifixion of Jesus," Jewish Telegraphic Agency News Bulletin, 1 May 1964.

4 As Ben-Johanan has revealed, theological tensions between Jews and Catholics have remained for decades after the Second Vatican Council, despite the spirit of dialogue initiated by *Nostra aetate* and the genuinely positive steps

of the postconciliar decades. See her *Jacob's Younger Brother: Christian-Jewish Relations after Vatican II* (Harvard University Press, 2022).

5 John Connelly, *From Enemy to Brother: The Revolution in Catholic Teaching on the Jews, 1933–1965* (Harvard University Press, 2012).

6 On American Catholic denunciation of Nazi antisemitism in the immediate wake of Kristallnacht, see Maria Mazzenga, "Condemning the Nazis' *Kristallnacht*: Father Maurice Sheehy, the National Catholic Welfare Conference, and the Dissent of Father Charles Coughlin," *U.S. Catholic Historian* 26, no. 4 (Fall 2008): 71–87.

7 "Mgr. Ryan Raps Nazi Persecution of Jews," *Michigan Catholic*, 14 July 1938, 3–4.

8 "Archbishop Scores Attack on Jews," *Michigan Catholic*, 8 June 1944, 1.

9 Edward H. Flannery, *The Anguish of the Jews: Twenty-Three Centuries of Anti-Semitism* (Macmillan, 1965).

10 Ibid., 277.

11 John F. Cronin, Francis X. Murphy, Ferrer Smith, eds, *The Encyclicals and Messages of John XXIII* (TPS Press, 1964), 423.

12 For a synopsis of American Catholic contributions to the drafting of *Nostra aetate*, see Joseph P. Chinnici, *American Catholicism Transformed: From the Cold War through the Council* (Oxford University Press, 2021), 240–7.

13 George Irani, *The Papacy and the Middle East: The Role of the Holy See in the Arab-Israeli Conflict* (University of Notre Dame Press, 1986), 35.

14 "Israel Refuses Jerusalem Changes," NCWC News Service, 13 September 1967.

15 "Pope Receives Israeli Foreign Minister Abba Eban," NCWC News Service, 6 October 1969.

16 "Vatican Policy on Jerusalem Veers," *Voice* (Diocese of Miami), 5 January 1968, 16. The statement also outlined a strategic case for maintaining Israeli control in the city. "The experience of cities like Vienna and Berlin have had under four-power rule should stand as a warning," it posited. "To bring these powers into the Holy City would turn it into a nest of intrigues, a meeting place of spies, a home of professional revolutionaries."

17 Paul Merkley, *Christian Attitudes towards the State of Israel* (McGill-Queen's University Press, 2001), 144.

18 See Robert F. Drinan, *Honor the Promise: America's Commitment to Israel* (Doubleday, 1977).

19 See Joseph Constance, "Rev. Robert F. Drinan and the Jewish Democratic State: Shaping Catholic Perspectives, 1970–1980" (Unpublished manuscript in the author's possession).

20 Drinan, *Honor the Promise*, 121.

Index